Dissecting Stephen King

A RAY AND PAT BROWNE BOOK

Series Editors
Ray B. Browne and Pat Browne

Dissecting
Stephen King

From the Gothic to
Literary Naturalism

Heidi Strengell

THE UNIVERSITY OF WISCONSIN PRESS
POPULAR PRESS

The University of Wisconsin Press
1930 Monroe Street
Madison, Wisconsin 53711

www.wisc.edu/wisconsinpress/

3 Henrietta Street
London WC2E 8LU, England

5   4   3   2

Printed in the United States of America

Library of Congress Cataloging-in-Publication Data
Strengell, Heidi.
Dissecting Stephen King : from the Gothic to literary naturalism /
    Heidi Strengell.
    p.   cm.
    "A Ray and Pat Browne book."
    Includes bibliographical references and index.
    ISBN 0-299-20970-9 (hardcover : alk. paper)
    ISBN 0-299-20974-1 (pbk.: alk. paper)
    1. King, Stephen, 1947- —Criticism and interpretation.
2. Horror tales, American—History and criticism.
3. Gothic revival (Literature)—United States.
4. Naturalism in literature.   I. Title.
PS3561.I483Z885   2005
813'.54—dc22   2004025717

For
HEIKKI,
JUHO, and
JUHANA

I believe that we are all ultimately alone and that any deep and lasting human contact is nothing more nor less than a necessary illusion—but at least the feelings which we think of as "positive" and "constructive" are a reaching out, an effort to make contact and establish some sort of communication. Feelings of love and kindness, the ability to care and empathize, are all we know of light. They are efforts to link and integrate; they are the emotions which bring us closer together, if not in fact then at least in a comforting illusion that makes the burden of mortality a little easier to bear.

Stephen King, *Danse Macabre*

Contents

Abbreviations

In the course of this study, King's works are abbreviated as follows. The list does not include his individually published short stories or e-published works.

B8   *From a Buick 8* (2002; novel)
BB   *Bag of Bones* (1998; novel)
BH   *Black House* (with Peter Straub, 2001; novel)
CA   *Carrie* (1974; novel)
CE   *Cat's Eye* (1985; original screenplay)
CH   *Christine* (1983; novel)
CS   *Creepshow* (1982; comic strips collection)
CU   *Cujo* (1981; novel)
CW   *Cycle of the Werewolf* (1983; novella)
DC   *Dolores Claiborne* (1993; novel)
DCA   *Dreamcatcher* (2001; novel)
DE   *Desperation* (1996; novel)
DH   *The Dark Half* (1989; novel)
DM   *Danse Macabre* (1981; nonfiction book)
DS   *Different Seasons* (1982; novellas)
DT   *The Dark Tower II: The Drawing of the Three* (1987; serial novel)
DTO   *The Dark Tower VII: The Dark Tower* (2004; serial novel)
DZ   *The Dead Zone* (1979; novel)
ED   *The Eyes of the Dragon* (1987; novel)
EE   *Everything's Eventual* (2002; short stories)
FPM   *Four Past Midnight* (1990; novellas)

FS	*Firestarter* (1980; novel)
GG	*Gerald's Game* (1992; novel)
GM	*The Green Mile* (1996; novel)
GS	*The Dark Tower I: The Gunslinger* (1982; serial novel)
GWLTG	*The Girl Who Loved Tom Gordon* (1999; novel)
HA	*Hearts in Atlantis* (1999; novel)
IS	*Insomnia* (1994; novel)
IT	*It* (1986; novel)
LW	*The Long Walk* (as Richard Bachman, 1979; novel)
MI	*Misery* (1987; novel)
ND	*Nightmares and Dreamscapes* (1993; miscellanea)
NS	*Night Shift* (1978; short stories)
NT	*Needful Things* (1991; novel)
OW	*On Writing* (2000; nonfiction book)
PS	*Pet Sematary* (1983; novel)
RA	*Rage* (as Richard Bachman, 1977; novel)
RE	*The Regulators* (as Richard Bachman, 1996; novel)
RM	*The Running Man* (as Richard Bachman, 1982; novel)
RMA	*Rose Madder* (1995; novel)
RW	*Roadwork* (as Richard Bachman, 1981; novel)
SC	*Storm of the Century* (1999; original television miniseries)
SK	*Skeleton Crew* (1985; miscellanea)
SL	*'Salem's Lot* (1975; novel)
SH	*The Shining* (1977; novel)
SKGY	*Stephen King's Golden Years* (1991; original television series)
SS	*The Dark Tower VI: Song of Susannah* (2004; serial novel)
ST	*The Stand* (1978; novel)
SW	*Sleepwalkers* (1992; original screenplay)
TA	*The Talisman* (with Peter Straub, 1984; novel)
TH	*Thinner* (as Richard Bachman, 1984; novel)
TK	*The Tommyknockers* (1987; novel)
WC	*The Dark Tower V: Wolves of the Calla* (2003; serial novel)
WG	*The Dark Tower IV: Wizard and Glass* (1997; serial novel)
WL	*The Dark Tower III: The Waste Lands* (1991; serial novel)

Dissecting Stephen King

Introduction

During his literary career, Stephen King has published four dozen novels, about a dozen novellas, and over a hundred short stories. He has also written two nonfiction books, a number of screenplays and e-books, even a comic book. Stephen J. Spignesi maintains that the total body of King's fiction includes an astonishing 550 individual works (*Essential Stephen King*, 10). Michael R. Collings, who has reviewed national bookseller lists and drawn the conclusion that King can be referred to as "a bestselling bestseller" or simply "the Stephen King phenomenon," also notes "the remarkable extent and durability of his popularity" (*Stephen King Phenomenon*, 36). Obviously, King's appeal is broader than that of a genre writer. But what makes him such a popular author? Ben P. Indick states that it is the combination of fear and realism in King's fiction ("What Makes Him So Scary?" 9). Edwin F. Casebeer, on the other hand, claims that King writes in all the major popular genres: horror, fantasy, science fiction, the Western, the mystery, and the romance, thus offering every reader something ("Art of Balance," 42). Perhaps both critics are partially right. Undeniably King shares traits with several genres, and he could have developed into both a literary naturalist and a capable novelist outside the horror genre. However, he has chosen the horror formula and enriches it with other literary genres. How and with what results the Gothic, myths and fairy tales, as well as literary naturalism are displayed in King's oeuvre is the focus of this monograph.

Until recently the notion of character in literature—like that of the author—has been disdained. Since I, like Baruch Hochman, believe that "characters in literature have more in common with people in life than contemporary critical discourse suggests" (7), the analysis of King's characterization plays a decisive role in this study. However, I do not offer a general discussion on character in literature. Suffice it to say that literary characters and people in real life seem to have in common a cognitive model of the nature of human beings. Since both fictional characters and real people are cognitively understood in a person's consciousness, they are understood in much the same terms. They are not identical, however. As Hochman aptly points out, literature reflects life with regard to character, just as it mirrors other aspects (7). Similarly, King lays great emphasis on his characters and openly admits that he induces fear in his readers by making them love the characters (Underwood and Miller, *Feast of Fear*, 246). In horror fiction, King claims, readers are not frightened by monsters; rather their fear is an expression of empathy with the main characters (Underwood and Miller, *Bare Bones*, 86; Winter, *Faces of Fear*, 251). When identifying with the characters, the reader fears for them, feels sympathy, and takes a stand—that is, actively participates in the development of King's stories. Presumably King's popularity can partly be explained through his Gothic, mythical, fairy-tale, and naturalistic characters.

In *Wizard and Glass* (1997), the fourth volume of *The Dark Tower* series, Stephen King maintains that although he has written enough stories to "fill a solar system of the imagination," he is coming to understand that Roland's worlds contain all the others of his making. Roland the Gunslinger is the protagonist of *The Dark Tower* series, and his heroic journey is tracked through several King stories. All of King's characters seem to finish up in Mid-World, because it "was here first, before all of them, dreaming under the blue gaze of Roland's bombardier eyes" (*WG*, 697). King began to write Roland the Gunslinger's story in the spring of 1970, and it has its origins in Robert Browning's poem "Childe Roland to the Dark Tower Came" (1855). This volume also analyzes Roland's worlds and their citizens, especially Gothic, mythical, fairy-tale, and naturalistic characters in King's universe. Stanley Wiater, Christopher Golden, and Hank Wagner identify it as a multiverse, "a cluster of universes existing in parallel dimensions" (xiii). Most of King's stories are in fact interrelated. For instance, *Gerald's Game* (1992) was written at the same time as

Dolores Claiborne (1993). In both novels the total eclipse of the sun on July 20, 1963, plays a decisive role in the lives of the female protagonists, Jessie and Dolores. Having experienced the worst imaginable nightmares, they have visions of each other later that day. Furthermore, in *Dreamcatcher* (2001) King returns to Derry, one of his fictional towns, and refers to the disaster of 1985, which occurred in *It* (1986). Spignesi notes that this narrative continuity positions *Dreamcatcher* as a "spin-off" of *It*, because it relates another story of the town, thereby once again emphasizing the point that King "has been writing one massive book his entire life and just breaking it up into individual volumes" (*Essential*, 103).

Among other King critics, George Beahm, Michael R. Collings, and Tony Magistrale refer to King's body of fiction as "the fictional universe of Stephen King" (*Stephen King: America's Best-Loved Boogeyman*, 188), "King's imagined universe" (*Stephen King as Richard Bachman*, 17), "King's universe," and "King's fictional universe" (*Landscape of Fear*, 26), respectively. Wiater, Golden, and Wagner argue that "it is all of a piece" and that "there is a seemingly eternal struggle between good and evil, chaos and order taking place throughout the Stephen King universe and its myriad parallel realities and dimensions" (xiv). It seems dubious, however, that King would deliberately have been building his empire from the days of *Carrie* (1974). It is more likely that he has constructed it in the same way as he usually writes his stories: if he notices underlying patterns in the first draft, he focuses on them in the second (*OW*, 197). Obviously, many characters, themes, and symbols recur in King. More significant than any geographical world King has created is the integrated view of the way in which things in life happen and why they happen. He suggests that his work repeatedly emphasizes that he is "not merely dealing with the surreal and the fantastic but, more importantly, [is] using the surreal and the fantastic to examine the motivations of people and the society and institutions they create" (Magistrale, *Stephen King: The Second Decade*, 15). Thus, both the fictional towns of Castle Rock, Derry, Jerusalem's Lot, and Roland's dimension and the actual towns of King's Maine reveal the contradiction between the fantastic and the real, the two poles King creates. For instance, the Gothic vampire town, Jerusalem's Lot, represents King's Gothic heritage. This he readily admits, regarding the obsession with the past as "an unpleasant thing," both in his own writing and in all Gothic literature (10). Hence, the Gothic, myths, fairy tales, and literary naturalism together constitute the cornerstone of King's immense popularity.

Finally, let me introduce King's Constant Reader, the permanent resident of his multiverse. In King's vocabulary the Constant Reader is anyone who reads his fiction on a regular basis. I would not go as far as Wiater, Golden, and Wagner to define the reader as a character of King's imagination (xvii). However, there is no doubt that King attempts to make his reader participate in the communication process. Popular-culture and brand-name references ensure that the reader feels at home in King's fictional world, however fantastic it might be, and the anticipation of future horrors is embedded in innocently realistic settings and seemingly true-to-life characters. No doubt King's deep-seated respect for his Constant Reader contributes to his success as a writer. Evidently his attitude would please Stanley Fish and be compatible to his notion of "interpretative communities." Fish states that these communities "are made up of those who share interpretative strategies not for reading (in the conventional sense) but for writing texts, for constituting their properties and assigning their intentions" (483). Hence, these strategies exist prior to the act of reading and therefore determine the shape of what is read. Interpretative communities can be applied to King and his Constant Readers in the sense that in close interaction with his audience the writer is able to produce texts that meet the audience's expectations. A sensitive author is capable of interpreting the fears and the emotions of the community and of expressing them in language that his readers can understand.

What is also worth noting is both King's and his Constant Reader's imagination. In *Stephen King as Richard Bachman,* Collings argues that King's "dedication, coupled with a visual and visceral imagination and a lucid style has resulted in novel after novel" (7). More recently Bo Pettersson has presented a double definition of imagination as "an activity or function of the individual mind," on the one hand, and as "the shared frame of popular imagination," on the other hand ("On the Study of Imagination and Popular Imagination," 23). In his works King has repeatedly relied on the healing power of imagination: many a time imagination saves the day—and even the lives of his characters.

In King's world imagination and laughter are the most powerful weapons against any evil. In short, the reader and his imagination act in close interaction with the writer and his imagination in King's works—a crucial reason for the author's popularity. In addition to effective genre blending and memorable characters, this reader-writer interaction constitutes the bedrock of King's appeal.

King, His World, and Its Characters

The central aspects of Stephen King's fiction and his choice of genre can be analyzed in the context of both American society and the course of his personal life. Four factors have contributed to his worldview of the United States: Puritanism, the Gothic mode, "the Emersonian drive," and naturalism. King writes within the American cultural tradition in regard to all but the Emersonian drive, whereas some aspects and themes derive from his personal history. Since a writer with about 550 individual works has dealt with a great number of themes, my analysis is confined primarily to the aspects centering on the American literary heritage and on King's characters.

The roots of American Puritanism date back at least to 1630, when John Winthrop in his "Model of Christian Charity" used mild religious terror to create a particular political identity. Six years later John Cotton and his first-generation Puritan divines pursued a provisional polity to counter the nation's spiritual and civic decline and used the language of witchery (Ingebretsen, 10–13; for the origins of "persecuting society," see Moore). The unfortunate events culminated in the Salem witch hysteria of 1692–93, the echoes of which can be heard in King's first published novels, *Carrie* (1974) and *'Salem's Lot* (1975). These events show how closely connected religion and political identity actually were at the time. In those times of political "dis-ease," somebody had to be found guilty of witchcraft and punished accordingly to ease the minds of the Puritans. John Demos in *Entertaining Satan* argues that witchcraft was a necessary part of communal life, because it served the group by "sharpening its boundaries, reinforcing its values, and deepening the loyalty of its membership" (Demos, 14; Trevor-Roper 165, 189). Thus, although framed in

religious terms as *maleficium*, witchcraft constituted a civil offense, and the witch's body became a site of public strife (Ingebretsen, 16; for the witch's person, see Thomas). Whereas witchcraft focused on social unrest within a divided community, it also
"allowed Satan entrance to the self," thus underscoring the tension between internal conflict and social confusion (Hall, 146–
47). In the same way, although silenced by law, such religious
discourse still makes itself heard today, "surfacing in places pre-
sumed to be dismissible—particularly in the genres of the horror
sublime, or those texts we call dark fantasy" (Ingebretsen, 12).
The deeply religious framework of the American cultural heritage is explicitly about power and implicitly about fear, and,
therefore, Puritanism and horror are often blended in popular
fiction. In fact, Edward J. Ingebretsen goes as far as to claim that
American popular culture begins with the Salem witch trials (12–
13). Marion Starkey even notes that the "hangings were made a
spectacle by intention" (208).

One might even venture to claim that religious discourse has
in part been shifted from churches to horror fiction. Victor Sage
in *Horror Fiction in the Protestant Tradition* offers a similar view
and goes on to contend that the primary determinant in the formation of the Gothic is the religious one. In his historical reading,
Sage points out that the formation of a Protestant orthodoxy essentially generated all the major symbols of the Gothic tradition
(11). Ingebretsen distinguishes the two traditions by arguing that
in Gothic lore monsters typically haunt the margins of society,
whereas in political realities social deviants, such as witches,
emerge from within communities (15). King's stories provide examples of how disowned theologies return, ghostlike, as moralistic social memory (14). King has been influenced by the Bible,
and he professes a faith in the Christian God (Magistrale, *Decade*,
3; Underwood and Miller, *Feast*, 64). Brought up in the atmosphere of Methodism and "fascinated by the trappings and so-
lemnity of Catholicism" (Underwood and Miller, *Feast*, 64), King
has been preoccupied with religious themes throughout his writing career. Religious frenzy finds its expression in such characters as Margaret White *(Carrie)*, Henrietta Dodd *(The Dead Zone)*,
Vera Smith *(The Dead Zone)*, and Sylvia Pittston *(The Gunslinger)*.
Unworthy priests are represented by such characters as Father
Callahan *('Salem's Lot)*, Reverend Lester Lowe *(Cycle of the*

Werewolf), and Sunlight Gardener (*The Talisman*). Good prophets are portrayed in the characters of Nick Andros (*The Stand*), Mother Abagail (*The Stand*), and David Carver (*Desperation*); evil in that of Randall Flagg (*The Stand, The Eyes of the Dragon,* and *The Dark Tower* series). Hence, King has been dedicated to religious themes both because of his national, Puritan heritage and for reasons of personal interest.

The concept of the Gothic is an emotional coloration, which may be called mood or more precisely mode, because, as Alastair Fowler in *Kinds of Literature* notes, "modal terms tend to be adjectival" (67, 106). In other words, although the Gothic began as a separate genre in the latter part of the eighteenth century, the genre no longer exists as such. Instead it is a mode that lends an atmosphere to literature, among other cultural artifacts. In fact, Leslie Fiedler in *Love and Death in the American Novel* argues that both the most serious and the funniest American writers have found the Gothic mode an apt one for telling the truth about the quality of American life (preface to the second edition, 2). Furthermore, he maintains that the Gothic atmosphere derives from the guilt that America's bloody past has produced. Not surprisingly the last desperate attempt to get rid of guilt is to pretend that all sinister events are nothing but jokes (6–7). Ingebretsen aptly links this guilt with the Calvinistic civic cosmology of expiation: the Salem witch trials, for example, were a means of self-definition (15). The witch-hunting rites were both expiatory and explanatory, socially just as clarifying and purgative as the Gothic literature less than a hundred years later.

The reasons for the proliferation of the Gothic may well be in part religious. Although most Americans believe in God, few seem to believe in his presence. In *Nightmare on Main Street*, Mark Edmundson argues that peace of mind can be gained by accepting the belief that the world is infested with evil, that all power is corrupt, that all humanity is debased, and that nothing can be done about it (67–68). The disenchantment with religion has caused a twofold reaction. Some seek confidence in the Gothic, others in naturalism—in either case, one ends up losing hope and dreams of benevolent, divine forces. Perhaps the essence of the Gothic mode is, however, the fall from innocence or the bargain with the devil, that is, the Faustian pact. These themes are visible in King's oeuvre from the beginning to the present. In particular they have found their direct expression in *Needful Things* (1991) and *Storm of the Century* (1999), where the pact is literally made. *'Salem's Lot* (1975), *The Shining* (1977), *Pet Sematary* (1983), *Misery* (1987), and even *The Dark Tower* series (1982–2004) are often referred to as Gothic novels because of their characters and settings. *The Dark Half* (1989) includes the Gothic motif of the double, and in *Gerald's Game* (1992) the same motif has been internalized in Jessie Burlingame's troubled mind. Finally, *Bag of Bones* (1998) can be labeled a Gothic romance, because it includes an unhappy love story. Of course, it takes more to make a Gothic novel than a single characteristic, and it seems more justifiable to argue that the Gothic mode is one important facet of King's oeuvre.

The third factor in King's American literary heritage is what I call "the Emersonian drive," namely, the self-reliance that, according to Harold Bloom, is "the Emersonian answer to Original Sin" (*Poetics of Influence*, 284) in the sense of personifying the confident spirit to clear whatever obstacles fate has chosen to put in one's way. The Emersonian drive seems to embody everything that eludes the Gothic: youthful drive and self-reliance. More significantly, for Emerson there is no fate to foil the efforts of a confident spirit, and each man is "greater than all the geography and all the government of the world" (*Nature,* 3). In fact, Emerson does not even believe in fate, and for him there is no original sin. In his view we succumb to fate out of fear, because in the Emersonian universe fate is an excuse and little more. The only sin is limitation; therefore, guilt, among other things, must go. Edmundson clarifies this point: "Whatever our faults in the past, we need to forget them or redeem them, if in sustaining them we're impeded from doing our work in the present" (72). By comparison, as an example of an anti-Emersonian, Bloom refers to Edgar Allan Poe, one of King's literary predecessors. He states that Poe's characters were never young (*Poetics*, 285). Edmundson, too, emphasizes that Poe's characters were struck by fate and Poe's "every story was a burnt offering on [fate's] altar" (72).

The Emersonian drive is continuously thwarted by fate in King. Born in 1947 to a lower middle-class family, King seems to exemplify the traditional American success story. However, the theme of success is rarely found in his fiction. In light of what we have learned from the contradiction between the Gothic and the Emersonian drive, this seems more than understandable.

Although, for instance, the members of the so-called Losers' Club in *It* reach the top of the ladder in their individual lives, they are all haunted by their childhood memories. Not even King's most fantastic works have attempted to depict a truly Emersonian character. For instance, *The Talisman* (1984), which in Wiater, Golden, and Wagner's words is "about youth, hope, and innocence that harkens back to the simpler times depicted in Mark Twain's work" (66), finds its depressing epilogue in *The Tommyknockers* (1987). Here Jack Sawyer, the protagonist of *The Talisman*, heroically saves his mother's life only to see her killed by a drunk driver. Jack's journey to hell and back leads to nothing. Charlie McGee *(Firestarter)*, Peter, the elder son of King Roland of Delain *(The Eyes of the Dragon)*, and Trisha McFarland *(The Girl Who Loved Tom Gordon)* may provide the rare exceptions of this rule in King's oeuvre, but only by a very narrow margin. Obviously, Charlie will all her life be under constant surveillance, since she possesses an ability to start fires with her mind; Trisha, will not be able to reunite her divorced parents; and Peter will be in charge of a kingdom that sooner or later will again be attacked by Flagg. Thus, even in King's most fantastic works, his characters are shaped by deterministic forces and fate.

The fourth and final factor in King's literary heritage is literary naturalism. In *Backgrounds of American Literary Thought*, Rod W. Horton and Herbert W. Edwards call the genre "the product of despair," because it reflects the shattering of the optimism of the Enlightenment: the faith in the democratic system, the hope for human growth, and the belief in the dignity of man (254). In its adherence to observed nature, literary naturalism is derived both from the natural sciences and from sociohistorical theories. As M. H. Abrams points out, the post-Darwinian thesis of literary naturalism holds that the human being belongs in the order of nature and does not have a soul or any connection with a spiritual world beyond nature. Therefore, a human being is merely a higher-order animal whose character and fortunes are determined by two kinds of natural forces, heredity and environment (Abrams, 153–54; Barton and Hudson, 117). Martin Gray, too, emphasizes that literary naturalism is a particular branch of realism with a focus on the miserable and poverty-stricken whose spiritual and intellectual aspirations prove meaningless, or on characters driven by their animal appetites, such as hunger and sexuality (135). As Horton and Edwards note, whereas the scholar of the Enlightenment probed the mysteries of nature as a means of self-justification, the naturalist found in scientific discovery only a confirmation of humankind's helplessness in the face of indifferent and inscrutable forces (255).

Since King has repeatedly acknowledged the existence of personal good and evil forces beyond human control, it is mainly the deterministic view of human beings that relates King to literary naturalism and which, according to Horton and Edwards, is regarded as the "most prevalent literary attitude [in the United States] during the first half of the twentieth century" (259). In *The World according to Kurt Vonnegut,* Bo Pettersson states that the origin of naturalism is manifold, including the modification of what is narrowly labeled as Calvinism into a philosophical determinism (29) and "the moral sterility of undisciplined material and political growth in America" (Horton and Edwards, 260). In King the following aspects of naturalism seem conspicuous: his view of human beings as a product of their environment, his view of humans at the mercy of indifferent forces, and his profound mistrust of scientific progress. Significantly, King shares the latter two attitudes with H. P. Lovecraft, one of his major literary influences.

The deterministic view of humankind also links the Gothic and literary naturalism in King's fiction. In Gothic fiction, fate rules human beings, and they are driven by their instincts; the deterministic view also holds these notions but assumes that humans, as rational beings, can make moral choices. Stephen J. Spignesi points out that in King's world "man possesses free will, but fate will often conspire to put things right" (*Lost Work of Stephen King,* 9). Apparently, King came to embrace the deterministic view of the world at a very early age, because it can be found in unpublished short stories such as "The Thing at the Bottom of the Well" and "The Stranger," both written as a young schoolboy. However, since King's naturalism is colored by the Gothic, the supernatural elements alternate between softening his naturalistic tones and making them even grimmer. At any rate, King's naturalism has kept its faith in the dignity of human beings and close-knit communities, within which emotional needs can be fulfilled and responsible acts committed. As Jeanne Campbell Reesman rightly claims, through supernatural realism

King explores both the attractions and the failures of naturalism (109). Thus, he examines naturalistic themes by means of horror. In conclusion, King is a distinctly American writer in that he deploys motifs and themes deriving from the nation's common source of memory and experience and has continued to use the same motifs and themes throughout his career.

King has said about his work that "probably all the significant experience shows up in the fiction" (Magistrale, *Decade,* 2). The aspects of King's fiction that derive from his personal experiences are primarily (1) regionalism and the writer's home state of Maine and (2) character description, including outsider motifs, child depictions, female characters, and his fairy-tale Everyman. In this connection I will focus on the character-centered aspects of King's fiction, instead of, for instance, the more typical view of horror as an unexpected and catastrophic event, because the notion of character will be crucial to the development of my argument. Let us briefly consider the settings and people of King's formative years: After his father had gone out for a pack of cigarettes and never returned, his mother, Ruth, and adopted brother, Dave, led a restless life moving around the country. When Stephen was eleven years old, the family moved to Durham, Maine, where King stayed until he graduated from the University of Maine in 1970. In the following year he married Tabitha Spruce, whom he had met in college. The couple has stayed in the Maine area, and they have three children (Spignesi, *Lost Work,* xix–xx).

King can with good cause be called a regionalist with a distinct narrative voice, often colored by the Maine dialect. The close-lipped declaration of his love for Maine reads as follows: "For me, it has always been a case of being here, living in Maine all my life. The settings are here" (Magistrale, *Decade,* 10). Undoubtedly, the setting comes through, casting its own shadow over whatever King is writing, and for him the importance of region is linked with how people have been disconnected. *Dolores Claiborne* and *Storm of the Century* are set on an island, and through the fictional microcosms of Castle Rock, Derry, and Jerusalem's Lot, he examines a small-town pathology with its calm surface and rotten heart. James E. Hicks notes that the horror of, for instance, *'Salem's Lot* is the reader's "realization that the American pastoral is corruptible, that small town America is not a bulwark against depravity" (76). The xenophobia of small-town America has been dealt with in *Carrie, 'Salem's Lot, The Dead Zone, Cujo, It, The Dark Half, Needful Things, Insomnia, Bag of Bones,* and in several short stories. Equally, many of the names of King's characters have personal significance: while some appear as little more than jokes, others refer to the names of local people or allude to friends and acquaintances. King admits that he has used symbolic names since he was a writer in college: "I don't always do it, but John Smith was certainly the most obvious case, and I chose [that name] on purpose" (Magistrale, *Decade*, 3).

The roots of the outsider motif are also embedded in the writer's own childhood. All of King's works have been preoccupied with this motif, from *Carrie* (1974) to *The Dark Tower* (2004). Introduced to horror by a radio adaptation of Ray Bradbury's story "Mars Is Heaven" at the age of four, the writer has up to *It* (1986) explored "the mythic power that childhood holds over our imagination and, in particular, the point at which the adult is able to link up with his or her own childhood past and the powers therein" (Magistrale, *Decade*, 5). King has been depicting children throughout his writing career, regarding *It* as his "final exam covering the subject" (5). Despite such characters as Trisha McFarland in *The Girl Who Loved Tom Gordon* (1999) and the handicapped Duddits in *Dreamcatcher* (2001), it holds true that King's child characters have grown older at the rate of his own children. For instance, in *From a Buick 8* (2002), King introduces the eighteen-year-old Ned Wilcox, whose relationship to his deceased father is thematized in the novel.

For King imagination, in essence, separates a child from an adult. In *Danse Macabre* he points out: "The imagination is an eye, a marvelous eye that floats free. As children, that eye sees with 20/20 clarity. As we grow older, its vision begins to dim" (407). Adults without imagination are the worst of his monsters, and the child or adolescent protagonist can merely hope for an encounter with an adult who is able to reenter the world of childhood. Such adult characters are almost without exception represented as writers—they seem to have immediate access to their childhood memories and to be able to perceive other dimensions. Although perfect victims, children possess strength that adults have lost in the process of maturing. Thus, when Matt Burke faces a vampire, he is stricken by a heart seizure brought on by fright. But when Mark Petrie encounters one, he is able to fall asleep ten minutes later: "Such is the difference between men and boys" (*SL*, 243).

Ever since the publication of *Carrie* (1974), King has been blamed for depicting his women characters as stereotypes. Since eight of his novels feature female protagonists (*Carrie, Firestarter, Cujo, Misery, Gerald's Game, Dolores Claiborne, Rose Madder,* and *Song of Susannah*); seven depict them as wives or partners (*The Shining, The Drawing of the Three, The Tommyknockers, The Dark Half, The Waste Lands, Insomnia,* and *The Dark Tower*); and four include them in minor roles (*The Stand, It, Needful Things,* and *From a Buick 8*), the accusation must be discussed in brief. Carol Senf notes the disagreement among critics commenting on King's portraits of women ("*Gerald's Game* and *Dolores Claiborne,*" 92). At one end of the spectrum, Clare Hanson regards King as a misogynist who attempts to resolve his Oedipus complex by means of his fiction (150). In the middle we have Chelsea Quinn Yarbro, who in 1985 expressed how disheartening it is "when a writer with so much talent and strength and vision is not able to develop a believable woman character between the ages of seventeen and sixty" (65); Tony Magistrale, who in 1989 complained that King's oeuvre features few complex women, that is, "multidimensional blends of good and evil" (*Moral Voyages of Stephen King*, 51); and Mary Pharr, who in 1992 argued that although female characters are plentiful enough in King's works and although women clearly matter to him, they lack substance ("Partners in the *Danse*," 20). Finally, at the other end of the spectrum, Burton Hatlen considers King a feminist influenced by his feminist wife (Magistrale, *Voyages*, 104), and Mark Jancovich considers King's female characters at least as strong as his male characters (101–2).

In fact, Fiedler in *Love and Death in the American Novel* maintains that no American novelist has been able to treat the passionate encounter of a man and a woman, but instead they shy away from permitting in their works "the presence of any full-fledged, mature woman, giving us instead monsters of virtue or bitchery, symbols of the rejection or fear of sexuality" (4–5). Instead of love, American novels depict "comrades in arms" (5). King regards Fiedler's book as "a motivating force behind the writing of *Carrie*" (Magistrale, *Decade*, 5): "A lot of my efforts in writing about women were made because I wanted to under-stand women and try to escape the stereotyping that goes on in so much male fiction" (5). Although King has made an effort since the very beginning of his writing career to avoid female stereotypes, especially since *Gerald's Game* (1992), he has more consciously concentrated on women, the emphasis shifting from child characters to women characters.

As "the guru of the ordinary," King also celebrates ordinary men (Magistrale, *Decade,* 10). Like Johnny Smith in *The Dead Zone,* King's Everyman struggles against indifferent forces and triumphs over evil by discovering his inner strength. The victory is reached more by the protagonist's essence of being than by his heroic acts. As Magistrale notes, King has endowed most of his male protagonists with certain powers, such as imagination, which serve them in their struggles against evil forces (11). Sev-eral novels feature either outsiders (for instance, *Roadwork, The Running Man, The Dark Tower* series, and *It*) or writers (for in-stance, *'Salem's Lot, The Shining, Misery, The Dark Half,* and *Bag of Bones*) as protagonists. King argues that writing about writers has been an effort to understand what he is doing and what writ-ing is doing to and for him (11). In fact, King's characters are de-veloped in an unusual way, which in part results from the combi-nation of archetypes and realism implicit in the characters. For instance, Johnny Smith epitomizes unselfish love for human-kind, but he becomes flesh and blood through his realistic feel-ings and actions, such as the love for his girlfriend and the pain-ful decision to shoot a maniac. Similarly, Norman Daniels, whose Christian name apparently refers to the protagonist of Robert Bloch's *Psycho,* personifies pure evil. Daniels is a police detective whose quick temper leads him to beat his wife and brutalize sus-pects and who becomes realistic through the detailed depiction of his hideous crimes.

King's writing has now been placed in the context of both American society and his personal life. Significantly, the central aspects of King's American heritage seem to center on the notion of fate. Fate played a decisive role in Puritan thought, bordering on the concept of God, who led the Puritans to the Promised Land of New England (Bercovitch, 136); in Gothic literature fate often implies evil destiny or even death, thus punishing the wrong-doings of such villains as Manfred of Otranto; and in literary naturalism parallels can be drawn with chance (as in King's Bachman books). In the section "Cosmological Determinism and Fate" in chapter 3, fate will be defined according to this tripartite division, but suffice it to note in this connection that the only aspect of the American literary heritage that cannot be applied to King, the Emersonian drive, focuses on life *after* fate has struck, thus providing an optimistic view of the future. When the exploration of fate intertwines with the central concerns deriving from King's personal experience, such as religion and human psychology, we have largely discovered the very essence of King's writing: the human being at the mercy of whimsical and indifferent forces where the best comfort can be found in empathy with one's fellow sufferers.

Interpreter of the Postmodern Condition

The heart of this monograph is my belief that King (when he is not Richard Bachman, the naturalistic pseudonym) is a traditionalist writer in our post-traditional world, a man whose work suggests that conscious choices together with predestined inner quality determine a character's destiny and whose multiverse presents the moral message that dedication, determination, and will power may sometimes overcome seemingly impossible odds. In her critique of this monograph, Mary Pharr aptly notes that "King's determination to have it both ways parallels the uncertain hopes and fears of his postmodern readers—and in that respect he is very much a product of the middle class of our time. That is, he has a postmodern perspective and a yen for premodern faith."

Postmodernism, however, is so contradictory a term that it can easily become useless, unless carefully defined. In what follows I make use of Bo Pettersson's reasoning and definition of American postmodern fiction (*Vonnegut*, 12–21). Indeed, King's relation to postmodernism can be clarified by first defining postmodernism qualified by *American* and *fiction*. Doing so can then lead to a discussion of his particular brand of horror. There are, as Pettersson has pointed out, three essential aspects of American postmodern fiction: its relations to reality, to society, and to literature (*Vonnegut*, 12).

In both the fantastic and modernism, Brian McHale has noted, what is in doubt is not so much the existence of reality as its true nature. In "Writing about Postmodern Writing," McHale argues that there is an *"epistemological* hesitation" between various interpretations. But in postmodern fiction, according to McHale, "we hesitate between competing structures of reality, alternative worlds—an *ontological* hesitation" (223, italics in original). As Pettersson notes, this distinction acknowledges the modern hesitation of postmodernism as well as the change in perspective (*Vonnegut*, 13). Moreover, it shows that "the radical skepticism about ultimate questions" Richard Chase considers typical of the traditional American romance or romance novel is still inherent in, and at times thematized by, American postmodern fiction (x). In fact, the American postmodern novel seems to have inherited the "symbolic or ideological, rather than realistic, plausibility" of the romance novel and the "mythic, allegorical, and symbolistic forms" it takes (13).

The ontological hesitation in postmodernism may in part derive from the cultural and social pluralism ensuing on the breakup of middle-class values (Pettersson, *Vonnegut*, 13). Patricia Waugh suggests that the modernist *"opposition* to existing social institutions and conventions" no longer works:

The power structures of contemporary society are . . . more diverse and more effectively concealed or mystified, creating greater problems for the post-modernist novelist in identifying and then representing the object of "opposition."

Metafictional writers have found a solution to this by turning inwards to their own medium of expression, in order to examine the relationship between fictional form and social reality. (10–11, italics in original)

The Everyman lost in the labyrinths of power is, as Pettersson points out, a theme at least as old as Kafka. Yet the postmodernist's formal means of expressing skepticism of ontological explanations and middle-class socioeconomic forces differ from the explorations of the psyche of modernism (*Vonnegut*, 14).

If modernists were aware of fiction as an artistic medium, postmodernists are conscious of fiction as artifice and turn to the tradition of the novel to revitalize their fiction (Pettersson, *Vonnegut*, 14). Waugh claims—rightly, I think—that the continual revision of our view of the universe in this century suggests that reality itself, like fiction, is a contradiction. By conspicuous use of a genre—the realist novel—postmodernists can simultaneously tell a story and reveal its artifice (6). In her view this presenting and unmasking is mirrored in explicit and implicit analyses of contemporary society and the power structures that rule it. Waugh summarizes these social aspects of postmodern metafiction as follows: it "converts what it sees as the negative values of outworn literary conventions into the basis of a potentially constructive social criticism" (11). At the same time, postmodern fiction is not simply an appropriate medium for an American writer to express his worldview. Part of the impetus behind it is also an urge to explore new means of literary expression (Pettersson, *Vonnegut*, 15; Fokkema, 236).

As Pettersson summarizes, American postmodern fiction shows a deep skepticism of ontological explanations as well as of middle-class values and socioeconomic forces in society and confronts the outside world by self-reflexive and playfully innovative use of literary tradition and technique (Pettersson, *Vonnegut*, 15; Wilde, 129, 12). This seems true of most American writers who are usually labeled postmodern: John Barth, Donald Barthelme, Tom Robbins, Terry Southern, Kurt Vonnegut—and Stephen King, who is a postmodern writer in all three senses, though his work contains other elements as well.

Presumably, King has been so concerned with ontology that he constantly writes about multidimensional worlds, universes within universes, and the essence of good and evil (see "Cosmological Determinism and Fate" in chapter 3). In his fiction final answers are seldom given to the existential questions of his characters. Similarly, socioeconomical aspects run throughout King's oeuvre (see "Genetic and Sociological Determinism" in chapter 3). By means of the horror genre, he strongly criticizes American politics and socioeconomics in most of his stories. The postmodern element also plays, I believe, into my discussion of metafictional determinism (see "Metafictional Determinism" in chapter 3). Like Alfred Hitchcock and Kurt Vonnegut before him, King defines himself within his own works by his narrative means of indicating the shape of those works, by their ties to our universe (the brand-name focus), by the increasingly unified universe in which they take place, and by his own presence (seen or implied) within his oeuvre. In her critique of this work, Mary Pharr points out that King is clearly a reflexive creator. Unlike, say, Peter Straub, King *is* his work and *is* his own Constant Reader (see especially *Song of Susannah* and *The Dark Tower*, where he literally becomes a character of *The Dark Tower* series). He has blended not only genre but also his persona and his reality—for good or for ill. He really is a creator for our time.

In fact, King characterizes himself as a medium, a writer who draws on primary instincts and deeply embedded memories— with a direct Jungian line to the American crisis center. Walter Ong in *Orality and Literacy* notes that in preliterate and oral cultures language is "a mode of action rather than [a] countersign of thought." The Hebrew term *dabar*, which means "word," also means "event" (75). Preliterate societies had no categories for abstracting knowledge as concepts; these remained "embedded within the human lifeworld," the world of action (Badley, *Writing Horror and Body*, 19). In his essay "Imagery and the Third Eye" (1980), King advises aspiring writers to focus on "story," situation, and scene. For King books "happen": first a situation occurs, then an opening scene (Underwood and Miller, *Bones*, 122). The essence of all is "story," that "simple caveman invention ('I was walking through the forest when the tiger leaped down on me') that held [an] audience spellbound around the fire" (King, "Imagery," 11). For King "story springs from image: the vividness of place and time and *texture*" (11, italics in original). In *On Writing*, he points out that "story" is not a linear plot but an existential situation or locus (163). Drawing on the post-Jungian psychology of James Hillman and others, Edwin Casebeer explains King's characters in comparable terms: "A writer such as King does not create personas. Instead his psyche becomes a locus available for personas to emerge and interact with one another" ("Ecological System of Stephen King's 'The Dark Half,'" 128). In other words, the resulting story is "a nexus upon which King and his readers converge for psychic dialogue" (128). Character is "coextensive with the archetypal. We are visited (or possessed) by identity" (129).

Similarly, King says that he writes out his nightmares in order to stay sane ("Novelist Sounds Off," 80). In a *Rolling Stone* interview with Abe Peck, he describes the "actual physical act" of writing as being "like autohypnosis, a series of mental passes you go through before you start" (Underwood and Miller, *Bones,* 108). As Linda Badley in *Writing Horror and Body* notes, in *The Dark Half,* for instance, professor-author Thad Beaumont performs a ritual—smoking, drinking, picking up a pencil—enters a trance, and becomes the best-selling writer of gruesome pulp thrillers (*Body,* 20). Like Beaumont, King has a third eye, a special vision- ary faculty to which he attributes animistic—and very Jungian— power. This "inner" eye has evocative power, but rather than re- cording events, it projects them, with the reader completing the act: "Imagery does not occur on the writer's page, it occurs in the reader's mind" (King, "Imagery," 12). King's characters, as the *Time* critic Paul Gray points out, are always watching movies in their heads (87). A character in "The Raft" tells the monster to "go to California and find a Roger Corman movie to audition for" (*SK,* 305). As Badley aptly notes, King gives postmodern sub- stance to the validated nightmare cliché. He applies naturalistic methods to an environment produced by popular culture and thus creates the sense of a shared nightmare (*Body,* 20). In this cul- turally produced virtual reality, ideas of evil "take the bodies of large beasts with powerful jaws; memories . . . become ghosts; and unwholesome impulses and animal instincts tend to pop into being as doubles" (Rafferty, 106). Thus, King's brand of hor- ror draws directly on psychoanalytic imagery and symbolism.

Undoubtedly, King can be placed into the context of post- modern America and middle-class America. This reluctant in- terpreter of postmodern humankind is simultaneously driven by the contradictory urges of his postmodern values and his middle-class fear of postmodernism. After all—as Pharr in her assessment of this monograph aptly notes—"what could be more postmodern than the blending of genres, and what could be more anti-postmodern than King's rejection of the purity of tech- nology? Yet here is the writer who tried selling a short story ('Riding the Bullet') over the Web and who loves tinkering with modes of publication delivery. He is everywhere contradictory in his perspectives—but so, too, are the rest of us, his Constant Readers."

With his postmodern perspectives here and there, King cer- tainly has formed a postmodern argument (see the sections "The Antihero as a Generic Hybrid (Randall Flagg)" and "Adapted and Revised Myths and Fairy Tales" in chapter 2 for examples). I believe that he needs his special brand of horror to express his essence as an avid *and* reluctant postmodern writer.

King's Brand of Horror

King's fictional art consists of generic hybrids. In combining elements of the Gothic tale with other genres—such as realism, literary naturalism, myths, fairy tales, romanticism, and other elements of the fantastic—King enriches his fiction at the same time as he challenges the traditional limits associated with these genres. His brand of horror is the end product of a kind of genre equation: the Gothic + myths and fairy tales + literary naturalism = King's brand of horror. As I see it, the Gothic provides the background; myths and fairy tales make good stories; and literary naturalism lends the worldview implicit in King's multiverse. Without disparaging their importance, other genres, such as science fiction, suspense fiction, and fantasy, recur more or less regularly.

When defining *genre,* a classic starting point is Aristotle's theory that fiction must be considered a characteristic of literature. In other words, what literary genres define is fiction. In addition to the function of genre, another characteristic seems of crucial importance in regard to a blender of genres like King: employing one genre does not rule out making use of another (see also Hawthorn, 137). Therefore, as Fowler points out, genres are not considered classes but types, because generic types do not require that all traits be shared by other embodiments of the same type (37–38). Hence, on the one hand, a single work of art can belong to more than one genre; on the other, different works of art can be placed in the same genre if they share its most characteristic traits. Regardless of his genius, every writer changes the genres he writes within. Fowler argues—rightly, I think—that "the character of genres is that they change" (18); all genres are in flux, and this seems the way in which literature itself changes (23). What makes King different from most other blenders of genres is his apparently systematic and deliberate attempt to do so. In fact, this blend of genres and modes has added to his versatility as a writer and contributed to his popularity. In sum, I define *genre* as a literary type that undergoes a continuous change. Like Northrop Frye in *Anatomy of Criticism* (131–40) and Cawelti in *The Six-Gun Mystique* (57), I acknowledge the existence of certain underlying patterns of action that seem universal, but in regard to the purposes of this work the discussion of universality remains irrelevant.

When defining *horror*, it is necessary to emphasize not only the contrast between the actual experience of horror and its artistic presentations but also to stress the effects of the horror genre. The distinction between actual experience and the aesthetics of representation has been made as early as in Aristotle's *Poetics* and Edmund Burke's essay on the sublime (1757). Both suggest that the instinct to enjoy works of horrific imagery is inborn in humans (Aristotle, 6–7; Burke, 53). Noël Carroll in *The Philosophy of Horror or Paradoxes of the Heart* develops the distinction between what he calls *natural horror* and *art-horror*, arguing that in the latter the emotive responses of the audience run parallel to the emotions of the characters, and that this mirroring effect is a key feature of the horror genre (17–18). In addition to identification, he distinguishes disgust (19), revulsion (19)/nausea (22), and impurity (23)/uncleanliness (21) as features of art-horror, stating that art-horror is an emotion (24).

In *Powers of Horror*, Julia Kristeva traces horror, or rather *abjection* in her terminology, to the Freudian primal scene. Compared to Carroll's list of the emotional effects art-horror causes in audiences, Kristeva's analysis results in a slightly more detailed one: revulsion/nausea (2), shame (1), desire (1), violation of the natural order (4), identification (5), and fear (11). She also suggests a solution to combat a threat by naming it in the manner of primitive societies (11). In *No Go the Bogeyman*, Marina Warner distinguishes different "states of mind or feelings" in horror, as, for instance, disgust and fear, and regards amusement as the defining mood of the horror genre (7). This modern sensibility first found its expression in the perverse and ironical fairy tales of the late seventeenth century, where fear was cultivated as an aesthetic thrill (4). Regardless of their vastly different approaches to literature as such, Carroll, Kristeva, and Warner largely agree on some aspects of horror. On this basis I define *horror* as an emotion that includes most such aspects, the experience of which in the reader runs parallel to the emotions of the characters.

King identifies himself as a horror writer. When he had already sold *Carrie*, *'Salem's Lot*, and *The Shining* and was planning to publish *Firestarter*, his literary agent from Doubleday, Bill Thompson, voiced his concern that King would be labeled a genre writer. King concluded, however, that he could be in worse company and cited others in the field whom he holds as his literary predecessors: H. P. Lovecraft, Clark Ashton Smith, Frank Belknap Long, Fritz Leiber, Robert Bloch, Richard Matheson, and Shirley Jackson (*DS*, 500–501). Thus, he takes the horror genre seriously and even analyzes it in *Danse Macabre*. In this nonfiction study, he repeatedly refers to our "phobic pressure points," contemporary concerns, and common anxieties (*DM*, 5). The symbolic expression of the horror genre, for King, divides into two aspects: cultural fears and personal fears (Hoppenstand and Browne, 11). Cultural fears include political, economic, and psychological threats, such as the fear of invasion, which he identifies in the films *Invasion of the Body Snatchers* (1956) and *Earth vs. the Flying Saucers* (1956) (*DM*, 5–9). As regards personal fears, he surveys them in the essay "The Horror Writer and Ten Bears" (12). King's ten "bears" are fear of the dark, fear of squishy things, fear of deformity, fear of snakes, fear of rats, fear of closed-in places, fear of insects (especially spiders, flies, and beetles), fear of death, fear of others (paranoia), and fear for someone else.

Both cultural and personal fears are thoroughly documented in King's fiction. In fact, one of the reasons for his success as a writer is that, as regards fear, he is a kind of Everyman. King believes that humankind has a so-called pool of fears and that "we all can come and see our own faces or wet our hands in it" (Underwood and Miller, *Bones*, 109). In *Carrie*, for instance, King charts the transgressive oppositions of a Calvinist cosmology, where an insistence on law and order organizes and essentially creates the conflict they enact, and where transgression and scrutiny organize the community (Ingebretsen, 19). In *The Shining* the supernatural motif of the novel is the haunted hotel, but the actual horror elements of the story thematize the disintegration of the Torrance family (Hoppenstand and Browne, 6). Virtually all of King's stories attempt to touch the reader on more than one level.

King's works can now be placed in the context of the horror genre. As regards his adolescent writings, King states that although these stories had the trappings of science fiction, they were really horror stories (Winter, *Art*, 19; Underwood and

Miller, *Bones*, 57, 62, 65). In *The Many Facets of Stephen King*, Michael R. Collings calls them "horror in disguise" (17). This statement holds true for the rest of King's writing as well: "the trappings" may vary, but, paradoxically, his brand of horror consistently combines horror with other genres (Russell, 22). In the afterword of *Different Seasons* (1982), King claims that he writes true to type and that elements of horror can be found in all the tales, because sooner or later, his mind always seems to turn in that direction (501–2). In Douglas E. Winter's *Faces of Fear*, King affirms this stance, arguing that writing horror fiction is his "fate" (239–40).

When emphasizing the horror genre at the heart of his fiction, King by no means undermines the influence of other genres. In fact, in the essay "On Becoming a Brand Name" (1985), he somewhat contradictorily maintains that his four earliest (if not published) novels can be labeled either suspense or, in one case, science fiction (20). Since one of the four, *Sword in the Darkness* (1970), allegedly depicts a race riot in a high-school setting and is influenced by John Farris's *Harrison High* novels and Don Robertson's *The Greatest Thing since Sliced Bread* (1965) and *Paradise Falls* (1965) (Spignesi, *Lost Work*, 66), I presume that King refers to the science-fiction traits of his first written but unpublished novel *The Aftermath* (written at the age of sixteen), which takes place after a nuclear war has destroyed a large part of the world's population. However, *The Sword in the Darkness*, *Rage* (written as a high school senior), and *The Long Walk* (written during his freshman year of college) would fall into the suspense category. Disregarding King's personal views of his brand of fiction, I think it is fair to say that none of his novels is purely either suspense or science fiction—or purely anything, for that matter. In his fiction the emotions of fear and fascination are thus combined in the genres they have inspired.

The versatility and diversity of King's blend of horror is a case in point. Here is a final illustration of my position: While the horror genre is frequently placed in one category, King's brand of horror covers four categories in Tzvetan Todorov's classic study. As a branch of popular fiction, horror fiction often poses the question: What if? (Winter, *Art*, 4; see also Deleuze and Guattari, 192). In his well-known study *The Fantastic*, Todorov classifies

literary genres. According to him, the fantastic occupies the duration of uncertainty, that is, as long as we are uncertain of the
credibility of a story, it remains in the territory of the fantastic
(25). If we decide that the laws of reality remain intact, we say
that the work belongs to the uncanny; if, on the contrary, we decide that new laws of nature must be adopted to account for the
phenomena, we enter the marvelous (41). While myths and fairy
tales are classified under the heading of the marvelous, because
their worlds do not abide by our scientific laws but have their
own laws (Carroll, 16), horror stories present a challenge to Todorov's classification.

Todorov argues that the literature of horror in its pure state belongs to the uncanny (47). Nevertheless, he uses Henry James's
classic *The Turn of the Screw* (1898) as an example of a story where
the ambiguity persists (43). Winter claims that "The Reach"
presents another example of this kind of ambiguity. In his view
the ghosts Stella Flanders sees cannot be proved to exist (*Art*, 69).
It seems, however, that King's stories more often are marred
by his obsession with giving an explanation of every possible detail. As an illustration, in "The Reach," the cap of Bill Flanders,
Stella's deceased husband, has mysteriously appeared on Stella's
head when she is discovered dead. This seems to imply that the
ghosts Stella sees before her death are real. While Carroll argues
that horror falls under the label of *the fantastic/marvelous* (16),
he argues persuasively that the notion of the fantastic/marvel-
ous fails to focus on the specific effect that the horror genre is
predicated upon. He also rightly notes that even if labeled the
fantastic-marvelous, horror constitutes a distinctive species (16–
17). Indeed, King's works include stories in all these fields: *The
Eyes of the Dragon* even exemplifies the fairy-tale characteristics
of the marvelous.

The premise of my argument has now been established: King
is a horror writer with an uncommonly wide interest in other literary genres. The following chapters will view him as a Gothic
writer, as a writer of myths and fairy tales, and as a literary naturalist. I have chosen to focus on the Gothic first, because it provides King's brand of horror with a historical background and
perspective. Since the Gothic atmosphere permeates King's
myths and fairy tales, the fantastic genres have been placed next
to each other. King has been simultaneously influenced by the

contradictory impulses of free will and determinism, which highlights a core tension in his oeuvre. Since the discussion leads to this contention, literary naturalism, as a realistic genre, precedes my conclusion, in which the fantastic and realistic genres and modes are connected through determinism. This blend is called Stephen King's horror fiction, and it remains to be seen whether it can even be labeled horror in the strict sense of the word.

1

The Gothic in King's Works

The term *Gothic* is used in a number of different fields: literary, historical, artistic, and architectural. As David Punter in *The Literature of Terror* (1:1) points out, in a literary context alone, it has several uses. First, *Gothic* is applied to a group of novels written between the 1760s and the 1820s, when such authors as Horace Walpole, Ann Radcliffe, Matthew Lewis, C. R. Maturin, and Mary Shelley stand out. In this instance the Gothic novel is characterized by a focus on terrifying, archaic settings, an indefinite past, the use of the supernatural, the presence of stereotypical characters, and the attempt to deploy and develop techniques of literary suspense.

Second, *Gothic* is applied to a certain kind of contemporary American fiction and to writers like John Hawkes, Joyce Carol Oates, Flannery O'Connor, and James Purdy. This *New American Gothic* deals with psychic grotesquerie and landscapes of the mind with little or no access to an objective world.

Third, and confusingly, *Gothic* refers to horror fiction itself. Punter maintains that many of the best-known horror writers—for example, Algernon Blackwood, M. R. James, and H. P. Lovecraft—derive their techniques of suspense, their sense of the archaic, and many of their crucial symbols of the supernatural from the original Gothic fiction (1:1–2). Remarkably, relying on its themes and styles, much of twentieth-century horror fiction has its roots in the Gothic. Both the second and the third definition of the Gothic can be applied to Stephen King's. Indeed, when listing contemporary writers of the Gothic mode, Tony Magistrale mentions such American writers as Harlan

Ellison, Thomas Harris, Joyce Carol Oates, Peter Straub, and Stephen King (*Decade,* 31). Furthermore, King has repeatedly acknowledged that his literary roots are deeply embedded in the Gothic (10).

The Gothic has formed a part of popular culture ever since the eighteenth century, since it can measure tensions in the society it addresses and reveal the darkest impulses of social humans (Magistrale, *Decade,* 27). Along the lines of the original Gothic, modern horror operates on two levels. King emphasizes that an effective horror story must be a well-balanced blending of reality and surreality and possess a "pleasing allegorical feel" (*DM,* 5). In King's vocabulary allegory signifies a symbolic way of saying "things that we would be afraid to say out straight," a way for the audience to "exercise emotions which society demands we keep closely in hand" (31). Through the symbolic subtext, the reader has the opportunity to confront his personal and collective anxieties from a safe distance (Gallagher, 38). Magistrale points out that the personal and cultural nightmares represented by the horror tale allow us to vent the subconscious phobias we repress with the conscious knowledge that tales of horror cannot be taken seriously (*Decade,* 27). If Theodore Ziolkowski is right in his claim that the Gothic "marked a shift from faith in a simple dualism to a fascination with the more complex interrelatedness of good and evil" (84), then *fear,* the mainspring in King's stories, expresses this aspect in King, who in other respects has largely preserved dualism. Ben P. Indick maintains:

> Walpole's school had foundered when fear lost its rationality. Drs. Van Helsing and Freud rediscovered it beneath Prince Albert coats. King has put it into a shopping basket, next to the tomato sauce, the Sanka and the Tab. Fear has become a commonplace, no longer the evil dispensation of noble or supernatural villains. No one can be trusted, not teenaged school kids, not a cop or a prosaic motel keeper, not even a small baby. It is a world with neither security nor stability.
>
> We all live in Otranto. ("King and the Literary Tradition of Horror and the Supernatural," 188)

More horrific than the monsters themselves is a faulty perception of them, that is, seeing them as harmless. Gary Hoppenstand and Ray B. Browne maintain that King frames this warning as an extended joke (13). Instead of a nerd teenager, Carrie White in

Carrie turns out to be a goddess of destruction; Father Callahan in *'Salem's Lot* is petrified, not in front of the vampire but facing his cozy childhood monster, Mr. Flip; and behind the smiling face of Pennywise the Clown in *It* we meet our personal household monster. Like the original Gothic writers in the eighteenth and nineteenth centuries, King is able to recognize the threatening and dangerous in the seemingly harmless and innocent.

In "The Gothic Romance," Frederick S. Frank establishes categories to define the major themes and tendencies of Gothic literature. King's works can be placed in "high Gothic," because, as Magistrale argues, he appears to have inherited the moral perspective Frank associates with it. Also, King seems to belong in the category of "didactic or philosophical Gothic" (Magistrale, *Landscape*, 25), because the supernatural phenomena of the Gothic are "used to symbolize various political or religious concepts; the aim is to revolutionize or radicalize the thinking of the reader" (Frank, "Romance," 8). However, like most Victorian novelists, in his Gothic works King makes use of the technology of early Gothic fiction: the haunted castle, dark corridors, supernatural surprises, the mysterious villain, tormented and tormenting spirits, the menaced maiden, and corpses (Frank, *Guide to the Gothic*, x–xi; Johansson 12–16). When discussing the individual Gothic pressure points, King's works conform to Richard P. Benton's definition of high Gothic, which centers on problems of self:

> The Gothic makes us think: how much do we know about reality, about life and death, about the universe and God, about human personality and motivation, and about the course of our destiny? How much do we know about good and evil, about what we should do and what we ought not to do? These are the kinds of questions that high Gothic proposes through the psychological archetypes dredged out of the darker depths of human experience, symbols of our "primitive" thinking, the tigers we ride on within the unconscious depths of our inner selves. (7–8)

In other words, the Gothic in King is more than supernatural thrills and excess: by means of these devices he discusses our political, economic, and psychological fears, which seem little different from those of the original Gothic (*DM*, 5).

All four sections of this chapter deal with monsters. They are essential features of the Gothic, and each of them embodies certain social motifs with which the Gothic era was concerned and with which King has been concerned during his writing career: "'Abnormal and Repressed Sexuality (the Vampire)': 'Salem's Lot—savage desires and repressed hopes; 'Hubris and Death (Frankenstein's Monster)': *Pet Sematary*—hubris and death; 'The Gothic Double (the Werewolf)': *The Dead Zone, Christine, Cycle of the Werewolf, The Talisman, The Dark Half,* and *Black House*—the hidden self; and 'The Gothic Melodrama (the Ghost)': *The Shining* and *Bag of Bones*—familial discord and romance." Each of the subtitled sections poses the question of sexuality and mortality from a moral perspective, and the sections follow an inner chronology. To be more precise, the vampire ("Abnormal and Repressed Sexuality [the Vampire]") epitomizes the passion that never dies and thus links sexuality with death. Both the vampire and Victor Frankenstein ("Hubris and Death [Frankenstein's Monster]") attain the knowledge of reproduction through death. While the Creature in *Frankenstein* constructs part of its creator's essential nature, the dialectic between monster and maker is portrayed in *The Strange Case of Dr. Jekyll and Mr. Hyde* as a conflict in a single body ("The Gothic Double [the Werewolf]"). Finally, the contradiction between personal freedom and social virtue develops into a net of Gothic relationships, enlarging the scope and including romance and familial discord, both of which often lead to death ("The Gothic Melodrama [the Ghost]").

In *Danse Macabre* King explains why we need monsters: "We love and need the concept of monstrosity because it is a reaffirmation of the order we crave as human beings" (39). This statement, with its distant echoes of the canonical American memory of the Salem witch trials, also testifies to the effective interplay between cosmological and sociological determinism in King: the former becomes a vehicle for societal and personal oppression in much of his fiction. Judith Halberstam in *Skin Shows* (1995) draws on Freud's theory of paranoia to suggest the ways in which fear and desire seem to be produced simultaneously within the Gothic narrative. Thus, for instance, she analyzes "Frankenstein's projection of his own desires onto his monster and the subsequent translation of his desire into fear of the other's desire" (Halberstam, 107). Apparently, King draws on the same source without psychoanalytic terminology when he maintains in *Danse Macabre* that the vampire in Bram Stoker's *Dracula* was created to attribute the sexual drive to a source beyond human control (64).

Leslie Fiedler, too, distinguishes the terms *monster* and *freak* at some length in *Freaks*. He argues that *monster* remained the preferred term for freaks from the time of Chaucer to that of Shakespeare and beyond. Although the etymology of the word *monster* is obscure—it is unclear whether it derives from the Latin *moneo* (to warn) or *monstro* (to show forth)—the implication remains the same: instead of a whim of chance, human abnormalities are the products of the design of Providence. Perhaps the awe we feel for monsters partly derives from the omens and portents they represent. Fiedler goes on to state that the terms *monster* and *freak* were distinguished after 1930 when C. J. S. Thompson wrote his study *The Mystery and Lore of Monsters*. Thompson does not make the distinction, but refers to both freaks and monsters as freaks. Fiedler maintains, on the one hand, that the term *monster* has been preempted to describe creations of artistic fantasy, such as Dracula, Mr. Hyde, the Wolf Man, King Kong, and the nameless metahuman of Mary Shelley's *Frankenstein*. Freaks, on the other hand, exist and may evoke both fear and pity, whereas monsters are primarily experienced as alien or hostile (22–23). King considers the Gothic archetypes of the Vampire, the Thing without a Name (Frankenstein's monster), Dr. Jekyll/Mr. Hyde, and the Ghost to be the basis of the monsters in all horror fiction (*DM*, 50; Magistrale, *Decade*, 29).

Three of the Gothic archetypes that King distinguishes in *Danse Macabre* embody the central issues with which the era was concerned. To be more precise, Mary Shelley's *Frankenstein, or the Modern Prometheus* deals with the refusal to take personal responsibility for one's actions because of pride; Robert Louis Stevenson's *The Strange Case of Dr. Jekyll and Mr. Hyde* exploits the possibilities provided by the discovery of the human psyche during the Gothic period, that is, the question of the Gothic double; and, finally, Bram Stoker's *Dracula* portrays perverse or, in medical terms, abnormal and repressed sexuality as well as double standards of sexuality. While the hidden secrets are concerned with the repressed, they frequently revolve around sex, which connects the Vampire, Frankenstein's Monster, and Dr. Jekyll/Mr. Hyde. In *The History of Sexuality*, Michel Foucault pinpoints the contradiction between desire and respectability as well as notes the power that is exercised to control the former. His argument, to my mind, can be applied to any repressed desire: "[S]ince sexuality was a medical and medicalizable object, one had to try and detect it—as a lesion, a dysfunction, or a symptom—in the depths of the organism, or on the surface of the skin, or among all the signs of behavior. The power which thus took charge of sexuality set about contacting bodies, caressing them with its eyes, intensifying areas, electrifying surfaces, dramatizing troubled moments. It wrapped the sexual body in its embrace" (1:44).

In addition to these three Gothic archetypes, Punter names a fourth, namely, the Wandering Jew, which features, for instance, in Charles Maturin's *Melmoth the Wanderer* (*Terror,* 1:124–30). In King the character of Randall Flagg reflects the image of wandering evil and recurs in *The Stand, The Eyes of the Dragon,* and *The Dark Tower* series. In a sense, Roland the Gunslinger, too, personifies the wanderer figure in King's oevre. When Roland reaches the Dark Tower at the end of his hero's journey, he begins the quest all over again. Roland's deadly sins are overly developed determination, dedication, pride, and ambition, which make him repeat the same mistakes in all of King's fictional works. What is more, since King has on numerous occasions been referred to as a writer of melodramas, a fifth Gothic archetype, the Ghost, represents this side of King's writing. King himself excludes ghosts from his so-called Tarot hand, which includes "the Vampire, the Werewolf, and the Thing Without a Name," because the Ghost is not limited to a single book (*DM,* 50). However, the reason for the exclusion seems insufficient, because King agrees that the Ghost represents an archetype and even claims that it is "the Mississippi of supernatural fiction" (50).

Now, dear reader, enter freely and of your own free will, meet—the vampire.

Abnormal and Repressed Sexuality (the Vampire)

Stephen King can be considered a Gothic writer because of, among other things, his treatment of the Gothic theme of abnormal and repressed sexuality. First, I will discuss varieties of sex and sexual abuse in Stoker and King (especially in *'Salem's Lot*), beginning with the vampire motif and with an analysis of repressed sexuality in the form of homosexuality. Then, I will present instances of destructive heterosexual relationships (adultery and violent/dominant relationships) and sexual abuse in the form of incest, pedophilia, and sexually threatening parents. Finally, sex and the supernatural will be dealt with in the form of inanimate objects and natural phenomena. Obviously, the secrets of 'Salem's Lot are primarily sex related, because even the reputable Lawrence Crockett defines his sublegal real-estate procedures in sexual terms. In this respect he feels like "going into the tunnel of love with girl A, screwing girl B behind you, and ending up holding hands with girl A on the other side" (*SL*, 80).

'Salem's Lot is influenced by Shirley Jackson's *The Haunting of Hill House* and Thornton Wilder's play *Our Town* (King, "Brand Name," 29–30). The town in King's novel epitomizes the vampire's evil. The town "knew about the darkness that comes on the land when rotation hides the land from the sun, and about the darkness of the human soul" (*SL*, 208). The short form of the town's name "'Salem" resonates with both the book of Genesis and the place for the witch trials and burnings of 1692. "Lot," in turn, refers to the Genesis and has as a secondary meaning "fate" or "fortune" (Reino, 18–19). Hence, since King repeatedly argues that evil places draw evil men (*SL*, 113; Winter, *Art*, 44), it seems plausible that evil in 'Salem's Lot is closely related to religion and hypocrisy. When Ben Mears returns to his childhood town after the tragic death of his wife, he does not remember what kind of people hide behind the doors and shutters of the houses of the morally doomed 'Salem's Lot: "wife-abandoned Albie Crane, absent-minded Coretta Simons, self-abusing Hal Griffin, panty-wearing George Middler, lecherous Reverend John Groggins, the unnamed pyromaniac valedictorian of the 1953 class" (Reino, 31; *SL*, 208–12). Like the demon Andre Linoge of *Storm of the Century*, the vampire Kurt Barlow reveals the secrets that the town keeps with "ultimate poker face" (*SL*, 212).

THE VAMPIRE MOTIF

What distinguishes *'Salem's Lot* from a number of contemporary vampire stories is that it includes sexual innuendoes and ambiguities to match its Gothic predecessor, Bram Stoker's *Dracula*. King has not confined himself to this single novel in his treatment of the theme but has explored it throughout his writing career. Written in 1879, Bram Stoker's *Dracula* derives its symbolism, at least in part, from John Polidori's *The Vampyre* (1819) and

J. Sheridan LeFanu's "Carmilla" (1870) (Reino, 19-20). King suggests that Polidori, in turn, might have been influenced by Lord Byron's "Burial" (*DM*, 61), whereas his vampire novel, *'Salem's Lot,* "was inspired by and bears a fully intentional similarity to" *Dracula* (Underwood and Miller, *Bones,* 56). He regards *Dracula* as "a frankly palpitating melodrama" (*DM*, 49) and as "one of English literature's most remarkable and engaging tricks, a *trompe l'oeil* that has rarely been matched" (64). As a horror fan, King has a thorough knowledge of the field, and, as Don Herron points out, "*'Salem's Lot* serves as a virtual *catalog* of vampirism and kindred horrors" ("Horror Springs in the Fiction of Stephen King," 81, italics in original). In his novel King refers to Samuel Taylor Coleridge's "Christabel" (1797) (*SL*, 164) and the Hammer films starring Christopher Lee (175), and Father Callahan even visits the local library in order to find material on vampires: "He read the titles before putting them back. '*Dracula. Dracula's Guest. The Search of Dracula. The Golden Bough. The Natural History of the Vampire*—natural? *Hungarian Folk Tales. Monsters of the Darkness. Monsters in Real Life. Peter Kurtin, Monster of Düsseldorf.* And . . . *Varney the Vampire, or The Feast of Blood*'" (296–97). Somewhat delighted, he even finds a copy of a *Vampirella* (297).

At the heart of *Dracula* is sexuality, blood, and otherness, which are interrelated themes all found in King's *'Salem's Lot.* Polidori, LeFanu, and Stoker wrote their classics for a Victorian readership, and the stories consequently adopted the sexually repressed attitudes of the society of the time. The sexual double standard of the era thrived, even to the extent of Victorian gentlemen maintaining secret rooms in their houses for sexual pleasures. King notes that, apart from a monster story, *Dracula* was the secret room of Victorian literature (Winter, *Art,* 45). While Count Dracula and his brides are "dead from the waist down," the sexual basis of the novel is "an infantile oralism coupled with a strong interest in necrophilia" (*DM*, 66). Since perverse sexuality could not be shown as emanating from the individual, the vampire was created to attribute the drive to a source beyond the realm of human control. Moreover, having lost control over his actions under the influence of the vampire, the victim was allowed to enjoy the sexual pleasures offered to him by the monster. As King points out, the count's evil seems as predestined as Jonathan Harker's ordeal at his castle or Lucy Westenra's death

(64). Similarly, when one of the vampire's brides at the castle of Dracula bends over Harker, he can do nothing but enjoy the sensation (Stoker, 52). Harker may enjoy the act, because he is not responsible. Similarly, when Dracula preys on women, both Lucy Westenra and Mina Harker lose control (*DM*, 65). In short, "Stoker revitalized the vampire legend by writing a novel which fairly pants with sexual energy" (64).

When comparing *'Salem's Lot* to *Dracula*, King has discovered that "there was not much steam left in the sexy underclothing of Dracula." Instead, "the unspeakable obscenity" in *'Salem's Lot* deals with his own disillusionment and fear for the future. Hence, the secret room in the novel is paranoia, the prevailing spirit of the early 1970s (Winter, *Art*, 45–46; Underwood and Miller, *Bones*, 13). Despite King's statement, *'Salem's Lot* includes sexual innuendoes and ambiguities to match its predecessor. First, the novel depicts variations of sexual activity. Second, following the Gothic tradition the novel links death to sensuality. Several times the refrain of Wallace Stevens's poem on sensuality and death, "The Emperor of Ice Cream," is quoted: "Let it be the finale of seem" (*SL*, 181, 406; Reino, 31). Third, the vampire himself manifests obvious sexual features. In a sociologically focused study, Halberstam argues that Dracula's sexuality is feminized, because it is nonphallic (98). Unlike the strictly heterosexual Dracula, the "effeminate" Kurt Barlow makes no difference between his victims' gender; also the infected become bisexual in their afterlife existence (*SL*, 352). Moreover, Barlow and his assistant, Richard Throckett Straker, are regarded as "queer for each other" by one of the town's furniture movers (86).

A writer who claims that his vampire version lacks sex and simultaneously adds these details as if to underscore the close relationship between the two male heroes of the novel has either missed his own point or is intentionally ambiguous. Because of the relation between blood and sex, Count Barlow can be regarded as bisexual, like Anne Rice's vampires in *Interview with The Vampire* (1976). Although modern vampires tend to be bisexual or homosexual, the fact that King has deliberately chosen to imitate Stoker and deviates from his model at this crucial point seems so significant that it will be discussed in greater detail in connection with characters such as Ben Mears and Mark Petrie.

Although sexual morality has changed since Victorian times, King deals with both abnormal and repressed sexuality in his works. In *Kaplan and Sadock's Synopsis of Psychiatry*, Harold I. Kaplan, Benjamin J. Sadock, and Jack A. Grebb argue that *abnormal sexuality* is "sexual behavior that is destructive to oneself or others, that cannot be directed toward a partner, that excludes stimulation of the primary sex organs, that is inappropriately associated with guilt and anxiety, or that is compulsive" (653). They state that homosexuality is now considered "an alternative life-style" that "occurs with some regularity as a variant of human sexuality" (658). Although homosexuality does not appear to be a matter of choice, its expression is. When viewed in the Gothic context and in King's treatment in *'Salem's Lot*, homosexuality falls into the category of repressed sexuality.

It is King who adds both heterosexual and homosexual implications to his depiction of the vampire's appearance. Dud Rogers, the local garbage-dump custodian, encounters the man of the world whose hair is "white, streaked with oddly virile slashes of iron gray" and who looks "like one of those fag concert pianists" (*SL*, 144). With "a black moustache," "high and Slavic" cheekbones, "pale and bony" forehead, and "dark hair swept straight back" (234), Barlow resembles his classic predecessor. Jonathan Harker describes his distinctly masculine host accordingly: "His face was a strong—a very strong—aquiline, with high bridge of the thin nose and peculiarly arched nostrils. . . . His eyebrows were very massive. . . . The mouth, so far as I could see it under the heavy moustache, was fixed and rather cruel-looking, with peculiarly sharp white teeth; these protruded over the lips, whose remarkable ruddiness showed astonishing vitality in a man of his years. [T]he chin was broad and strong, and his cheeks firm though thin" (Stoker, 28). Halberstam views the vampire as an aggregate of race, class, and gender (88). Otherness personified, Dracula can be considered a paradox: monster/man, feminine/masculine, parasitical/wealthy, repulsive/fascinating, and eternal/mortal. She notes that Dracula's striking appearance, his aversion to all the trappings of Christianity, his blood-sucking habits, and his niggardly relation to money resemble stereotypical anti-Semitic nineteenth-century representations of the Jew (86). Halberstam then traces the vampire to the myth of the Wandering Jew, an image that in many respects unites the characteristics of the most threatening King villains: Kurt Barlow (see also "Adapted and Revised Myths and Fairy Tales" in chapter 2), Randall Flagg (see "The Antihero as a Generic Hybrid [Randall Flagg]" in chapter 2), Leland Gaunt (see "Genetic and Sociological Determinism" in chapter 3), and Andre Linoge (see "The Antihero as a Generic Hybrid [Randall Flagg]" in chapter 2 and "Cosmological Determinism and Fate" in chapter 3). The threat posed by the wanderer can vary considerably: King identifies Flagg as all-devouring; Gaunt and Linoge collect souls; and Barlow constitutes a sexual threat. A wanderer figure, the vampire carries his coffins with him and nests in populated areas. Halberstam states that "[h]ome, with its connotations of marriage, monogamy, and community, is precisely what Dracula is in exile from and precisely what would and does kill him in the end" (99).

If Dracula threatened Victorian familial life with his perverse sexuality, Barlow reveals that there is not much left to be endangered. However, both King and Stoker tend to fuse the image of the virtuous, that is, sexually continent, woman with that of the Virgin Mary, whereas sexual activity indicates evil lust. Mina and Lucy, the dark and the fair heroine, respectively, of *Dracula*, represent the ideal of Victorian womanhood. If Halberstam is right in her claim that Stoker makes "Englishness a function of quiet femininity and maternal domesticity" (89), then by seducing both women with his foreign sexuality, Dracula attacks nothing less than the national pride of the country. Lucy is severely punished for her wanton desire for three men, whereas Mina remains true to Victorian ideals and is rescued by the same men who stake Lucy's vampiric body.

Tony Magistrale maintains that the two genres most influential for King's fiction include the Gothic romance and popular pulp fiction. Rather surprisingly, he goes on to argue that King "relies rather heavily on frequent and explicit sexual references" (*Voyages*, 42). If the scholar is referring to vulgar language, the statement holds true, but explicit sex scenes are rather rare exceptions in King's works—and they are nonexistent in *Dracula*. In fact, King deliberately shies away from graphic portrayals of sex (*OW*, 73). On the one hand, he claims that the physics of sex "are so familiar to everyone that it is hard to do in a novel way"

(Underwood and Miller, *Bones*, 195). On the other hand, this discomfort stems from a more general problem with creating plausibly romantic relationships. "Without such strong relationships to build on," King argues, "it's tough to create sexual scenes that have credibility and impact or advance the plot" (54). Hence, one of the traits King seems to have in common with the Gothic romance and Stoker is that balanced heterosexual relationships seldom occur in his fiction. Magistrale points out that, unlike much of the work in the Gothic and the pulp-fiction traditions, King does not employ scenes of sexual contact for the mere purpose of titillation, but uses sexuality to highlight important themes relevant to a certain story and "often incorporates a character's sexual response as a way of signalling his or her place on the moral continuum of good and evil" (*Voyages*, 42).

Blood is associated with the idea of sacrifice; for women it is linked with reaching physical maturity and the ability to bear children; in religion it is symbolic of both sin and salvation; and it is also associated with the handing down of family traits and talents (*OW*, 199). Both Stoker and King make use of most of these connotations, focusing, however, on the relation between sex and blood. According to Professor Van Helsing, the doctor-lawyer in *Dracula*, the vampire "can flourish when that he can fatten on the blood of the living" (Stoker, 286). Apart from this religious inversion of "the blood is the life," blood is also equated with sex and reproduction in both novels. Blood rites are performed on the necks of sleeping or hypnotized persons in both works, and their respective monsters thus evince a kinship with the blood-oriented creatures of myth and folklore (Reino, 23).

The origin of the vampire myth reinforces the sexual implications of blood, because, for instance, in Hellenic magical belief, Hecate's foul blood-sucking and child-stealing offspring, the Empusae (literally, "one-footed") disguised themselves as lovely girls to seduce victims (Warner, *From the Beast to the Blonde*, 121–22), and Louis XV was rumored to suck blood and bathe in the fresh blood of vigorous young bodies (Warner, *Bogeyman*, 130). Both Count Dracula and Kurt Barlow epitomize the sexually predatory boogeyman, who, as Marina Warner notes, has become far more insistent since Charles Perrault introduced him in "Little Red Riding Hood," a fairy tale that colors the whole range of images in stories about devouring and being devoured (38). In fact, in one of Perrault's versions Little Red Riding Hood feeds on her grandmother and presumably sleeps with the wolf (37). In sex the eating fantasy may include "power over the hungry, control of the consumer" (140). Finally, then, the question of who devours or drinks whom can be answered differently. The French philosopher Jacques Derrida maintains in the spirit of the predestined evil of *Dracula* and *'Salem's Lot* that "Good can also be eaten. And it must be eaten well" (115).

Concerning reproductivity, *Dracula* dramatically differs from *'Salem's Lot*. Blood substitutes for other bodily fluids such as milk and semen, and only male vampires reproduce in *Dracula*. Halberstam notes that Lucy and Dracula's three brides in Transylvania feed from children but do not create them (101). In order to reproduce a new race of his own kind, the count symbolically subjects Mina's maternity to his sway by giving her "what Van Helsing called 'the Vampire baptism of blood'" (Stoker, 383). Paradoxically, this virtuous woman, who maternally nurtures all the men around her by day, drinks blood from the bosom of the king vampire by night (Halberstam, 101). In King both sexes reproduce, and vampirism appears to be both incestuous and pedophilic. As Laurence A. Rickels in *The Vampire Lectures* has observed, first Ralph Glick gets vampirized, then he returns to infect his brother (198). Also, somewhat ironically, Kurt Barlow baptizes Father Callahan, which can perhaps be considered another homoerotic implication in the novel (for both scenes, see "Free Will and Responsibility" in chapter 3). Furthermore, the virtuous Mina gives birth to a son whose paternity can be regarded as both shared and multiple. Halberstam argues that the birth of little Quincey at the end of the novel signifies a culmination of the transfusion scene, when all the men who fight for the two women's virtue give blood to Lucy's depleted body (101). Significantly, however, Dracula has drunk from Lucy, and Mina has drunk from Dracula, which makes the count one of Quincey's many fathers.

HOMOSEXUALITY

Although the encounter between Susan Norton and Ben Mears is undoubtedly meant to serve as a counterforce against the necrophilia of Kurt Barlow, their mutual relationship is from the beginning shadowed by the future close relationship between Ben

Mears and Mark Petrie, "a local boy who is the double of Ben" (Rickels, 192). Even the two encounters resemble each other in their image of fate (for Ben and Susan, see *SL,* 9), but Ben and Mark's encounter appears more powerful with homosexual innuendoes such as "queer stretching" and "queerly heavy": "[F]or Ben the moment seemed to undergo a queer stretching, and a feeling of unreality swept him. [—] It made him think of the day he had met Susan in the park, and how their light conversation had seemed queerly heavy and fraught with intimations of the future" (*SL,* 314). Although King seemingly defends the homosexual Adrian Mellon of *It* against his bullying attackers, he would appear to be taking pains to avoid expressing a sense of distrust. The ambiguous attitude toward homosexuality and "sissy boys" is also to be found in the depiction of Mark Petrie. Mark, just as many other King's heroes, has a slender body structure and wears glasses. Mark is called a "four-eyes" "queer" boy who "suck[s] the old hairy root" by the school bully, Richie Boddin, but he triumphs in a schoolyard fight by his wit (46). Joseph Reino hints that King's affectionate male bonding might include homosexual implications (26–33), whereas King's fatherless childhood provides another angle on the question. Concerning Ben and Mark, King argues: "People say to me since then that what I wrote there was a classical sub rosa homosexual relationship. I say bullshit, it's father-son" (Underwood and Miller, *Bones,* 130). Since I agree with E. D. Hirsch Jr. that "no logical necessity compels the critic to banish the author in order to analyze his text" (12), I think that King should be taken at his word. However, this point will be developed and questioned in the following discussion.

Hence, although he has authored a novel with a homosexual rape scene that takes place in prison, Ben Mears appears completely heterosexual. So does his young duplicate, Mark Petrie. Clearly, however, the nature of their mutual relationship goes beyond friendship. Reino argues that it falls "somewhat short of raw sexual attraction, yet they are clearly beyond friendship, paternal affection or mere resemblances of things past" (29). Their first encounter reminds the reader of the ambiguities of the opening sentence of the novel: "Almost everyone thought the man and the boy were father and son" (*SL,* xi). But if they were not, what then? To me it seems a combination of a romanticized father-son relationship (as in Poe's "Lionizing," 1–2, 6) and that of soul brothers (as in Poe's "Fall of the House of Usher," 139–40, 142–43; Reino, 29). In demonstrating my point further, I would like to draw a parallel between the opening scene of *'Salem's Lot* and the depiction of Charlie McGee and her father in *Firestarter*. Almost everyone whom the two fugitives encounter on their flight assume that something sexually perverse is going on between the father, Andy McGee, and his daughter, Charlie. Ironically, Reino notes that these average American characters consistently seem to assume the worst of Andy and Charlie. As if implications of incest were not enough, suggestions of androgyny are subtly reinforced: of course, Charlie refers to Charlene (44–45). Hence, despite the innuendoes nothing explicitly sexual occurs between Andy and Charlie or between Ben Mears and Mark Petrie. Nevertheless, how are the following desperate exclamations to be interpreted: "I love you," "I want you," "I need you" (*SL*, 398, 405, 409; see also xix)?

Although the uttered words include at least platonic homoeroticism if not outright homosexuality, King manifests a twofold significance in the characters of Ben and Mark. On the one hand, he has on a number of occasions stated that the loss of his father can be found in the numerous older male characters in his works. We need only compare the relationship of Ben and Mark to those of Dick Hallorann and Danny Torrance in *The Shining*, Roland the Gunslinger and Jake Chambers in *The Dark Tower* series, Lester "Speedy" Parker and Jack Sawyer in *The Talisman* and *Black House*, and Sandy Dearborn and Ned Wilcox in *From a Buick 8*, among others, to draw the parallels and to note that none of these relationships appears to be homosexual in nature. The contradiction between the seemingly homoerotic but in reality innocent relationship between Ben and Mark, on the other hand, creates a counterforce to the truly bisexual vampire. This is probably why Reino argues that King has consciously positioned these two suspicious-looking males among the innocent, although the hypocritical residents of 'Salem's Lot would readily accuse them of sexual deviation. Against the vampire's perverse sexuality, the innocent relationship of vampire-resisters Ben and Mark defies analysis and adds to the psychological complexity of the novel. Despite his slender body structure, Mark Petrie turns out to be virile in both will and determination—a strong virginal male in the tradition of a little-known piece of folklore whereby a male virgin used to ride on a white stallion around the grave of a suspected vampire in order to destroy him (32).

Characters other than those separated by the generation gap can have affectionate same-sex relationships in King. In *Christine* the teenagers Dennis Guilder and Arnie Cunningham share an unexpected moment of tenderness. Dennis comforts Arnie in his grief and realizes that they "looked like a couple of queers" (66). Edward Madden defines their relationship as "homosexual desire," thus maintaining that to dismiss the novel as a narrative of two childhood friends growing apart is "to dismiss the overwhelming homosociality the novel inscribes, indicts, and evades" (150). Repressed homosexuality may also be disguised in hostility between the two (Reino, 30). For instance, in *The Shining* Jack Torrance cannot help noticing the pure beauty of his former male student, George Hatfield. Despite his hatred for the student, Jack regards George as "almost insolently beautiful" (123). In "Apt Pupil," the old Nazi Dussander and his young protégé Todd Bowden develop a relationship that includes both affection and hostility and which Dussander expresses in sexual terms: "[W]e are fucking each other—didn't you know that?" (*DS*, 194). What is more, in "Graveyard Shift" Hall thinks about his hated boss Warwick, "trying to place what it was about Mr. Foreman that drew him, that made him feel that somehow they had become tied together" (*NS*, 41). These examples show that King deliberately plays with homosexual innuendo, despite his pronouncement to the contrary. Also, *'Salem's Lot* includes more homosexual ambiguities than *Dracula*, which primarily hints at unrestrained sex and heterosexual aberrations.

As an American writer, King cannot claim immunity to the nation's literary tradition of male bonding. Leslie Fiedler argues that the failure of the American fictionalist to depict adult heterosexual love and his consequent obsession with death, incest, and innocent homosexuality are not merely matters of historical interest or literary relevance. On the contrary, they affect both the personal lives of average Americans and influence American writers (*Love*, preface to the first edition, 5). He puts it straightforwardly: "Paul Bowles, writing highbrow terror-fiction in the middle of the twentieth century, cannot escape the limitations that plagued Charles Brockden Brown at the beginning of the eighteenth; and Saul Bellow, composing a homoerotic *Tarzan of the Apes* in *Henderson the Rain King,* is back on the raft with Mark Twain" (5). Fiedler, indeed, discovers homosexual connotations in Twain—one of King's major literary influences. "With Jim, of course," he tells us, "Huck does not dream of any sexual relation. . . . Yet they pet and sustain each other in mutual love and trust: make on their raft an anti-family of two" (278–79). Despite a variety of similar depictions, homophobia seems a prevalent attitude among such different male writers as Hemingway, Melville, Stevenson, Stoker—and King.

In *Between Men* Eve Kosofsky Sedgwick uses the term *homosexual panic* to denote the perceived social threat of "blackmailability," the interiorized homophobia inherent in Western homosocial bonding, which enforces the disjuncture between homosocial relations and homosexual desire (89–90). Later, in *Epistemology of the Closet,* she enlarges the definition to cover the legal use of the term, *homosexual panic* being a defense used in courts to lighten or prevent the sentencing of those who commit antigay bias crimes (gay bashing, assault, or even murder), a defense based on the "assumption that hatred of homosexuals is so private and so atypical a phenomenon in this culture as to be classifiable as an accountability-reducing illness." Sedgwick notes that the defense is so widely accepted that it in fact proves just the opposite, that hatred of homosexuals is "even more public, more typical, hence harder to find any leverage against than hatred of other disadvantaged groups" (19–21; see also Madden, 143–58). To me it seems that King's male bonding in part reflects the contradictory urges of homophobia and the desire for closeness and friendship, even for the father he never knew in his own life.

To prove his heterosexuality once and for all, King has a character called Stephen King answer to this question under hypnosis. When Jake Chambers saves King's life towards the end of *The Dark Tower* (2004), Roland fittingly asks the hypnotized King:

> "Do'ee dream of love with men?"
> "Are you asking if I'm gay? Maybe a latent homosexual?" King sounded weary but amused.
> "I don't know," Roland paused. "Think so."
> "The answer is no," King said. (*DTO,* 373)

Case closed.

Destructive heterosexual relationships can be considered in terms of adultery and violent/dominant relationships. When Jonathan Harker visits Castle Dracula at his employer's request, Dracula tells him never to leave the guest suite or sleep in any other part of the castle. As Laurence A. Rickels notes, "[A]s soon as the law gets issued, we see Jonathan quickly rush to transgress it" (45). Like a father, Dracula rescues Harker, who, like a wayward child, does not wish to be rescued from the female vampires' embraces. Harker gets excited by the ladies and contemplates adultery (Stoker, 51). Although Harker never consummates a bloody union with the vampire's brides, Lucy Westenra "is coming her brains out," as King puts it in graphic terms (*DM*, 65). Similarly, Stoker's depiction of the vampire kiss resembles an orgasm: "I have a vague memory of something long and dark with red eyes . . . and something very sweet and very bitter all around me at once; and then I seemed sinking into deep green water, and there was a singing in my ears, as I have heard there is to drowning men; and then everything seemed passing away from me; my soul seemed to go out from my body and float about the air" (121).

Hardly unwittingly, Stoker has added the lighthouse to the seaside scenery to indicate a phallus: "I seemed to remember that once the West Lighthouse was right under me, and then there was some sort of agonizing feeling, as if I were in an earthquake, and I came back" (121). When interpreting adultery in *'Salem's Lot* and elsewhere in King, we have no trouble recognizing it for what it is. In *'Salem's Lot* the hypersexed Corey Bryant is first beaten by his mistress's husband and then vampirized by Kurt Barlow. Similarly, Donna Trenton's secret liaison with the oversexed Steve Kemp leads to destruction in *Cujo*. Bonnie Sawyer never realizes the consequences of her own actions, whereas Donna Trenton regrets that she ever was intimate with the sex-obsessed drug addict who reveals the liaison in order to get revenge on Donna for rejecting him as a lover (Reino, 77–79; Stump, 134–35).

King argues that the vampire impersonates "sex based upon relationships where one partner is largely under the control of the other; sex which almost inevitably leads to some bad end"

(*DM*, 68). As for Dud Rogers, vampirism provides new options with regard to Ruthie Crockett, whom he has long lusted after. Count Barlow, after reading the hunchback's mind and realizing it is full of insecurities about inadequate masculinity, promises to fulfill his wish (*SL*, 146). And shortly thereafter Ruthie, who sleeps in an abandoned freezer, finds "his advances among the heaped mounds of garbage very acceptable" (310). Similarly, Ed "Weasel" Craig gets another chance to enjoy Eva Miller's charms in their shared afterlife existence. During their first time together, "they had slept like spoons in a silverware drawer" (45), and now "she loved him again . . . more than ever. She yearned for his kiss" (372, ellipsis in original). Hence, both Dud Rogers and Weasel Craig finally get the woman of their dreams, but not through their own charm.

By taking the woman's point of view, *Rose Madder* (1995) transposes the situation and setting into a kind of female Gothic. In the novel, violence and sex make a Gothic fusion in a modern American context. Rose Daniels is trapped in an abusive marriage: her husband Norman, a police detective, has beaten her for most of their fourteen-year marriage, including one particularly vicious attack that resulted in Rose's miscarriage. Finally, a single drop of blood makes her leave him: "It was on the top sheet, her side, close to where the pillow went when the bed was made" (26). Instead of hiding the spot or changing the bed linen, she leaves Norman and the brutal reality for another dimension—apparently, the one inhabited by Roland the Gunslinger—to fight back. Alluding to classical works of mythology, King turns Norman into a bull and thus evokes Greek mythology and the legend of the Minotaur with its sexual connotations. In this way *Rose Madder* clearly displays how King deploys realistic and fantastic themes to advance his ideas.

Both *Dracula* and *'Salem's Lot* link negative sexuality to the woman's role as an amoral seductress. When the "Un-Dead" Miss Lucy makes advances to her fiancé, Arthur Holmwood, she seems full of lust. Although poor Arthur falls back and hides his face in his hands, he cannot help responding: "There was something diabolically sweet in her tones—something of the tingling of glass when struck" (Stoker, 253–54). Similarly, the "Un-Dead" Susan Norton makes advances to Homer McCaslin: "'Sheriff?' A light, carefree voice, like tinkling bells" (*SL*, 313).

In like fashion Chris Hargensen of *Carrie* is portrayed as a vamp. Employing her body to manipulate the males in her life, she is fully aware of the potential power that sex represents and of her ability to advance her goals (Magistrale, *Voyages*, 45). Chris never recognizes love and tenderness but only the exploitative side of the very act of lovemaking. She has realized her power when in high school and exercised it on older, college males: "They began by treating her with patronizing good fellowship . . . and always ended up trotting after her with panting, doglike lust" (*CA*, 133). Although Billy Nolan is regarded as a juvenile delinquent, it is Chris who seduces him to fetch pig blood from Irwin Henty's farm and thus further her efforts to bring about Carrie White's destruction. In other words, Billy is submerged in a passion that is out of control. Victimized by Chris's sexual domination (Magistrale, *Voyages*, 46), Billy "would have done murder for her, and more" (*CA*, 117). Having brought about Carrie's destruction, he and Chris celebrate the victory in a way that reveals their moral corruption. Sexually aroused, they punch and slap each other, ripping off their clothes and backing toward the bed:

> "You gave me a shiner, you bitch."
> "I'll give you more."
> "You're goddam right you will."
> They stared at each other, panting, glaring. Then he began to un-button his shirt, a little grin beginning on his face. (221)

Along the same lines as in the original Gothic, sex in King frequently illustrates moral corruption. Magistrale points out that as a manipulative force the passion of love turns into the aggression of self-destruction (*Voyages*, 47). While denying the voice of conscience, King's characters succumb to deeper evil and lose their identities as well as their ability to possess control over their destinies. Compared to a healthy sexual response that affirms life and the love between human beings, perverse sexuality leads to an evil end.

SEXUAL ABUSE

King explores sexual abuse in the form of incest, pedophilia, and sexually threatening parents. As he argues, "[C]onsidering Lucy in her role as the 'bloofer lady' [that is, a female vampire], *Dracula* even borders on pedophilia" (*DM*, 66). In order to drive the stake through her heart, the rescue team follows Lucy to the cemetery, where she attacks a fair-haired child. Moral corruption makes the characters in *Dracula* ugly: "The sweetness was turned to adamantine, heartless cruelty, and the purity to voluptuous wantonness" (Stoker, 252–53). In a similar vein, before driving the stake through her heart, the rescue team notes Susan's dark beauty. However, her face reminds Jimmy Cody of young Saigon prostitutes: "Yet with those girls, the corruption hadn't been evil but only a knowledge of the world that had come too soon. The change in Susan's face was quite different" (*SL*, 338).

Like Donna Trenton, the economically and socially privileged Jessie Burlingame feels inadequate in her marriage. Childless and in her own eyes significant only as her husband's sexual object, she shares an incestuous past with both Beverly Marsh of *It* and Selena St. George of *Dolores Claiborne*. While *Misery* blames a sadistic and all-devouring matriarchy for the protagonist's victimization, *Gerald's Game* condemns patriarchy. In both *Misery* and *Gerald's Game*, the setting is the bed (Badley, "Stephen King: Viewing the Body," 184). While *Gerald's Game* is a survival story based on a classic Gothic situation (the woman trapped in the house and terrorized by her husband), King modernizes it by using a bondage game. The simultaneously written *Gerald's Game* and *Dolores Claiborne* focus on two female protagonists. Through their telepathic awareness of each other and through their experience of the same eclipse as the most important incident in their lives, King establishes the typical features of these two different women. Both Jessie and Dolores are whole only before and after men enter their lives. Jessie experiences the eclipse through the seduction and domination by her father; Dolores exits the eclipse by murdering her husband, who also seeks to exploit his daughter sexually (Casebeer, "The Art of Balance," 53; T. Thompson, 48). The molestation of Jessie was witnessed by Dolores Claiborne, who during the same eclipse of the sun by the moon, associated with female power, saw to it that her husband, Joe, fell down a well shaft, thus ending the molestation of their thirteen-year-old daughter, Selena. Dolores recalls the telepathic vision: "I saw somethin else, as well, somethin that made me think of Joe: her Daddy's hand was on her leg, way up high" (*DC*, 232). Apparently, Dolores's vision has been documented to reinforce

Jessie's recollections. More importantly, Dolores's unsophisti-
cated interpretation of the incident emphasizes the horrid nature
of the molestation. At the request of her father, Jessie is dressed to
seduce, without herself being aware of it. Dolores, in contrast,
pays attention to the too short dress, unnecessary lipstick, and
the exaggeratedly feminine hairstyle (231–32).

Monstrous and physically large women frequently people
King's fiction, and perhaps they reflect his horror as a child
finding himself alone with his grandmother's corpse, as in
"Gramma" *(Skeleton Crew)*, and watching his mother die of cancer, as in "Woman in the Room" *(Night Shift)*. Although different
in nature, Myra Kaspbrak of *It* and Annie Wilkes of *Misery* can be
considered objects of incestuous desires. Myra's husband, Eddie,
"did not need a shrink to tell him that he had, in a sense, married
his mother" *(IT*, 94). In essence Eddie marries Myra out of fear
and insecurity. Because of fear and insecurity, too, Myra overeats
and becomes a sexless mother monster, totally dependent on
Eddie. Like other incestuous mothers in King, Annie Wilkes is a
big woman who seems to have "no feminine curves at all" *(MI*,
7). Keeping the writer Paul Sheldon as her prisoner, his "number
one fan" exercises a kind of emotional slavery by forcing him to
write a new Misery Chastain story along the lines of *The Thousand and One Nights*—in other words, he must "tell a story or die"
(Beahm, *Stephen King Story*, 167). A nurse by profession, Annie
is doubly linked to the maternal sphere. Having had access to
drugs, she turns Paul into a drug addict, and he becomes as dependent on her as an infant on its mother. On the other hand, a
sexual tension becomes obvious when Annie brings Paul pills for
his pain and he has to suck them off her fingers in a parody of
both a nursing child and sexual activity (Gottschalk, 124–25; *MI*,
8, 209). While ensuring Paul's childlike dependence on her with
the addiction to the drug, Annie also treats him like a child who
must be educated: she tells him what happened in the car accident and disciplines him if he has been naughty, although she
later comforts him in motherly fashion. Like an ancient goddess,
Annie not merely sustains life but can take it away as well. In the
manner of an "Angel of Death," she keeps a detailed book of the
murders she has committed (Gottschalk, 125–26). Paul attempts
to kill the goddess Annie by burning her up like a sacrifice with
his manuscript. When stuffing the manuscript in her mouth to

"rape" her with it (129), he shouts: *"I'm gonna rape you, all right, Annie. . . . So suck my book. . . . Suck on it until you fucking CHOKE"* (*MI*, 317; italics, ellipses, and capitals in original). Not surprisingly, Kathleen Margaret Lant argues that Paul uses his pen as his penis, raping his reader as his last resort (178). Hence, in this scene of vengeance King links the Gothic motif of rape with the vampire sex "based upon man's domination and woman's submission" (*DM*, 69).

SEX AND THE SUPERNATURAL

Finally, then, abnormal and repressed sexuality can also be directed toward the forces of nature and inanimate objects in King. In both examples the all-devouring evil force sucks the victim's will and life force in a vampirelike manner. The former is found in "Strawberry Spring," in which sexual arousal is connected with a mysterious femme fatale. King is definitely aware of medieval symbolism, which invests the strawberry with sexual significance. As Magistrale points out, in Hieronymus Bosch's "Garden of Earthly Delights," for example, sexual promiscuity has transformed some individuals into walking strawberry hybrids (*Voyages*, 44). In this short story, fog has transformed itself into a sexually arousing woman who leads a killer by the name of Springheel Jack to commit crimes under her influence. The narrator, who turns out to be the killer himself, describes the evil presence in marital terms: "It was as if our little school was caught between them, squeezed in some crazy lover's embrace, part of a marriage that had been consummated in blood" (*NS*, 177). Significantly, too, the narrator's wife accuses him of having an affair: "She thinks I was with another woman last night. And oh dear God, I think so too" (180).

In *Christine*, the high school misfit, Arnie Cunningham, falls in love with a 1958 Plymouth Fury called Christine. Arnie's liaison with Christine appears complexly motivated. The car possesses stereotypical feminine qualities, for instance, in that it appears distinctly jealous of Arnie's contacts with females (Egan, "Technohorror," 51; Madden, 147). Arnie, for his part, treats Christine as if she were a lover. In James Egan's view, he and Christine share the car's black-magical powers as if they were a lover's secret. As Christine's list of victims grows, Arnie's union with her becomes more intimate, more overtly sexual. Christine develops into his closest companion when his girlfriend, Leigh Cabot falls for his best friend, Dennis Guilder (51–52). Early in the novel, the car seller's brother expresses his opinion of love: "Love is a cannibal with extremely acute vision" (*CH*, 108). Undoubtedly, this King maxim finds its perfect target in the lonely and love-seeking Arnie. Very soon the car exerts control over Arnie, and the relationship is expressed in sexual imagery. Dennis observes that it looks like "love at first sight" (75). Hence, Magistrale notes that Arnie responds to the car "on a highly charged sexual level" (*Voyages*, 52). Dennis also compares Christine to a sexually excited woman (*CH*, 77). An act of sexual intercourse is even mimicked when Arnie pushes Christine back to Darnell's garage after the car has been vandalized (382). Apparently, Arnie has an orgasm inside Christine, but—like the fog in "Strawberry Spring" or the ghost woman dancing with Jack Torrance in *The Shining*—Christine seduces Arnie merely to entrap him.

Characters in King's Gothic works remain as well developed as the rest of his characters with the notable exception of those with dark sexual obsessions, who seem prone to stereotyped treatment. The Gothic line can in this respect be said to continue in King, for his female characters frequently either act as seducers or are themselves victimized, thus resembling, for instance, the seducer-demon Matilda in Matthew Lewis's *Monk* or the virginal Emily St. Aubert in Ann Radcliffe's *The Mysteries of Udolpho*. Fiedler states that women are characterized as either Madonnas or whores in American literature (*Love*, 4–5). A negative kind of sexuality is often displayed through the latter. For instance, the male distrust of women is manifested in *Christine*, in which the car represents the vamp—seductive but dangerous (Magistrale, *Voyages*, 53): "Oh he loved her and loathed her, he hated her and cherished her, he needed her and needed to run from her, she was his and he was hers" (*CH*, 381). Hence, King, too, frequently links the perversion of the sexual bond to the woman as a modern Eve: an amoral seductress preying on masculine weaknesses. I think, however, that Magistrale exaggerates when maintaining that these female characters as such would reinforce the Madonna-whore stereotype, which has in part sustained the general distance that exists between men and women (*Voyages*, 51).

Although vampiric sexuality as it appears in both *Dracula* and *'Salem's Lot* can be described as homoerotic and as heterosexual exogamy, it is both and more. Instead of merely lesbian, homosexual, or heterosexual sexuality, the vampire represents sexuality itself. King seems to emphasize the homosexual angle, but both novels discuss varieties of sexual activity: Stoker hints at these variations, whereas King presents them more openly according to contemporary standards. However, Stoker's novel veritably throbs with an undercurrent of wild sexual energy, suggesting that wild sex is the secret desire of the Victorian gentlemen, whereas King underscores the moral corruption of vampire sex, focusing on such real-life incidents as Watergate and the political secrets of the early 1970s. More frightening than the vampires, King tells us, is 'Salem's Lot in daytime, the silent town with people hiding in closets and under beds (Underwood and Miller, *Bones,* 13). In other words, the vampires become the metaphor for the Watergate hearings, which were pouring out of the television when King was writing the novel.

In addition to *'Salem's Lot,* King has in passing dealt with the vampire theme in *Black House* (2001), in which an ancient hospital with vampire nurses is the link between the worlds of Roland the Gunslinger and Jack Sawyer's Territories, and in five short stories: "Jerusalem's Lot" (*Night Shift,* 1978), "One for the Road" (*Night Shift*), "The Night Flier" (*Nightmares and Dreamscapes,* 1993), "Popsy" (*Nightmares and Dreamscapes*), and "The Little Sisters of Eluria" (*Everything's Eventual,* 2002), all of which feature the vampire as a Dracula-like hero-villain. In the three last volumes of *The Dark Tower* series King distinguishes three types of vampires according to their degree of mortality and threat to humans. Significantly, Father Callahan from *Salem's Lot* returns to fight his arch enemies, the vampires, and finds a living god and a redemption in the final encounters with the type one vampires at the beginning of *The Dark Tower* (2004). Father Callahan dies, whereas Roland barely survives an attack by a type one vampire called Joe Collins towards the end of his quest. Entering an old cottage Roland the gunslinger and Susannah of New York, encounter an old man with rosy cheeks, "the picture of wintry good health" (*DTO,* 529). The smile, "showing a lot of white teeth," arouses Susannah's suspicions (*DTO,* 544). She barely manages to rescue Roland from the vampire who does not survive on blood but on human emotions. Clearly, the Vampire remains a prominent archetype throughout King's oevre.

Carol Senf maintains that the vampire in the twentieth century is frequently an attractive figure, although she mentions *'Salem's Lot* as one of the exceptions ("Blood, Eroticism, and the Vampire in Twentieth-Century Popular Literature," 27). In general, however, while vampires become more appealing—attractive physically, morally, and intellectually—their human counterparts become more appalling (Carter, 126). For instance, Chelsea Quinn Yarbro interprets the vampire no longer as a mirror of humankind's worst violence, but as an outsider who comments on the cruelty thus perpetrated (Senf, "Blood," 23). Likewise, as early as 1921, Hans Heinz Ewers in *Vampir* depicts a vampire who drinks blood for the good of his country. Manley Wade Wellman in "The Horror Undying" (1936) and David Drake in "Something Had to Be Done" (1976) reveal humankind's cruelty and so put the vampire's bloodlust into a less horrifying perspective (21). The list could be made longer, but Anne Rice's *Interview with the Vampire* (1976) should also be mentioned, because the novel restored the vampire as a claimant to the monster throne.

At this point, dear reader, we should perhaps consult a doctor. Would you like to meet Dr. Frankenstein?

Hubris and Death (Frankenstein's Monster)

Like the vampire, Victor Frankenstein is an individualist, who attempts to reproduce a new race. Both constitute an implicit threat to society by attacking the whole concept of morality. The vampire, as Punter notes, is the logical culmination of the Gothic hero, "in whom power and attraction are bent to the service of Thanatos, and for whom the price of immortality is the death of the soul" (*Terror*, 2:22). However, the vampire's evil is predestined, whereas Victor Frankenstein makes a conscious decision to do an evil deed, which makes his Gothic confrontation with death all the more personal. Through their portrayals of Victor Frankenstein and Louis Creed, respectively, Mary Shelley and Stephen King discuss the refusal to take responsibility for one's false actions and hubris, that is, false pride and defiance. They also pose questions such as: Who is the real monster? and Who made whom? In other words, if the Gothic attempts to express the unspeakable, or, in the words of Sedgwick, if the unspeakable is buried alive within the speakable (*Coherence of Gothic Conventions*, 20; *Men*, 94–96), then *Dracula* focuses on hidden sexual desires and *Frankenstein* on identity itself (Halberstam, 35). An assortment of living dead typically features in King's fiction, and therefore a brief discussion of life after death and resurrection is also included in this section.

Mary Shelley's *Frankenstein* blends Gothic horror and romance in a story that has become a seminal myth of modern technology, in that it reveals that "uncontrolled science ma[kes] man more demonic than deific" (Pharr, "Dream of New Life," 115). Stephen King has dealt with this theme in a number of works, such as *The Stand* (1978), *Firestarter* (1980), *The Running Man* (1982), *The Talisman* (1984), and *Pet Sematary* (1983). Mary Ferguson Pharr points out another invaluable theme in *Frankenstein* as well as *Pet Sematary*, that is, the dream of new life, "a dream both seductive and malefic, the stuff finally of nightmares made flesh" (116). A retelling of W. W. Jacobs's "Monkey's Paw" (1902), the short story about parents who literally wish their son back from the dead, *Pet Sematary* also displays King's interest in funerals and modern customs of death and burial (Winter, *Art*, 146). Finally, King considers hubris to be a key theme in both *Frankenstein* and *Pet Sematary*:

> All tales of horror can be divided into two groups: those in which the horror results from an act of free will and conscious will—a conscious decision to do evil—and those in which the horror is predestinate, coming from outside like a stroke of lightning. The most classic horror tale of this latter type is the Old Testament story of Job, who becomes the human Astroturf in a kind of Superbowl between God and Satan.
>
> The stories of horror which are psychological—those which explore the terrain of the human heart—almost always revolve around the free-will concept; "inside evil," if you will, the sort we have no right laying off on God the Father. This is Victor Frankenstein creating a living being out of spare parts to satisfy his own *hubris*, and then compounding his sin by refusing to take responsibility for what he has done. (*DM*, 62)

By refusing to acknowledge and thus repent his wrongdoing, Victor Frankenstein, on the one hand, succumbs to the mortal sin of pride—the same sin that resulted in Lucifer's fall from heaven and Faust's pact with the devil. On the other, defiance is embedded in the Gothic tradition in the character of its hero-villain. Both Victor Frankenstein and Louis Creed of *Pet Sematary* embody this disputable Gothic ideal. Both *Frankenstein* and *Pet Sematary* also analyze the concept of free will, hence apparently suggesting that although fate undeniably rules and the mechanistic worldview of the Gothic is in place, the characters still possess free will to make moral choices.

In *Pet Sematary* King reworks traditional material to make a connection with the reader's real-life anxieties. Since his horror fiction is grounded in American social reality, King interprets Shelley's classic to suit his purposes by commenting on twists of fate, dissolving marriages, hubris, and death in the novel. Aptly Pharr argues that he does not copy Shelley but rather amplifies the cultural echo she set in motion so that its resonance is clearer to the reader of Gothic fantasy today ("Dream," 120). In the same way, King refers to Shelley's work as "caught in a kind of cultural echo chamber" (*DM*, 65). In addition he has written more than one introduction for editions of *Frankenstein* (see bibliography for Shelley) and commented on the novel as well as its film adaptations in *Danse Macabre*, acknowledging a somewhat reluctant admiration "for a work both less vivid and more important than anything he has yet produced" (Pharr, "Dream," 120). King characterizes *Frankenstein* as "a rather slow and talky melodrama" (*DM*, 52) and Shelley herself as "not a particularly strong writer of emotional prose" (58). At any rate, King's respect for this Gothic archetype is expressed in *Pet Sematary* and other works, for instance, in *It*, where the Creature appears with nearly every other imaginable monster.

Pet Sematary can be viewed as a retelling of Nathaniel Hawthorne's fictional allegories. Tony Magistrale has compared the novel to Hawthorne's oeuvre by claiming that King's stories owe much of their formulation to the romance tradition in nineteenth- and twentieth-century American literature (*Voyages*, 57). Acknowledging his debt to Hawthorne's tales (*DM*, 25), King, like Herman Melville, Flannery O'Connor, and Edgar Allan Poe, frequently places his protagonists in situations where they face the reality of evil and must make choices that will influence the rest of their lives. How his characters react to the loss of innocence and what they learn from the fall from grace have a decisive effect on their survival. Undoubtedly, the journey into the wilderness links Hawthorne's Aylmer, Chillingworth, Goodman Brown, and Rappuccini to King's Louis Creed, who, entering the woods behind the Pet Sematary, refuses to recognize sin or exert self-discipline and therefore loses his soul. If Ralph Waldo Emerson and the other nineteenth-century transcendentalists are right in their claim that nature offers a vehicle to self-knowledge, then the self disclosed by Thoreau among the pines at Walden Pond differs dramatically from the "self's essential darkness and the human affinity to sin" in the woods of Hawthorne and King (Magistrale, *Voyages,* 59).

Yet another way to analyze *Pet Sematary* is to view it as a kind of Greek tragedy. King has repeatedly argued that entertainment often seems the only goal of what he terms *fearsomes,* but clearly these tales of horror become art when they manage to touch our "phobic pressure points" (Mustazza, 73; *DM,* 4). In doing so they suggest that horror fiction at its best is not make-believe at all, but "a literature whose essence is our single certainty—that, in Hamlet's words, 'all that live must die'" (Winter, *Art,* 152). In King we sense the tragic element in life and the effects of the Aristotelian emotions of fear and pity produced by watching his characters, just as characters in great tragedies do. For the ancient Greeks, the character flaw *(hamartia)* and fate cause the fall of a person of high station. Renaissance tragedy also involves the suffering and death of an aristocratic person, although that outcome results not from fate but from human agency. However, modern America has preferred the form known as "domestic tragedy" or "tragedy of the common person," in which the aristocrats or historical personages are replaced by common people, and the tragedy is the result of the collision of character and dire circumstance (Mustazza, 74). Besides interfering with the natural order, Louis Creed is pushed along the path of destruction by the flaw in his character. Significantly named, Creed's "creed" turns out to be rationality, which convinces him wrongly that he has the ability to return the dead to life, and he cannot help but use it (Winter, *Art,* 151). In King's view Louis Creed "never ceases to be the rational man. Everything is plotted out—this is what can happen, this is what can't happen. But nothing that he thinks can happen is eventually what does happen" (151).

A number of critics have attempted to address the issue of moral responsibility in the novel. Most of King's characters retain a fair amount of free will when confronting evil, and, as Magistrale points out, the majority of his protagonists are like Louis Creed: they choose their own course of action (*Landscape*, 62). He goes on to argue that, as in the case of so many of Hawthorne's young idealists, the awareness of sin forces King's characters to proceed in one of two possible directions, either toward moral regeneration or toward moral degeneration. That is, the characters are offered a double-edged deal: the danger of Faustian temptation as well as the possibility for rebirth and transcendence (*Voyages*, 57, 59). In fact, Louis consciously chooses to liberate the malevolent energies residing in the Micmac burial ground and freely elects to avail himself of its delusive magic (64). Tim Underwood and Leonard Mustazza also acknowledge Louis's responsibility for the disaster, emphasizing that King has created a character with whom it is easy to identify and sympathize, an essentially good man in a difficult situation (Underwood and Miller, *Kingdom of Fear*, 309; Mustazza, 78).

In my reading of *Pet Sematary*, the flaw in Louis's character is hubris—not merely the lack of emotional and intellectual resources that Underwood suggests (*Kingdom*, 309). Since the notion of hubris includes both pride and defiance, two emotions that call for conscious action, I regard Louis as responsible for his actions. Struck by fate, he deliberately chooses evil, and "maybe the worst thing about it was that he didn't feel bad, didn't feel guilty at all" (*PS*, 146). Also, King has Jud Crandall, Louis Creed's surrogate father, state: "[B]ringing the dead back to life . . . that's about as close as playing God as you can get, ain't it?" (168, ellipsis in original). Douglas E. Winter notes that *Pet Sematary* focuses on the question of moral responsibility for having interfered with the natural order (*Art*, 150). Instead of feeling rage and defiance, Louis Creed ought to understand the lesson taught by Jud Crandall: "Sometimes dead is better" (*PS*, 166) or the one that another surrogate father, Dick Hallorann, teaches Danny Torrance in *The Shining*: "You grieve for your daddy. [—] That's what a good son has to do. But see that you get on. That's your job in the hard world, to keep your love alive and see that you get on, no matter what" (463). Furthermore, Louis carries out his quest in secrecy, which clearly indicates that he feels that he has something to hide. Apparently, however, he lets evil seeds grow in his heart. Winter notes that secrets constitute the dark undercurrent of the novel: the secrets that divide man and woman, the secrets of the mortician's room, and the secrets of the burial place that lies beyond the Pet Sematary (Winter, *Art*, 152; *PS*, 141).

Despite the difference in background and personal experience, Louis Creed's and Victor Frankenstein's individual lives culminate in a similar disaster for the same reason: hubris. Louis loses his father when only three years of age, whereas Victor's childhood and youth seem the paradigm of happiness. The loss of the father contributes to Louis's overly rational attitude toward death—as does his cousin Ruthie's violent car accident. Similarly, at the age of seventeen Victor loses his mother, who dies of scarlet fever, and his separation from the enclosure of the family begins. He leaves his Genevan home for the University of Ingolstadt and soon surpasses even his professors in the search for the elixir of life. Like Louis Creed, who keeps a personal record against death, whispering to himself at the moment of victory: "won one today, Louis" (*PS*, 161), Victor is first driven by the purest of motives: "Wealth was an inferior object: but what glory would attend the discovery, if I could banish disease from the human frame, and render man invulnerable to any but a violent death!" (Shelley, 39). Louis epitomizes normality and takes pride in his common sense, whereas Victor is alienated first from his family and then from humanity itself by his dreams of success. However, as the story progresses, Louis develops into a madman in the course of his personal tragedy, while Victor becomes increasingly insane due to his inhumane experiments and personal losses. Although grief-stricken, Louis excludes the facts concerning the nature of his daughter's resurrected cat and finds an odd fascination in the idea of resurrection as an act itself (*PS*, 255). By hypothesizing that the secret of life is the first step to the secret of resurrection (Pharr, "Dream," 117), Victor rationalizes his dreams of glory (Shelley, 52). Ultimately, however, like Lucifer, he wants to become God and create a master race (like another Gothic loner, the vampire): "A new species would bless me as its creator and source; many happy and excellent natures would owe their being to me" (51).

Dedicated to the mission of resurrecting his son, Louis acts in desperate haste. And when he takes his wife killed by the "Creature" (that is, his own resurrected son) to the Micmac burial grounds, Louis is, to quote King, "in a state of transcendence," beyond sanity (Magistrale, *Decade*, 9). Also, when creating the Creature, Victor is in a trancelike state. The protagonist recalls later that he "seemed to have lost all soul or sensation but for this one pursuit" (Shelley, 52). When the Creature opens its eyes, the beauty of Victor's dream vanishes and disgust fills his heart. Both Elisabeth Frankenstein and Rachel Creed die at the hands of the monsters their husbands have created. While Victor's mother rests in peace (like Norma Crandall in *Pet Sematary*), the innocent Creature (like the innocent Gage Creed) stalks its innocent victims. However, the guilty parties, that is, the creators of these monsters, are not able to realize the truth. Lying on his deathbed, Victor warns a friend of ambition, adding, however, that somebody else might succeed where he failed (210). Thus, he dies unfulfilled and somewhat defiant—indeed, a pitiable man who is unable even to destroy the creature he has resurrected. The faithful Creature, however, voluntarily follows Victor into death. Louis, insane and beyond such an emotion as hubris, is united with his resurrected wife, Rachel. Hence, both novels reaffirm order, showing in graphic terms that hubris leads to disaster.

In my reading of *Pet Sematary* and *Frankenstein*, the relationship between Louis/Victor and their Creatures has a twofold function. On the one hand, it reflects the conflict between God and the human being as well as that between an author and his creation. On the other, the Creature reveals the Gothic Janus face of its creator, posing the same question as, for instance, Robert Louis Stevenson's *Strange Case of Dr. Jekyll and Mr. Hyde* (1886) and Oscar Wilde's *Picture of Dorian Gray* (1891): Who made whom? or, as Halberstam puts it: "*Who* rather than *what* is the object of terror?" (28, italics in original). In other words, the Creature remains a victim who never asked to be born, but who, since given the gift of its miserable and disreputable life, returns to its creator to claim its hereditary rights. In King the resurrected Gage is possessed by external evil, whereas only when rejected by its creator does Shelley's Creature become genuinely evil. In addition to works by William Beckford, Charles Brockden

Brown, William Godwin (Shelley's father), Matthew Lewis, Ann Radcliffe, and several of the German terror novelists, Mary Shelley was influenced by the myths of Prometheus and Faust (Punter, *Terror*, 1:106). Despite her mentor Percy Bysshe Shelley's belief in Prometheus unbound, that is, in transcending human limitations, Mary Shelley creates a modern Prometheus in the character of Victor Frankenstein, bound by science to nightmare. She emphasizes that man is mortal (Pharr, "Dream," 116) and that hubris turns man not into God but into the devil. Although it is Creed/Frankenstein who defies God by creating life, it is Gage/the Creature who bears part of the punishment. Punter points out that Mary Shelley tries to present the latter in the light of Rousseauistic and Godwinian theories, a morally neutral, innocent creature who is made evil by subsequent hardships (*Terror*, 1:106–9). In King the soul of the deceased has been replaced by an ancient evil demon.

HUBRIS IN *PET SEMATARY*

Hubris leads to death in *Pet Sematary*. Each of the novel's three parts begins with a biblical paraphrase that continues from part to part. Obviously, the paraphrases both frame the story and make it resonate with the resurrection of Lazarus (John 11:11–44), thus providing a contradiction between God's will and Louis Creed's consciously evil act. The first paraphrase clearly indicates that for someone possessing power, death equals sleep and can thus be reversed. Since his power, however, proves insufficient, is exercised with the wrong attitude, and lacks humility, Louis fails in his effort. On the narrative level, the first part introduces the Creed family: the father, Louis (a young physician), the mother, Rachel (a housewife), Ellie (dedicated to her pet cat, Church[ill]), and Gage (Ellie's younger brother). When the family moves from Chicago to Ludlow, Louis Creed attains a position as a manager of a university infirmary. Subscribing merely to rationality, "[h]e had pronounced two dozen people dead in his career and had never once felt the passage of a soul" (*PS*, 22). Rachel Creed, in contrast, fears the very thought of death, having witnessed the final agonies of her sister ravaged by spinal meningitis. When Jud Crandall takes the family to the Pet Sematary in the woods, the five-year-old Ellie intuitively apprehends the message implicit in the cemetery and fears for her cat and her family (70). Undoubtedly, the deaths of Pascow, a college student, and Church function as warnings, because the third one to die on the same road will be Gage.

Louis Creed's metamorphosis from a rationalist to a hubris-driven scientist to a raving lunatic begins with his encounter with the dying Victor (!) Pascow. The fact that not even Pascow's final gruesome appearance makes any difference to Creed bears witness to either his inability or his reluctance to see beyond rationality as well as the feeling of superiority he takes from this realization—in a word: hubris. Although Victor Pascow plays only an introductory role, repetitive allusions—even in dreams (83–87, 314–19)—strengthen the force of Pascow's imperative: "The door must not be opened," "The barrier was not made to be broken" (87). Alongside the other Gothic beasts—the Byronic vampire, Dr. Jekyll/Mr. Hyde, and the Wandering Jew—both Victor Frankenstein and Louis Creed represent the seeker of forbidden knowledge. The ultimate forbidden knowledge links sex with death, because both the vampire and the seeker of forbidden knowledge attain the knowledge of reproduction through death. Ironically Louis's initial act of love turns into that of death when he reproduces his son for the second time. Also, the knowledge of eternal life condemns these characters to social isolation, because, as Punter points out, the knowledge itself transgresses the boundaries between the natural, the human, and the divine (*Terror*, 1:105). The warning is also found in a number of fairy tales. For instance, Bluebeard's bloody chamber, which the villain's latest wife opens with the key he has forbidden her to use, reveals the dead bodies of her predecessors and warns her of her impending doom (Warner, *Beast*, 241). Disobedience, in turn, is condemned in "Little Red Riding Hood" and "Goldilocks and the Three Bears," who "should have been better brought up," to say the least (243). Finally, a number of fairy tales can be viewed as replayings of one biblical master plot, the Genesis account of the Fall, or of Greek myths, such as the fall of Icarus—a kind of hubris (Tatar, *Off with Their Heads*, 96). As in fairy tales, Creed ignores the deaths of Pascow and Church and the three warnings by Pascow. By repeating the warnings and emphasizing their serious character, King makes clear that Creed has voluntarily chosen to ignore them and is therefore responsible for the grim consequences.

The next phase in Louis Creed's gradual transformation turns him into a Victor Frankenstein: Church the cat dies at the age of three years (for the number three, see *PS*, 15, 52, 402). Winter argues that Ellie's cat is named with a purpose. In the death of Church, King signals that at the heart of *Pet Sematary* is "the rational being's struggle with modern death: death without God, death without hope of salvation" (*Art*, 149–50). However, aware of the pain that Church's death will cause Ellie, her rational father realizes that theoretical explanations prove worthless within the framework of a personal tragedy and consequently takes Jud Crandall's advice to bury the cat in the Micmac burial ground. Reino argues that at this point Church's return from the dead and the Lazarus quotation from the Gospel of John begin to conjoin, and the perceptive reader begins to suspect a connection between the cat's nickname ("Church"), the Hebraic name Pascow (suggesting Passover), the raising of Lazarus from the dead, and the theme of the Easter resurrection (96). Unlike Reino, who regards *Pet Sematary* as a "revolt against Christian resignation" (96), I believe that the novel reinforces Christian values by showing that humans destroy themselves when they attempt mechanistic miracles. Even the hard-headed protagonist's last name ("Creed") testifies to human helplessness before death, and the unfortunate outcome of his proud and defiant struggle against the natural order suggests that certain barriers are not made to be broken. Church's return, finally, turns Louis Creed into a believer, in what he believes are shared opinions.

Louis Creed's destiny is sealed when in his hubris he decides to avail himself of the destructive energies of the Micmac burial grounds. Since Louis Creed does not believe in the Christian revelation but in the furious Wendigo, the "creature that moves through the north country [and whose touch can] turn you into a cannibal" (*PS*, 46), he has neither piety nor patience to wait till the Judgment Day to encounter his son. The second paraphrase anticipates the terror drawing closer to the Creed family. Like a modern Martha praying for Lazarus's return, Ellie prays to God for Gage to come back (250). Unfortunately the wish is brought about through her own father by the evil Wendigo, and, since the former exerts no power and the latter possesses it merely in an evil form, Ellie loses not only her brother but her whole family. Part 2 begins with Gage's funeral and culminates in Louis's reclaiming of his son's body. Louis's controlled attitude toward death turns out to be nothing but a veneer that is shattered when his own son is killed. In an action that recalls his comforting Ellie in the face of death, Louis rocks his lifeless son in his arms. He no longer speaks the scientist's language but reassures him: "Gage, it will be all right, this will end, this is just the night, please, Gage, I love you, Daddy loves you" (343). Mustazza maintains that the protagonist knows that things will not be "all right," and that the lie proves how much he has changed (78). I believe, however, that at this point Louis has both made up his mind to resurrect Gage and is losing his sanity—he would not deliberately bother to lie. This exactly constitutes the tragedy of the novel: following his rational mind, the protagonist repeats the same mistakes over and over again and simultaneously falls deeper and deeper into his misery. Similarly, Bernadette Lynn Bosky notes the irony inherent in the novel, claiming that Louis begins to follow his intuitions only when he should begin to doubt them ("Mind's a Monkey," 268).

Like Victor Frankenstein and Hawthorne's idealists, the protagonist finds no consolation in his desperate acts. His encounter with evil leads to self-destruction and isolation, and the abyss of death only discloses a grotesque version of his love. Indeed, while Gage was his joy, the joy has now left Louis Creed. The bitter nature of this separation alienates Louis from both his family and his calling. Since he is a healer by profession, Dr. Creed is expected to take care of his wife and daughter, but he concentrates on his plans to resurrect Gage (*PS*, 232). Therefore, I consider Louis's mourning a combination of the driven ambition of Lucifer/Faust/Frankenstein and madness. The protagonist's urge to resurrect Gage is not based on pure love but on a selfish need, for he is aware of the qualitatively altered life of the house cat and the risks he is taking with his own son (160). Ironically, Jud Crandall, who introduced Louis to the Micmac burial grounds, now warns him: "You make up reasons . . . they seem like good reasons . . . but mostly you do it because you want to" (168, ellipses in original). The repeated Ramones quotation "Hey-ho, let's go" refers to the beginning of the tragic action in the Micmac burial grounds, where Louis Creed turns from a loving father and a capable physician into a madman. In fact, the quotation recurs any time the natural course of life seems threatened (see, for instance,

246, 252, 344, 402). As the second part progresses, the reader watches the mental collapse of Louis Creed, and, because of the emotional groundwork in the first part, the reader feels the Aristotelian fear and pity—fear that Louis Creed will attempt to resurrect his son, pity for a decent man's suffering (Mustazza, 78).

Both the third paraphrase and the third part of *Pet Sematary* focus on resurrection. Both Lazarus and Gage Creed have been dead for several days, but, unlike Lazarus, Gage does not "come forth" unaltered and alive but emerges deteriorated, deformed, and transformed into an amoral devourer and demon. The latter quotation links both with the fairy tale "Three Wishes" and to the short story "The Monkey's Paw." In *Danse Macabre* King argues that the speculation about what might have been "makes these stories such quintessential tales of terror" (22). Also, the third part of *Pet Sematary* contains several horrific scenes: the blood and guts for which the horror genre is infamous (Mustazza, 81).

The flaw in Louis's character, that is, hubris, exposes him to the Wendigo. Natalie Schroeder maintains that King leaves Louis's ultimate motives ambiguous: he is either completely controlled by the evil Wendigo or, in his grief, ready to reach for any possible way to get his son back—even to committing what he knows is blasphemy, by playing God, knowingly this time, and resurrecting Gage (137). Clearly, evil places in King's work exert power of their own and on their own, but it is of crucial importance to notice that this power is rarely exercised without human assistance. In some cases, such as the alien spacecraft in *The Tommyknockers* and the Chinese mine in *Desperation,* evil is inactive if left untouched. In other cases, "evil places call evil men" (*SL*, 113; Winter, *Art*, 44). For instance, the Marsten House preserves the evil of Hubie Marsten and actuates an even greater evil in the character of Count Barlow. Having introduced the Micmac burial ground to the Creed family, Jud Crandall assumes that he himself might be responsible for the death of Gage Creed. In his view the resurrected Church activated the Wendigo, which deliberately exerted its power, killing Gage on the road and exposing Louis to the temptation to revive his son (*PS*, 275). Anticipating an accident, Rachel returns from Chicago earlier than expected and, like Jud Crandall, feels that something is trying to keep her from Louis (368). In King evil often occurs in cycles: like the spider-monster of *It*, feeding on children every twenty-seven years, the Wendigo, too, seems to rest periodically. Hence, it becomes obvious that Schroeder need not choose "either—or" but "both" of her two options: Louis is exposed to the evil Wendigo because of his own flawed character.

DEATH IN KING'S FICTION

Pet Sematary focuses on death from two angles. One states that "except perhaps for childbirth, [death is] the most natural thing in the world" (56), finding its manifestation in the death of the eighty-year-old Norma Crandall. The other symbolizes death as Oz the Gweat and Tewwible, finding its expression in the painful death of the ten-year-old Zelda Goldman. Clearly, the Wendigo is connected with the latter. Reino points out that, accordingly, the name "Norma" refers to normality, whereas "Zelda" begins with the same letter of the alphabet as zombie. Indeed, her final illness and death, according to Rachel, evokes the figure of the "living dead" (97). Oz the Gweat and Tewwible is symbolic of an unpredictable, indifferent, and evil death. Before getting sick, Zelda had hung a picture of Oz the Great and Terrible on her wall, calling him Oz the Gweat and Tewwible, because she could not make the *r* sound. Besides Jud Crandall's inability to pronounce some words and the many misspellings that appear on the cemetery tombstones, the misspelling of Oz the Gweat and Tewwible seems to emphasize two points. First, even children too young to speak correctly may yet succumb to death. Second, as Reino notes, L. Frank Baum's *Wizard of Oz* is frequently referred to as a parable of the American dream of success, emphasizing the wonder and joy of a fairy tale without sorrows and nightmares (147). With the childish misspelling, however, King redesigns the friendly concept, emphasizing the nightmare of American society. The repetition of the concept intensifies its force (see, for instance, *PS*, 213, 247, 284). Undoubtedly, Oz the Gweat and Tewwible can be equated with both unnatural and painful death as well as the amoral forces of the Wendigo, since both seem to reside in the Micmac burial grounds: "*No, not Christ. These leavings were made in propitiation of a much older God than the Christian one. People have called Him different things at different times, but Rachel's sister gave Him a perfectly good name, I think: Oz the Gweat and Tewwible. God of dead things left in the ground. God of rotting flowers in drainage ditches. God of the Mystery*" (*PS*, 344, italics

in original). Given over by the Micmac to the Wendigo, a malevolent cannibal demon, the Indian burial ground is "an evil, cur-
dled place" (274). Jud used it as a boy to revive his dog, and now
the spirit uses him to get at Louis through Gage.

On the first page of *Pet Sematary,* King maintains: "*Death is a
mystery, and burial is a secret*" (italics in original). Although many
characters have lost their lives in his fiction, and the reader frequently obtains a detailed as well as often gory or grotesque description of the very act of dying, King only seldom penetrates
beyond death to any kind of vision of afterlife. The following examples, however, focus on his characters' inner observations of
the approach of death. Let me begin with Jake Chambers in *The
Gunslinger,* who does not personally experience the transgressing of the boundary between two dimensions. Jake dies in his
own world only to reappear alive in Roland's world later in the
novel. Possessing merely a few recollections of his own dimension, Jake feels similarly estranged in Roland's dimension:

> *Jake feels nothing but surprise and his usual sense of headlong
> bewilderment—is this how it ends? He lands hard in the street and looks at
> an asphalt-sealed crack some two inches from his eyes. [—]*
>
> *Somewhere a radio is playing a song by the rock group Kiss. He sees his
> own hand trailing on the pavement, small, white, shapely. He has never
> bitten his nails.*
>
> *Looking at his hand, Jake dies.* (83, italics in original)

The detailed, introspective observations of death are embedded
in intense realism implicit in all of King's oeuvre. It has often
been stated that an individual experiences his death as a slow-
motion picture. In order to gain invaluable time to defend oneself, regain strength, or flee, the brain slackens the perception of
time. Perhaps Jake, too, has attained a higher level of consciousness, being able to observe every detail of his death scene. Additionally, possibly because of the oft-noted adrenaline flow linked
with a stress situation, Jake feels no pain but retains full possession of his senses to the very end.

The act of Jake's dying is summed up in a single sentence,
whereas Carrie White of *Carrie* enters death through a tunnel,
another widely envisaged passage to the unknown. Sue Snell
senses Carrie's presence in her mind, traces her through this connection, and, finally, witnesses her death: "For a moment Sue felt

as if she were watching a candle flame disappear down a long, black tunnel at a tremendous speed. (she's dying o my god i'm feeling her die) And then the light was gone, and the last conscious thought had been (momma i'm sorry where)" (241). The ultimate question goes unanswered: either Sue as a living human being is unable to follow Carrie beyond the barrier, or Carrie's sad life ends in the abyss of oblivion. More than even attempting an answer, King emphasizes the true nature of Carrie White. In spite of her loveless existence, the abused and mocked teenager remains true to her mother, begging her forgiveness during the last moments of her sordid life.

While Carrie White disappears like a "candle flame" "down a long, black tunnel," Johnny Smith of *The Dead Zone* enters "limbo, a weird conduit between the land of the living and that of the dead" during his coma, and he is given the choice to live or to die (93). Johnny decides to live because of his responsibility for Sarah: "His girl was sick. He had to get her home" (94). Having fulfilled his macrocosmic destiny, that is, having saved the world, Johnny finds himself in the same corridor between life and death again: "The sweet hum of the voices faded. The misty brightness faded. But he was still *he*—Johnny Smith—intact" (385, italics in original).

"The Reach" (*Skeleton Crew*), too, provides a rare glimpse of life after death in King's oeuvre. Not surprisingly, King presents a third popular idea concerning the afterlife existence, that is, relatives and family receiving the deceased, pointing out the vast difference between the desperation of *Pet Sematary* and the gentle transcendence in "The Reach": "There was a bit of pain, but not much; losing her maidenhead had been worse. They stood in the circle in the night. The snow blew around them and they sang" (*SK*, 565). Since it is accepted and natural, Stella's death provides a painless and for a horror writer surprisingly comforting view of death. Indeed, the difference between Louis Creed and Stella Flanders lies in their ability to love and give up. While capable of both, Stella obtains access to truths of which Louis Creed gets merely a distorted and grotesque view. The latter can similarly be applied to Victor Frankenstein, who, like Louis Creed, never learns his lesson.

In *Pet Sematary* no Christian resurrection occurs. As Magistrale notes, by promising the miracle of resurrection, the deceitful

Wendigo manipulates Louis's human frailty only to deliver a grotesque version of the miracle (*Voyages*, 61). What is more, in his deepening involvement with the dark powers of the Wendigo, the hero-villain of the novel, Louis Creed, is first alienated from his family and community and, finally, totally ruined with nothing left but his Frankenstein-like monsters. Exploring the dark emotions of the human mind, *Pet Sematary* is concerned with death, decay, and disorder. A Gothic novel with a Gothic atmosphere, it includes direct references to the genre by the comparison between Rachel Creed's pain and Gothic penny dreadfuls: "That day's penny-dreadful events were only complete when [Rachel] was pulled, screaming, from the East Room of the Brookings-Smith Mortuary" (*PS*, 229). Although minor observations in themselves, they, too, manifest the function of the Gothic along the same lines as Julia Briggs: "Irrational fear [caused by the death of a student] can split open the known world to reveal the underlying nightmares" (212). For this reason *Pet Sematary* seemed too frightening to be published at first. When King realized that Gage Creed would have to die, he also realized that he "had never had to deal with the consequences of death on a rational level" (Winter, *Art*, 147).

In King's words, "Let's flip up the third card in the uneasy Tarot hand. [—] Gaze, if you dare, on the face of the *real* Werewolf. His name, gentle reader, is Edward Hyde" (*DM*, 69, italics in original).

The Gothic Double (the Werewolf)

The core themes of sexuality and immortality of the previous sections have been taken two steps further in Robert Louis Stevenson's *The Strange Case of Dr. Jekyll and Mr. Hyde*, which views them as drives of our human nature and places them in a social context. The archetype of the Werewolf demonstrates that one of the central issues of the Gothic era, namely, the paradoxical existence of both good and evil in a single person, remains an important issue in the fiction of Stephen King. This perpetuation reveals our inability to evolve past our base instincts, to purge them completely from the human psyche. The appearance and reappearance of the Gothic double shows us that popular fiction provides a useful repository for our deepest fear—specifically the fear that each of us is capable of great evil (see also Romero, 255–56). It is clear that the traditional Gothic double has found its modern counterpart in the two-faced serial killer, who partly represents an old threat in a new disguise. In part the character of the serial killer, however, adds to the tradition of the randomness of evil threat. In other words, while the discovery of the human mind in the nineteenth century internalized a number of our fears, the serial killer—apart from showing a familiar face with a sinister mind—chooses his victims randomly. Along the same lines as the Gothic tradition and King in particular, everybody must be suspected, and, moreover, anybody can become a victim.

The themes of Robert Louis Stevenson's *Dr. Jekyll and Mr. Hyde* will first be traced to King's relevant works and then analyzed according to the following classification: (1) the werewolf stories: *Cycle of the Werewolf* (1983) and *Christine* (1983); (2) the doubles: *The Dark Half* (1989); and (3) the serial killers: *The Dead Zone* (1979) and *Black House* (2001). All three focus on the duality within a single character, in which the duality revolves around the poles of good and evil. In addition the werewolf stories presume a change in the character's appearance. Apart from the transmogrifying werewolf, King also introduces Wolf of *The Talisman* (1984), a werewolf by birth, that is, a nontransforming werewolf.

Let me begin by distinguishing the *Gothic double* from the terms related to it. Alongside Frankenstein's monster, the Wandering Jew, and the Byronic vampire, Punter sets a fourth Gothic character, the *Doppelganger*, which, in his view, signifies "the mask of innocence" and which is found in, for instance, *Dr. Jekyll and Mr. Hyde* (*Terror*, 2:1). On another occasion, he refers to the novel as a record of a *split personality* (2), and since the terms are far from identical, they need to be defined at the outset. The term *Doppelganger* denotes both a person exactly like another and a wraith, especially of a living person. Since the German equivalent, too, primarily assumes that the word refers to two separate entities, the term *Doppelganger* is rejected in this context, although it is widely used in literary criticism. The term *split personality* is not included in modern medical dictionaries, rightly so, because such a diagnosis is no longer considered scientifically valid. After Eugen Bleuler in the late nineteenth century coined the term *schizophrenia* to replace the old one, *dementia praecox,* the lay public mistakenly understood it as an equivalent of the term *split personality*. The confusion of the terms meant that the lay term *split personality* was replaced in scientific usage by *dissociative identity disorder* (Kaplan, Sadock, and Grebb, 457). The latter includes various states and signifies a personality disorder in which the person is unaware of what his "other half" is doing. Whether Dr. Jekyll/Mr. Hyde can be diagnosed as a dissociative disorder patient or possibly as a borderline personality may concern psychiatrists, but the Gothic double will do for King's characters.

Like *Doppelganger,* the term *double* elicits ambiguous interpretations and therefore needs to be defined. As the unity of the personality was put in question by Freudian notions, similarly many Gothic narratives were consumed "by a paranoid terror of involution or the unraveling of the multiformed ego" (Halberstam, 55). *Dr. Jekyll and Mr. Hyde* fittingly displays this juxtaposition of the smooth surface of Dr. Jekyll and the "dwarfish" (Stevenson, 18), "ape-like" (27) Mr. Hyde. While Dr. Jekyll is pleasant and sophisticated, Mr. Hyde, stunted, crumpled, and ugly, is designed to shock. Indeed, the "Gothic effect depends upon the production of a monstrous double" (Halberstam, 54). Thus, for my purposes the term *Gothic double* refers to the essential duality within a single character on the presumption that the duality centers on the polarity of good and evil.

Like many of King's works, Stevenson's novella discusses the conflict between the free will to do either good or evil as well as hypocrisy. King believes the conflict between good and evil is the conflict between, in Freudian terms, the id and the superego and refers also to Stevenson's own terms: the conflict between mortification and gratification. In addition King views the struggle in both Christian and mythical terms. The latter suggests the split between the Apollonian (person of intellect, morality, and nobility) and the Dionysian (physical gratification) (*DM,* 75). Influenced by James Hogg's *Confessions of a Justified Sinner* (1824) and Edgar Allan Poe's "William Wilson" (1839), Stevenson wrote his novella in three days in 1886 (Punter, *Terror,* 2:2; *DM,* 69). King expresses his admiration for *Dr. Jekyll and Mr. Hyde,* regarding it a "masterpiece of concision" (*DM,* 69, 80–81).

Dr. Jekyll and Mr. Hyde is the story of a Victorian gentleman who leads a secret life of vice. It uses multiple narrators to relate the story of a man doomed by the chemical reproduction of his double. "[M]an is not truly one but two" says Dr. Jekyll, tormented by a sense of "the thorough and primitive duality of man" (Stevenson, 70). Through chemical experimentation, he discovers a potion that dissociates the "polar twins" of the self, transforming his body into that of his other self (70). The other self, Mr. Hyde, allows Dr. Jekyll to satisfy his evil desires untrammeled by moral scruples. Haunting the streets of London, this small and indescribably ugly character "spring[s] headlong into the sea of liberty," which finally leads him to murder a respectable gentleman (75). Frightened, Dr. Jekyll determines never to use the potion again. However, the metamorphosis has become spontaneous, and, as King notes, Dr. Jekyll "has created Hyde to escape the strictures of propriety, but has discovered that evil has its own strictures" (*DM*, 73). In the end Dr. Jekyll has become Mr. Hyde's prisoner, and Jekyll/Hyde's life ends in suicide.

Many of the themes of *Dr. Jekyll and Mr. Hyde* appear in King's work. While the Gage creature in *Pet Sematary* constructs part of its maker, the dialectic between monster and maker is resolved in, for instance, *Cycle of the Werewolf* as a conflict in a single body. Gage Creed's monstrosity depends on the fragility of his father's humanity, whereas the repulsive nature of the werewolf can only be known through the failed respectability of Reverend Lester Lowe in *Cycle of the Werewolf* (see also Halberstam, 53). Arnie Cunningham of *Christine* illustrates one aspect of the werewolf myth: the werewolf as an innocent victim, predestined to its destruction. Reverend Lester Lowe, in turn, bases his influence on moral superiority, and his high views of himself produce morbidity in his relations with his own appetites. King characterizes Lowe as genuinely evil, whereas Jekyll, although a hypocrite and self-deceiver, only desires personal freedom and keeps certain pleasures repressed. Punter points out that while Hyde's behavior manifests an urban version of "going native," Jekyll struggles with various pressures (*Terror*, 2:3). Similarly, Lester Lowe, who embodies social virtue, takes great pleasure in his bloody nocturnal adventures.

Thad Beaumont's alter ego in *The Dark Half* expresses the violent part of the protagonist's character, of which he himself is not constantly aware. Likewise, the degree to which Dr. Jekyll takes seriously his public responsibilities determines the "hiddenness" of his desire for pleasure. Punter notes that since the public man must appear flawless, he must "hide" his private nature, to the extent of completely denying it (2:3). Defying all logic, Beaumont's "dark half," George Stark, has somehow come into existence, and Beaumont must literally face his dark half in a confrontation in which either Beaumont's Jekyll or Stark's Hyde must die.

The Drawing of the Three introduces a dissociative patient, Odetta Holmes/Detta Walker, who through Roland the Gunslinger's and Eddie Dean's intervention is able to merge her two personalities into the woman named Susannah Dean. Odetta had developed a second personality as a young girl, when Jack Mort dropped a brick on her head. Her two personalities—the sophisticated and wealthy Odetta and the uneducated and vulgar Detta—lead separate lives, completely unaware of each other. Since both are aspects of her self, she cannot become whole until those "polar twins" are united in Susannah Dean. When the compassion of Odetta and the strength of Detta merge into Susannah, she becomes a worthy gunslinger in Roland's team.

The dark halves of King's Gothic doubles express unrestrained sexuality. Lester Lowe "wolf-rapes" Stella Randolph, and Arnie Cunningham is transformed into a vulgar senior citizen in the form of the beast. In a similar vein the sexually insatiable Detta Walker uses foul language and teases men, whereas George Stark commits a sexually charged murder of Miriam Cowley—not to mention the rape-murders of Frank Dodd and the child murders of Carl Bierstone/Charles Burnside. Gothic monsters underline the meaning of decadence and are thus concerned with the problem of degeneration. Punter maintains that they pose, from different angles, the same question appropriate to an age of imperial decline: "how much can one lose—individually, socially, nationally—and still remain a man?" (Punter, *Terror*, 2:1; Sedgwick, *Men*, 92). The question has remained a central issue in the modern Gothic and in King's fiction in particular.

Dr. Jekyll and Mr. Hyde was published at a time when the problem of prostitution was receiving considerable public attention in England. As in *Frankenstein* and *Dracula*, the protagonist's vice and decadence are once again sex related, but also clearly sadistic—the serial killers, Frank Dodd *(Dead Zone)* and Charles Burnside *(Black House)*, manifest these sadistic traits in King. Stevenson had read W. T. Stead's series of articles on child prostitution and was aware that the demand for child prostitutes was being stimulated by the sadistic tastes of Victorian gentlemen (Clemens, 123). More importantly, the theme is evoked at the outset of the novella when Mr. Hyde tramples on a young girl. The violation of the girl's body is settled with a hundred pounds, which reinforces the prostitution motif. Also, the foggy night side of Mr. Hyde's London gives a glimpse of the Victorian gentlemen's subculture: "Once a woman spoke to him, offering, I think, a box of lights" (Stevenson, 85)—clearly, she was offering something else. As in *Black House,* in which the Fisherman lusts for a young boy's buttocks, the hints of sexual exploitation also suggest male victims, as, for instance, in the scene in which Mr. Utterson, "toss[ing] to and fro" on his "great, dark bed," imagines Mr. Hyde blackmailing Dr. Jekyll. This dark "figure to whom power was given" would stand by Jekyll's bedside, "and even at that dead hour he must rise and do its bidding" (20). A disturbing novella, *Dr. Jekyll and Mr. Hyde* gives a detailed depiction of some upper-class gentlemen, but, as Valdine Clemens notes, criticizes moralistic middle-class sexual repression (for instance, prostitution and the prevalent homosexual abuse in public schools) and patriarchal power (124, 132).

King has been concerned with the theme of moral responsibility in scientific research in a number of his works, but not once in connection with the Gothic double. Briggs suggests that the issue of the relations between the human and the bestial, for instance, in Stoker and Stevenson derives from the attempt to analyze Darwinian revelations about the nature of evolution (Briggs, 20–21, 79–81; Punter, *Terror,* 2:5). However, as a child of our times, King finds it more relevant to lay the emphasis of the scientific threat elsewhere than on post-Darwinian fears of degeneration. As Punter notes, *Dr. Jekyll and Mr. Hyde, Frankenstein,* and H. G. Wells's *Island of Dr. Moreau* (1896) rely on public anxieties about scientific progress and about the direction of this progress if undertaken in the absence of moral guidance, but this aspect seems largely metaphorical (*Terror,* 2:3–4). Likewise, the striking similarities between Mr. Hyde's appearance and Charles Darwin's account of highly developed primates in *The Descent of Man* have to be bypassed, because Darwinism has no direct relevance to King. Apart from moral and social aspirations, however, King's Gothic doubles share Dr. Jekyll's desire to "make another man," which in fact stems from personality disorders. Although struck by fate, Reverend Lester Lowe enjoys his metamorphosis, and so does in part Arnie Cunningham before his Gothic confrontation with the consequences of his nocturnal adventures. Furthermore, Thad Beaumont profits financially from the violent imagination of his writing dark half. Similarly, Frank Dodd and Charles Burnside deliberately seek the pleasures provided by their alter egos.

In King the serial killer is portrayed in the character of the rapist-killer Frank Dodd, who strangles women in *The Dead Zone* and figures as a haunting threat in *Cujo*. The serial killer is also found in *Black House,* which introduces a new kind of serial killer from a dimension called the Territories—an allusion to a fantasyland in Twain's *The Adventures of Huckleberry Finn.* The original archetype of Jack the Ripper emphasizes class differences and assumes that, when unmasked, he might come from the working class. However, both Dr. Jekyll/Mr. Hyde and Frank Dodd are the cornerstones of bourgeois society. Somewhat ironically, the Fisherman even represents aristocracy: the Crimson King. Significantly, *Dr. Jekyll and Mr. Hyde* introduces the original archetype of the serial killer, namely, a kind of Jack the Ripper. Martin Tropp compares the characters in terms of violence derived from the contradiction between the inner and the outer man. He claims that both the actual murders and *Dr. Jekyll and Mr. Hyde* became a central issue, because they undeniably conveyed "a sense of precariousness of a culture caught between outward respectability and secret violence" (110). In a similar vein Halberstam claims that Buffalo Bill and Hannibal Lecter, perhaps the most famous fictional serial killers of our time in Thomas Harris's *The Silence of the Lambs* (1991), resemble Dr. Jekyll and Mr. Hyde or Dorian Gray and his portrait (180). In brief, although Stevenson's classic finds no single counterpart in King, its motifs occur in several of King's works.

THE WEREWOLF

Cycle of the Werewolf and *Christine* introduce us to another Stephen King double: the werewolf. Perhaps nowhere else in King's fiction is the Gothic double more pronounced than in this figure. Beginning as a calendar, displaying twelve colored drawings by Bernie Wrightson with a brief accompanying text by King, *Cycle of the Werewolf* evolved into a novella of twelve chapters (Blue, 67; Collings, *Annotated Guide to Stephen King*, 10). Each successive segment takes place on a specific holiday of the year, from January to December, relating the story of the recurring appearance of a werewolf in isolated Tarker's Mills, Maine, and its destruction at the hands of a crippled boy. King defines the predestined nature of the disaster: "It is the Werewolf, and there is no more reason for its coming now than there would be for the arrival of cancer, or a psychotic with murder on his mind, or a killer tornado" (*CW*, 14). Although the werewolf arouses fear and suspicions, only in October do the residents take systematic action to defend themselves. Like Castle Rock, Derry, or 'Salem's Lot, Tarker's Mills keeps its secrets, and, similarly, the residents of Tarker's Mills embody "all of the diversifying virtue and ugliness found in everyday people" (Larson, 104).

What is more, each of the werewolf's victims expands the constant sense of isolation, due to the flaws of their physiques and in their characters (Collings, *Many Facets of Stephen King*, 80). As an illustration, the February victim, Stella Randolph, is isolated by her skewed romanticism and by her corpulence. However, this Valentine's Day the lonely old maid receives a visitor: "a dark shape—amorphous but clearly masculine" (*CW*, 21). King depicts Stella's encounter with the werewolf in Gothic terms, combining dreams, sex, and death (21–24). He uses the common French metaphor "orgasm is a little death" to reinforce the Gothic effect of the February section. Indeed, what takes the place of the Valentine figure is a "beast" with "shaggy fur in a silvery streak" (22), its breath "hot, but somehow not unpleasant" (23). Despite Bernie Wrightson's illustration of a lustful redhead embracing a werewolf, King never graphically describes the wolf-rape and killing of the fat old maid, but veils it in quasi-romantic images that might have derived from John Keats's classic poem "The Eve of St. Agnes" (Reino, 136).

Like the wheelchair-bound protagonist Marty Coslaw, the Reverend Lester Lowe did nothing to deserve his destiny. Until May he remains as unaware of the werewolf's identity as anybody else in Tarker's Mills. On the night before Homecoming Sunday, however, he has a most peculiar dream. In his dream Lowe has been preaching with fire and force but has to break off, because both he and his congregation are turning into werewolves. Lester Lowe's relief after the nightmare turns into shocking awareness when he opens the church doors next morning and finds the gutted body of Clyde Corliss.

King refers to the werewolf in biblical terms as "the Beast" and "the Great Satan," and in the Gothic manner the Beast can be anywhere or, even worse, anybody (*CW*, 45). Unlike a number of other monsters, however, werewolves frequently arouse pity. Aptly Michael R. Collings states that the werewolf is more sinned against than sinning and that the curse works in two ways: on the level of plot, it transforms an otherwise sensible man into a rapacious monster; on the level of theme and symbol, it divorces him from reality and isolates him from society and from his personal standards of morality (*Facets*, 78).

Although Reverend Lester Lowe shares a fate similar to that of Arnie Cunningham in *Christine*, he does not evoke fear and pity to the same extent. In the same way as his hypocritical predecessor in *Dr. Jekyll and Mr. Hyde*, Lester Lowe makes excuses for his behavior without fighting against it. In November, having learned that hunters have been sent out after the werewolf, he deliberately takes the role of the beast and defends himself by comparing the hunters with irrational animals. Ignoring the threat of these adult men, Marty Coslaw's lined notepads and his direct question—"*Why don't you kill yourself?*" (*CW*, 108, 111, italics in original)—force the Reverend Lester Lowe to analyze his situation. With hubris like that of Victor Frankenstein, he turns to God: "*[I]f I have been cursed from Outside, then God will bring me down in His time*" (111, italics in original). In other words, against the advice of his own creator, Stephen King, Reverend Lester Lowe readily lays the guilt on "God the Father" and refuses either to take responsibility for his actions or to fight his werewolf instincts (*DM*, 62). Moreover, blinded by his own logical reasoning, Lester Lowe succumbs to even greater evil by deliberately contemplating the murder of Marty Coslaw—this time both premeditated and in full possession of his senses (*CW*, 111).

While many contemporary treatments tend to glamorize the virtues of evil, King's approach is more traditional (Larson 106–7; Barker [appendix]). Randall D. Larson regards Reverend Lowe as a man unable to free himself from the overwhelming influence of evil, and he is eventually only able to do so through the aid of an outside agency, through the sympathy and concern of Marty

Coslaw (107). Despite his fear of the werewolf, Marty recognizes the human being inside the beast. While aiming his pistol with silver bullets toward the attacking werewolf, he says: "Poor old Reverend Lowe. I'm gonna try to set you free" (*CW*, 125). In the same way, Mina Harker pities the vampire in *Dracula:* "The poor soul who has wrought all this misery is the saddest case of all" (Stoker, 367). Clearly King's allusion to this sentiment reinforces the moral tradition that has traditionally lain at the heart of the horror genre, and which has been much absent in contemporary horror fiction (Larson, 108).

Undoubtedly, King takes a traditional stand by letting evil perish at the end of the novella, but, unlike Larson or Magistrale (in *Voyages*, 57–67), I argue that evil can often be conquered in King's fiction. Although Jack Torrance of *The Shining* succumbs to evil and takes the mallet to attack his family, Dick Hallorann is able to resist the same evil influence of the hotel—similarly, Lowe could have acted otherwise. In *The Talisman* we encounter Wolf, a slow-witted werewolf from the Territories. When he senses that the full moon is rising and that his instincts might lead him to hurt Jack Sawyer, who has become his "herd" and whom he is thus expected to defend against all imaginable threats, this righteous creature takes measures to prevent possible accidents and locks up the herd, that is, Jack Sawyer, in a shed for three days: "He Would Not Injure His Herd" (321). Unlike the godly Lowe, who attempts to silence his crippled eyewitness, the animal-like Wolf avoids killing people. Lowe considers his werewolf nature alien to his true self and allows this alien part to commit even grimmer crimes, which pushes him toward greater levels of moral corruption. Wolf, in contrast, lives by the laws of nature, takes into account the facts caused by his instincts, and respects himself. Just as in *Dr. Jekyll and Mr. Hyde*, the outwardly cultivated surface is hypocritical, while as a child of nature Wolf has nothing to hide.

Arnie Cunningham of *Christine* perishes because of his desperate loneliness. An unattractive teenager who finds little solace at home or at school, Arnie falls in love with a 1958 Plymouth Fury. Possessed by the evil spirit of Christine's earlier owner, Roland LeBay, Arnie is alienated from his family, his best friend Dennis, and even his high school sweetheart, Leigh Cabot. Like *Dr. Jekyll and Mr. Hyde*, *Christine* focuses on "humanity's vulnerability to dehumanization," which coexists with the fear of internal evil: "the upsurge of the animal, the repressed unconscious, the monster from id," or, as Winter points out, "the monster from the fifties" (Winter, *Art*, 137, 139; *DM*, 75; Badley, "Love and Death in the American Car," 84). The novel also discusses the conflict between the will to do evil and the will to deny evil. The car becomes a symbol of the duality of human nature, which is as telling as the two sides of Henry Jekyll's town house, which bordered both a graceful Victorian street and a slumlike alley (Winter, *Art*, 139–40; *DM*, 75): "It was as if I had seen a snake that was almost ready to shed its old skin, that some of the old skin had already flaked away, revealing the glistening newness underneath" (*CH*, 57–58). As Christine magically returns to street condition, Arnie also begins to change, at first for the better, but then he matures beyond his years: "a teenage Jekyll rendered into a middle-aged Hyde" (Winter, *Art*, 140).

While Halberstam views the Gothic double in *Dr. Jekyll and Mr. Hyde* as the duality of the form, distinguishing the concise and artistic surface of the novel from the grim reality of the content (64), the ultimate duality of *Christine* is crystallized by Dennis Guilder when he muses on growing up: "If being a kid is about learning how to live, then being a grown-up is about how to die" (53). Along the familiar lines of the Gothic, death awaits Arnie Cunningham in the form of a car accident. Luckily for him, however, Arnie solves his free will problem for the victory of Dr. Jekyll. LeBay had attempted to possess Arnie in the car, but Arnie fights him and earns "at least a draw" (585). In brief, Wolf takes full responsibility for his actions, whereas Reverend Lester Lowe views himself as an innocent victim and secretly enjoys the state of affairs. Arnie Cunningham of *Christine* ultimately evokes our fear and pity, because in the end he takes responsibility for his actions.

THE DOUBLE

Another variation of the Gothic double in Stephen King's work is Thad Beaumont/George Stark or the writer/his pseudonym. In the author's note to *The Dark Half*, King notes his gratitude to his pseudonym, Richard Bachman, maintaining that the "novel could not have been written without him." In an interview with Walden Books (1 [Nov./Dec. 1989]), King acknowledged prior to

the publication of *The Dark Half* that Richard Bachman is the
darker, more violent side of Stephen King, just as Stark is the dark
half of Thad Beaumont (Magistrale, *Decade*, 66). The pseudonym
of Richard Bachman was so completely developed that King in-
vented a persona to fit Bachman's name and so pervasive that
New American Library included a dust-jacket photograph of
"Bachman" (Collings, *Bachman*, 3). In the preface of *The Bachman
Books* (1986), King gives reasons for the pseudonym in familial
terms: "My 'Stephen King' publishers were like a frigid wifey
who only wants to put out once or twice a year, encouraging her
endlessly horny hubby to find a call girl. Bachman was where I
went when I had to have relief" (ix). More importantly, King in-
vented Richard Bachman to find out if his success as a writer had
not been merely an accident and if he could do it again (Winter,
Art, 208). Remarkably, then, the Gothic double resides within the
Gothic double, that is, the reality of the novel reflects reality.
Tony Magistrale notes that the details surrounding the union
between Beaumont and Stark underscore King's intimate relationship with Bachman. Furthermore, even information relevant
to those trusted persons who knew, protected, and finally revealed King's pseudonym corresponds to the fictional events that
the reader discovers in *The Dark Half* (*Decade*, 63–64).

Like Dr. Jekyll/Mr. Hyde, whose transformation is occasioned
by scientific explanation, King attempts to establish credibility
by means of medicine. Having suffered from constant head-
aches, the eleven-year-old Thad Beaumont is operated on, and,
instead of a supposed brain tumor, a fetal twin is discovered
in his brain. In addition to being Thad's physical twin, George
Stark has his origin in the writer's imagination. Considering
George "a very bad man," Thad knows that he has "built George
Stark from the ground up" (*DH*, 155). The symbolic funeral of
George Stark becomes a moral stand on Thad's part, because he
has both indulged his dark fantasies in Stark's fiction and prof-
ited financially from his success (Magistrale, *Decade*, 64). Wendy
and William, Beaumont's identical twins, underscore the symbiotic relationship of Stark and Beaumont. While responding with
similar affection to these different-looking men, Wendy and
William sense their identical nature. Sharing identical finger-
prints and a capacity for mental telepathy, George obviously has

a right to feel insulted (*DH*, 331). Not even Thad can make a clear distinction between himself and George: "*Who* are *you when you write, Thad? Who are you* then?" (129, italics in original).

Since George constitutes an integral part of Thad's psyche, he does not seriously attempt to get rid of his brother. Elisabeth compares the relationship with alcohol or drug addiction, stating that Thad revealed George's identity only through the force of circumstances: "If Frederick Clawson hadn't come along and forced my husband's hand, I think Thad would still be talking about getting rid of him in the same way" (202). Indeed, this contradiction has resulted in alcohol addiction, a suicide attempt, and lifelike dreams. However, only as Stark threatens Beaumont's immediate circle does he realize the intimacy of their relationship and its fatal consequences. Starting as a thriller, the final confrontation of the two brothers and its victory for Thad receives a mythological explanation. Conducting human souls back and forth between the land of the living and the land of the dead, sparrows are able to distinguish the original brother from the dead one and to take the latter where he belongs. Nevertheless, Thad's victory may prove of short duration, and he is mentioned in a less pleasant context later in King: in *Needful Things* (1991) we learn that Thad Beaumont has broken up with his wife and in *Bag of Bones* (1998) that he has committed suicide.

Autobiographical references can be found throughout the novel. Thad Beaumont's alcohol problem is linked with George Stark's life span, 1975–88—the years that were marked by King's own heavy drinking. A similar oak desk dominated both Thad Beaumont's and King's own study—King got rid of his when he stopped drinking (*DH*, 131; *OW*, 100). And, of course, both had a pseudonym. Despite these references the union of the two brothers remains both vague and unconvincing. Magistrale argues that King depicts Stark both as an independent agent and as fatally dependent on Beaumont, which confuses the reader (*Decade*, 65). Hence, while King is elsewhere often masterful at bridging the gap between reader and text, this Gothic double does not convince the reader in the manner of its counterpart in *Dr. Jekyll and Mr. Hyde*. Since Bachman and King were never antagonists to the same extent as Stark and Beaumont, even the fictional contradiction remains somewhat unconvincing.

THE SERIAL KILLER

The serial killer represents the modern counterpart of Dr. Jekyll/ Mr. Hyde. *The Dead Zone* concerns the removal of masks, both political and psychological. The Gothic duality is displayed even in the novel's central symbol, the wheel of fortune, which, apart from representing blind chance, reveals a second disc. Winter explains that at its heart is the presidential seal, a symbol of a different game of chance—politics—and its paradoxes (*Art*, 76). Greg Stillson is a congressional candidate whose name is an intentional conjunction of "still" and "Nixon" (263). Stillson takes the Vietnamese masquerade game of the Laughing Tiger a step further: "[I]nside the beast-skin, a man, yes. But inside the man-skin, a beast" (*DZ*, 297). *The Dead Zone* also connects the fates—and masks—of Johnny Smith and Frank Dodd. Smith's resemblance to Everyman is signaled in the prosaic simplicity of his name, whereas Dodd is the strangler-rapist of Castle Rock, whose identity is withheld until one of "Faithful John's" psychic revelations. The names "Frank" and "Johnny" may allude to the old, famous blues song "Frankie and Johnny" about two heterosexual lovers, one of whom kills the other because he is unfaithful.

As a consequence of a car crash, Johnny lies in a coma for four and a half years. Awakening in May 1975 at the age of twenty-seven, he discovers that the world has changed: the war in Vietnam has ended, a vice president and president have resigned, Johnny's girlfriend is married and has borne a child, Stillson has made his political move, and an unidentified rapist is killing young women in Castle Rock. Apart from regaining consciousness, Johnny has acquired occult powers of precognition and telepathy. Both cause his estrangement from his past life and force him to take a moral stand: whether to stop Stillson and Dodd. Although this Faithful John serves the purpose of good, his Jekyll-and-Hyde mask haunts his girlfriend, Sarah Bracknell (later Sarah Hazlett), throughout the novel (14). The Hyde aspect of the mask is personified by Sarah's abusive ex-boyfriend Dan and symbolizes inescapable fate (24, 39, 78).

While Johnny is comatose, the policeman Frank Dodd commits his brutal rape-stranglings. Reino maintains that the crimes seem to emerge from the blankness of the coma, as if they were

merely the dark side of an otherwise sunny personality and as if
Frank was Johnny's evil "other"—the two thus possess something like Edgar Allan Poe's "bi-part soul" (67). As Reino points
out, "bi-part souls" are found throughout King's oeuvre, and
Frank and Johnny are undoubtedly interrelated. Frank Dodd is
introduced with a single sentence: "The killer was slick" (*DZ*,
64). Despite the grim verdict, King provides the character with a
background that explains some of his hideous acts. While Dodd
awaits a young victim (Alma Frechette) to walk into his trap, his
mind is momentarily obsessed with an embarrassing childhood
memory: a lesson in sexual education given by his abusive
mother. When Frank was innocently playing with his penis, his
mother, a huge woman, caught him in the act and began to shake
him back and forth. King emphasizes parental responsibility for
aberrant personality development, arguing that Frank "was not
the killer then, he was not slick then, he was a little boy blubber-
ing with fear" (65). Albeit somewhat simplistically, King underscores the significance of the formative years. When Alma Frechette appears, fate plays a decisive role in a genuinely Gothic
manner, and again everybody must be suspected. Familiar with
the killer, Alma does not suspect anything but wonders at his Little Red Riding Hood outfit (66). She is strangled at the moment of
Dodd's ejaculation. "Surely no hometown boy could have done
such a dreadful thing," states the pious narrator, and from then
on almost two years pass without more killings (68).

Significantly, Johnny Smith's awaking from the coma coincides with the fourth murder. However, it takes deep self-
exploration on the recovered Johnny's part before he accepts
Sheriff George Bannerman's request to assist in the murder investigation. By acknowledging his psychic abilities and acting
accordingly, Johnny humbles by fate. In King's world nobody escapes his destiny, and, at any rate, a well-developed brain tumor
would cause Johnny's death within a few months. However, by
bearing responsibility for his next, Johnny prevents Greg Stillson's presidency and its likely consequence, a nuclear war, as
well as Frank Dodd's continuing his murder series. After all, the
investigation turns out to be of short duration, since the deputy
Frank Dodd commits suicide the same evening the two men
meet at the police department. Remarkably, a childish face hides
the Gothic mark of the beast, underscoring that evil actions have

their root in childhood. Having gathered enough evidence, Bannerman and Smith visit Dodd's house and find him dead: "*Knew,* [Johnny] thought incoherently. *Knew somehow when he saw me. Knew it was all over. Came home. Did this*" (253, italics in original). In other words, the two men are connected, and their interrelations are further reinforced by the nature of their mothers: the sexual neurotic, Henrietta Dodd, who "knew from the beginning" (252), and Vera Smith, who marks her son with her religious frenzies: "God has put his mark on my Johnny and I rejoice" (61).

The opening page of *Cujo* repeats the story of Frank Dodd, stating that "[h]e was no werewolf, vampire, ghoul, or unnameable creature from the enchanted forest or from the snowy wastes; he was only a cop named Frank Dodd with mental and sexual problems" (3). Like Buffalo Bill in *The Silence of the Lambs* (1991), Frank Dodd personifies a victimized human being who does not "suit in his skin." Although regarded as a respected resident of Castle Rock, Frank Dodd lacks identity and is perhaps therefore a master of disguise. Unlike Dodd, Charles Burnside aka. Carl Bierstone and the Fisherman of *Black House* is born evil, and he justifies cruelty as an end in itself.

Black House is a kind of sequel to *The Talisman;* both works are jointly authored by Peter Straub and Stephen King. A Victorian novel with allusions to Charles Dickens's *Bleak House,* Dickensian characters, and references to Edgar Allan Poe and Mark Twain, *Black House* reads as a tale of horror or a detective story with a blend of thriller and fantasy. The narrative reintroduces the twelve-year-old Jack Sawyer of *The Talisman*. Now a retired, burned-out LAPD homicide detective, he lives in the small Wisconsin town of French Landing—interestingly, in scenery resembling Tom Sawyer's and Huckleberry Finn's foggy riverside. Children are being abducted from French Landing by a cannibal named the Fisherman, who has disguised himself as an Alzheimer's patient in the local old people's home and is aided in his evil deeds by a talking crow called Gorg. The Fisherman is a pawn in the hand of the Crimson King, evil monarch of End-World, who attempts to abduct a wunderkind in order to annihilate the universe with his powers. Jack and a gang of philosophically inclined motorbikers called the Hegelian Scum take action to save the wunderkind, Ty Marshall, and arrest the Fisherman.

Parodying the thriller formula, the narrator takes us to the
murder scene of Irma Freneau: "We are not here to weep. [—]
Humility is our best, most accurate first response. Without it, we
would miss the point, the great mystery would escape us, and
we would go on deaf and blind, ignorant as pigs. Let us not go
on like pigs. We must honor the scene—the flies, the dog worry-
ing the severed foot, the poor, pale body of Irma Freneau, the
magnitude of what befell Irma Freneau—by acknowledging our
littleness. In comparison, we are no more than vapors" (*BH,* 35–
36). The Fisherman himself is named after Albert Fish, a real-life
child-killer and cannibal, whose crimes he imitates in the novel's
fictional world. In his study of the interrelationship between the
reader and the novel, Edward Bullough states that a work of fiction has succeeded when the reader participates in the communication process so completely as to be nearly convinced that the
art is reality (758). In *Black House* the authors bridge the gap
between the reader and the text by equating the reader with the
narrator (a first-person plural narration), by using the present
tense, and by even letting the reader choose the story ending that
best serves his or her purpose. Perhaps the otherwise too fantastic occurrences of the story become more realistic by these means,
since they are combined with King's usual artillery: lifelike characters and initially realistic settings.

The serial killer turns out to be one of a kind: a tall, skinny, and
senile old man (*BH,* 22). In *Dreamcatcher* and *Black House,* King
deploys gross humor as a device to bridge the gap between the
reader and the text and perhaps even to shock his readers. Having previously heard that Burnside, who snatches, kills, and eats
the town's children, has ejaculated in his dreams, we are then
introduced to his anal functions (109–10). But to regard Burnside
as an empty shell possessed by an outside force would definitely
be a wrong interpretation. "Chummy"/"Burny" Burnside has
voluntarily succumbed to evil. Although a soul brother to the
other men who reside at the Maxton Elder Care Facility, with
his "sly, secretive, rude, caustic, stubborn, foul-tongued, mean-
spirited, and resentful" character (23), Charles Burnside hides
his true self: "Carl Bierstone is Burny's great secret, for he cannot
allow anyone to know that this former incarnation, this earlier
self, still lives inside his skin. Carl Bierstone's awful pleasures,
his foul toys, are also Burny's and he must keep them hidden in

the darkness, where only he can find them" (26). In this case the Gothic double is deployed to introduce a monster. The secrets with which Charles Burnside indulges himself turn him into a loner, forcing him to hide his misdeeds. As a tool in the hands of a greater evil, Burnside takes his pleasure feeding on children who are not worth sending to the End-World to the Crimson King, a creature who ultimately hides beneath the Fisherman mask.

Assisted by Gorg, the speaking crow, Charles Burnside addresses the End-World like a vassal or a stray dog fed with crumbs. When action is needed, the senior citizen undergoes a transformation. Carl Bierstone and something inhuman take Charles Burnside's place (111). The inhuman inside Burny's head signifies Mr. Munshun, the Crimson King's close disciple and servant, a vampirelike figure. Nearing the end of his usefulness, Burny is at Mr. Munshun's request forced to take Ty Marshall, a promising "breaker," to an appointed meeting place. The term *breaker* is used for those slaves of the Crimson King who break the beams leading to the Tower, thus aiming at the total annihilation of King's multiverse. Driven by contradictory urges, this odd serial killer is afraid of the consequences of his actions (541) but, despite a deadly wound, still lusts for Ty Marshall's "juicy buttocks." Like the witch in "Hansel and Gretel," he is reluctant to hand over his prey: "A good agent's entitled to ten percent" (550). Only seldom can a parallel be drawn between a serial killer and a wicked witch from a fairy tale, which perhaps bears further witness to King's genre blending.

The Gothic double of *Dr. Jekyll and Mr. Hyde* shares some traits with characters in King's work. First, flawed humanity moves between the two poles of good and evil, causing contradiction and anguish to the subject. Second, the Gothic gnome, that is, the "dwarfish" and "apelike" half of the personality is hidden at the cost of hypocrisy and often hideous crimes. Therefore, a disguise is needed, which causes further tension and the fear of getting caught. Tension intensifies from the constant threat of transformation. These works also separate the good from the bad, the pure from the dirty, the beautiful from the ugly, and the sexual from the spiritual. Hence, the descendants of Dr. Jekyll/Mr. Hyde all perish in King, with the notable exception of Wolf, who accepts his duality and lives by it. The Gothic double seems to be directed toward the two polarities of good and evil: the Hyde part toward the monstrous; the Jekyll part toward the virtuous. Thus, the tension is produced by the constant threat of Dr. Jekyll's transformation. Aptly Halberstam argues that for the moments the monster stands apart from humanity, the reader witnesses the ways in which the Gothic deploys monstrosity to attach negative meaning to bodies with specific sexual, racial, and class codings (59).

Monsters of the nineteenth century scare us from a distance, while, as Halberstam notes, "We wear modern monsters like skin, they are us, they are on us and in us" (163). King, too, states "that the monsters are no longer due on Maple Street, but may pop up in our own mirrors—at any time" (*DM,* 252). Presumably, both convictions are based on two facts: good and evil can and do exist within a single person, and, concomitantly, we are ultimately unable to evolve, to purge our baser selves from our psyche. King puts it straightforwardly: "Werewolf, vampire, ghoul, unnameable creature from the wastes. The monster never dies" (*CU,* 4).

King has maintained: "When we turn over the whole card, the one that makes the hand, we find the central card of our Tarot hand: the Ghost" (*DM,* 260).

The Gothic Melodrama (the Ghost)

Instead of maniacal outsiders, the sexual threat may also take the familiar face of the father/the husband, who lives in the same household with his female victims. In this section the problems of self are viewed as reflected in the family, which connects them to a larger whole. In other words, the contradiction between personal freedom and social virtue discussed in the previous section develops into a net of Gothic relationships, enlarging the scope and including romance and familial discord, both of which often lead to death. In fact, the archetype of the Ghost seems to embody the Gothic melodrama. Furthermore, many of the themes of the first Gothic novel, Horace Walpole's *The Castle of Otranto,* recur in King's distinctly melodramatic works. My analysis focuses on the Gothic archetypal characters that can be detected in King.

The main concerns of Stephen King's Gothic melodramas are clearly expressed in *Bag of Bones* and *The Shining:* (1) domestic violence, incest, and rape as well as romance (2) the revisiting of the sins of the fathers on their children, and (3) the archetype of the Ghost. King has frequently been referred to as a writer of melodramas. Somewhat ironically, another writer, Mike Noonan of *Bag of Bones* (1998), is called "V. C. Andrews with a prick" (*BB*, 25, 26; note that V. C. Andrews is a female writer of serialized melodramas). *Bag of Bones* can be viewed as equal parts a ghost story, a thriller, a romance, a mystery, and a psychological suspense story. A love story with supernatural overtones, it evokes Daphne du Maurier's *Rebecca* (1938); other literary connections include Herman Melville's "Bartleby the Scrivener" (1856) and Thomas Hardy. Among its several genres, the melodrama and the horror genre seem to stand out, and the most Gothic features about the novel are its sexually blurred relations between the protagonist, his dead wife, and his new lover. Originally structured as a five-act Shakespearean tragedy, *The Shining* introduces the Torrances, who have locked themselves in with the ghosts of the past. The novel focuses on domestic violence and the past haunting the present.

King and Walpole share several traits. E. J. Clery argues that Horace Walpole established a modern Gothic style of fiction: *Gothic* was no longer a historical description but marked the initiation of a new genre (ix, xv). Furthermore, Punter maintains that *Otranto* was the earliest and most important manifestation of the late eighteenth-century revival of romance, that is, of the older traditions of prose literature that had been supplanted by the rise of the novel (*Terror*, 1:44). Although Walpole's use of nonrealistic or romantic historical setting and wooden characterization differs from King, in King's melodramatic works one can distinguish the traditional male archetypes of the hero and the villain as well as the female archetype of the heroine. Also, both believe in the power of terror to awaken and sustain interest: King in retaining his position as a guardian of traditional values; Walpole in launching *Otranto* as an assault on Enlightenment norms. Both blend genres (in fact, Walpole's assumed resemblance to Shakespeare is based on his mixing of kinds and genres), and both have an inclination to portray excess and exaggeration (Punter,

Terror, 1:44; Clery, xv). Moreover, both exploit the supernatural in order to amuse: King by creating "gray men" with an appetite for raw bacon *(Dreamcatcher),* "alien-weasels" born of adult males *(Dreamcatcher),* and serial killers who are not housebroken *(Black House);* Walpole by combining devices from folklore with Elizabethan motifs to produce an armory of magical helmets, speaking pictures, and ghostly giants. Finally, both expose themselves to self-parody and irony (Punter, *Terror,* 1:45–46; Clery, xviii).

Apparently, King has adopted the Gothic castle from Otranto, which in turn was modeled on Walpole's own Strawberry Hill: it is portrayed in the Overlook Hotel *(The Shining)* and, to a lesser degree, in Sara Laughs *(Bag of Bones).* In fact, the castle literally is the protagonist in both *The Shining* and *Otranto.* However, more important than the physical presence of the Gothic castle is the atmosphere of oppression and the powerlessness of the characters, who are manipulated by forces they cannot comprehend (Clery, xv). Both King and Walpole use the forces of nature to emphasize the possibility that evil forces shape their characters' fate (Hennessy, 327). King also modernizes the devices Walpole handed down to his successors: underground vaults become basements, and ill-fitting doors lead to forbidden rooms in his treatment (Birkhead, 22–23). In *Danse Macabre* King discusses the haunted house and the archetype of the Bad Place, maintaining that the past is a ghost that haunts our present lives constantly and that the haunted house is turned into a kind of symbol of unexpiated sin in *The Shining* (265). He places the age-old notion of the past haunting the present in a contemporary setting throughout his oeuvre, and the theme of the revisiting of the sins of the fathers on their children is emphasized in *The Shining* and *Bag of Bones.* Hence, King is aware of this specific theme in the Gothic classics. He notes that Horace Walpole's *Castle of Otranto,* Matthew Lewis's *Monk,* C. R. Maturin's *Melmoth the Wanderer,* and even Mary Shelley's *Frankenstein* are books in which the past eventually becomes more important than the present (254–55). Punter points out that the tyrant Manfred in *Otranto* signifies a social anxiety that has a historical dimension: threat to convention was to some extent regarded as originating in the past, in the memory of previous social and psychological orders *(Terror,* 1:47).

The large readership of both King's melodramas and *Otranto* can in part be explained by the latent motif of domestic and sexual violence. Clemens in *The Return of the Repressed* claims that *Otranto* captivated so many readers because they were actually "haunted" by this taboo topic. The novel offered emotional confirmation of a social problem that was still denied conscious recognition (29). *Otranto* was published at a time when the institution of marriage had become a matter of public controversy in England (32). An MP since 1742, Walpole seems to have taken a stand for clandestine marriages and marital equality by his ironical representation of the Manfred figure as well as his emphasis on the righteous young love of Theodore and Isabella. Apart from the most developed Manfred figure, *Otranto* introduces Isabella and Matilda as two virtuous ladies in distress, Hippolita as the prototype of a long series of victimized wives, and Theodore as the hero whose "soul abhors a falsehood" (Walpole, 53). Both familial contradictions and sexual violence as well as romantic relations are included in King's melodramas. The reader identifies with the character, and violence is therefore viewed as violence and nothing more, not as humor or a moral lesson.

Similarly, the topic of rape and incest would not in itself have shocked Walpole's readers, who were used to Samuel Richardson's and Henry Fielding's treatment of the themes, but they may have been struck by Walpole's presentation of unruly masculine sexuality (Clemens, 34). In abandoning the conventional humorous or moral/sentimental treatments in favor of one that vividly conveys the victim's sense of terror, Walpole seems to confirm the existence of domestic violence. In Walpole, as Clemens notes, the incest/rape motif is played out through the Freudian dream displacement strategy, in which the individuals' identities become blurred (35). In King dreams have a wide range of functions: they warn, predict, carry the narrative forward, and even form their own subplots. Thus, while the post-Freudian King consciously exploits psychoanalytic theory to advance his ideas, the pre-Freudian Walpole and his audience appear to have subliminally apprehended the rich imagery of sexual symbolism (31). Instead of physical imagery in the form of gigantic swords and helmets or subterranean passages, King refers to father-son and mother-daughter relationships and older males' infatuation with young women, and in some cases he even internalizes the Ghost in a character's psyche, as in Tony of *The Shining*.

The major themes of *Otranto* are expressed through the archetype of the Ghost. The idea for *Otranto* came to Walpole in a dream: "I had thought myself in an ancient castle . . . and . . . on the uppermost bannister of a great staircase I saw a gigantic hand in armour" (Walpole, vii). In the novel the hand grows into a gigantic statue and the nemesis of the story. Although William Shakespeare had already introduced the Ghost in *Hamlet,* it had never before had a distinct function in a novel. King's view of the archetype seems more refined than that of Walpole: on the one hand, he notes the tension between the Apollonian and the Dionysian in the Ghost and, on the other, traces it back to humans: "What is the ghost, after all, that it should frighten us so, but our own face? When we observe it we become like Narcissus, who was so struck by the beauty of his own reflection that he lost his life. We fear the Ghost for much the same reason we fear the Werewolf: it is the deep part of us that need not be bound by piffling Apollonian restrictions. It can walk through walls, disappear, speak in the voices of strangers. It is the Dionysian part of us . . . but it is still us" (*DM*, 258, ellipsis in original). Furthermore, King maintains that of the four Gothic archetypes, the "Ghost is the most potent," because it sums up all the rest and traces them to the original antagonist, the devil (259).

King embraces Peter Straub's view of the Ghost. While analyzing this archetype in *Julia* (1975), *If You Could See Me Now* (1977), and *Ghost Story* (1979), he notes the resemblance of Straub's ghosts to those of Henry James, Edith Wharton, and M. R. James, stating that the characters in Straub recognize a Freudian kinship. As in James's "Turn of the Screw," in Straub's and King's works ghosts adopt the motivations and the souls of those who behold them; if the ghosts are evil, they have adopted the evil from their beholders (*DM*, 257). In King's fiction Nick Andros can be seen as a primary example of a good ghost. In *The Stand* he returns from the dead to tell the half-witted Tom Cullen how to heal the novel's hero, Stu Redman, after he has fallen ill with pneumonia. Apart from *The Stand, The Shining,* and *Bag of Bones,* King has deployed the archetype of the Ghost in, for instance, *The Dead Zone* (Johnny Smith returns to comfort Sarah [Bracknell] Hazlett on his grave at the end of the novel), "The Reach" (relatives and family receive the deceased), *It* (the victims of

Pennywise the Clown invite the children who are still alive to join the dead ones), *The Dark Half* (George Stark rises from the dead), and *Rose Madder* (Wendy Yarrow delivers justice as a maid of the devourer-goddess).

Although King argues that "for the purposes of the horror novel the ghosts must be evil," his fiction is stalked by good, evil, and neutral ghosts (*DM*, 260). The latter type seems significant, because it illustrates King's view of free will. For instance, Victor Pascow approaches Louis Creed to deliver a message, nothing more. Only when Louis Creed begins to seek forbidden knowledge does Pascow become truly threatening. In other words, the character transfers his own nature to the ghost. This is not true in all cases, however, and the reality of both good and evil marks the whole of King's oeuvre. He clearly embraces the moral stance of Straub's ghosts, which is reactionary and defends traditional values. What may distinguish Straub's ghosts from those in King is their gender. Straub's evil ghosts are female, whereas King in *Bag of Bones* introduces two female ghosts: Jo Noonan as a guardian ghost and Sara Tidwell as a seeker of vengeance. However, both Straub in *Ghost Story* and King in *Bag of Bones* blur the concept of evil in an intriguing way by explicitly and implicitly asking the question: "Which evil is the real evil?" Horror novels, King tells us, can usually be divided into those that explore "inside evil" *(Dr. Jekyll and Mr. Hyde)* and those that explore "outside" or predestinate evil *(Dracula)*. However, in *Ghost Story*—and in King's *Bag of Bones*—the reader is not able to determine which category the books fall into (262).

BAG OF BONES

Four years after the sudden death of his wife, the forty-year-old Mike Noonan is still grieving. He is experiencing threatening dreams centering on his vacation home at Dark Score Lake, Maine. Unable to write and plagued by the nightmares, Mike reluctantly returns to the summerhouse, which he calls Sara Laughs and which plays the part of the Bad Place in the novel. The place was christened after a black blues singer, Sara Tidwell. Her extraordinary laughter was extinguished in the late nineteenth century when a gang of white boys raped Sara and killed both her and her son. The details of the revengeful Sara taking vengeance on the killers and their descendants is revealed to Jo Noonan, who returns to the cottage shortly before her death to gather newspaper clippings concerning the incident.

Mike, too, realizes that the residence is inhabited by ghostly presences. Since he recognizes Jo as one of the ghosts, he gets used to the harmless ways the spirits make their presence known. As Jo's messages become more urgent, Mike begins to sense evil presences haunting the environs of Sara Laughs. What is more, Mike finds the whole town held in the grip of a powerful software magnate, Max Devore, who is engaged in a bitter custody struggle with his daughter-in-law, Mattie Devore, over his three-year-old granddaughter, Kyra. Mike meets Mattie after rescuing Kyra from a busy local highway, develops romantic feelings toward the twenty-year-old widow, and makes her problems his own. As so often in King, *Bag of Bones* is concerned with the theme that monsters live inside ordinary people. Although Stanley Wiater, Christopher Golden, and Hank Wagner refer to Sara Tidwell as "the root cause of evil" (122), the question of *Ghost Story* remains: "Which evil is the real evil?" (*DM*, 262). Although Mike breaks Sara's hold over the town by uncovering and destroying her remains, the old curse has already given birth to new monsters: Mattie Devore is fatally shot before she and Mike can consummate their relationship.

The central Gothic characters consist of the bold villain, who is both admired and feared, the pale and melancholic hero, and the sensitive and innocent suffering heroine (Birkhead, 223). Drawing on Freud's theory of paranoia, Sedgwick in *The Coherence of Gothic Conventions* claims that if the heroine of the Gothic romance is "a classic hysteric," the hero of Gothic monster fiction is "a classic paranoid" (vi). For Sedgwick the paranoid hero is locked into a homosocial relation with his feared and desired double, typically the monster (ix). Apart from the main characters, the minor characters, too, represent two categories of identity: archetypal masculinity and archetypal femininity. William Patrick Day in *In the Circles of Fear and Desire* defines the masculine archetype as a character who personifies egocentric impulses frequently manifested as a desire to become godlike and who satisfies this desire with illegitimate power (76).

Manfred of *Otranto*, Max Devore of *Bag of Bones*, and, to some extent, Jack Torrance of *The Shining* represent the archetypal male tyrant, the feared villain. As Day points out, the villain's struggle aims at preserving his individual identity and patriarchal power (93). Indeed, Manfred seems on the verge of losing both when his son dies and his inheritance of Otranto proves illegitimate. Devore's actions are quickly sketched: (1) action for pleasure (2) action to defeat the past, and (3) action to protect his interests. In King's world even the meanest villain is provided with a background that to a certain extent explains the crimes he commits. Unlike Manfred, who is declared evil without any reasons, both Max Devore and Jack Torrance act within the framework of their personal history. Unable to subject his son, Lance, to his sway or to pay the low-class Mattie to leave Lance, Max fails to exercise patriarchal power. Estranged from Lance, he cuts off all contact with him, but after his son accidentally dies, he finds another target for his pursuit, engaging in a custody battle over his granddaughter. Although individualism is considered acceptable or even desirable in the hero, the trait turns into egotism in the villain. Devore, too, views himself as all-powerful, regarding merely his own opinions as significant.

For the villain no amount of power is sufficient; in his quest for more, he readily sacrifices anything and everything regarded as important in a traditional sense. Ending up a monstrous parody of the god he is attempting to be, he is capable only of terror and destruction, never of creation and love of creation (Day, 96). Ready to sacrifice his marriage in order to gain power, that is, the claim to the castle of Otranto, Manfred attempts to replace his recently deceased son by marrying his bride, thus, ironically, becoming his own son. Threatening the protagonist over the telephone, Max Devore makes his first contact with Mike Noonan. Devore's sophisticated exterior, however, is exposed as a sham when he meets with resistance, and, as with a number of other villains in King, his madness is open to view. "Devore was mad, all right, mad as a hatter" (*BB*, 395), Mike Noonan states, having barely survived an attempted murder.

As Frederick S. Frank in *The First Gothics* points out, the villain may seem remorseless and cold, but he is actually a character "of titanic and destructive passion" (437). Indeed, the senior citizen Max Devore is capable of both surprisingly foul language and, despite his wheelchair, acts of physical strength. In other words, Devore's inner transformations mark the typical Gothic villain, who is subjected to endless metamorphoses (Day, 7). Before the final act of violence, Max Devore's force takes on vast dimensions when he assumes the role of the devil, giving Mike one last chance to save his soul (*BB*, 403). Although Noonan does not recognize anything supernatural about Devore, King consciously repeats the reference to human souls, which the villain regards as mere playthings. Mad characters in King's fiction possess the willpower to clear any obstacles in their way. Devore, dedicated to his mission, does not hesitate to take advantage of even his own suicide to attack Noonan and his own disobedient relatives.

In high melodrama it takes only one encounter to fall in love with one's destiny. Along the same lines as the original Gothic romances or contemporary romance, *Bag of Bones* is centered around Mike Noonan's barely restrained sexuality and his attraction to Mattie Devore. Apparently, his feelings are reciprocated, but this Gothic hero—"a lonely, stalwart and black-browed man of beautiful countenance, whose spiritual life is in the grip of some secret influence" (Railo, 31)—struggles with his inner urges, since his rational mind considers Mattie young enough to be his daughter. Obviously, *Bag of Bones* draws from the same spring as the Gothic classics, where the hero-villain, full of desire and lust, pursues the heroine in the narrow corridors of a decayed castle or locks her up with the intention to rape her.

As a Gothic hero, Mike Noonan, however, discovers his true identity as a human being and muses: "I don't believe that people automatically have a right to what they want, no matter how badly they want it. Not every thirst should be slaked" (*BB*, 472). Indeed, Noonan's friend Bill Dean warns him to keep his distance from Mattie and not to meddle in Devore's interests. In fact, Mattie seems doomed from the start, as her lawyer, John Storrow, observes (358). Of course, Dean's and Storrow's statements emphasize the vast dimensions of the heroic act the protagonist is planning by underscoring simultaneously the power of the antagonist and the cowardice of the town residents. This clearly places the hero in the foreground of the action and the heroine in the position of a damsel in distress.

The sexually blurred relations between Mike, his dead wife, Jo, and Mattie make *Bag of Bones* a genuinely Gothic novel. As a kind of latter-day version of *The Scarlet Letter*, the Christian names of the local children begin with the letter *k*, which seems to mark the town residents' shared guilt for having murdered Sara Tidwell and her son, Kito. Also, when Jo Noonan died, she was pregnant with a child who was supposed to have another Christian name beginning with the letter *k*, Kia. Significantly, Mattie's daughter calls herself by that name, which indicates that she might actually be Jo and Mike's unborn baby. Hence, this Gothic love triangle consists of the teenager Mattie, the sexually aroused, middle-aged Mike, and his dead wife, Jo, who demands that Mike helps Mattie or, in fact, helps their mutual child, Kyra.

Obviously, the guilt-stricken hero is drawn in two directions by two women. In one of his masturbatory dreams, he makes loves to both Mattie and Jo, of which the latter instance, of course, exemplifies a Gothic case of necrophilia. Both women encourage Mike to do what he wants, which leads to a Gothic confrontation with death. Again both women affirm that everything culminates in death. These interrelations are further emphasized and complicated by the characters' telepathic connections, shared dreams, and even hauntings throughout the novel. Although in love and struggling with his urges, Mike acknowledges how things stand. While promising to support Mattie and Kyra financially and while requested to give his reasons for the unselfish act, he initially thinks that he wishes to be part of something in which he can make a difference. Despite his heroism Mike is also tempted by another alternative: Mattie could also become his mistress (426). Despite his strong feelings toward Mattie, Mike also remains aware of the social gap between them and the power he could possibly exert over her. As a Gothic hero, he is able to resist the temptation.

In *Bag of Bones* King through supernatural themes comments on communal guilt and prejudices as well as on familial discord. His prose style is deceptively simple, his characters seem "open and accessible" (Winter, *Faces*, 251), "and the ease with which one of his imaginary worlds envelops the reader represents another reason for his popularity" (Magistrale, *Landscape*, 13). Magistrale points out that the insecurities of modern life lead readers to King, who as a "child of [our] times is able to express them in modern terms" (Magistrale, *Landscape*, 13; *DM*, 10–15). Hence, his fiction has a political and social relevance that is both serious and significant (Magistrale, *Landscape*, 13).

The haunted house that loomed in the background of *'Salem's Lot* also becomes the centerpiece of King's third published novel, *The Shining.* Inspired by Shirley Jackson's Hill House and Edgar Allan Poe's haunted palace in "The Masque of the Red Death" (1842), the Overlook Hotel stands in the Rocky Mountains, forty miles from the nearest town, over roads that are impassable through six months of cold winter (Winter, *Art,* 51). Overlooking and obviously contributing to the ruination of a family unit, the hotel is recognized by the five-year-old Danny from the warnings of his imaginary friend, Tony. What Danny senses as hiding beneath the seemingly settled order of this isolated hotel is revealed as the ruined castle of Gothic literature with its labyrinthine corridors, forbidden rooms, rattling chains (in the elevator shaft), and ghosts. Winter notes that like its Gothic predecessors, the Overlook Hotel epitomizes the pride and guilt of genuine tragedy (51). Built at the turn of the twentieth century and beset by scandal and financial problems ever since, the resort hotel remains shackled to its past by the same events repeated night after night.

A caretaker is hired annually to maintain the Overlook until it reopens in the spring. A former drinking companion assists Jack Torrance in landing the position, which seems his last chance to finish his play, to improve his marriage with Wendy, and to leave his violent past behind him. Unfortunately the family is already haunted by emotional problems that make them perfect potential victims of the malevolent hotel. Despite his attempts to overcome his problems, Jack gradually succumbs to the evil spirit of the hotel, which works through him to get hold of Danny. Danny has a cardiokinetic ability called "the shining," which enables him to find lost objects, read minds, and glimpse the future. By the unintentional action of his abilities, the hotel starts coming to life, causing situations that threaten the child. As Michael N. Stanton argues, it seems obvious that the power of the hotel also lies in its ability to harm most those who perceive most accurately its true nature (13). As Jack's personality becomes submerged, Danny calls Dick Hallorann, the hotel cook, who also "shines," to rescue him. More importantly, the boy refuses to cooperate with the spirit in front of his father, and Jack himself manages to surface for a brief moment to tell Danny that he loves him and that he should escape. Having forgotten to tend the hotel boiler, Jack and the evil spirit are blasted in the explosion that follows, whereas Danny, Wendy, and Hallorann flee in a snowmobile.

For obvious reasons Jack Torrance of *The Shining* can be regarded as a Gothic villain (see, for instance, *SH*, 203, 341, 445), but this well-developed character is also a tragic hero. Apart from addiction to alcohol, Jack's problems include a negative family history and a fractured personality. King himself regards Jack Torrance as a dysfunctional personality who keeps looking for a geographical change in order to start all over again: "What I was trying to say in that novel is that wherever you go, the same asshole gets off the plane" (Magistrale, *Decade*, 18). *The Shining* opens with Jack Torrance applying for a new chance to change his life. He offers no flattering views of his future employer but takes a defensive attitude toward him from the beginning. In search of a fresh start, "his pride was all that was left" (*SH*, 48), but pride equals sin in the Gothic world and inevitably leads to disaster. As a Gothic hero-villain, Jack, full of hubris, directs himself toward his own doom. The observant reader realizes the inevitable fate from the beginning, and King fulfills his expectations. At one point Jack has the opportunity to choose differently, but the form of this novel, modeled on Shakespearean tragedy, limits his behavior. In other words, whatever is going to happen to Jack has already been decided. Although an organization is at work at the Overlook, King views it primarily as a supernatural recreation of Jack's previous problems (Magistrale, *Decade*, 18–19). To return to the original question of this study—What makes King so popular?—*The Shining* offers at least a partial answer. That readers know the final outcome of the story in chapter 1 and are still willing to wade through about four hundred pages undeniably reveals that the work has a striking appeal. We should remember that King holds that love of characters makes an effective horror story: "There is no horror without love and feeling. . . . [B]ecause horror is the contrasting emotion to our understanding of all the things that are good and normal. Without a concept of normality, there is no horror" (Winter, *Art*, 52; see also Straub, 9).

To arouse fear and pity in the reader, King includes biographical information about Jack's abused childhood and "his regrettable relationship with the wealthy and irresponsible surrogate father-figure, Al Shockley" (Manchel, 87). Indeed, the shadow of his father has fallen on Jack, whose childhood was clouded by his father's drunken viciousness, which included wife and child abuse. Drawing parallels between Jack and Danny, King depicts the innocent and forgiving Jack waiting for his father's home-coming. After the detailed depiction of the mother's severe beat-ing, he then draws parallels between the two marriages: Jack's mother corroborates the father's story about the beating, just as Wendy affirms Jack's story about Danny's arm-breaking in-cident. When Jack's father, a six-foot-two-inch tall male nurse, dies, he goes on living in his own son. King clearly underscores this stance by using the archetype of the Ghost. When alive, Jack's father is referred to as "some soft and flapping oversized ghost in his hospital whites" (*SH,* 237). When dead, he resembles "the Ghost-God" and, more remarkably, in a reference to William Golding's *Lord of the Flies,* "the Pig-God," which drives the frag-ile and sensitive Simon to madness and death (241). Indeed, de-spite a number of supernatural ghosts in *The Shining,* the real ones of the characters' personal past have the strongest effect on the reader. Again the horror in King does not ultimately derive from the supernatural monsters but from the reader's realization that he himself could be Jack.

The threat of divorce sways constantly over the family, and in the manner of the modern melodrama, it is viewed from the angle of every family member in turn. As a modernized Gothic heroine, Jack's fragile and attractive wife, Wendy, who has been raised in the shadow of a voracious mother, awaits her husband's return home from the job interview. Day's definition of a typical feminine archetype as a character with childish qualities and with love for as well as obedience to the male figure (79) fittingly de-picts her at the beginning of the novel, where we encounter her weeping. Unable to protect Danny from Jack's violent outbursts, unstable condition, and the threat of their divorce, she has a num-ber of reasons for her anguish. However, just as her counterparts in the Gothic classics, Wendy unwaveringly but hesitantly fol-lows her husband to the Overlook, telling her son: "If it's what your father wants, it's what I want" (*SH,* 26).

In fact, she has no choice, although "[l]ove was over" (57). Am-biguously King begins chapter 6 by dealing with Wendy's noc-turnal thoughts with this sentence, which literally refers to the couple's lovemaking but perhaps on a deeper level to her inner fears. Wendy stays in her abusive marriage because she feels both guilty of having caused her parents' divorce and grateful to Jack, who has provided her with the privileged status of a married woman. She then submits for the wrong reasons to Jack's whims at the cost of Danny's well-being. Insightfully King sketches the contradictory dependencies implicit in the relationship. He seems to underscore the fact that in an abusive relationship a price must always be paid. However, after the arm-breaking incident, Wendy decides to leave Jack for her own and Danny's sake. Against her better judgment, Wendy's resolve is weakened by Jack's improved behavior. However, Wendy cannot be regarded as a stereotypical Gothic heroine, because she gradually develops from an dependent girl into a mature woman. Aptly Jeanne Campbell Reesman notes that Wendy demonstrates to the reader that succumbing to evil is not the only possible response to evil. She responds to the call for survival but bases her decisions on what she believes to be right (112). Wendy's maturing is shown by her appearance at the end of the novel. As Dick Hallorann notes, some nine months ago she had been a mere girl. Now she was a woman, "a human being who had been dragged around to the dark side of the moon and had come back able to put the pieces back together" (*SH*, 460).

Like his mother the five-year-old Danny waits for his father to come home from the job interview. Nicknamed "Doc," the innocent and forgiving child loves Jack unreservedly. His warm feelings are reciprocated, but since the novel is structured as a Shakespearean tragedy (primarily *Hamlet*), Jack seems to destroy the people he loves best—just as he has been destroyed by his own father. King illustrates the interrelations of the three generations by using the characters' names as a uniting factor. As Reino points out, Jack's father by the name Mark Anthony Torrance is connected with Jack, whose full name is John Daniel Torrance, and, finally, with the youngest of the three, Daniel Anthony Torrance. The interrelationship between the middle names suggests that Danny's imaginary friend, Tony, is a composite of the three (38), thus affirming King's conviction that the present results from the past. While encouraging Danny before the final battle, Tony explains that he is part of Danny. However, the stamp on Tony's features is that of Jack Torrance, "as if Tony—as if the Daniel Anthony Torrance that would someday be—was a halfling caught between father and son, a ghost of both, a fusion" (*SH*, 437).

After this detailed portrayal of the Torrance family, we as readers are aware even before Jack returns home from the job interview that tragedy awaits. Having failed "as father, husband, caretaker, and, most maddening of all, playwright" (Reino, 39), Jack becomes fused with his father, and Mark Anthony's credo becomes John Daniel's credo with disastrous consequences: "You must kill him, Jacky, and her, too. Because a real artist must suffer. Because each man kills the thing he loves" (*SH*, 241). To summarize, despite King's suggestion that Jack carries his doom with him, this Gothic hero-villain or Shakespearean tragic hero makes conscious choices that contribute to his self-destruction. King sums up the tragedy in the Torrance family by implying that the decision Jack has to make is one that illustrates free will, that he must articulate what is wrong at the hotel and leave it or succumb to evil. In his view Jack is like Hamlet, who reaches a certain point and gets pulled into the machinery. Focusing on the couple's marital problems, King takes a clear stand. The tragedy, he tells us, might have been averted if the couple had been able to communicate (Magistrale, *Decade*, 19). Although I will close the subject of *The Shining* for now, the novel with its rich content is additionally discussed in chapters 2 and 3. In those chapters I develop the point that King's fiction is created as a fusion of several genres, which also contributes to its large readership.

Both *Bag of Bones* and *The Shining* discuss all the aspects detected in *Otranto:* melodrama, the past haunting the present, and the archetype of the Ghost. Similarly, both evidently have a Gothic character gallery. Manfred of *Otranto* corresponds to the villains Max Devore of *Bag of Bones* and, to a minor extent, to Jack Torrance of *The Shining*. Theodore, Danny Torrance, and Mike Noonan can, in turn, be regarded as heroes in the respective novels, whereas Isabella of *Otranto*, Wendy Torrance of *The Shining*, and Mattie Devore of *Bag of Bones* are the heroines. *The Shining* and *Bag of Bones* are multidimensional novels that make use of multiple plots and dream sequences and that have drawn from several genres and modes. Influenced by Daphne du Maurier's *Rebecca*, *Bag of Bones* avails itself of melodramatic plot development and archetypal characters, whereas *The Shining*, as an early King novel, seems more inclined to literary naturalism, with its strong emphasis on the past shaping the present. In *Bag of Bones* a kind of resolution is achieved in regard to the theme of the past shaping the present, whereas *The Shining* focuses on the naturalistic struggle that leads to the destruction of the Gothic hero-villain.

In Gothic fiction the story line consists of three parts: introduction, pursuit, and destruction. Day argues that Gothic literature is marked by energetic motion, in spite of which no action can ever achieve its intended result but always remains circular (44). In *Otranto* both statements hold true. For instance, although the retired Manfred is left to lead a seemingly peaceful life with his loyal wife at the end of the novel, he never genuinely changes his wayward habits, since—if possible—he would start anew. Indeed, Manfred begins to pursue Isabella at the end of the first chapter, and the introduction therefore remains short. Hannele Kinnunen notes that the pursuit can be considered the most traditionally Gothic part, since it follows the pattern of a labyrinth and can take place on different levels: in the dream world of the mind and in reality. Remarkably, while the violator pursues the heroine, he himself is pursued both by the ghosts of the past and by the hallucinations of his own mind (56–57). Thus, the pursuit evolves into a never-ending circle, where the physical pursuit symbolizes the inner and eventually unresolved struggle of the villain, who is the Gothic double.

In King the reader is slowly led to the scene of the events, and the introduction therefore takes much longer in both *The Shining* and *Bag of Bones* than in *Otranto*. Despite the threatening atmosphere, the actual pursuit of Danny's life does not begin until the last few chapters when the clock strikes twelve and the masks are removed. In *Bag of Bones* the front lines are drawn and the starting shot is fired for the pursuit when Max Devore attempts to drown Mike Noonan in chapter 17 (395–599). The destruction of evil remains partly unresolved in this book, since, despite the final confrontation of Mike and Sara Tidwell as well as the suicide of Max Devore, violence stays alive in the rural Maine town. In other words, both *The Shining* and *Bag of Bones* include the three parts typical of the Gothic novel. Because of his well-developed characters and multilevel plot development, King needs a large canvas to introduce his scenes of events, unlike the traditional Gothic, which focuses on the pursuit. The destruction part, however, takes approximately the same number of pages both in King and in a traditional Gothic novel. In other words, half of a typical novel by King deals with the introduction, whereas the remaining half is divided into the pursuit and the destruction. In *Otranto* half of the novel is concerned with the pursuit, whereas the introduction and the destruction cover the other half.

Obviously, the Gothic double relates to the masculine and the feminine archetype in that the taboo themes of the Gothic are centered on the collapse of archetypal identity. Love and affection find their expression in the feminine archetype, whereas the masculine figure uses the members of the family as instruments of power. Day points out that both feminine and masculine features exist within the self, but as they are unable to fuse into a whole, their relationship becomes destructive (76–77). Similarly, in King a constant battle is going on between two sides of the self within the respective protagonist. Whereas the realistic novel would resolve the conflict between the two archetypes or within a single character, the Gothic denies such a resolution. Day argues that the conflict is caused by the denial of the androgynous self that results from the fusion of the masculine with the feminine. Significantly, too, he connects the masculine and the feminine archetype to the discussion of repressed sexuality and asks what would happen if the most obvious signs of identity, that is, sexuality, would be called into question (77–78). For instance, Jack Torrance's double identity results in attempts to escape, he becomes a twisted version of a human being, and the collapse inevitably follows. While Jack directs violence outward, it backfires, because the violence is in fact directed at his double nature.

The synthesis of the two halves of the self into a single androgynous being often fails. Day suggests that this is because the nature of the identities remains archetypal, and, hence, the character's attachment to the archetypes makes any alternative a threat to the security of separate male and female identities (132). Moreover, this crisis of identity and inability to accept the energy of pleasure embodied in sexuality results in the loss of identity and the final solution to the struggle within the self, namely, death (183). In fact, Gilles Deleuze claims that "[b]oth sadism and masochism imply that a particular quantity of libidinal energy be neutralized, desexualized, displaced and put at the service of Thanatos" (110). But it seems questionable that the sadomasochism inherent in the Gothic derives from the denial of the masculine and the feminine archetype within a single character, that is, that pleasure is not reached through love but through pain. If indeed domestic violence and sadomasochistic sex resulted from the male protagonist's inability to fuse the feminine archetype into his self, this would suggest that the majority of males are cruel, violent, and sadistic by nature. Females, in contrast, would embrace the finer qualities of human nature. Somewhat surprisingly, King himself gives reasons for this rather dated view in an interview related to *Bag of Bones*. He states that most men are capable of performing acts of violence, because they are primitive creatures with a real inclination to violence (O'Hehir, 1–2).

Having traced the Gothic line to King, we can readily see that no clear difference between the notions of the *Gothic* and *horror* can be drawn. In a sense all of King's fiction that is related to the past tradition can thus be called Gothic. As a conclusion, I will now place King's fiction in this field by discussing what kind of Gothic references and features it includes and which writers have influenced King. The fact that King is aware of the Gothic inheritance is clear both from his own statements and the several references to writers and texts in much of his fiction. Indick has listed a few from *Carrie, 'Salem's Lot, The Shining,* and *The Dead Zone* ("King and the Literary Tradition of Horror and the Supernatural," 180–81). In *Carrie* an interviewer on the West Coast is depicted as having "an odd, pinched look that is more like Lovecraft than Kerouac out of Southern Cal" (27–28). Shirley Jackson's *The Haunting of Hill House* hints at the horror of the Marsten House in *'Salem's Lot*. Poe's "Masque of the Red Death" was inspiration for *The Shining* and is referred to in its climactic pages. *The Dead Zone* is a tribute to Ray Bradbury's *Something Wicked This Way Comes*. Algernon Blackwood, Washington Irving, Bram Stoker, J. R. R. Tolkien, and H. G. Wells also roam his pages. Although Bradbury, Poe, and Lovecraft have paved the way to King's Gothicism, King has forged his own integrity and style. Just as he enriches and deepens his texts with myths and fairy tales, King emulates influences from his Gothic predecessors. Bradbury, for instance, seems to have provided him with small towns, a natural vernacular, and ordinary people.

As with Poe, King's work seems to share some traits of the notion that all people carry within themselves the seeds of their fate. The protagonists of *The Shining* and Poe's "Masque of the Red Death" are comparable in this respect. In Poe the misery is brought about by the plague, which reaches the indulged and indifferent idlers in the middle of their ball; in *The Shining* the same effect is caused by Jack Torrance living in the evil hotel. Furthermore, psychological honesty marks the writing of both Poe and King. According to Indick, neither Poe nor King accept *the fantastic* as simply fantastic but make it *real* ("Supernatural," 182). King does not settle for depicting Frank Dodd of *The Dead Zone* merely as a blatant rapist-killer but provides him with a history that explains some of the horrid acts. As in Poe, Dodd becomes aware of his acts, albeit too late. Furthermore, Poe's poetic language finds its often bizarre expression in King, despite the fact that he is no poet. Not surprisingly, Indick states that Poe's feverish narration is antithetic to King's terse style, although King is capable of expressive imagery (181): "The womb of his young wife had borne a single dark and malignant child" (*ST*, 14: a metaphor for cancer); and "Overhead, the moon rode the sky, a cold sailor of the night" (*DZ*, 60: a moment of foreboding).

King can be listed in company with Robert Bloch, Clark Ashton Smith, Frank Belknap Long, Fritz Leiber, and Ray Bradbury as authors whom H. P. Lovecraft's work initiated into the fold. In *Danse Macabre* King advises us to keep in mind that Lovecraft's "shadow, so long and gaunt . . . overlie[s] almost all important horror fiction that has come since" (97). To be more precise, Sam Gafford, Ben P. Indick, Fritz Leiber, and Robert M. Price have devoted essays to Lovecraft's influence on King. Gafford focuses on the aspect of literary style and technique, but neither Gafford in his essay nor King in *Danse Macabre* (112–13) is able to identify much that is Lovecraftian in King's style. Indick argues that the influence is grounded on the presentation of fantastic elements as scientific reality. In such novels as *Carrie, The Shining, The Dead Zone*, and *Firestarter*, King must establish scientific credibility in order to make his reader accept different extrasensory abilities (Indick, "Supernatural," 185). *Carrie,* for instance, is set a few years into the future when we may have acknowledged telekinetic powers as an existing phenomenon.

However, as Price points out, more important than questions of style is Lovecraft's worldview of horror, according to which the universe is indifferent to humanity and in its blindness will eventually crush our race, just as we crush an ant without even noticing (110). In Lovecraft's stories the merciless yet impersonal superhuman forces of nature are represented by "the Great Old Ones," a group of extracosmic entities who seek to regain their domination in the universe. Cthulhu, Yog-Sothoth, and the rest of Lovecraft's "Cthulhu Mythos" (so named by August Derleth) do not have any antagonistic feelings for us; we just happen to be in their way. Price points out—rightly, I think—that, rather than depicting supernatural events, Lovecraft is really describing science. The ultimately terrifying for him is the realization that humanity is nothing but "a freak in history, with neither purpose nor destiny" (110-11). Thus, Lovecraft explores, and for fictional purposes mythologizes, the disorientation caused by Copernicus and Darwin (Price, 111; Leiber, "Literary Copernicus"). Copernicus taught us that our home planet is not the center of things, whereas Darwin told us that we are not qualitatively removed from or superior to animals. In "The Dunwich Horror," Lovecraft puts it straightforwardly: "Nor is it to be thought . . . that man is either the oldest or the last of earth's masters" (128). In *Danse Macabre* King seems to understand what Lovecraft was doing: "The best of [Lovecraft's stories] make us feel the size of the universe we hang suspended in, and suggest shadowy forces that could destroy us all if they so much as grunted in their sleep" (63).

King, by his own admission, also stands in the shadow of Lovecraft, but, as Price points out, he had no real "Lovecraftian period," and, more importantly, he has moved on (120). However, King has retained two essential facets of Lovecraft's influence: the distrust in the progress of science and the sense of cosmic fear. From *The Stand* (1978) to *Dreamcatcher* (2001), he has mocked scientific pretensions but also expressed a deep-seated fear of their consequences. Similarly, the indifference of fate to human pain can be detected in the early Bachman books, just as it can be found in *From a Buick 8* (2002), where a drunk driver accidentally deprives the young Ned Wilcox of his father. However, most of the time King seems to be pursuing completely different, non-Lovecraftian directions: first, his characters have a choice between good and evil; second, love, mercy, and responsibility for one's fellow human beings can often beat the indifferent forces in King's multiverse.

King's debt to the American romance tradition of the nineteenth century is also evident. He owes as much to Nathaniel Hawthorne, Herman Melville, and Mark Twain as he does to German vampire legends and his literary contemporaries William Blatty and Ira Levin. As Magistrale points out, the most obvious trait that King shares with nineteenth-century authors is his reliance on Gothic settings and atmospheric techniques. Magistrale considers Hawthorne's woods "a place of spiritual mystery" where Young Goodman Brown, Reuben Bourne, and Arthur Dimmesdale face their darkest urges much in the same way as Louis Creed confronts his in King's *Pet Sematary* (*Landscape*, 16–17). He goes on to point out assorted workplace dungeons in Melville's "Bartleby the Scrivener," *Benito Cereno*, and *Moby Dick* and draws parallels to such depictions of work experience in King as "Graveyard Shift" (*Night Shift*), "Trucks" (*Night Shift*), and "The Mangler" (*Night Shift*). He argues that for both writers, the Gothic is frequently "evoked as [a vehicle] for underscoring a sterile and rotting economic system" (18). Magistrale then notes that the journey motif in *The Stand, Pet Sematary, The Talisman*, and *Thinner* becomes the metaphor for the journey into the self. The westward journey across contemporary America or down the Mississippi River is fraught with fear, because King's characters, like those of Twain, realize that true moral development is achieved only by confronting evil, not by avoiding it (20). In brief, the strength of King's stories is found in his characters' moral search for selfhood in terms of the nineteenth-century romance tradition.

In sum, with regard to the detailed depiction of the scenes of events, King seems to reach the essence of the original Gothic to a larger extent than, for instance, Walpole owing to the intense realism of his works. Since every literary work reformulates its genre, and, as Alastair Fowler maintains, "the character of genres is that they change" (18; see also Jameson, 86), King, far from imitating the traditional Gothic, has assimilated Gothic features such as mood, monsters, and, to some extent, plot into his horror fiction and thus created modern Gothic fiction. In combining elements of several genres and modes, King adds depth to his fiction at the same time as he expands the traditional limits associated with these genres and modes. King's blend may be labeled horror, but in its diversity and versatility his brand of horror appears to be unique by virtue of the many genres and modes merged.

If the Gothic basement of King's fictional chamber of horrors provides his stories with a historical perspective, then myths and fairy tales reside in the very building in an airy atmosphere of timelessness. In the attic we have literary naturalism, because it features in all of King's fiction regardless of its degree of realism. To be more precise, King has been simultaneously influenced by the contradictory impulses of free will and determinism, a factor that highlights a core tension in his oeuvre. My discussion also leads to this contention, and chapter 2 introduces the building block that bridges the seeming gap between the Gothic and literary naturalism in King: myths and fairy tales.

2

Myths and Fairy Tales in King's Works

In the 1989 interview with Tony Magistrale, King argued: "To my mind, the stories that I write are nothing more than fairy tales for grown ups" (Magistrale, *Decade,* 4). From a functional angle this statement seems to hold true. King has in *Danse Macabre* given the horror genre both personal and social functions. Magistrale summarizes these functions (*Decade,* 21–24), and Sharon A. Russell presents them in the form of a list (19–22):

1. Horror allows us to prove bravery, and we can test our courage without risking our lives.
2. Horror allows us to re-establish feelings of normality.
3. Horror confirms our positive feelings about the *status quo.*
4. Horror allows us to feel we are part of the larger whole: identifying with the group and working together for a good cause, we identify with the good.
5. Horror allows us to penetrate the mystery of death: horror, on the one hand, shows a way to cope with death and, on the other hand, even suggests what might happen beyond death.
6. Horror allows us to indulge our darkest collective and social fears, connecting our anxieties to a larger concern.
7. Horror allows us to return to childhood.
8. Horror allows us to transcend the world of darkness and negation.

Significantly, the horror genre and myths and fairy tales have these functions in common.

Mircea Eliade in an essay "Myths and Fairy Tales" in his *Myth and Reality,* Jack Zipes in *Fairy Tale as Myth/Myth as Fairy Tale,* and in part Bruno Bettelheim in a psychoanalytic guise in *The Uses of Enchantment* (1975) elaborate the symbiotic connection between myth and fairy tale, tracing both back to initiation rites (see also Franz, 24–36). Eliade claims that although in the West the fairy tale has long since become a literature of diversion or of escape, it takes up and continues initiation on the level of imagination and dream (201–2). He goes on to point out that the fairy tale constitutes an "easy doublet for the initiation myth" (202), and initiation is one of the functions that King explores in his fiction. King's first point suggests that horror allows us to prove bravery without risking our lives (Magistrale, *Decade,* 22; Russell, 20). This is close to Olle Sjögren's notion that horror movies are modern rites of passage (14). Sjögren refers to Arnold van Gennep's *Rites of Passage,* according to which, the rite of passage includes three parts: separation, transition, and incorporation (96). When breaking away from family ties, teenagers gather together in dark cinemas in order to confront their fears and prove their bravery. A successful experience both reinforces the feeling of togetherness and provides the Aristotelian catharsis (Aristotle, 10; *DM,* 13). Although the modern reader enjoys the fairy tale and the tale of horror as a private activity, the three parts of the rite of passage can also be distinguished in the reading process. Russell notes that King provides us with skills that allow us to cope with the evil we encounter in our lives. While identifying with those who are tested, we see what is crucial for our own survival. We learn that we must face our fears and believe in the power of good in our lives (22).

The paradox that myth and the fairy tale are both fictitious yet true resembles that of horror fiction. Zipes points out that although we regard myths and fairy tales as lies, saying "oh, that's just myth/a fairy tale," these so-called lies often govern our lives (*Fairy Tale,* 4) or, rather, as Bettelheim puts it, tell the truth about our lives through allegory (6–7). Both in myth/fairy tale and the horror genre, "a pleasing allegorical feel" softens the occasional blows of harsh reality (*DM,* 5). Zipes could be referring to horror fiction rather than fairy tales when in *Spells of Enchantment* he states that both the oral and the literary forms of the fairy tale emanate from specific battles to humanize bestial and barbaric forces that have terrorized our minds and communities in concrete ways, threatening to destroy free will and human compassion. The fairy tale sets out to conquer this concrete terror through metaphors, and therefore these tales are marks that leave traces of the human struggle for immortality (xi–xii). This statement runs parallel to King's functions 5 and 6: horror permits us to indulge our darkest collective and social fears and provides an opportunity to penetrate the mystery of death (Magistrale, *Decade*, 22–23).

In our attempt to establish types and values, we classify, categorize, and preserve classical myths and fairy tales that always seem to have been with us. John Stephens in *The Oxford Companion to Fairy Tales* argues that a small number of literary fairy tales have become mythical in the sense that they have naturalized formulaic ways of thinking about individuals and social relationships and thus become bearers of grand cultural narratives (331). The classics have become almost part of our nature, because, as Zipes notes, we feel safe with the familiar. These tales make it appear that we are all part of a universal community with shared values and norms, striving for the same happiness and trusting that a certain type of behavior will produce guaranteed results (*Fairy Tale*, 5). Virtually anything can become a modern myth. Joseph Campbell argues that "[t]he material of myth is the material of our life, the material of our body, and the material of our environment" (*Transformations of Myth through Time*, 1; see also Frye, *Myth and Metaphor*, 3–17). In *Mythologies* Roland Barthes refers to myth as frozen speech, stolen and restored. Although myth, in his view, assumes the appearance of generality, its form serves its intention, and consequently anything can become a myth (114–15, 124–25). Barthes's definition of myth can be applied to both canonized fairy tales and myths in King's fiction. Similarly, functions 2, 3, and 4 correspond to Zipes's argument in King's kind of horror: horror fiction reestablishes feelings of normality, confirms our good feelings about the status quo, and lets us feel we are part of the larger whole (Magistrale, *Decade*, 22).

Function 7 suggests that horror fiction also allows us to return to the world of our childhood (Magistrale, *Decade*, 23). If we regain its fears, we also regain its beliefs. Russell points out that King wants the reader to realize that the horror genre moves him through horror to the world where basic human values have been tested and reaffirmed. Those who succeed in overcoming evil face a world that has been cleansed. Hence, there is hope for the world we live in, since in the final analysis good can prevail, and we learn how to work toward the defeat of evil (22). Finally, then, horror allows us to transcend the world of darkness and negation (Magistrale, *Decade*, 23), which, in turn, refers to the often neglected dark side of the fairy tale. In this sense King has, indeed, been telling fairy tales for grown ups for almost thirty years now.

King has repeatedly emphasized both the oral tradition of storytelling and the interaction between the teller and the listener (see also Plato, *Republic*, 49; Warner, *Beast*, 14). Zipes claims that in ancient times oral tales served as the basis for literary fairy tales and were closely tied to the rituals, customs, and beliefs of tribes and communities. Fostering a sense of belonging and hope, they instructed, amused, warned, instructed, initiated, and opened windows to imaginative worlds. They were to be shared, exchanged, used, and modified according to the needs of the tellers and the listeners (*Spells*, xii). Tracing his storytelling tradition back to the ancient Greek bards, King has compared a horror writer to the Welsh sin eater who gathers all evil feelings and fears of his society and regurgitates them (*NS*, xviii). King feels that he and his fellow horror writers are absorbing and defusing all the fears, anxieties, and insecurities of their community and taking them upon themselves: "We're sitting in the darkness beyond the flickering warmth of your fire, cackling into our cauldrons and spinning out our spider webs of words, all the time sucking the sickness from your minds and spewing it out into the night" (Underwood and Miller, *Bones*, 62).

The Gothic atmosphere prevails in the majority of classic fairy tales. King states in *Danse Macabre* that many horror films and novels have "more in common with the Brothers Grimm than the op-ed page in a tabloid paper" (131). Magistrale, too, states that King has inherited fairy-tale archetypes from the Brothers Grimm and recast them in a particularly Gothic format (*Decade*, 37). King considers fairy tales the scariest existing stories, arguing that the stories for children form a conduit leading to what adults call horror stories. Not only frightening in themselves, these stories also provide access to a time in our lives when we were more scared and more vulnerable than we are as adults. Just as a hypnotist is capable of hypnotizing a subject by using a special word, fairy tales perform a similar feat, making us regress instantaneously into childhood. King deliberately employs fairy tales in his fiction to evoke a specific effect: "In the writing I am working on right now, I've been able to play off two—'Little Red Riding Hood' and 'Goldilocks and the Three Bears'—in my mind, two of the scariest fairy tales ever written" (4). In this way he wishes to address the child inside every adult. By gaining access to his or her imagination, the adult is more capable of coping with real-life fears. In other words, through the fairy-tale formula adults can be transferred back to their childhood to deal with their pressure points in an authentic environment. In this sense King uses the formula story as a magic spell to expose the reader to the subtext of horror, and since horror and fairy tales so often overlap, he should not find any difficulty in doing so.

Horror fiction and myths/fairy tales largely have similar themes. Magistrale argues that both rely on primal phobias—the breakup of familial relationships, death, and isolation—and in both the reader is forced to confront these issues and participate in attempts to resolve them (*Decade,* 34). Maria Tatar adds sex and violence to the list, especially in the form of incest and child abuse, starvation, and exposure (*Hard Facts of the Grimm's Fairy Tales,* 10). Remarkably, King deals with all the above-mentioned themes, even starvation in the short story "Survivor Type" (*Skeleton Crew),* in which the protagonist ends up feeding on himself. In addition to the common themes, King's plots frequently follow the fairy-tale formula as his child-heroes at some point must fight against and finally conquer the evils affiliated with adulthood (Magistrale, *Decade,* 36). As in fairy tales, King's language consists of simple sentences and colorful, even vulgar, vernacular. His characters, too, resemble the fairy-tale Everyman with which the reader can effortlessly identify. Chelsea Quinn Yarbro argues that King has merely changed the setting of the fairy tale and shows us the malignant forms not in castles or caves but in contemporary settings (62).

Because of their seemingly innocent, harmless, and natural appearance, myths and fairy tales have undergone the process of duplication and spread throughout the world in various forms of presentation, for instance, books, films, and musicals. The act of doubling something imitates the original and reinforces the traditional modes of thinking that provide our lives with structure. The audiences are not threatened, challenged, excited, or shocked by the duplications, and their socially conservative worldview is confirmed. Revisions, however, are different, because the purpose of producing a revised story is to create something new that incorporates the critical thinking of the producer and corresponds to the changed demands of audiences or may even seek to alter their views of traditional patterns (Zipes, *Fairy Tale*, 8–10). Both duplication and revision also feature in King's use of myths and fairy tales. Virtually every King novel alludes to at least one particular tale: "Cinderella" in *Carrie;* the vampire myth in *'Salem's Lot;* "Goldilocks and the Three Bears," "Bluebeard," "Little Red Riding Hood," and Lewis Carroll's *Alice in Wonderland* in *The Shining;* "Faithful John" in *The Dead Zone;* "Beauty and the Beast" in *Firestarter;* L. Frank Baum's *Wizard of Oz* in *Pet Sematary;* "Snow White and the Seven Dwarves" and "The Three Billy Goats Gruff" in *It,* to mention a few. Fairy tales provide King with a close relation to myth, and this, in turn, gives his popular fiction a sense of timelessness (Curran, 43). In this way King, who has been criticized for popular-culture references that would in time deprive his works of a lasting standing in English literature, in fact secures the durability of his fiction by means of myths and fairy tales.

What is of central importance for this study is that the vague and ambiguous notion of myth can be replaced with a conception of literary structures that can be precisely defined. In *Adventure, Mystery, and Romance,* John G. Cawelti defines *literary formulas* as conventional ways of representing and relating cultural images, symbols, themes, and myths in a work of art (20). The conventional story pattern, or the formula, has two advantages over the notion of myth. First, the formula focuses on the entire story rather than on an arbitrarily selected mythical image, symbol, or theme. Second, the relation between formulas and cultural phenomena can be explored directly without metaphysical assumptions of superpersonal ideas (29–30). I view myths and fairy tales in Stephen King's work as formulaic stories, that is, entities with separate story lines. In analyzing the works of an author of about forty novels, it seems important to distinguish the numerous mythical symbols, such as the rose and the key of *The Dark Tower* series, from the formulaic myths and fairy tales.

The fact that the two genres can be considered literary formulas is reinforced by Vladimir Propp's *Morphology of the Folktale,* in

which he outlines thirty-one basic functions that constitute an archetypal story form. By functions he means the basic components
of a tale that are the acts of a character, necessary for the development of the story (Zipes, *Spells*, xiii). Similarly, Campbell's stages
of the hero's journey discussed primarily in connection with
myths can also be applied to King's fiction. Although Propp's
and Campbell's categories at times appear so broad that virtually
anything can be included, my point is to demonstrate that King
applies such formulas and, more importantly, to show why he
does so. Since Zipes conveniently summarizes Propp's functions
of the fairy tale (*Spells*, xiii; Propp, 25–65), I place King's story of
Roland in relation to them. It should be noted, however, that not
every fairy tale includes all of Propp's functions, nor do the functions always follow one another in direct succession. In Propp's
view they can also be performed by different characters (71).

1. The protagonist is confronted with an interdiction/prohibi-
tion, which he violates.

By discovering his mother's infidelity and by taking an early
test of manhood, Roland is alienated from his family.

2. Departing/banished, the protagonist has been given/as-
sumes a task related to the interdiction/prohibition. The protagonist's character will be marked by the task that is his sign.

After the discovery of his mother's infidelity and the trial of
manhood, Roland is dispatched, along with his friends Cuthbert
and Alain, to the oceanside town of Mejis for their safety. There
they discover a plot against Roland's father. Roland's character is
thus clearly marked by the task of pursuing the Man in Black and
saving the multiverse.

3. There is an encounter with (a) a villain; (b) a mysterious in-
dividual/creature, who gives the protagonist gifts; (c) three different animals/creatures, who are helped by the protagonist and
promise to repay him; or (d) three animals/creatures who offer
gifts to help the protagonist, who is in trouble. The gifts are often
magical agents, which bring about miraculous change.

On his quest Roland encounters both the villain, who also
takes up the task of donor or helper, and a mysterious creature in
the form of the oracle trapped in an enchanted circle of stones.
The necessary gifts are then given in the form of useful information. As in Bettelheim, King's hero is helped by his being in touch

with primitive creatures or things, guided step by step, and given help when needed (11).

4. The endowed protagonist is tested and moves on to battle and conquer the villain or inimical forces.

Roland leaves behind the young boy (Jake Chambers) he has recently encountered and grown to love, and his dedication to the quest is hereby tested.

5. There is a peripety, or sudden fall in the protagonist's fortunes, that is a temporary setback. A wonder is needed to reverse the wheel of fortune.

Contemplating his agony at losing Jake, Roland experiences a setback in his fortunes. The miracle that is needed to save the hero appears in the form of three doors standing freely on the beach. Each door opens, for Roland, to our world. He visits New York at three points, both to save his own life and to draw out the three who must accompany him on his quest for the Tower.

6. The protagonist makes use of endowed gifts (including the magical agents and cunning) to achieve his goal. The result is (a) three battles with the villain; (b) three impossible tasks that are nevertheless made possible; or (c) the breaking of a magic spell.

Roland makes use of endowed gifts, including useful information and his recently formed *ka-tet,* to achieve the goal. The result is three impossible tasks that are nevertheless made possible (for instance, kill Shardik the Bear, enter the city of Lud, and travel on Blaine the Monorail).

7. The villain is punished, or the inimical forces are vanquished.

Roland beats his enemy.

8. The success of the protagonist usually leads to (a) marriage; (b) the acquisition of money; (c) survival and wisdom; or (d) any combination of the first three.

Roland survives and gains in wisdom.

Virtually all of King's novels can likewise be placed in relation to Propp's functions or, as we will see later in this discussion, to Campbell's stages of the hero's journey, and virtually all of them also include references to myths and fairy tales. In *Bag of Bones,* for instance, King draws on these parallels when referring to Mattie and Max Devore as "The Damsel in Distress versus The Wicked Stepfather" (169). Mattie's childhood family is depicted in the same manner: "Talk about your Brothers Grimm, huh? Subtract the Fisher-Price toys behind the house, the two pole hairdryers in the basement beauty salon, the old rustbucket Toyota in the driveway, and you were right there: *Once upon a time there lived a poor widow and her three children*" (196, italics in original). The recurrent brand names place the fairy tale in the present, and the contrast between the mythical past and the modern age aids reader identification with the story. Having set the time, King goes on to give detailed information about the individual characters: "Mattie is the princess of the piece—poor but beautiful. . . . Now enter the prince. In this case he's a gangly stuttering redhead named Lance Devore" (196). Lance has majored in forestry, and his preferences in clothing entitle him to the role of the woodcutter (200). Again, the contrast between the looks of a fairy-tale prince and Lance Devore reinforces the reader's sense of reality.

How and why King avails himself of myths and fairy tales is outlined in the following discussion. The section titled "The Hero as a Generic Hybrid (Roland the Gunslinger)" focuses on the original tales written within this formula, with special attention to the mythical hero Roland the Gunslinger. "The Antihero as a Generic Hybrid (Randall Flagg)" also deals with King's original myths and fairy tales, in particular the mythical/folk-tale/pop-culture antihero of Randall Flagg. "Adapted and Revised Myths and Fairy Tales" analyzes King's adaptation of Bram Stoker's *Dracula* with a focus on the story lines in relation to mythical themes. By thus revising classical tales, King comments on social ills, such as Nixon's secretive politics in the 1970s, familial contradictions *('Salem's Lot)*, and societal and personal oppression *(Carrie)*. Among other things this section also discusses *Carrie* as a revised Cinderella myth. Finally, as the section "Mythical and Fairy-Tale Themes" suggests, King weaves mythical and fairy-tale themes into his stories in order to reinforce the thematic concerns of the main story. Thus, each section is intended to advance the linear trajectory of my argument as I enlarge the scope from individual characters to larger patterns of mythical and fairy-tale themes. Furthermore, King's reliance on mythical paradigms and fairy tales throughout his writing career creates a balance between the Gothic and literary naturalism and thus unifies his fiction. In brief, my chapters follow an inner logic as each of

them adds a new aspect to the discussion and leads to my contention that the idiosyncratic blend of free will and determinism
combines the different aspects of the fantastic and realistic in
King—and ultimately makes his horror fiction unique.

Although the next two sections are dedicated to the mythical
stories and fairy tales of King's own creation, the emphasis is
placed on two characters for three reasons. First, since Roland
the Gunslinger and Randall Flagg recur in most of King's original myths and fairy tales, these stories are discussed through his
most ambitious presentations of the hero and the antihero. Second, these characters recur in works that feature traits of several
genres. For instance, *The Dark Tower* series can be labeled a Western, a Gothic novel, an apocalyptic fantasy, a tale of horror, and a
myth. Third, these individual characters also embody traits of
several genres.

The Hero as a Generic Hybrid (Roland the Gunslinger)

Throughout his literary career, Stephen King has reworked the
stereotypes and the conventions of a number of literary formulas
to express our cultural and personal fears, and he has established
the generic, structural, and thematic framework of *The Dark Tower*
series by combining several genres. James Egan's essay "*The Dark
Tower:* Stephen King's Gothic Western" analyzes the Western, the
Gothic, and the apocalyptic fable in the series, whereas I wish to
emphasize the myth and fairy-tale formula as its generic bedrock.
From there I go on to present the genres that *The Dark Tower* series
features, focusing on the character of Roland the Gunslinger as a
generic hybrid. Indeed, little academic work has been done on
The Dark Tower series, although Robin Furth has compiled a concordance to the first two volumes, thus documenting the phases
and backgrounds of the story. Similarly, a study by Bev Vincent (*A
Road to the Dark Tower*) has recently been released (2004). Hence,
this section develops threads treated only minimally if at all by
James Egan and Anthony Magistrale.

The Gunslinger first appeared as five short stories between October 1978 and November 1981. They were collected as *The Dark
Tower: The Gunslinger* and published in limited hardcover editions
of ten thousand copies in October 1982 and April 1984. Inspired in

part by Robert Browning's poem "Childe Roland to the Dark
Tower Came" (1855), King wrote the first story in March 1970
while still in college. Browning's poem, in turn, is indebted to
Edgar's Song in *King Lear*. *The Dark Tower* has recently been completed (2004), and it includes six follow-up volumes: *The Drawing
of the Three* (1987), *The Waste Lands* (1991), *Wizard and Glass* (1997),
Wolves of the Calla (2003), *Song of Susannah* (2004), and *The Dark
Tower* (2004). Over the years King has grown less satisfied with
the quality of the first book, *The Gunslinger*, because in his view it
was too forced. In order to "simplify it a little bit," he set about revising his college work while finishing the final three books (King
in Reese, 1). In a review of *The Dark Tower* series, John Mark Eberhart notes that in the latter version, "King has subtracted some
things, added others and tinkered with the prose" (2). This section, however, deals with the original, since the twenty-two years
between the first and the latest volumes so eloquently shows
King's development and maturation from a naturalist-oriented
young philosopher into a gentle-minded and wise writer.

The *Dark Tower* series was greatly inspired by J. R. R. Tolkien's
Lord of the Rings and related fantasy genres, as King has admitted. In an interview with Ben Reese, he considers Tolkien's work
as a starting point for Roland's tale. Many young fantasy writers
at the end of the 1960s and in the early 1970s were influenced
by those books, including Robert Jordan, Terry Brooks, Stephen
Donaldson—and Stephen King. King was one of those writers
who read Tolkien's classic and were "knocked out by the magic
of the stories, by the idea of the quest, and just by the scope, the
broadness of it, by how long it took to tell the tales and how
thrilling they were" (4). He has also been aware of the danger of
imitating such a strong work. King made a conscious effort not to
duplicate what Tolkien had done, but he loved the idea of the
quest. He wanted his story to be "more closely tied to our world"
and not to be "entirely a fantasy world" (4). Roland's tale has "a
connection with our own world," but it also has a connection to
King's other stories (4). Reese notes that King's novels have always been notable for their self-reference, the way characters in
one story will mention events or characters from another story,
connecting the story lines of all of King's titles (3). This all began
when King realized that Father Callahan from Jerusalem's Lot
(*'Salem's Lot)* was going to be a character in *The Dark Tower* series.

In fact, shortly thereafter he understood that everybody from all the books in which the Tower is mentioned will turn up in *The Dark Tower* series. As such characters, King mentions Ted Brautigan from *Hearts in Atlantis* (1999), Dinky Earnshaw from *Everything's Eventual* (2002), Shimi from *Wizard and Glass*, and Stephen King from the real world(!) (King in Reese, 3–4). In a sense *The Dark Tower* sums up King's writing career. As he says, "[I]t puts a real bow on the whole package" (5). After the series everything else would be a kind of "epilogue" to what he has done with his life work, King adds (5). The essential similarity to Tolkien's work is that King, too, places both his characters and his readers in the middle of the eternal struggle between good and evil. The moral survivors of their stories must act ethically and take responsibility for their fellow human beings. This moral message lies at the heart of both Tolkien and King.

In the afterword of *The Gunslinger,* King maintains that he had played with the idea of writing a long romantic novel embodying the feel of Browning's poem. Unable to offer what he calls his Constant Reader a synopsis of what is to come, King promises that "at some magic time, there will be a purple evening (an evening made for romance!) when Roland will come to his dark tower, and approach it, winding his horn" (220–24). Thus, he seems to be referring to the final stanzas of Browning's poem:

> XXXIII
> Not hear? when noise was everywhere! it
>   tolled
>   Increasing like a bell. Names in my ears
>   Of all the lost adventurers my peers,—
> How such a one was strong, and such was
>   bold,
> And such was fortunate, yet each of old
>   Lost, lost! one moment knelled the woe
>   of years.
>
> XXXIV
> There they stood, ranged along the hill-
>   sides met
>   To view the last of me, a living frame
>   For one more picture! in a sheet of
>   flame

> I saw them and I knew them all. And yet
> Dauntless the slug-horn to my lips I set,
> And blew. *'Childe Roland to the Dark*
>   *Tower came.'*
>   (362, italics in original)

The series consists of interlocking short stories that are approximately equivalent to one self-contained stanza of the poem. Overall the plot of the stories we have from King are thus paralleled by that of Browning's poem. Browning's protagonist has spent his adolescence dreaming of and training for the sight of the Tower. As a persevering knight, he presses toward this goal, disregarding the mental and physical dangers that he faces. King's Roland, too, seeks a vision he neither understands nor precisely knows where or how to pursue. As Magistrale points out, the very pursuit of an idea, a person, or a thing to its most profound level of meaning or being is an occupation Browning praises in many of his poems; such tests of perseverance strengthen the individual's spiritual resolve (*Decade*, 142). King's protagonist comes to parallel Browning's heroes in each of the aforementioned aspects, but—as Magistrale notes—his spiritual evolution is slow and as tentative as the quest to find the Tower (*Decade*, 143). Influenced by such naturalist writers as Theodore Dreiser, Thomas Hardy, and Jack London, King seems unwilling and unable to offer straightforward solutions to his protagonists' problems and spiritual ponderings. Only after a long road of trials does King's Roland find peace of mind and closeness with his fellow warriors.

THE HERO'S JOURNEY

As King has been "particularly taken" by Joseph Campbell's *Hero with a Thousand Faces*, and it has "definitely had some effect" on him (Magistrale, *Decade*, 3), I begin by comparing Campbell's stages of the hero's journey to Roland the Gunslinger to demonstrate that Roland, indeed, can be regarded as a mythical hero. The mythical hero will then be discussed in connection with the other genres implicit in the character and in *The Dark Tower* series as a whole. Elucidating the reason why King prefers to shift and blend genres as well as to transgress the boundaries of the horror genre remains my ultimate objective.

Like Bruno Bettelheim, Mircea Eliade, and Jack Zipes, Campbell traces the various stages of the mythical hero to rites of passage, arguing that the three parts of the rites of passages (in Campbell's terms, departure/separation, initiation, and reintegration) are reflected in the various stages of the hero's journey (*Hero*, 30), which he, drawing on James Joyce's term in *Finnegans Wake*, calls the nuclear unit of the monomyth (581). In other words, the monomyth consists of the various stages of the hero's journey. Analyzing myths and fairy tales together, he claims that the fairy-tale hero achieves a domestic, microcosmic triumph, whereas the mythical hero achieves a macrocosmic triumph. The first great stage, that of the departure or separation, includes five subsections: (1) The Call to Adventure (2) Refusal of the Call (3) Supernatural Aid (4) The Crossing of the First Threshold, and (5) The Belly of the Whale (*Hero*, 36–38).

The signs of the vocation of Roland the Gunslinger are revealed in passing when he discovers that his mother has become the mistress of Marten, an advisor to his father. In order to avenge his father's honor, Roland is forced to an early test of manhood at the age of fourteen. As in Bettelheim and Campbell, King's hero proceeds for a time in isolation, and the moment of violating a certain prohibition or interdiction coincides with his adolescence (Bettelheim, 11–12; Campbell, *Hero*, 51). The interdiction he violates seems related to his sexual awakening, and this molds Roland's destiny, as he later relates to Jake Chambers: "'I suppose the coming of age was part [of my destiny], too,' he said almost grudgingly. [—] 'Love and dying have been my life'" (*GS*, 158). Due to his clever choice of weapon (a falcon), Roland passes the test of manhood and heads north in his pursuit of the Man in Black. Since Roland accepts the challenge, the next subsection, "Refusal of the Call," is omitted: he cannot refuse something he has already accepted.

Unsuspected assistance often comes to the one who has undertaken his proper adventure (Campbell, *Hero*, 36). In *The Gunslinger* the Man in Black himself appears to be this supernatural aid, since, despite their mutual differences, Roland and the Man in Black do not seek each other's death. Guiding Roland to his destination, this "furthest minion of the Dark Tower" (205–6) possesses considerable powers of supernatural origin. Similarly, the oracle Roland encounters midway through the story, and who in exchange for Roland's sexual favors foretells his future, acts as a supernatural aid. The hero then comes to the guardian at the entrance to the zone of magnified power. Campbell points out that mythologies tend to place deceitful and dangerous presences in deserted places outside the normal traffic of the village (*Hero*, 77–78). Having left the security of his privileged court life, Roland heads for the desert, which is characterized as "the apotheosis of all deserts" (*GS*, 11). There he encounters Jake Chambers, his symbolic son, and crosses the first threshold by sacrificing him: "Given a choice between the Tower and child, possibly between damnation and salvation, Roland chooses the Tower" (*DT*, 12). Thus, as I see it, Roland chooses responsibility for humankind over personal wishes. Finally, "the passage into the realm of the night" (Campbell, *Hero*, 36) signifies the agony Roland feels having abandoned the child he has grown to love as his own son. Roland's despair is reflected in the Gothic atmosphere of *The Drawing of the Three*, when the hero awakes on the edge of the Western Sea "in the middle of the night to discover that the incoming tide has brought a horde of crawling, carnivorous creatures—'lobstrosities'—with it" (2).

In Campbell the stage of the trials and victories of initiation is presented in six subsections: (1) The Road of Trials (2) The Meeting with the Goddess (3) Woman as the Temptress (4) Atonement with the Father (5) Apotheosis, and (6) The Ultimate Boon (*Hero*, 36). Having drawn Eddie Dean, Odetta Holmes/Detta Walker/ Susannah Dean, and Jake Chambers into his dimension, Roland considers his *ka-tet* (that is, his group sharing the same destiny) formed, and together the group goes on a classic hero's journey. For instance, they kill Shardik the Bear, discover the Path of the Beam, visit the Gothic city of Lud, and travel on Blaine the Monorail. It is clear that *The Dark Tower* series follows the tradition of myth-adventures discussed by Campbell and Northrop Frye (Campbell, *Hero*, 97; Frye, *Anatomy*, 187).

The ultimate adventure is frequently represented as a mystical marriage between the protagonist and the Queen Goddess of the World, whose image is not always benign (Campbell, *Hero*, 109). King seems to split the mother archetype into three separate characters in *The Dark Tower* series: Roland's soul-mate, Susan Delgado, as a benevolent and desirable figure; Rhea of Cöos Hill, a witch who lives on the outskirts of Hambry and who uses magic to manipulate Roland into murdering his mother; and, of course, Roland's actual mother, whom the hero accidentally kills. Subsections 3 and 4 in Campbell's second stage of the hero's journey ("Woman as the Temptress" and "Atonement with the Father") are both mutually interrelated and also linked with the second subsection. An idealized woman figure, Susan is characterized as natural, unspoiled, and pure. Roland and Susan are evidently suited for each other, and the couple is "nearly torn apart by their desire for each other" (*WG*, 317). Aware of the Oedipal implications of Roland's family, King has Susan tell Roland the story of Oedipus. Roland absorbs it in silence, musing on the quadrangle formed by his father, his mother, Marten, and himself. Having survived the trial of manhood, Roland goes into the lower town to make love to a woman for the first time. He awakes the next morning at the arrival of his furious father, Steven Deschain, who calls him stupid. Roland is devastated to learn that the adultery has not escaped Steven's attention, and that his father has allowed it to continue because of the greater issues at hand. Steven also expresses his deep love for his son, and the two of them embrace passionately (116).

As Browning's "Childe Roland to the Dark Tower Came" suggests, the exultation of Roland the Gunslinger is inevitable. This is also the case with regard to Campbell's third stage of the hero's journey: the return and reintegration with society (*Hero*, 36). Only Roland keeps repeating the stages of the hero's journey for ever and ever. As a modernized wandering Jew he fulfills his ka ("destiny") and seeks redemption for his sins.

THE WESTERN

In *The Dark Tower* series, King has taken the Western as a starting point and modified it with the Gothic in order to explore a post-apocalyptic society or rather our fears of such a prospective nightmare. In *The Six-Gun Mystique*, Cawelti both distinguishes a Western formula and notes the growing awareness of the Western as a genre and a myth, which, in turn, has resulted in the increasing use of Western materials by contemporary novelists who otherwise would not be concerned with the evocation of the traditional mythology (4). Despite his fondness for blending genres and playing them off against one another, King has not so far written a Western novel as such. Because he likes the Western as a mode, however, Western influences can also be distinguished in King's college serial novella "Slade" (Spignesi, *Lost Work*, 282), which was published in the university newspaper *The Maine Campus* during the summer of 1970, and whose main character was a gunslinger (Winter, *Art*, 262). Undoubtedly, Stu Redman of *The Stand* shares traits with a Clint Eastwood–type of Western hero. Clearly, King knows his Western classics very well. In Wister's *Virginian*, the Virginian utters his famous line, "When you call me that, smile," directed at his rival, Trampas. The same line is echoed in King when Roland the Gunslinger refers to a remark made by his antagonist, the Man in Black, by stating: "I hope he smiled when he said that" (*GS*, 55). In *The Waste Lands* King uses Susannah Dean as his mouthpiece while listing Western influences: "*Cheyenne, The Rifleman*, and, of course, the archetype of them all, *Gunsmoke*" (257).

My discussion on setting, situation, and character in *The Dark Tower* series emphasizes the role of the hero. Even though Noël Carroll argues that the Western is identified primarily by virtue of its setting (14), I would side with Cawelti, who claims that setting, character, and situation, when structured in a particular way, together constitute the formula of the Western (*Mystique*, 61). The second paragraph of *The Gunslinger* establishes a setting that corresponds to the primary qualities Cawelti has identified in the Western setting (62–73). Similarly, King's desert is huge, white, blinding, waterless, and burning hot. The mountains sketch themselves on the horizon, and the devil-grass brings sweet dreams, nightmares, and death. An occasional tombstone sign points the way on an ancient highway: "The world had moved on since then. The world had emptied" (*GS*, 11). On his quest to save the multiverse and find the Tower at its nexus, Roland the Gunslinger carries two guns. After a lengthy description of these guns, King goes on to describe the hero's Western-style clothing: "His shirt was open at the throat, with a rawhide thong dangling loosely in hand-punched eyelets. His pants were seam-stretched dungarees" (12). Roland clearly journeys somewhere in the western United States, where certain styles of clothing are worn (Cawelti, *Mystique*, 62). Mike Wheelan's illustrations reinforce the impression of a formulaic hero from the 1950s: masculine, stereotypical, and slightly homoerotic.

Social relations between different classes of people feature in Westerns because of the specific history of the United States, and, as Cawelti notes, such aspects of setting may play a more decisive role than geography in defining the Western formula (*Mystique,* 65). In chapter 1 in the section "Abnormal and Repressed Sexuality (the Vampire)," we noted that Leslie Fiedler maintains that the complex relationship between a young white boy and an African American or a Native American is a central theme of major American novels. King has replaced Twain's Jim with a black woman, Odetta Holmes/Detta Walker/Susannah Dean, another healed multiple personality in his fiction, who is a member of Roland's *ka-tet.* The skillful gunslingers who replace Roland's childhood friends, Eddie, Susannah, and Jake, Roland's symbolic son, undoubtedly fit in both Fiedler's character gallery and King's typical Losers' Club, whose members end up as heroes. However, by repeatedly emphasizing the notions of *ka* (destiny), *ka-tet* ("a group of people bound together by fate" [*WL,* 259]), and *khef* ("closeness and sharing of minds" [260]), King gives *The Dark Tower* series mythical proportions. Endlessly dedicated to the exploration of free will, responsibility, determinism, and fate, King seems to have created a whole mythology in order to study these dilemmas. The essential points he keeps repeating can be summarized in two arguments: "*Ka* does not rule all, and coincidences still happen" (260); "Denigrating free will by confusing it with *ka* was worse than blasphemy; it was tiresome and stupid" (269). Of course, these are also American myths and therefore found in many Westerns such as *High Noon, The Virginian,* and Walter van Tilburg's *Ox-Bow Incident.*

The character of Roland the Gunslinger largely conforms to the Western hero archetype. How he does so and where he departs from the archetype will now be discussed. Skillful formula writers make use of stereotype vitalization to add a slightly different angle to the formula narrative and sustain the reader's interest in the story. Cawelti argues that two sorts of stereotype vitalization seem effective: (1) the stereotypical figure who also embodies qualities that appear contrary to the stereotypical characteristics and (2) the addition of touches of human complexity or frailty to a stereotypical character (*Adventure,* 11–12). Both sorts of vitalization reveal themselves in Susannah's depiction of Roland the Gunslinger. Let me first, however, discuss the stereotype. She had "seen him as an existential version of that make-believe Kansas peace officer, whose only mission in life (other than an occasional drink in The Longbranch with his friends Doc and Kitty) had been to Clean Up Dodge" (*WL,* 258). In other words, the stereotype implies "a cop riding a Daliesque range at the end of the world," a drink every now and then, an all-American gruff-faced buddy, and a girlfriend called Kitty (258). In his roles as a diplomat, a mediator, a teacher, and a soldier, Roland does not depart from the Western hero archetype. The first sort of vitalization is made by references to the mythical past and Roland's status as a knight of high nobility (258). Roland's *ka-tet,* for instance, is impressed by the fact that the people of River Crossing still kneel in the dust to receive his blessing.

Having defined the hero in terms of his many duties and mission, King focuses on his personal traits. Referring to President Kennedy as the last gunslinger of the Western world, King has Susannah link Roland's character with the romance tradition of the Western, adding to the traditional list of heroic virtues the notion of guile: "She suspected that Roland possessed little of Kennedy's imagination, but when it came to romance . . . dedication . . . charisma . . . *And guile,* she thought. *Don't forget guile"* (*WL,* 258, italics and ellipses in original). Evoking the reader's admiration for Roland the Gunslinger by equating him with the martyred president of the United States, King offers his readers an idealized role model of such superhuman proportions that he remains beyond the reach of mere mortals (Bettelheim, 41). To bridge the gap between Roland's perfection and the reader's assumed imperfection, King makes use of the second type of the stereotype vitalization, depicting the protagonist as being without imagination (*WL,* 276) or without a sense of humor (*GS,* 168), but with a heart for romance (11). Obviously, King takes his Western hero very seriously, because even the slightest concession to Roland's essential humanity must be counterbalanced — here by Roland's ability to handle a gun faster and shoot straighter than any of his peers (*WL,* 276).

Roland conforms to the Western hero archetype also in that he, too, is surrounded by the supporting characters of Doc and Kitty. During the quest Roland the Gunslinger also discovers the strength and special abilities of the individual members of his *ka-tet.* He learns to respect Eddie's sense of humor and quick tongue, which save the group from the rage of Blaine the Monorail, Susannah's dark half, which she now is able to control, and Jake's innocence and courage, which will presumably play a decisive role in the final confrontation. King's tale of Roland the Gunslinger is more than a story of the triumphant journey of a group of individuals, for the hero dares to reveal his hidden and guiltridden past to his new friends. Cawelti maintains that, for instance, the mystery formula, which is derived from the Gothic (especially Poe) and which, in turn, lends its atmosphere to *The Dark Tower* series is based on the theme of hidden guilt (*Adventure*, 102). By revealing his frailty, Roland becomes a true member of the *ka-tet*, and this, rather than the group's overcoming of obstacles on its moral mission, seems to be the true focus of interest in this adventure story. Tracing this story type back to the myths and epics of earliest times, Cawelti distinguishes two types of heroes: the superhero with exceptional strength or ability and the hero as "one of us," a figure marked by flawed abilities and attitudes shared by the audience (40). Despite or because of the flaws in his character, Roland the Gunslinger appears to be a superhero in the mode of the American Western.

The third aspect of the Western formula is situation. A mysterious stranger and a loner, Roland acts outside social codes. Manipulated by the Man in Black, Sylvia Pittston, a religious maniac, rallies the town of Tull against Roland, who protects himself by shooting virtually every resident of the town. The moral corruption of Tull reveals itself shortly after Roland enters the saloon. But although Roland is violent and carries guns, he nevertheless avoids needless killing (*GS,* 27–28). As in Cawelti, *The Dark Tower* features the tripartite division of characters that dominates the Western pattern of action, including Roland as the Western superhero; an assortment of characters, such as the Slow Mutants and the residents of Lud as the Indians or the outlaws; and the townspeople who defend their settlement and seem virtually incapable of moving beyond it (*Mystique,* 67). However, pursuing the Man in Black, who is both his personal enemy and the holder of dark secrets, Roland leaves behind a Gothic, rather than a Western, collection of decadent and immoral people but also the dead body of Allie, a local woman who has offered him sexual favors. In other words, the tripartite division of characters conforms to the formula Western, but the decadent and immoral quality of the characters deviates from the formula characterization.

So far I have maintained that both the character of Roland the Gunslinger and *The Dark Tower* conform to the Western formula. Now I will show how they depart from it. If the climactic shoot-out embodies the crucial battle that moves the hero from alienation to commitment (Cawelti, *Adventure,* 96), then both King's outlaw motif and his revenge motif, which Egan adds to the formula Western ("Western," 98), depart from the typical pattern. Manslaughters in Tull, for instance, mark Roland as an outlaw who seeks to avenge his father's honor. Unlike the Western formula, which avoids ambiguities, the Man in Black remains an ambiguous figure and eludes the definition of the stereotypical villain. More importantly, if Roland kills the Man in Black, the gunslinger loses the secrets of his antagonist. When Roland spots his adversary and fires away at him, the adversary merely laughs, stating: "You kill me no more than you kill yourself" (*GS,* 192). Unable to prove the Man in Black guilty of any crimes, Roland even remains uncertain of his antagonist's true identity. Frye has noted that although the enemy in a quest may be an ordinary human being, the nearer the *mythos* of romance is to myth, the more attributes of divinity will cling to the hero and the more the enemy will take on demonic qualities (*Anatomy,* 187). Despite his exceptional qualities, Roland the Gunslinger remains human, whereas the Man in Black seems to be of supernatural origin.

Roland the Gunslinger also departs from the Western hero archetype in that the formula typically avoids ambiguities concerning violence, sexism, and racism (Cawelti, *Mystique,* 15–21), whereas King emphasizes the complex character of his hero whose choices have long-term consequences for the human race as such. Significantly, if the Western formula aims at a dynamic but reassuring regularity of form (29) and a plot in which the hero always carries out true justice (59), Roland cannot be placed within this pattern. In order to right the wrongs he has caused earlier in his life, Roland relentlessly heads for the Tower, letting even Jake Chambers, the young boy dependent on him, die for the sake of his mission. As Cawelti points out, an average Western hero resolves the conflict between pioneers and savages (82), whereas pioneers are difficult to find in the apocalyptic world through which Roland travels. Egan also notes that the issue of savages and savagery is blurred in *The Dark Tower* series ("Western," 99), because the Man in Black does not stand in opposition to the townspeople. Furthermore, Roland's quest has macrocosmic proportions of myth, because his destiny is to save King's entire multiverse.

In addition to the classical myth and the formula Western, the Gothic and the apocalyptic fable can be distinguished in *The Dark Tower* series. The series opens with a Western setting that shortly turns into Roland's Gothic quest of the Dark Tower and the apocalyptic allegory of the radioactive wastelands. King incorporates into his Western Gothic conventions, characters, and in part setting as well as apocalyptic imagery. In doing so, he leaves the clarity, regularity, and resolution of the Western for the ambiguity and ambivalence of the Gothic. Not surprisingly, however, Egan refers to an important characteristic that links these two genres. If the Western can be regarded as a *mythos* of quest romance, as Cawelti and Frye suggest (Cawelti, *Mystique*, 95-96; Frye, *Anatomy*, 187), so can the Gothic. The principal difference is the mysterious quality of the Gothic quest. A primary example of dark romanticism, the Gothic does not contradict the Western qualities of *The Dark Tower* series but rather expands them, so that the two genres define and explore the limits of each other (Egan, "Western," 102). Let me now survey these Gothic features, which, as Egan notes, amount to a modern rendering of themes that have permeated the genre for over two centuries: the power of the unknown, the irrationality and unpredictability of the human psyche, as well as good and evil as moral principles (101).

THE GOTHIC

The most Gothic features of *The Dark Tower* series are its ambiguities as regards the moral poles of good and evil. In fact, it so worried the writer that he was initially reluctant to authorize a trade edition of *The Gunslinger:* "I believed then and believe now that more general readers would feel both shocked and cheated by the book's lack of resolution—it is after all, the first section of a much longer work" (Beahm, *Stephen King Companion*, 198). Indeed, Roland's chase after the Man in Black brings him into intimate contact with evil and its "insidious ability to corrupt even the most noble intentions" (Magistrale, *Decade*, 144). The gunslinger's Gothic sense of guilt deepens into soul-sickness when he is forced to sacrifice the people he loves. True to Browning's poem, the protagonist has "descended into the underworld and ascended to the mountaintops, penetrated into himself and expanded beyond the limits of the universe" (Collings and Engebretson, 117). After completely eliminating Tull's residents, Roland recovers quickly. We learn that "he ate hamburgers and drank three beers. [. . .] That night he slept in the bed where he and Allie had lain. He had no dreams" (*GS*, 64). Roland learns his lesson slowly, but, as Magistrale notes, he no longer eats hamburgers after he loses Jake (*Decade*, 144).

Reminiscent of the monsters common in Gothic tales, the Slow Mutants add to the Gothic character gallery of *The Dark Tower* series. Apart from the oracle and the Man in Black, these repulsive, carnivorous, and humanoid creatures, who live beneath the earth, are encountered by Roland on his journey into an unknown territory that seems to be nightmarishly expanding. The setting changes from the wide desert and the clear, blue sky of the Western to the subterranean passages of the deserted subway stations and the dark, Gothic atmosphere of the Browning poem. The change is echoed in the character of Roland, which explores the theme of hidden guilt. The psychological explorations of the Gothic seem to culminate in Sigmund Freud's distinction between eros and thanatos, the basic human drives toward sex and death. In other words, this tension between confidence and guilt lies at the heart of Roland. In the manner of the master narratives of Greek mythology, he brings about the death of his own mother and witnesses the painful death of his lover, Susan Delgado. Having also sacrificed Jake Chambers for the sake of the Tower, Roland, guilt ridden, ashamed, and desperate, suspects that he sows death wherever he wanders. The hidden guilt marks the lonely rider of the Western. Only after the climactic shootout and supported by the love of the right woman does the hero typically leave his past behind him and move from alienation to commitment. A mythical hero with a Gothic sense of guilt, Roland will reach his decisive victory, but there will not be a new "Kitty" for him.

Furthermore, the Gothic double of such classics as Edgar Allan Poe's "William Wilson," Robert Louis Stevenson's *Dr. Jekyll and Mr. Hyde,* and Oscar Wilde's *Dorian Gray* permeates *The Dark Tower* series in the characters of Roland the Gunslinger and the

Man in Black. The two characters resemble each other more than Roland wishes to admit. Egan points out that the Man in Black may not be Roland's alter ego, "but rather the embodiment of what Roland might become, the sum of his negative capabilities" ("Western," 104). When Roland threatens to kill him for the second time, the Man in Black maintains: "You can't. But you can gather wood to remember your Isaac" (*GS*, 198). Sarcastically he thus refers to John "Jake" Chambers, whose initials suggest that he is considered "a sacrificial lamb" (198) as well as "a poker chip" (175) by Roland. Significantly, just as in Frye's definition of the hero-Messiah (*Anatomy*, 187), Roland is also Jake. In this sense he sacrifices himself for humankind: "He had become the boy; the boy had become him" (*GS*, 192). In fact, it is the Man in Black himself who has brought Jake into Roland's path as his final trial before the real quest can begin (99). Like Jesus this Messiah is tempted: he could turn around and take Jake with him, "make him a new center of a new force" (184). Able to resist this temptation, Roland realizes that going back west would mean either death or entombment with the Slow Mutants. By sacrificing Jake, Roland has made himself worthy of a dream vision of the Tower and earned the right to continue the quest.

THE APOCALYPTIC FABLE

Interacting and reinforcing each other, the Western and the Gothic contribute to the apocalyptic allegory that links the seemingly disparate themes of *The Dark Tower* with King's very real concern with the world situation and technological development. Presumably written with *The Stand* in mind, King has Roland's *ka-tet* visit a train station of Stu Redman's world and discover several mummified bodies of Captain Trips's victims. While traveling with Blaine, the *ka-tet* must have passed "a thinny" leading into another dimension. "Thinnies" are characterized as "sores on the skin of existence, able to exist because things are going wrong . . . in *all* worlds," and they emphasize the justification of the quest (*WG*, 81, italics in original). Roland explains that either Captain Trips or other plagues could contaminate several dimensions. The apocalyptic catastrophe may have resulted from warfare, because, while crossing the desert, Roland must avoid devil-grass, a narcotic and an obvious product of nuclear radiation. Later Jake and Roland pass through an underground railroad terminal in which a deadly gas has been used: "Somewhere a converter was turning the air over and over, as it had for thousands of years. . . . [—] The boy was standing, transfixed, at the book stall. Inside, sprawled in the far corner, was a mummy. The mummy was wearing a blue uniform with gold piping. . . . [—] The mummy's face was like an old shriveled apple. Cautiously, the gunslinger touched the cheek. There was a small puff of dust, and they looked through the cheek and into the mummy's mouth. A gold tooth twinkled. 'Gas,' the gunslinger murmured. 'They used to be able to make a gas that would do this'" (*GS*, 182–83). Again King shows that he is first and foremost a horror writer. Horror is an essential ingredient in *The Dark Tower* series, and as a genuine craftsman of the genre— and a capable literary naturalist—King focuses on the gruesome details of the mummified body.

Although the apocalypse is frequently associated with the end of the world and the postcatastrophic scene, it also celebrates the birth of a new world, because, as Egan notes, "the apocalyptic paradigm is circular" ("Western," 102). The recurrent references to "life as a wheel" (for instance, *IS*, 656) reinforce this impression in King, who has drawn the themes and images of *The Dark Tower* series from the book of Revelation. The medieval court of Roland's youth suggests that one civilization has been destroyed and another is about to grow. Indeed, the setting indicates that Roland's world differs dramatically from the technological world that preceded it. Following an ancient highway, he encounters a few survivors, mostly lepers and madmen. King sums up this sad vision by using "an old man of thirty-five" as his mouthpiece. When the gunslinger asks the man if he believes in an afterlife, the man maintains that "this is it" (*GS*, 19). Hence, Roland's apocalyptic existence seems a blend of the genres King deals with in *The Dark Tower* series: medieval customs of the mythical past, Western frontier conditions, and an assortment of Gothic characters. Frye analyzes demonic apocalyptic imagery in terms of the world of the nightmare and the scapegoat; the world of bondage, pain, and confusion; the world of perverted work, ruins, catacombs, and monuments of folly. He even refers to King's influences, Browning's "Childe Roland to the Dark Tower Came," and T. S. Eliot's *Waste Land,* with regard to their emphasis on wilderness and tragic destiny (*Anatomy*, 147, 149).

The atmosphere of tragic destiny and fate mark both apocalyptic imagery and *The Dark Tower*. Roland does not accept his destiny, because innocent outsiders, such as Jake, the populace of Tull, and Allie have become part of the chess game between him and the Man in Black. He has "not asked to be faced with a choice between the obsession of his duty and his quest and criminal amorality" (*GS*, 78). Jake, too, has an aura of destiny, although he looks small, peaceful, and harmless: "The gunslinger did not believe he was harmless. There was a deadly feeling about him, and the stink of predestination" (84). As in Frye (*Anatomy*, 147), the demonic divine world of *The Dark Tower* personifies the irrational forces of nature as they appear to a technologically underdeveloped society. Similarly, King frequently views the machinery of fate as administered by an assortment of remote gods, who both exclude humans and intervene in human affairs mainly to protect their own interests. Fate seems to take the role of God in *The Dark Tower* by demanding sacrifices and enforcing obedience to moral law.

King's characters also fit the apocalyptic character gallery. In the midst of the Tull residents lives the religious leader Sylvia Pittston, who, by calling Roland "the Interloper," turns the town into a crazed mob intent on killing the gunslinger. Just as in Frye's analysis of apocalyptic imagery, this close-knit society is held together by loyalty to the group or the leader, and social relations are based on the mob. In fact, according to Frye (*Anatomy*, 147–49), there are kinds of fulfillment in the apocalyptic conception of human life: individual, sexual, and social. In the same way Roland begins his quest as a powerful, independent, and self-sufficient individual but becomes a member of his *ka-tet* as the quest proceeds. In addition to courage and individualism, cooperation and sense of community are qualities necessary for survival in the postapocalyptic world. Significantly, the same qualities are required in the frontier conditions inhabited by the archetypal Western hero.

The character of Roland also personifies the twofold role of the villain in demonic apocalyptic imagery. Just as in Frye (*Anatomy*, 148), King presents these two poles as the tyrant-leader (inscrutable, ruthless, melancholy, and with an unfaltering will) and the *pharmakos*, or sacrificed victim. The two may also become the same. As I argued earlier, both the Man in Black and Jake provide

Roland with an alternative self-image. Despite his deep-seated individualism, Roland also possesses qualities of the tyrant-leader at the beginning of the quest. He is ready to sacrifice anything to reach the Tower and uses others as tools to achieve this goal (*DT*, 170). Roland also acknowledges his dark side (*GS*, 58). In light of Roland's recurring dreams, it seems possible that Jake has been sacrificed for the gunslinger's sins (120, 139). Presumably, the three characters are interrelated, representing different qualities of Roland the Gunslinger.

The Man in Black, too, belongs to the character gallery of both Gothic and apocalyptic literature. As a Gothic figure he seems an occult character disguised by a monkish robe; as an apocalyptic one he appears to be, in Frye's terms, "the hooded heretic, the black man" (*Anatomy*, 149). Although Egan claims that the Man in Black possesses many of the traits of the shape-shifting Trickster ("Western," 103), Barbara Babcock's list of Trickster characteristics does not support his claim (see the section "The Antihero as a Generic Hybrid [Randall Flagg]"). Despite his tricky behavior, such as making Roland meet Jake and possessing Sylvia Pittston, the Man in Black guides Roland to his destination as a kind of helper or donor. Jake regards him as a priest because of his hood and robe, but during the final council Roland identifies him as an old acquaintance from the court. It was he who made Roland's father and broken him; it was he who came to Roland's mother in the shape of Marten and took her. It has been written that "[e]arth has been given into my hand," he triumphantly declares (*GS*, 205–6). In Tull the Man in Black performs a demonic parody of Christ's raising of Lazarus by raising a devil-grass addict from the dead, and during the council he puts Roland in a trance, giving him a Genesis-like vision of the world's creation and a glimpse of the Tower. Although his actions resemble those of the apocalyptic false prophet (Egan, "Western," 103), the Man in Black seems to serve a narrative purpose, fulfilling his preordained destiny rather than functioning as an active and independent agent as such.

King describes Roland the Gunslinger as a Western law enforcer, a diplomat, a teacher, and a soldier of the mythical White force. Despite the Gothic and apocalyptic traits of his character, such as the Gothic double and the double role of the villain, Roland largely conforms to the archetype of the Western hero. The main distinction between the Western, which is considered a modern myth, and a traditional myth lies in the scale of the hero's journey. The Western focuses on resolving conflicts between pioneers and savages, whereas Roland's quest determines the future of the entire human race. In other words, Roland and his quest go beyond the microcosmic battle of the Western to the macrocosmic proportions of myth. Hence, I regard Roland the Gunslinger at once as a classical mythical hero and as a Western superhero.

Interacting and reinforcing each other, the Western and the Gothic, on the one hand, contribute to the apocalyptic allegory of Roland's quest. On the other hand, King gives the Western mythical proportions by means of apocalyptic imagery, which increases the magnitude of Roland's quest through epic conflicts, the cosmic role of the hero, and the enlargement of time and space continuum. Jenni Calder notes the "gothic quality" of the West's dying towns (71), whereas Egan points out that King redefines the conception of *frontier* in *The Dark Tower* ("Western," 104–5). Like King, Fiedler sees the frontier as "the margin where the theory of original goodness and the fact of original sin come face to face" (*Love*, 6–7). Similarly, while comparing the Gothic hero-villain with the Western hero, Fiedler could be depicting Roland. To him Cooper's Natty Bumppo seems a Faust in buckskin. Faust/Roland knows that his quest is ambiguous, and that he must pay in suffering for his freedom of social codes. As a Westerner, however, Roland knows that what he does is the right thing (184–85). Because of the ambivalence of his character, Roland remains a mythical hero with a Gothic sense of guilt.

King's claim that he has "redefined the genre of horror-writing in [the United States]" can also be applied to *The Dark Tower* series (Goldstein as quoted in Beahm, *Stephen King from A to Z*, 99; Dyson, 5, 39; C. Bloom, 215). By blending the Western, the Gothic, the apocalyptic fable, and, in my view even more importantly, horror and classical myths, King expands and redefines the limits of the genres. King prefers to shift and blend genres as well as to transgress the boundaries of the horror genre in part because of his abiding interest in literary naturalism: by means of fantastic genres he explores the collective and personal anxieties of modern humans. Drawing on his personal blend of literary and film influences, he links these archetypes and stereotypes

with the threat of technological advances beyond human comprehension *(The Stand and Firestarter)*, the Middle East oil crisis in
1973–74 *(Roadwork)*, Nixon's politics of paranoia in the 1970s
('Salem's Lot and *The Dead Zone)*, the inability of social institutions to provide citizens with security *(The Running Man* and
Needful Things), and familial contradictions *(The Shining* and *Bag
of Bones)*, to mention but a few. Thus, King both recycles age-old
literary formulas and gives them new content.

The Antihero as a Generic Hybrid (Randall Flagg)

Stephen King blends genres not only in his plots but also—and
at least as importantly—in his protagonists. A generic hybrid,
Randall Flagg is a composite of many traits, primarily those of
the Dark Man and the Trickster. King's genre blending becomes
all the more obvious, because, for instance, the Antichrist and
the Trickster exist in different cultural realms: the former in the
realms of myth, religion, and advanced civilizations; the latter in
those of folk tale and myth. In the following discussion I analyze
Flagg in the works in which he appears in order of their publication to reveal the essential paradox of both this complex character and King's oeuvre in general: despite seemingly supernatural
characters, story lines, or phenomena, the bedrock of King's credibility lies in his intense realism. In the final analysis we are forced
to face our own flawed humanity in the amorality of Randall
Flagg, who appears to be a recurring incarnation possessed by an
outside force. In brief, King views both good and evil not as ab-
stract metaphysical concepts but as very real forces, which in turn
challenge us to fight for the values we respect. Hence, Randall
Flagg, on the one hand, embodies much of King's genre blending
and genre shifting and, on the other, reflects the tension between
the supernatural and the realistic—two of the most typical characteristics in his writing.

The discussion about Randall Flagg (aka. the Ageless Stranger,
Ahaz, Anubis, Astaroth, Russell Faraday, Raymond Fiegler, Ramsay Forrest, Richard Fry, Nyarlahotep, R'yelah, Seti, and the Walkin Dude) opens with a paradox, because the true identity of the
object of the study cannot be verified. Apparently, King leads his
Constant Reader astray by providing contradictory information,

as Flagg is characterized as a blatant liar. In order to solve the dilemma of Randall Flagg's true nature, I will briefly consider the
discussion Roland the Gunslinger conducts with his hooded antagonist, Walter, toward the end of *The Gunslinger,* where Walter
refers to the Ageless Stranger (aka Maerlyn/Merlin) as his master (212). If Randall Flagg can be traced to the Ageless Stranger,
then he may also be equated with the mythical Merlin of Malo-
ry's *Morte D'Arthur* or, in King's vocabulary, *King Arthur's Tales*
(Magistrale, *Decade*, 3). Both King Arthur's and King Roland's
(The Eyes of the Dragon) advisors are depicted as ambiguous and
dangerous characters. The former, however, plots for the good of
his king in the original story, whereas the latter embodies pure
evil. Paradoxically, in the author's note to *The Waste Lands,* King
equates Walter with the Ageless Stranger (422). All the more
contradictorily, toward the end of *Wizard and Glass,* Roland encounters his predestined antagonist, Randall Flagg, whom he
recognizes as Marten. In *The Gunslinger* Walter refers to this plotting figure as his vessel through which he has seduced Roland's
mother and brought about the destruction of the kingdom (205,
213). However, when Roland awakes after his seemingly eternal
council with Walter, he discovers Walter's laughing skeleton by
the ruins of the campfire, whereas Marten recurs fifteen years
later in *The Dark Tower* series as Roland's antagonist. Therefore, it
seems to me that Walter, Marten, and Flagg are all incarnations of
the same evil that aims at the annihilation of King's multiverse.
In the two latest volumes of *The Dark Tower* series King explicitly
states this fact (*DTO*, 99, 119, 143, 147).

Randall Flagg makes his first appearance in *People, Places, and
Things*, a collection of eighteen one-page science-fiction and horror short stories in typescript written by King and his childhood
friend Chris Chesley in the late 1950s (Spignesi, *Lost Work,* 5). The
collection includes the short story "The Stranger," which reintroduces Kelso Black of "The Hotel at the End of the Road" (also included in *People, Places, and Things*), a petty criminal who makes
a pact with a stranger. Having shot a guard during a robbery,
Black celebrates his victory by drinking cheap whisky. He is,
however, visited by a stranger, "who wore a black coat and [had]
a hat pulled over his eyes" and who reminds him of the implicit
pact the two of them had made when Kelso killed the guard
("The Stranger," as quoted in Spignesi, *Lost Work,* 9). The stranger

has now come for Kelso Black, who is terrified. The stranger laughs horribly, and in a moment the room is empty, though the smell of brimstone remains. Spignesi argues that in "The Stranger" King for the first time employs the Dark Man, a personification of evil, who would later become Randall Flagg (and other manifestations of this character) (9-10). However, the figure is not named Randall Flagg until *The Stand* (1978). In *The Eyes of the Dragon* (1987), Flagg recurs as a plotting magician and an evil advisor, but without a given name and with incarnations deviating from his character's typical pattern. *The Dark Tower* series (1982-2004) presents him as an old acquaintance from *The Stand* and as Roland's mythical antithesis. Flagg is also indirectly referred to in *Hearts in Atlantis* (1999), in which the mysterious leader of the group of war protesters, called Raymond Fiegler, is able to make himself "dim," that is, almost invisible, as Flagg does in *The Eyes of the Dragon*.

It was Robert Browning who introduced the dark and hideous creature who in turn inspired King's character in *The Dark Tower* series. The figure could be anyone of the three incarnations of evil—Walter, Marten, or Randall Flagg.

At the end of *The Dark Tower* King has Roland and Susannah discuss stanzas I and II in more detail. According to them, stanza the first refers to Joe Collins, also known as Dandelo, who attempts to destroy Roland by making him laugh himself to death: "Collins," Roland says. "Whoever wrote that spoke of Collins as sure as King ever spoke of our *ka-tet* in his stories" (*DTO*, 561). Stanza two, in turn, refers to the vampire's stick and the way he waves it. The poem is thus a description of what happens to Roland and his *ka-tet*. Regardless of the villain's personality, he epitomizes pure evil in *The Dark Tower* series. In fact, the epic poem "Childe Roland to the Dark Tower Came" opens with the depiction of Roland's antagonist:

> I
> My first thought was, he lied in every
>   word,
>   That hoary cripple, with malicious eye
>   Askance to watch the working of his lie
> On mine, and mouth scarce able to afford
> Suppression of the glee, that pursed and
>   scored

> Its edge, at one more victim gained
>   thereby.
>
> II
> What else should he be set for, with his
>   staff?
>   What, save to waylay with his lies, en-
>   snare
>   All travellers who might find him posted
>   there,
>   And asked the road? I guessed what skull-
>   like laugh
>   Would break, what crutch 'gin write my
>   epitaph
>   For pastime in the dusty thoroughfare.
>   (Browning, 359)

These two stanzas illustrate the essential qualities of the antagonist. First and foremost, the creature is characterized as a liar
crippled by his own evil. He is seldom seen at the site of action,
because he prefers to pull the strings behind the scene and van-
ish. Gloating over the misfortunes of humans, he creates havoc
wherever he wanders.

King could hardly have chosen his archvillain's name by accident. "Flagg," on the one hand, refers to the verb *flag*, that is,
"to give a sign" in the sense of taking a stand. On the other, it
can also indicate the unfortunate outcome of the pursuit, that is,
"to wither," "to weaken." In King good lasts (Underwood and
Miller, *Feast*, 65), whereas Randall ends up "flagging." The name
"Randall" may also allude to such well-known ballads as "Oh,
Where Have You Been, Lord Randall, My Son." Finally, Flagstaff
Mountain with its Sunrise Amphitheater rises above the town of
Boulder, where the Free-Zone people reside (*ST*, 1049, 1131).

Flagg's personality consists of many sides, of which the demonic will first be considered. Since King regards himself as a
Jungian freethinker and has been influenced by Jung's sense of
myth and symbol (Magistrale, *Decade*, 4), I turn to Jung for the
Dark Man. In *The Archetypes of the Collective Unconscious*, he
argues that the figure of the Wise Old Man symbolizes the spiritual factor (215). In fairy tales the old man appears when the hero
finds himself in a desperate situation in which a miracle is
needed to reverse the wheel of fortune (217–18). But just as all

archetypes have a positive side, they also have another that is in part negative but mostly neutral. Hence, the figure has an ambiguous elfin character; Merlin, for instance, appears good incarnate in some of his forms and in others an aspect of evil. Like the negative aspect of the Wise Old Man in Jung, King in *The Eyes of the Dragon* seems to view Flagg as the wicked magician who, from sheer egoism and pleasure, commits evil for evil's sake (226–27).

Also, in the role of the Dark Man, the Walkin Dude (another of Flagg's nicknames) possesses supernatural powers and appears at moments of utter despair to make his devilish offer. A seeker of souls—like Melmoth the Wanderer in Charles Maturin's novel by the same name, Leland Gaunt *(Needful Things),* and Andre Linoge *(Storm of the Century)*—Flagg repeatedly demands oaths of allegiance from his victims, often in the form of the sentence "My life/soul for you" *(ST,* 457, 718; *ED,* 37; *WL,* 388–89). The character of Flagg has been influenced by his Gothic predecessor, because just as Melmoth consummates his demon-marriage to Isidora, Randall Flagg pursues the virginal Nadine Cross. In fact, the two scenes are almost identical. By her marriage to Melmoth, Isidora moves to the world of shadows: "All was mist and darkness with her" (Maturin, 394). She becomes pregnant with Melmoth's child, just as Nadine Cross bears Flagg's child. Nadine, too, feels "a blackness creeping over her vision" when Flagg falls on her *(ST,* 1074). The sexual union seems to go on endlessly, because Flagg is tireless. Dead cold and older than earth itself, Flagg fills Nadine "with his nightspawn, screaming laughter" (1214–15). Nevertheless, Melmoth and Flagg differ at a crucial point. A tragic character, Melmoth has been cursed to wander eternally on earth, unless he passes the burden to an even worse sinner. However, neither the Walkin Dude nor King's other demonic villains suffer from a guilty conscience. Thus, the Dark Man in King represents evil, cruelty, malice, deceit, and unpredictability.

Indeed, Flagg has a number of demonic traits: he is a killer, a maker of ultimate mischief, a liar, and a tempter, and he sows the seed of evil in many ways. Like many evil beings, Flagg regards himself as omnipotent and can therefore be tricked. However, he is not merely either the Devil or a demon. Referring to King's college poem, "The Dark Man" *(Ubris,* Fall 1969), Douglas E. Winter considers Flagg "neither Satan nor his demonic spawn" *(Art,* 67). In an interview with Charles L. Grant, King affirms that "the

Dark Man isn't the Devil" (Underwood and Miller, *Feast,* 21). In another interview with Winter, he clarifies this statement by comparing Flagg to Colin Wilson's Outsider (see bibliography): not very bright, full of rage, and real (*Art,* 67). In yet another interview, with Richard Wolinsky and Lawrence Davidson, King views Flagg as embodying the most evil beings since Hitler: a composite of Charlie Starkweather; Charles Manson; Charles Whitman, the Texas tower killer; and Richard Speck (Underwood and Miller, *Feast,* 29). A truly Gothic villain, Flagg is a master of disguise with his collection of masks and elusive identity. Influenced by Campbell's *Hero with a Thousand Faces,* King, however, seems to take a reluctantly protective or benevolent attitude toward this "last magician of rational thought" (*ST,* 916). Just as evil is represented in Campbell (*Hero,* 294), the antagonist in King works in continuous opposition to the Creator, mistaking shadow for substance. Cast in the role of either the clown or the devil, Flagg imitates creation and seems to have his place in the cosmogonic cycle. By mockery and by taking delight in creating havoc and chaos, he activates good in order to create new order. This continuous dialogue or, rather, struggle maintains the dynamics of humankind's existence. There is thus more to Flagg's personality than his devilish traits.

The notion of the Trickster was first used by David G. Brinton in the nineteenth century to depict a mythical character who recurs in the oral tales of Native Americans. Brinton's term has no equivalent in any Native language, and therefore the Trickster is called Coyote, Rabbit/Hare, Spider, Raven, Jay, Wolverine, or Gluskabe in different parts of the country. Most of these epithets are names for animals, because in the earliest times no distinction was made between beings in animal form and those in human form. Excessive, gluttonous, obscene, incestuous, and wandering, the Trickster is usually male, but he is able to change sex when needed (Baym, 55). Destructive, amoral, selfish, and foolish, the figure threatens established order everywhere, but as Nina Baym points out, he is also a cultural hero and transformer whose actions in mythical times provided humans with a kind of order (Baym, 55; Deloria, 24). Arthur Cotterell notes that the difference between a folk tale and a myth lies in an emphasis on the supernatural, which also reflects a preoccupation with existential problems, as opposed to a mere interest in narrative. A violator of cultural norms, the Trickster-god of North American Indian mythology has entered popular culture through such figures as Wile E. Coyote, Batman's Joker, and Randall Flagg.

Non-Native writers have been criticized for simplifying the Trickster, since they often regard the figure as a devil. For instance, Jung refers to the demonic features exhibited by Yahweh in the Old Testament and finds in them reminders of the unpredictable behavior of the Trickster (256). The Jungian approach to the Trickster based on Paul Radin's study of the Winnebago Trickster myths, *The Trickster* (1956), has rightly been criticized by Vine Deloria, a Native American writer, and Barbara Babcock, a scholar of American literature. Deloria considers it a classic example of white psycho-anthropologizing of Native peoples (17–31), and Babcock criticizes Jung for viewing the Trickster as the symbol of an undifferentiated psychic state in the process of differentiation (165–66). By examining Babcock's roster of typical Trickster characteristics, we can see how these contradictory elements have been combined in the figure of Flagg. If he lacks positive features, he is a rather simplistic Trickster—if a Trickster at all. Babcock's list includes sixteen points (162–63), which I have summarized and applied to Flagg:

1. Flagg exhibits an independence from temporal and spatial boundaries by appearing in different places at the same time (*ST*, 1143).
2. Flagg inhabits places situated between the social cosmos and the other world or chaos (*DT*, 362).
3. Flagg is *not* involved in scatological episodes of any kind.
4. Flagg *cannot* partake of the attributes of Trickster-transformer-culture hero, because he aims at chaos and destruction.
5. Flagg exhibits mental abnormality as he is repeatedly considered insane (*ED*, 63).
6. Flagg has an enormous libido without procreative outcome (*ST*, 1214–15).
7, 9–10. Flagg has an ability to disperse and disguise himself and a tendency to be ambiguous, single/multiple, and young/old (*ST*, 229–31; *ED*, 60–63).
8. Clearly male, Flagg does *not* exhibit any androgynous features. However, he is associated with mirrors: "His mind was very complex, like a hall of mirrors with everything reflected twice at different sizes" (*ED*, 132).

11. Flagg exhibits a human/animal dualism and may appear as a human with animal characteristics and vice versa (*ST,* 341, 886, 1271).
12. Flagg is amoral, asocial, aggressive, and vain.
13. Flagg does *not* find his most abiding form of relationship with the feminine in a mother/grandmother form, because King has not provided him with any family ties or social life.
14. Flagg is *not* situated between life and death/good and evil as he favors death over life and evil over good.
15. Flagg is ascribed to roles with a certain freedom from social codes.
16. Flagg expresses a breakdown of the distinction between reality and reflection (*ST,* 230, 1008, 1207, 1420).

In brief, as a character, Flagg conforms to points 1, 2, 5, 6, 7, 9, 10, 11, 12, 15, and 16; whereas it is difficult to determine whether point 8 applies to Flagg; and points 3, 4, 13, and 14 cannot be applied to Flagg. Despite the several points he shares with Babcock's list, Flagg cannot be considered a Trickster through and through, because his clear intention to do evil contradicts too strongly with the Trickster's more ambiguous nature. It should also be noted that the Trickster characteristics constitute merely one side of Flagg's multidimensional personality. How Flagg embodies the traits of the Dark Man and the Trickster is outlined in the following discussion. Since I simultaneously try to reveal Flagg's true identity and track his path to the encounter with Roland the Gunslinger, the novels in which he appears are discussed in order of publication. In all of them, Flagg represents both the Dark Man characteristics and the Trickster traits.

THE STAND

Flagg makes his first appearance in *The Stand* as he is heading for Nevada. He is introduced as a rather harmless Trickster, but as the story evolves, the Dark Man characteristics clearly predominate until the very end of the novel, where his destruction inaugurates a fresh start for humanity, thus serving a positive purpose. A true patriot, Flagg loves his country, knows the roads, and walks them at night (*ST,* 226). Wearing sharp-toed cowboy boots, he is depicted as "a tall man of no age in faded, pegged jeans and a denim jacket" (226). He exemplifies Gary Snyder's characterization of Coyote: "always traveling, always lustful" (88). "[A] night-prowler and killer" as well as "a great survivor" (Shackleton, 54–55), Flagg is compared to a coyote, which is one of the animals he can command and take the shape of (*ST*, 341). In his human form, Flagg leads a number of separate lives. He is known as, for instance, Richard Fry, Robert Franq, and Ramsay Forrest. In all these roles, he has eagerly killed, raped, set towns on fire, and fed on human weakness, greed, and hate.

Obviously, King has also applied to Flagg Jung's conception of the Trickster as a reflection of a psyche that has barely left the animal level. In this Jungian view the disposition to mock and the otherness of the Trickster is derived from its origin in a primordial stage of consciousness, which existed before the birth of myth and which corresponds to id-motivated self-gratification. Both subhuman and superhuman, a bestial and a divine being, the Trickster is so unconscious of himself that his body is not a unity, and his two hands fight each other (Jung, 260–63). Similarly, Flagg does not know exactly where he comes from (*ST*, 230) or who he is (1008, 1420): "He was no longer strictly a man, if he had ever been one. He was like an onion, slowly peeling away one layer at a time, only it was the trappings of humanity that seemed to be peeling away: organized reflection, memory, possibly free will . . . if there ever had been such a thing" (1207, ellipsis in original). In many respects Flagg is more primitive than an animal and gets into one ridiculous scrape after another. However, unlike the original Trickster, who commits evil from sheer unrelatedness (Jung, 264), the Dark Man archetype in the character of Flagg is genuinely evil.

King places otherness in our own selves, which makes his monsters so horrifying. Paul Ricoeur puts it in related terms in *Oneself as Another*: "*Oneself as Another* suggests from the outset that the selfhood of oneself implies otherness to such an intimate degree that one cannot be thought of without the other, that instead one passes into the other, as we say in Hegelian terms" (3). Ricoeur's idea of "oneself inasmuch as being other" is reflected in the character of Flagg, whose frightening traits we so often share (3). Placed under hypnosis, Tom Cullen reveals further information about Flagg. An outsider who comes out of time, Flagg is not aware of himself. His real name, Legion, refers to the thousand demons that Jesus turned into a herd of pigs. Although this "king of nowhere" can command certain animals and knows magic, he is afraid of humans who are "inside," that is, care for one another (*ST*, 1008). Andre Linoge of *Storm of the Century* might be equated with Flagg for the following reasons: (1) He is described as "a tall man dressed in jeans, boots, a pea jacket, and a black watch cap snugged down over his ears" (*SC*, 6); (2) His name is evocative (Linoge/Legion); (3) Like Flagg, Linoge has lived thousands of years, but he is not immortal (*SC*, 324); (4) Like Mother Abagail (*ST*, 637), Mike Anderson refers to Linoge's relation with Satan (*SC*, 335); And (5) like the Ageless Stranger in *The Gunslinger*, Linoge has a wand "worthy of Merlin" (*SC*, 355).

As an embodiment of the Dark Man, Flagg consciously chooses evil. King defines evil as "the conscious will to do harm" (Underwood and Miller, *Feast*, 66). He also sees evil as being powerful but ultimately stupid, whereas good is powerful in a more subtle way and ultimately the force that has all the variation and all the excitement (94–95). To underscore the monotony of evil, on the one hand, and the very real threat of rearmament in the late 1970s with its doomsday countdown, on the other, King makes an effective use of sound imagery, especially clocking and knocking images (Reino, 58). Hence, Flagg "walked rapidly, . . . his . . . boots clocking on the pavement" (*ST*, 226); "[h]e hammered along" (228); and "[h]e rocked along" (229). The clocking sound is heard again as Bobby Terry fails to obey Flagg's orders in the Walkin Dude/Crow episode, which, according to Michael R. Collings, represents Flagg as both human and something beyond ("*The Stand:* Science Fiction and Fantasy," 85): "The clocking sound was speeding up. A fast walk, a trot, a jog, run, *sprint*, and Bobby Terry got all the way around, too late, *he* was coming" (*ST*, 1156, italics in original; see also 1018, 1030–31, 1149, 1167). Finally, then, these images culminate in the Trashcan Man's discovery of over a dozen cheap plastic timers, which he attaches to a copper ignition system in order to blow up, ironically, Flagg's own helicopters: "[I]nstead of going *ding* this time . . . they are going to go *bang*" (1254, italics in original). In other words, not only is humanity's existence threatened by national weaponry systems but, worse still, by the whims of maniacs who would eagerly push the red button.

The Dark Man, another of Flagg's nicknames, is equated with the Antichrist by some characters, thus emphasizing his devilish traits (*ST,* 226, 229; *ED,* 60). The superinfluenza, Captain Trips, expresses itself and sometimes even personifies itself as the character of Randall Flagg. Joseph Reino regards Flagg as King's version of a pestilent Big Brother who resembles both the Antichrist and the superflu with its 99.4 percent communicability (57). King depicts both Flagg and Captain Trips as shape-shifters, and the physician George Richardson's description of the disease could similarly be applied to Flagg's shape-and-name-shifting behavior. Resulting in inevitable death, Richardson tells us, the influenza changes every time one's body adopts a defense posture, shifting form until the body is used up (*ST,* 1399–1400). However, although some of the characters in *The Stand* believe that Flagg has started the plague himself (1172), that he is the Satan/ the Antichrist, whose coming was foretold in Revelation (1108), he is in fact as real as the superflu and atomic bombs (1201). Like Jean Baudrillard in *The Transparency of Evil,* King believes that evil is both real and omnipresent.

Hence, in King evil is depicted in very graphic terms. In this respect demonic attributes can be attached to Randall Flagg as the Dark Man. Describing Flagg, Mother Abagail maintains that he is "the purest evil left in the world" (*ST,* 636). She also thinks of Flagg as "the Imp of Satan" (625), "[the] Dark Prince," "[the] Man of Far Leagues" (1126), and "the Dark Prince's least minion" (1129), referring to his diabolic traits. In a dream Mother Abagail encounters Flagg as a Rocky Mountain timber wolf that is portrayed in biblical terms. Known as John the Conqueror, Flagg speaks for modern humankind, revealing that Mother Abagail's decent followers know him best (886). When Nick Andros doubts Flagg's existence, King uses Mother Abagail as his mouthpiece, reinforcing that evil/Flagg is as real as Nick himself. Ironically, even Nick's own name with its "Old Nick" connotations refers to the devil. The sociologist-martyr Glen Bateman suggests different names for Flagg (Beelzebub, Nyarlahotep, Ahaz, Astaroth, R'yelah, Seti, and Anubis), but emphasizes that all of them center on a single notion: his real name is Legion, and in the final analysis he is "an apostate of hell" (1310).

Robert M. Price points out that Beelzebub means "Lord of the Flies" and was used as a mocking name of the Philistine god

Beelzebub, "Lord of the House." It came to be used as an alternative name for Satan or as the name of his rival for the throne of
hell. Ahaz was a rather cowardly king of Judah in the time of the
prophet Isaiah. Seti—or Set—was the Egyptian god of evil, and
Anubis was the Egyptian god who guarded tombs. Nyarlahotep
and R'yelah are Lovecraftian names of evil and, as Price observes, suit particularly well the apocalyptic context of *The Stand*,
thus underscoring the aspect of the Dark Man. First, the name
"Nyarlathotep" (this is Lovecraft's spelling; King spells it without the first *t*) came to Lovecraft in a dream, which he wrote in
the form of the prose-poem "Nyarlathotep" (see bibliography).
In this dream-narrative an Egyptian called Nyarlathotep appears
in Province as a kind of traveling showman with a film presentation describing the end of the world so effectively that it hypno-
tizes audiences. Thus, in Lovecraft's conception Nyarlathotep is
an apocalyptic Antichrist figure. So is R'lyeh (King uses a variant
spelling "R'yelah"), which is a sunken island in Lovecraft's "Call
of Cthulhu," his seminal Cthulhu Mythos story. Lovecraft tells
us that the degenerate Cthulhu cultists are always seeking to
awaken the slumbering titan Cthulhu and to free him from his
palace in the sunken island city of R'lyeh. If R'lyeh rises from the
depths, humanity will de doomed (Price, 118–20). Hence, the
imagery is apocalyptic and appropriate in its association with
Randall Flagg as the Dark Man.

By his supernatural powers, ability to levitate, and divine
characteristics, Flagg resembles the Antichrist (Reino, 59) and
obviously regards himself as such, because he uses crucifixion as
a punishment among his people. Reminiscent of Stoker's Count
Dracula or Count Barlow in *'Salem's Lot,* he commands weasels
to frighten Mother Abagail and wolves to attack Charles Starkweather. In an attempt to push his troubles aside, Flagg levitates,
his chanting suggesting a parody of the Hebrew cabala and divine creation. The Hebrew cabala represents creation in a series
of the emanations of the "I am" of the Creator, and it is precisely
these words that Flagg keeps repeating when levitating (*ST,*
1247; Campbell, *Hero,* 271). In Flagg's pseudoreligious parody of
Christ, both Lloyd Henreid and Donald Merwin Elbert "the
Trashcan Man" hand over their lives and souls to Flagg, who in
return sets them to perform various tasks. Henreid becomes his
bloodhound, whereas the Trashcan Man is sent out to set fire to

things. Significantly, Flagg, a curious savior figure, appears in dreams and expects to encounter the Trashcan Man in Las Vegas, a city representing the very base of evil (*ST*, 718–19).

Like the demonic Sauron in *The Lord of the Rings*, Flagg is able to send forth his Eye. Reino traces this ability back to the cosmology of Heliopolis in ancient Egypt, where the single-armed deity, Atum, had the ability to send forth his single eye called Wedjet, thus representing the destructive aspect of the Egyptian mother goddess. The Eye, with its "search-and-seizure behavior," seems a fitting companion for Flagg, who uses it in a number of functions (59–60). Mother Abagail is able to sense the search (*ST*, 622), whereas Harold Lauder, who has recently crossed over to the side of evil, feels that the Eye is calling him (708). However, the ultimate purpose of the traveling Eye is to trace Flagg's enemies. In this function it approaches Dayna Jurgens and Tom Cullen, and Flagg is now about to send out his Eye to discover the secrets of Glen Bateman, Ralph Brentner, Stu Redman, and Larry Underwood. The Eye becomes separated from Flagg with a tug and flies like a hawk in the night sky. At one with the night, it becomes the eye of a crow, a wolf, a weasel, a cat, a scorpion, and a spider: "a deadly poison arrow slipping endlessly through the desert air" (1271). Reino points out that the Eye is able to overcome an eagle, a traditional medieval symbol of the apocalyptic triumph of Christ, but unable to overcome a dog, the traditional Gothic symbol of opposition of vampires (60).

Like Roland the Gunslinger, whose contradictory traits and alternative options are reflected in Jake Chambers and the Man in Black, so too Flagg's various stages of moral corruption are mirrored by Lloyd Henreid and Donald Merwin Elbert "the Trashcan Man." It would be tempting to draw parallels to Roland's "shadows" and view Henreid and the Trashcan Man as Flagg's alternative options. Presupposing a certain degree of predestination in King's multiverse, Flagg fulfills his evil destiny, and in this light his free will is confined to the choice between lesser and greater evil. Henreid's moral growth might serve the purpose of the former. However, the Trashcan Man cannot be regarded as the latter, because King depicts him as an abused outcast rather than as a willing agent of evil. Nonetheless, when "setting [the Trashcan Man] high in [his] artillery" (*ST*, 718), Flagg brings about his own destruction. The appearance of the "Hand of

God" in the sky at the moment of the atom-bomb explosion caused by the Trashcan Man testifies to God's intervention, and so does the discovery of the bomb. Before finding the bomb, the Trashcan Man contemplates suicide, but some powerful force stops him. He falls asleep, and the thought of redemption dawns on him. Ironically, his redemption includes a vision according to which "the righteous and unrighteous alike were consumed in that holy fire" (1337).

The true conclusion of the novel is not the burst of fire from the atomic device but the spontaneous burst of laughter from Glen Bateman (Collings, "Science Fiction," 88). Bateman realizes that he has been frightened for nothing, and he is now amused by both his own foolishness and Flagg's lack of substance (*ST*, 1318). Just as in Campbell (*Hero*, 294), Flagg disappears into nothingness at the end of *The Stand*, because, to King, evil is ultimately nihilistic. He believes that even genuinely evil people ultimately personify external evil (Underwood and Miller, *Feast*, 29, 95). In other words, the powers that Flagg has invoked pass to another (Winter, *Art*, 68–69) (for this view see "Genetic and Sociological Determinism" on Eduard Delacroix and "Cosmological Determinism and Fate" on the Crimson King, both in chapter 3). Shortly before the explosion, Flagg's clothes are suddenly empty. The motif of demonic possession runs through King's fiction: in *The Shining*, for instance, the demon flees from the hotel, leaving an empty shell (*SH*, 451); in *Desperation* the demon, Tak, leaves the China pit (*DE*, 542); and in *The Regulators* Tak possesses an autistic boy. However, in his Trickster aspect Flagg is not merely a menace to order but also serves a positive purpose by activating good forces to settle order in King's multiverse.

Indicating that Flagg remains a pawn of evil, King regards the character as terrifying, because he is real. Throughout *The Stand* King refers to the real-life incidents in which Flagg has participated. Regardless of his obscure origin, Flagg has obviously grown as a character in King's imagination since *The Stand*. At any rate, evil undoubtedly needs its willing agent to create new havoc, because shortly after the explosion we meet a man called Russell Faraday on a bone-white beach: "He awoke at dawn. He had his boots on" (*ST*, 1419). Reminiscent of the old Doors song "The End": "The killer awoke at dawn, he put his boots on" (http://www.malakoff.com/sking.htm), Flagg/Faraday soon adjusts to his new existence and begins to preach his gospel to the natives: "I've come to teach you how to be civilized!" (*ST*, 1421). And as King never tires of underscoring, the rest is history.

THE EYES OF THE DRAGON

While Flagg's Dark Man characteristics predominate in *The Stand*, *The Eyes of the Dragon* focuses on his more ambiguous Trickster traits, such as his role as a Merlin figure and the haphazard nature of his evil. However, the principal constituents of his behavior remain the same, and whether labeled an epic fantasy or a fairy tale, *The Eyes of the Dragon* reintroduces the same Randall Flagg, who was left to enjoy his well-deserved vacation on a primitive island at the end of *The Stand*. In addition to evil, deceit, cruelty, malice, foolishness, and the shape-shifting ability of the figure, *The Eyes of the Dragon* focuses on yet another of Flagg's characteristics: Flagg as the wizard/shaman/medicine man. Jung links the character of the shaman and the medicine man to the Trickster, because he, too, plays malicious jokes on people, only to fall victim to the vengeance of those whom he has insulted (256). From Flagg's angle this is precisely what the novel is about.

The opening page of *The Eyes of the Dragon* reveals Flagg as a plotter who wants to make sure that King Roland's younger son, Thomas, will be crowned king in the land of Delain (7). It was also Flagg who in order to raise the King's virility had mixed his impotent monarch a draught of double strength, which resulted in the birth of Thomas (15). Flagg had acted on the spur of the moment: "His instinct for mischief told him that this one might cause trouble, and Flagg simply obeyed his instinct" (81). To bring about the death of his opponent, the virtuous female character Queen Sasha, Flagg blackmails her midwife, Anna Crookbrows, to cut one of the queen's blood vessels during the birth of Thomas. Resembling Henreid and the Trashcan Man, Anna Crookbrows promises Flagg anything in exchange for healing her son (37). When Sasha dies, the indolent and somewhat slow-witted King Roland remains at Flagg's mercy, and Flagg poisons him, making it appear as the deed of Peter, Roland's elder son. When Peter escapes from prison—significantly, called the Tower—and the two brothers unite their forces against Flagg, the magician vanishes much in the same way as in *The Stand*: Flagg is suddenly gone.

Flagg's Dark Man characteristics and his Trickster traits alternate throughout the novel and cannot be separated from each other. In eliminating the queen, Flagg reveals the face of a murderer, and he is even called by the same name as in *The Stand*: sometimes the dark man, but sometimes also Flagg the Hooded (*ED*, 60). In this novel, too, Flagg shifts identities and aliases. A regular guest in Delain, he is always accompanied by misery and death. Despite a different name, a different face, and a different bag of tricks, he always appears hooded and almost faceless: never as the king, "but always as the whisperer in the shadows, the man who pour[s] poison into the porches of the King's ears" (62; note the reference to *Hamlet*). Like all evil creatures, Flagg needs power in order to make mischief. As in *The Stand*, he is referred to both as "the devil" (61) and as "a sickness, a fever looking for a cool brow to heat up" (62). Like "the First Citizen" of Las Vegas (*ST*, 773), the magician Flagg is afraid of independent, courageous, and righteous individuals who need no advisors. Accused of the murder of King Roland, Peter looks neither afraid nor confused, and Flagg feels "a faint stirring of fear" (*ED*, 147). Similarly, in both novels the character has preserved his inimitable, malicious laughter and strong teeth (160, 344).

As an evil enchanter, Flagg is capable of casting spells, versed in the ways of poisons, and proficient in the art of making himself almost invisible. Deceptively ordinary in appearance, all Flagg incarnations know how to become "dim" (*ST*, 226, 1175; *ED*, 77). In King evil has no face and therefore remains hidden, which is precisely what Flagg seeks: in his vocabulary *dim* is a synonym for *ghostly, transparent,* and *unobtrusive* (*ED*, 77). Dimness pleases villains such as Flagg, but it does not save him from his own warped mind. Regarding everyone with suspicion, he believes that everyone has hidden reasons for his or her actions (132). As a Gothic villain, Flagg is full of hubris, and although he sees much, he is strangely blind as regards variation, imagination, and love (167). Finally, then, fate or luck leads to his ruin when Thomas accidentally sees Flagg serve the poisoned drink to the king (75). Underestimating his "pet dog" (161), just as the Walkin Dude underestimated the Trashcan Man, Flagg brings about his own destruction.

As an example of King's interconnected multiverse, the land of Delain exists in the same world as Susan Delgado's Hambry of

Wizard and Glass: on windy nights old wives tell their husbands that Rhiannon, the Dark Witch of the Coos, is riding her broom (*ED,* 108). When doing so, Rhiannon/Rhea possesses one of the pieces of Maerlyn's rainbow. Reminiscent of the rings of *The Lord of the Rings,* Maerlyn's rainbow consists of thirteen powerful crystals, one for each of the twelve guardians of the portals, and one for the nexus point of the beams that connect those portals, that is, the Dark Tower (Wiater, Golden, and Wagner, 58). Flagg owns one of these crystals—whether it is the Mastercrystal or a minor glass ball remains unclear (*ED,* 84; *WG,* 671). The crystal brings us back to Maerlyn/Merlin and suggests the possibility that Flagg, indeed, could be equated with him. If Flagg provides Maerlyn/Merlin with a body to materialize into from time to time, King's conception of Maerlyn/Merlin differs dramatically from that of *Morte D'Arthur.* Whether the corruptive power of the glass ball has turned the wise and cunning wizard into the villainous and sly Flagg seems ultimately unclear even to King himself, but the provision of Flagg with a crystal is not an incidental detail. At any rate, in *The Eyes of the Dragon* the magician Flagg is recognized as a demon by the citizens of Delain (365). However, as a modified Trickster, he brings about order through disorder by prompting the two brothers to unite their forces against him. In this sense Flagg has his place in the cosmogonic cycle.

THE DARK TOWER SERIES

Finally, Randall Flagg recurs in *The Dark Tower* series, where, again, he embodies both the Dark Man and the Trickster with an emphasis on the former. The paths of Roland the Gunslinger and Flagg cross in *The Drawing of the Three,* and Flagg is mentioned in passing. Paying a visit to Katz's Drug Store in New York, Roland notes that among the magicians he has known in his time was a demon, "a creature that pretended to be a man and called itself Flagg" (361–62). Paradoxically, Roland here clearly distinguishes the characters of the Man in Black and Marten from Flagg: "Then there had been the man in black. And there had been Marten" (362). However, as we will shortly see, Marten, Walter, and Flagg are one and the same.

Randall Flagg is encountered again toward the end of *The Waste Lands,* where he, like Melmoth, appears at the moment of loss to make his devilish offer to Andrew Quick aka the Tick-Tock Man in the city of Lud. Recalling his memories of Henreid and the Trashcan Man from *The Stand,* Flagg recruits Quick to prevent Roland's *ka-tet* from reaching the Dark Tower: "Say, 'My life for you,' Andrew—can you say that?" (*WL,* 389). The fact that Flagg uses the Tick-Tock Man's given name, Andrew, which even he himself has forgotten, indicates that the demonic Flagg is once again sending out disciples to alter the balance of the multiverse. Able to read his mind and with a penetrating, hissing voice, Flagg does not seem human to Andrew (387). The boots reveal an old acquaintance, and while introducing himself, Flagg comes up with a long list of names, beginning with a Trickster poem about shifting identities, names, and aliases (387). Flagg then claims that he cannot be equated with Maerlyn/Merlin, but, of course, he might be lying (387–88). Not surprisingly, he wishes to be called Richard Fannin (388). Concluding a Faustian pact in modern terms, Flagg holds out a hand whose palm is utterly devoid of lines: "What do you say, pard? Shake the hand that shook the world" (388).

Near the end of *Wizard and Glass,* the hero and the antihero finally meet each other in an emerald palace reminiscent of that in *The Wizard of Oz.* Jake notes Flagg sitting in the middle of a throne. Although Flagg is casually clothed, Jake discovers that he is not a man but the wizard with a crystal ball in his bag (671). At this point Roland recognizes his age-old antagonist, Marten Broadcloak (672). Although both parties fire at each other, it seems predestined that the bullets miss their targets. Introducing himself as Flagg, the antagonist recalls his encounters with Roland as if they were meetings with an old acquaintance. Having warned Roland not to enter the Tower, Flagg vanishes, leaving the *ka-tet* a last-warning message decorated with two smile faces and a thundercloud (689). *Wolves of the Calla* (2003) does not discuss Randall Flagg, whereas *Song of Susannah* (2004) mentions him in passing. In the final volume of *The Dark Tower* (2004) Roland encounters the Crimson King as an embodiment of evil. Randall Flagg dies a cruel and violent death in the jaws of Mordred, the Crimson King and Roland's mutual son(!). In his pursuit of becoming "the God of All," Flagg attempts to use Mordred as a vehicle and underestimates the hybrid's powers (*DTO,*

139). Through their telepathic connection, Roland feels that Randall Flagg, "his old nemesis," is dead (*DTO*, 202).

Randall Flagg seems a composite of the Dark Man (the dark side of Jung's Wise Old Man) and the Trickster with its wizard, shaman, and medicine man connotations. The Dark Man characteristics seem to predominate, because Flagg's clear intent to do evil contradicts too strongly the Trickster's more ambiguous nature. Apparently, the embodiments of the Dark Man allow King to present his mythical view of the primordial dichotomy between good and evil. Possibly influenced by Jungian thinking, King tends to split the figure of the Wise Old Man into benevolent father substitutes and malevolent incarnations of evil. Aware of North American mythology, Campbell's presentation, and, presumably, Jung's interpretation of the Trickster, not to mention the pop-culture references, King has merged mythical, folk-tale, and popular-culture influences in Randall Flagg's character. Flagg is depicted as a mythical character by his preoccupation with existential problems in his role as the medicine man/wizard in *The Dark Tower* series and *The Eyes of the Dragon* as well as in his resemblance to the Antichrist in *The Stand*. As a killing night-prowler, a great survivor, and a smiling joker, Flagg thus shares traits with the mythical and the pop-culture Trickster. In this way King blends genres not only in his plots but also, and perhaps more importantly, in some of his most central characters.

Flagg is ultimately a grotesque character. Marina Warner defines *grotesque* as a style, a mood, or a sensibility expressed in art that beats to a double pulse: *terribilità* as well as *capriccio*, thus combining terror and laughter (as mockery instead of mirth) (*Bogeyman*, 246–47). The grotesque also links Flagg with reality, and this very combination appears to be his most significant trait. In the conclusion of *The Grotesque in Art and Literature*, Wolfgang Kayser distinguishes grotesque traits in art and literature (184–89), and Vernon Hyles has presumably applied them to King's fiction. Hyles views the grotesque as "new Gothicism" and in summary reaches three conclusions (56–57). Since all these conclusions can be applied to Flagg, they serve as a kind of summary of his character: First, the grotesque is the expression of the alienated world, that is, the familiar world is seen from a strange perspective that is experienced as either comic or terrifying, or both.

Similarly, Flagg's ordinary face reveals an insane, mocking, and dangerous monster. Second, blending laughter and terror, the grotesque deals with the deep absurdities of existence. As King puts it, "Flagg is always there, in the human capacity to do evil" (Underwood and Miller, *Bones*, 115). Third, the grotesque is an attempt to take control over the demonic elements of the world. In the character of Flagg, we as readers can externalize our fears, insecurities, and even our rage, hate, and frustration. What is more, his paradoxical failure and survival reestablish the laws of normality and teach readers to cope with their own failures in life.

Undoubtedly, King has created several myths and fairy tales. However, *originality* is an inappropriate word here, because personal mythologies are nearly always on closer inspection reworkings of traditional mythologies. In *Fear Itself*, a collection of critical essays, Don Herron criticizes King's work for being overly derivative. He contends that King's supernatural creations either suggest earlier work in the genre or are adopted as such ("Horror," 90-91). King concedes this point freely, maintaining that he has never regarded himself as "a blazingly original writer in the sense of conceiving totally new and fresh plot ideas." Neither have other writers, in his view, because in genre as well as in mainstream fiction, "most writers are essentially reworking a few basic themes." What he attempts to do is "to pour new wine from old bottles" (Underwood and Miller, *Bones*, 55). There is, however, a crucial difference between producing a mere echo and returning to a previous theme. Although allusions to *The Wizard of Oz* and *The Lord of the Rings* may create the specific atmosphere of *The Stand* and *The Dark Tower* series, in his works King has been able to create a whole mythology that transcends the limits of an individual work of art. Including cosmology, social order, and various species and languages, the roots of Roland's saga go back to the same cultural "mythpool" (Burton Hatlen's term frequently used by King, for instance, *DM*, 50) as its classical equivalents in, for instance, the Bible, Greek mythology, and such epic fantasies as *The Lord of the Rings*.

Hence, King blends genres, most significantly the Gothic and fairy tales, in his own myths and individual characters, which is a link between the discussion in chapter 1 and that in chapter 2 of this book. The Gothic lends King's stories both a historical perspective and a dark atmosphere, whereas myths and fairy tales link the fictional events with cultural and historical archetypes. In other words, mythical and fairy-tale symbols and narrative structure fuse the events and the personal relationships of King's stories with larger patterns of human behavior. Finally, literary naturalism frames the stories by providing them with common laws: those of free will and determinism. In what follows, I develop my argument by claiming that, in addition to myths of his own creation and mythical characters, most of King's stories have a fairy-tale structure. This, I would claim, is an important point, because it proves that King takes advantage of significant elements of various genres to create his unique brand of horror.

Adapted and Revised Myths and Fairy Tales

Stephen King uses literary formulas to describe contemporary scenes of horror by means of adaptations and revisions of literary classics. Drawing on everything he has read and seen, King blends the influences to create an original work of art. If his story line follows the spirit of the original myth or fairy tale, I regard it as an adaptation in this study. Hence, although *'Salem's Lot* differs in its details from *Dracula* (for instance, *'Salem's Lot* has only one setting), both novels describe the vampire as a threat to their respective communities against which the hero and his companions take action. Furthermore, King has repeatedly acknowledged the indebtedness of *'Salem's Lot* to *Dracula*, even to the extent of calling it his "*Dracula* look-alike" (Herron, "Horror," 81) and "a homage to *Dracula*" (Underwood and Miller, *Bones*, 129). Similarly, he regards *Carrie* as a revised "Cinderella" and maintains that it has a fairy-tale structure (Underwood and Miller, *Bones*, 93). Unlike the canonized fairy tales, which preserve the status quo, the revised tale aims to alter the reader's views of traditional patterns, images, and codes (Zipes, *Fairy Tale*, 10). This seems to be King's intention in *Carrie*, which also draws on a B-movie called *The Brain from Planet Arous* (Underwood and Miller, *Bones*, 56).

I discuss Bram Stoker's *Dracula* and King's *'Salem's Lot* partly in terms of Propp's functions of the Russian folk tale and partly according to King's functions of the horror genre in order both to analyze the story lines and to determine whether the functions of the two separate genres overlap. In this connection I wish to emphasize that although I use Propp's functions as a tool to compare *Dracula* and *'Salem's Lot*, the functions of the fairy tale cannot be applied to complex novels that, for instance, contain several subplots. Although both Propp's and King's categories are so general that they could be applied to a number of stories, the applicability of the fairy-tale structure to King bears witness to the archetypal nature of his work. I also wish to emphasize that, instead of Propp's thirty-one functions, I use Jack Zipes's summary of them as presented at the beginning of this chapter (see 3).

'SALEM'S LOT: KING'S "DRACULA LOOK-ALIKE"

Heading for Count Dracula's castle on the eve of Saint George's Day, Jonathan Harker both proves brave in inviting the reader to participate in an imaginary rite of passage and violates the interdiction of confronting evil without proper precautions (cf. function 1 in King and point 1 in Propp). In *'Salem's Lot* the violation of the interdiction is even called "the initiation" (28): To join the Bloody Pirates, an exclusive club of prepubescent boys, Ben Mears must go into the cursed Marsten House and bring out some booty. The ghost of the long-dead Hubie Marsten and the souvenir from the house, a glass snow globe, make the protagonist return to his childhood town and attempt to purchase the Marsten House. In fact, the glass globe, a recurring object throughout King, also allows readers to return to the world of their childhood, regaining both its fears and its beliefs (cf. function 7 in King). King's recollections of a similar glass globe were frightening in his own childhood, and the atmosphere of that moment finds its expression in Ben's experience (Underwood and Miller, *Bones*, 22). Hence, the glass ball symbolizes an attempt to control one's fears.

Arriving in his childhood town, Mears recognizes it, but realizes that he himself has become a stranger, an outsider. Marked by his obsession to rent the Marsten House, he hears that somebody has already acquired the haunted house, but the discovery merely intensifies his interest in and connection with it (cf. point 2 in Propp). The first tasks Mears undertakes is to discover the secret of the Marsten House and later, when he reveals it, to fight against the vampire. The two tasks are interrelated, and they also relate to the interdiction and prohibition of entering the house in the first place. Similarly, referring to his duties, which he can "allow nothing to interfere with," Harker ignores the villagers' warnings and departs (Stoker, 13). A marked man and a social outcast, he wishes to have his work done. In other words, Harker's character is marked by his very task.

When Mark Petrie and Susan Norton break into the Marsten House, Richard Throckett Straker (Barlow's servant, whose name is presumably a pun on Bram Stoker) captures them. Mark escapes, but Susan is vampirized by Barlow. Despite his instincts and the final warnings of his fellow passengers, Harker ascends Dracula's carriage and is taken to his castle. Harker's often-cited encounter with Count Dracula presents the monster as a sophisticated man of the world who, unlike Barlow, welcomes his guest to "[e]nter freely" and, more importantly, "of [his] own will" (Stoker, 26; cf. point 3 in Propp; and functions 5, 6, and 8 in King). Discovering that he is imprisoned in Dracula's castle, Harker decides to ignore his host's warning not to sleep anywhere but in his bedroom. In doing so, he encounters three female vampires (cf. three creatures in Propp), discovering the final truth about Count Dracula, who promises the ladies that when he is done with Harker, they may kiss him at their will, handing over a living child to them in exchange for Harker. An infanticide scene is also included in King's version, in which Straker sacrifices the child. As in *Dracula*, the scene is merely alluded to, not described in any detail, which, in King's view, "heightens the obscenity of the act" (Underwood and Miller, *Bones*, 58). Undoubtedly, the novel thus provides an opportunity to deal with death (cf. function 5 in King), permits us to indulge our collective and social anxieties (cf. function 6 in King), and lets us transcend the world of negation (cf. function 8 in King). The afterlife is not depicted as appealing in either *Dracula* or *'Salem's Lot,* and although Mears encounters Count Barlow only toward the end of *'Salem's Lot,* he is frequently confronted with the living dead in the course of the novel.

In King's adaptation of *Dracula*, Ben Mears, Susan Norton, Matt Burke, and Jimmy Cody unite their forces against evil, which relates to a larger whole (cf. point 4 in King). Ben Mears becomes a worthy hero at the loss of his recently found lover, Susan Norton. Like Lucy Westenra, Susan becomes the bride of the vampire, and in both novels the female protagonist is released from her suffering by her beloved. Harker, too, is tested, and he manages to escape from Count Dracula (cf. point 4 in

Propp). The emphasis shifts to Dr. Van Helsing during Harker's long recovery from the dreadful experience. In fact, Lucy Westenra becomes Dracula's victim before Harker even realizes that the vampire has arrived in England. As in King, a group of characters unite in order to conquer evil.

The deaths of Lucy and Susan can be regarded as temporary setbacks on the hero's journey (cf. point 5 in Propp). The sixth point in Propp focuses on the battle with the villain. Discovering his hiding places and sterilizing his earth boxes, the rescue team forces the count to leave and pursues him back to Transylvania. As the sixth point in Propp suggests, the pursuit results in three battles with the villain: the first in the Harker bedroom after the count's attack on Mina (Stoker, 336–37), the second in the count's Piccadilly house after the sterilizing of Dracula's earth boxes (364–65), and the third, and final, confrontation in Transylvania, which results in the destruction of the vampire (447). In King virtually all the townspeople turn into vampires, and consequently there are more than three battles with the villain. The final battle occurs between Kurt Barlow and Ben Mears, and it is depicted in graphic detail. Ironically, Barlow refuses to die neatly. To place the vampire in a prone position, Ben has to wriggle into the coffin himself, and while he hammers the stake through Barlow's heart, the antagonists have time to conduct a rather intellectual discussion before the vampire finally dies. Although the vampire eventually crumbles to dust, the process takes considerably longer than in *Dracula* (*SL*, 412–13).

In *'Salem's Lot* the protagonists survive and gain in wisdom: "'You and me,' Mark said and closed his fist. He face was no longer pale; bright color glowed there. His eyes flashed. They went back to the road and drove away" (427). In the final note of *Dracula*, Jonathan Harker maintains: "Seven years ago we all went through the flames; and the happiness of some of us since then is, we think, well worth the pain we endured" (Stoker, 449). He and Mina have a son, and Godalming and Seward are both married. In other words, feelings of normality have been reestablished and good feelings about the status quo confirmed (cf. point 7 in Propp; and functions 2 and 3 in King).

Throughout his fiction King reworks traditional material and uses the horror formula to depict American social reality. Although the vampire provides supernatural thrills and fun, King reveals familial discord, violence, and other social illnesses for what they are in *'Salem's Lot*. In King the fairy-tale Everyman encounters social taboos in modern terms, and, as Herron notes, the shock effect is created by means of detailed realism (Herron, "Horror," 76; Roberts, 36). Herron goes on to argue that *'Salem's Lot* cannot be considered a serious novel, because it relies on old scenes from *Dracula* or Hammer films starring Christopher Lee, unlike, for instance, Rice's *Interview with the Vampire* (1976), which introduces original scenes of horror (86). I believe, however, that by linking familiar archetypes with our collective and social anxieties, King does, indeed, create something new. Furthermore, contemporary readers may find King's version more accessible in language, style, and contemporaneity than Stoker's classic. In other words, King reworks traditional material in part to "the delight of the horror fan, who is always on the lookout for new tales of lycanthropy or necromancy" (Herron, "Horror," 82) and in part to make a connection with the reader's real-life fears (Underwood and Miller, *Feast*, 19). A popularizer who can make the supernatural interesting to the modern reader (Herron, "Horror," 89), King is also able to touch the reader at a deeper level in the way real art always does.

CARRIE: A MODERN CINDERELLA

If *'Salem's Lot* emphasizes the similarities with *Dracula* in order to entertain, achieve reader identification, and discuss sexual and social phobias, then *Carrie* deviates from "Cinderella" in order to do so. Hence, the function of King's adaptations and revisions in both books seems identical. A number of scholars have discussed *Carrie* in terms of fairy tale and myth. Instead of a typical heroine, however, Carrie White is called "a wimp" turned into "a bitch-goddess" by King (Underwood and Miller, *Bones*, 55). Various critics have described her in different ways: "Galatea" by Greg Weller (5–6), "a doomed victim" by Tom Newhouse (52), "a teenaged ugly duckling" by Douglas E. Winter (*Art*, 32), "Cinderella" by Joseph Reino (13) and Chelsea Quinn Yarbro (62), and "Kore"/"Persephone" by myself (*Women Characters in Stephen King's Novels*, 25). Because of the multitude of analyses, I discuss *Carrie* here in terms of the famous Perrault version of the "Cinderella" fairy tale, with the focus on the deviations from the classic.

King has seen high school society from two perspectives, as a student and as a teacher. *Carrie* deals with bullying and suggests that Carrie's desperate effort to become like her peers fails in part because of the bottomless conservatism and bigotry of high school society. King regards high school as a place where the adolescents "are no more allowed to rise 'above their station' than a Hindu would be allowed to rise above his or her caste" (*DM*, 171). King considers *Carrie* a story about a girl who does a terrible thing but who is justified, because she has been driven mad by all the teasing (Underwood and Miller, *Bones*, 93; *DM*, 208), and his exoneration of Carrie is equaled by his contempt for the peers who torture her. His sympathies are always with the socially rejected, who are not only victimized by the cruelty of their more popular peers, but who also by their intelligence and sensitivity deeply realize their status as pariahs (Magistrale, *Landscape*, 76). Thus, Carrie becomes doubly pitiful, because "she can only wait to be saved or damned by the actions of others" (*DM*, 174). In the character of Carrie, King attempted to create a well-developed female protagonist; even though she starts out as "a nebbish victim," she develops into "a bitch goddess" who destroys an entire town in her hormonal rage (55). Hence, she embodies male fears about menstruation and about dealing with all-devouring women. King also views *Carrie* as a parable of women's consciousness, since he regards women as the only humans exercising their brains, showing moral courage, and performing moral acts (102).

With the exception of the glass slipper, King has retained the essential elements of the classic fairy tale in his version of "Cinderella": familial discord, peer pressure, and sexuality with its bloody connotations. In fact, when first written down around AD 850–860, "Cinderella" already had a history (Bettelheim, 236; Warner, *Beast*, 202). "Cinderella" found its Western canonical form in Charles Perrault's "Cendrillon" (Warner, *Beast*, 202–3; Opie and Opie, 152), although Bruno Bettelheim points out that in ancient times "having to live among ashes" was a symbol of being debased in comparison to one's siblings, regardless of sex (236). Still, in addition to familial discord and social inequality, "Cinderella" focuses on sexuality. In Bettelheim the symbolic erotic significance of the slipper relates to the substitution of body parts effected by imagery (264–72), whereas Marina Warner states that Cinderella's shoe has both social and sexual connotations. The strained relations between women in the Chinese version of Cinderella are linked with the dangers of polygamy, whereas in Grimm's version the strains between stepmothers and stepdaughters find their bloody expression when the sisters hack off their toes and heels to make the slipper fit *Beast,* 203).

Just as in Bettelheim (25), King's stories often focus on the inner processes taking place in an individual, and the unrealistic nature of those processes seems an important device in achieving this end. King's stories, too, begin realistically and have everyday features woven into them. Douglas Keesey claims that the fantastic constitutes an integral part of *Carrie*'s social commentary (32). To be more precise, Carrie's telekinetic ability provides King's novel with a fantastic dimension, but the opening scene is depicted realistically enough: the other girls chuck tampons and sanitary napkins at Carrie White in the shower room when she has her first period. A classmate's furious yell indicates that Carrie lacks the looks of a typical fairy-tale heroine: "You're bleeding, you big dumb pudding!" (*CA,* 8). Whereas the fairy tale typically makes clear that it tells about Everyman, even to the extent that, instead of proper names, general or descriptive names are used to depict the protagonist (Bettelheim, 40), Carrie White has both a name and a broader identity. Clearly, the girl's name has significance. Edward J. Ingebretsen points out that her last name evokes the tradition in American letters in which whiteness and inscrutability are two points of a triangle whose third point refers to the futility of interpretation—a central theme in Edgar Allan Poe, Herman Melville, and Robert Frost. The name "Carrie" echoes the American history of social violence perpetrated in the name of public good. Both Martha Corey and Martha Carrier were executed at Salem for witchcraft in 1692 (20). Furthermore, Reino notes that the four-syllable "Carietta" (Carrie's real name) echoes the four-syllable "Cinderella" (14).

Innocence and a sense of superiority mark the character of Carrie White. In traditional retellings Cinderella is described as both good and beautiful, but capable of plotting against her stepmother. For instance, in Giambattista Basile's "La Gatta Cenerentola" ("The Cinderella Cat"), the heroine conspires with her governess to kill her wicked stepmother (Warner, *Beast,* 205;

Opie and Opie, 156). Also Bettelheim claims that only Perrault's story and those directly based on it depict Cinderella as sugar-sweet, insipidly good, and completely lacking initiative (251). In most variants, however, the heroine's innocence and virtue are stressed (Bettelheim, 246; Tatar, *Heads*, 98; Douglas, 28–29). Just as in King's version of "Cinderella," behind the surface of the character's humility lies in most variants the conviction of her superiority to stepmother and stepsisters (Bettelheim, 241). In the original fairy tale, the virtuous, diligent, and clever heroine outwits her evil and clumsy rivals, whereas not even King likes Carrie White. According to him, she "seemed thick and passive, a ready-made victim" (*OW*, 76). Emphasizing the difference between Carrie and her classmates, King depicts his humiliated and naked protagonist in the shower room: "She looked the part of the sacrificial goat, the constant butt, believer in left-handed monkey wrenches, perpetual foul-up, and she was" (*CA*, 4). Carrie's paranormal ability is apparently brought on by her first menstrual period: when five-year-old Tommy Erbter calls her names shortly after her period begins, she glares at him with rage, and his bike falls over. If *Carrie*, as King maintains, is about women finding their own channels of power (*DM*, 171), then Carrie is just discovering her endless source of power: "If only she could make something like that happen whenever she liked (just did)" (*CA*, 25). Undoubtedly, the telekinetic ability provides her with a feeling of superiority over her peers.

Blood is associated with female power in *Carrie*. It appears at all three crucial points of the story: the beginning (Carrie's first menstrual period), the climax (the prank with a bucket of pig's blood), and the end (Sue Snell discovers that she is not pregnant) (*OW*, 199). The innocent Carrie fails to understand her own sexuality, which further isolates her from her classmates, who are initiated into the mysteries of sex. Magistrale notes that Carrie's innocence produces a confused response to her body's menstruation, which in turn puts in motion the events that will finally destroy both Carrie and the whole town (*Voyages*, 45). Reino, too, compares Carrie's period to a bloody rite of passage, "from biological ignorance through sentimental fairy to massive myth" (17). In his view, as the fairy tale ends, the supernatural part begins, assuming almost Wagnerian dimensions. Relating Carrie's bloodbath to the Gothic, he goes on to compare the novel to the bloody revenge of Siegfried's wife, Kriemhild, for the murder of her husband in (the twelfth-century Middle High German epic romance) *Das Niebelungenlied* (16–17).

The good mother dies in "Cinderella," whereas the father's relation to her sufferings remains a mystery. An oddly passive figure, he steps aside to allow Cinderella's maltreatment, hoping that his daughter will combat the woman he has just married. King, in contrast, dares to depict the evil mother, maintaining that many fairy tales are thinly disguised hostility raps against parents. Children are aware that they would not survive without their parents, and this submission to their parents' domination frequently causes feelings of hate (Underwood and Miller, *Bones*, 206; *DM*, 102–4). In King's version of "Cinderella," the symbiotic relationship between Carrie and her mother excludes other human relations; hence, the father has died before the story begins. Appearing merely in short flashbacks in the memories of his wife, Margaret, and a neighbor, Stella Horan, Ralph White is described as his wife's equal in evil.

Maria Tatar claims that the *Nursery and Household Tales* by the Brothers Grimm include three types of ogres: (1) beasts and monsters (2) social deviants, and—outnumbering both other categories—(3) women (various cooks, stepmothers, witches, and mothers-in-law) (*Facts*, 139). As Greg Weller points out, the reader will instantly recognize Margaret White both as the Wicked Witch of the Gingerbread House and as a raving lunatic. On Carrie's prom night, when most mothers would be anxiously anticipating their child's return to hear about the date, Margaret White awaits Carrie's homecoming, sharpening a butcher's knife (8). Caught up in a prison with a mother who maltreats her because of her own twisted personality, Carrie shares a fate similar to Cinderella's. Of course, King takes his Cinderella version a step further, presenting Margaret as an actual threat to her daughter's life. Tatar claims that in spite of the oppression exercised by other family members, the fairy-tale heroine typically finds a way to escape and establish a new home. Significantly, however, she can only do this by being physically attractive and by proving her domestic skills (*Heads*, 137). Carrie, too, wishes to present herself as a dazzling beauty in order to find a source of salvation.

When Sue Snell acts as a fairy godmother, lending Prince Charming/her boyfriend Tommy Ross to Carrie for the prom

night, Carrie gets her chance to escape from home. Although Yarbro is right in her claim that Sue merely alleviates her shame for
having maltreated Carrie and that Prince Charming has to be returned by midnight (62), Carrie's beauty is acknowledged at the
prom. In fact, the reluctant escort falls for her, and the tragedy
implicit in the story includes the protagonist's close rescue and,
typically in King, fate. Tom Newhouse, too, refers to the complexity and the fatalistic ambivalence of the novel caused by
King's multiple explanations for the tragedy (53). Like the fairy-
tale Cinderella, Carrie both outwits her silly rivals and wins the
prince's heart. When one of her classmates, Norma Watson, wonders at her changed appearance, Carrie reveals that she has a famous lover (*CA,* 151). Tommy Ross, an athlete, an A student, a
good friend, and a fine young man (92–93), is characterized as a
true prince, and his feelings for Carrie grow from holding hands
to true love (90, 152). Reminiscent of a fairy-tale coronation,
Tommy ascends the stage as the King of the 1979 Spring Ball
with his Queen Carrie, thinking of her beauty and his own love
for her (169).

Carrie's beauty is also noted by her physical education
teacher, Ms. Desjardin (157), who represents both maternal care
and punishment in the novel: she takes care of Carrie after the
shower-room incident and mothers her at the prom as well as
punishes the other girls for their actions toward Carrie, thus re-
placing Carrie's incompetent mother. Weller compares Rita Desjardin to the goddess Artemis (7) with her "slim, nonbreasted"
body and "unobtrusive[ly] muscular" legs (*CA,* 5). She appears
in the girls' shower-room with "[a] silver whistle, won in college
archery competition" hanging around her neck (5). At the prom
she is "dressed in a glimmering silver sheath, a perfect comple-
ment to her blonde hair, which was up. A simple pendant hung
around her neck" (157). However, Artemis herself is unable to
hide her first reaction to Carrie's first period. Slapping the hys-
terical girl across the face, she "hardly would have admitted the
pleasure the act gave her, and she certainly would have denied
that she regarded Carrie as a fat, whiny bag of lard" (11). Hence,
both the original fairy tale and King's version include critical
portrayals of women.

King seems to echo Tatar's view of fairy tales in thinking that
nearly every character is capable of cruel behavior in his fiction

(*Facts*, 5). In King the ugly stepsisters have been replaced by the sexually initiated classmates. The inhumanity of the other girls in the locker room is evident (*CA*, 8). Rather than simply cruel or stupid, the other girls seem to be afraid of Carrie's obvious otherness. If Yarbro is right in her claim that the Cinderella myth in part deals with the proper programming of women in Western society (63), then Carrie's classmates must reject her to save their own skins in the high school pressure cooker. By her defiance of traditional femininity, Carrie is considered a threat. Significantly, however, when she brings her behavior and appearance into accord with them, the other girls are ready to welcome Carrie into their group. Voted the queen of the prom, she notes that the applause sounds "honest and deep, a little frightening" (*CA*, 168).

However, not everyone accepts Carrie. A Circe-like manipulator of men, Chris Hargensen appears to be the worst of Carrie's persecutors. Genuinely evil, she embodies Margaret White's vision of sex: "After the blood the boys come. Like sniffing dogs, grinning and slobbering, trying to find out where the smell is" (99). According to Weller, images of drunkenness and madness are embodied in the figures of Lilith and Circe, and the animalistic relationship between Chris and Billy Nolan emphasizes Chris's Circe-like transformative powers and illustrates the type of savage sexuality that Margaret White, ironically enough, imagines for her daughter and Tommy Ross (6, 11). Whether Weller is right in his claim that Billy plays Dionysus to Tommy's Apollo seems irrelevant to the final result of this modern Cinderella story (11): like God's holy fire, Carrie's rage sweeps away the whole town of Chamberlain.

Unlike in "Cinderella" nobody is victorious in *Carrie*, which seems the most obvious revision to the original fairy tale. Undoubtedly, King's version wishes to alter the reader's traditional patterns of thinking (Zipes, *Fairy Tale*, 10). The difference between King's retellings of *Dracula* and "Cinderella" lies largely in the final outcome of the stories: the adaptation provides a happy ending, whereas the revision shows no signs of mercy or redemption. Despite its criticism of small-town America, the two protagonists survive, and the vampire is destroyed in *'Salem's Lot*. In contrast, Carrie seems doomed from the beginning: both the protagonist and most of her oppressors lose their lives in *Carrie*. Yarbro argues that King has not knowingly written a latter-day

Cinderella story with an unfortunate outcome (63), whereas Reino claims that the Cinderella analogy seems deliberate (13). Well aware of King's tendency to draw from everything he has seen or read and to blend all the influences in order to create something new, I agree with the latter.

King's work is ample proof of his awareness of the archetypal forms of horror in myths and fairy tales. Instead of the exotic, he relies on the everyday world for his effect. King also avails himself of literary formulas in his plot development, and, as Yarbro notes, his style is low key and conversational, which allows him to use archetypes as they were once introduced in oral traditions (Yarbro, 69–70; Roberts, 36). Contradictory as it may sound, King's characters remain both developed and undeveloped at the same time, characters who in Samuel Schuman's terms are "at once unique and universal" (109). The characters' simple traits frequently represent the rather traditional worldview of the writer, and thus the reader has easy access to the story. This seeming paradox may result from the combination of fairy-tale characters and the intense realism in King's works.

Here is a final illustration of my point. In *The Eyes of the Dragon*, King introduces King Roland as lazy, slightly naive, exuberant, and unpolished. Spying his father through a peephole, Thomas sees his father often pick his nose when he is alone. Such details are seldom given in any kind of story, but King takes the reader's revulsion a step further: "He would root around in first one nostril and then the other until he got a plump green booger. He would regard these with solemn satisfaction, turning each one this way and that in the firelight, the way a jeweler might turn a particularly fine emerald. Most of these he would then rub under the chair in which he was sitting. Others, I regret to say, he popped into his mouth and munched with an expression of reflective enjoyment on his face" (97). Undoubtedly, the depiction of this "old man who fart[s] out stinking clouds of steam" and "pisse[s] into the fire, sending up more clouds of steam" has many functions in King (98). Throughout his fiction King has described his characters through their actions. In this example the reader is provided with both an unrefined picture of Roland the Good and an embarrassing but lifelike scene with which to identify. As a result King's fairy-tale characters become flesh and blood through their realistic actions and the author's insights into the human psyche.

Mythical and Fairy-Tale Themes

Mythical and fairy-tale motifs occur as an integral part of all of King's fiction. As products of their society, writers tend to rely on archetypal constructs in various degrees in order to prepare the ground for the reader. King is especially sensitive to these archetypes, and mythical and fairy-tale themes appear in virtually all his stories, including his shorter works. For instance, in *Night Shift* (1978) the stories "Jerusalem's Lot" and "One for the Road" relate to the vampire myth; "Night Surf" is thematically related to *The Stand* (1978); Reino regards "I Am the Doorway" as a twentieth-century Arthurian romance (112); "Children of the Corn" alludes to the Bible; "Strawberry Spring" invests the berry with mythical and sexual significance; and "The Lawnmower Man" refers to Pan. In the following discussion I will confine myself to three novels to illustrate my point: *The Shining* (1977), *Firestarter* (1980), and *It* (1986). These three have been chosen because they focus on mythical and fairy-tale themes in King from different angles: three fairy tales resonate throughout *The Shining; Firestarter,* although lacking direct references to any specific fairy tales or myths, includes a host of fairy-tale traits; and a fairy-tale motif echoes throughout *It.*

THE SHINING

"Hansel and Gretel," "that most cautionary of nursery tales" (*DM*, 174), and "Goldilocks" are alluded to when Dick Hallorann of *The Shining* commences to show the Torrance family the Overlook Hotel. Afraid of getting lost in the large kitchen, Wendy decides to leave a trail of breadcrumbs every time she goes there. Dwarfed by the sheer magnitude of the kitchen, Wendy reacts to the multiple ovens in the Overlook Hotel much as Goldilocks did to the parental furniture in the house of the three bears (Curran, 37; *SH*, 84–85). To underscore the imminent threat and the fairy-tale atmosphere of the novel, King has Wendy realize the ominousness of the situation: like fairy-tale creatures, the family will have to stay in the deserted Overlook, eating leftovers (*SH*, 85).

Aptly, Donald T. Curran notes that the fairy tales in *The Shining* both shape the lives of the characters and determine their general temperament, thus guiding the reader and the Torrances in their shared experience of primal fear (33).

When Danny introduces the third fairy tale, "Bluebeard" (*SH*, 100), the reader may already anticipate what the child hero will shortly learn. If "Hansel and Gretel" allows King to suggest a sibling relationship between Wendy and Danny menaced by the devouring-mother qualities of the hotel, then "Bluebeard" suggests a negative father archetype (Curran, 38–39). The drunken Jack Torrance reads "Bluebeard" to his son, and Danny later thinks that the tale is linked with the secret of Room 217, his father's short temper, and his mother's golden hair. The parallels are made clear enough:

Actually the story was about *Bluebeard*'s wife, a pretty lady that had corn-colored hair like Mommy. After *Bluebeard* married her, they lived in a big and ominous castle that was not unlike the Overlook. And every day *Bluebeard* went off to work and every day he would tell his pretty little wife not to look in a certain room, although the key to that room was hanging right on the hook, just like the passkey was hanging on the office wall downstairs. *Bluebeard*'s wife had gotten more and more curious about the locked room. She tried to peep through the keyhole the way Danny had tried to look through Room 217's peephole with similar unsatisfying results. (*SH*, 182–83, italics in original)

"Bluebeard" both allows Danny to write himself into the story and anticipates the future events (Curran, 39). Instead of the dead bodies of Bluebeard's seven previous wives, Danny encounters Mrs. Massey, the suicide of Room 217 (*SH*, 232).

King depicts the all-devouring qualities of the Overlook Hotel in graphic terms: "Inside its shell the three of them went about their early evening routine, like microbes trapped in the intestine of a monster" (225). Emphasizing the image of eating and being eaten, he introduces a new fairy tale, "Little Red Riding Hood," combined with the surrealistic images of "Bluebeard": "*(what big teeth you have grandma and is that a wolf in a BLUEBEARD suit or a BLUEBEARD in a wolf suit)*" (229, italics and capitals in original). The white rabbit of *Alice in Wonderland* leads Danny to the yawning abyss of Room 217, and the reference to the Red Queen's violent croquet party anticipates Jack Torrance's homicidal attack on his family with the roque mallet. Aware that he is violating an interdiction, Danny turns the key and encounters the Red Queen (230). Later, while escaping the corpse, Danny wonders if the fairy tale concerns the queen's croquet or his father's roque (232).

By employing fairy tales in *The Shining*, King takes the reader back into the world of childhood, where "our own shadow may once again become that of a mean dog, a gaping mouth, or a beckoning dark figure" (*DM*, 101). This is a world where magical thinking precedes ego defense and where parental power is absolute, despite the threat children may have of being abandoned and annihilated (Curran, 33). In King's view children, like Danny Torrance, are able to deal with fantasy and terror on their own terms better than adults because of the size of their imaginative capacity and their unique position in life (*DM*, 102). The fairy tales of *The Shining* also link the events within the text with cultural and historical archetypes. Their symbols and narrative structure fuse the events and the personal relationships of the fairy tale with larger, a priori patterns of human behavior. Magistrale claims that the matters of life and death assume larger dimensions than those of the personal issues in the domestic, time-bound realm of the Torrance family. He points out that several fairy tales resonate throughout *The Shining* and give its core scenes a rich intertextuality, providing passkeys that open the doors to altered states of mind that border on the realm of madness and the process in which a child's archetypal predispositions expose him to the personal flaws of his parents (*Decade*, 34–35).

FIRESTARTER

Although *Firestarter* lacks direct biblical, mythical, or fairy-tale references, it alludes to the persecution of both the child Jesus and the infant Heracles/Hercules and evokes the Greek myth of Pallas Athene; the fairy tale "Beauty and the Beast" also resonates throughout the novel. A victim of an immoral experiment, the eight-year old Charlene "Charlie" McGee of *Firestarter* is able to create a nuclear explosion by the force of her will. In the hopes of harnessing Charlie's power for its own twisted purposes, a secret government agency known as the Shop captures Charlie and her father, after having eliminated the mother. In her captivity Charlie becomes acquainted with John Rainbird, the Shop killer, with whom she develops an odd relationship, reminiscent of that between Beauty and the Beast. Yarbro notes that King depicts the protagonist as a fairy child or a changeling brought into the twentieth century. Simultaneously a mutant and one of King's wise children, Charlie allows the author to explore the strength and the power of childhood in great detail (68). An attractive child able to make moral choices, Charlie is capable of showing initiative and accepting responsibility (Leiber, "Horror Hits a High," 111). Even though Carrie White of *Carrie*, despite her older age, is mastered by her power, Charlie is determined to master hers (Bosky, "Stephen King and Peter Straub," 69). Charlie also seems deeper in the White force than her father, who has had too much time to think about his own ability (Grant, 169). To some extent Charlie's psychic powers appear to be a curse to her, because she must constantly control them and realize that they can never become a magic carpet of escape (Indick, "Horror," 182). However, she is torn by the pressure to use her pyrokinetic ability to save her father and herself from death, by the guilt stemming from her parents' training that the power is a "Bad Thing" (*FS*, 19), and by her increasing pleasure in making use of her ability (Winter, *Art*, 89).

Like the infant Heracles/Hercules, who was singled out by Hera and who survived several assassination attempts (Forty, 286), Charlie is tested by circumstances and escapes peril by using her inborn abilities (Yarbro, 68). There, however, the similarity to Hercules ends: Hercules went on to achieve superhuman feats (Forty, 286), whereas Charlie has been trained to hide her power. Driven mad by Hera, Hercules killed his family in a frenzy and undertook his twelve labors in repentance (286), whereas the innocent Charlie is persecuted by the government for her special qualities—like the child Jesus by King Herod. Hence, not one but several myths are intertwined in *Firestarter*. Referring to Charlie as a demigod who has remained true to her heritage and to herself, Yarbro regards Rainbird as Charlie's mythical antithesis, a demigod who has perverted his gift and therefore has the mark of the beast on his scarred face (69). Rather than a minister of an evil king or a pawn of the government, Rainbird seems to be a free enterpriser who takes assignments for the sake of pleasure. He clearly regards himself as such: "He was his own man, crippled soldier of fortune, copper-skinned angel of death" (*FS*, 340). Obsessed with death, this amoral, one-eyed

Polyphemus is motivated by neither greed nor revenge, but by an endless quest for an understanding of his own inescapable demise (Winter, *Art*, 90).

Similarly, the relationship between Charlie and her father can be viewed in terms of myth. Although implications of incest and child-molestation prove wrong, suggestions of androgyny seem to draw on the myth of Pallas Athene. Charlie looks like her mother (*FS*, 7), but her name (Charlene/Charlie [53]), her slender, agile body structure (229), Andy McGee's comparison of the pyrokinetic ability with the nocturnal seminal emissions of most teenage boys (176), and her love of fast horses (301) all emphasize Charlie's androgynous qualities. Held in captivity, Andy becomes fat, passive, and lazy (217), whereas Rainbird admires Charlie's warrior-like qualities and toughness "more than he could have said" (213). In an attempt to win Charlie's trust for their final "long waltz for death" (340), Rainbird pretends friendship. Unable to make her laugh, he reaches his goal by arousing sympathy in the empathetic girl. Similarly, Athena/Pallas Athene/Minerva, the warlike goddess of wisdom and the daughter of Zeus and Metis (Forty, 256), inherited her compassion from Metis, her displaced mother. To annul a prophesy, according to which the child that the pregnant Metis carried would surpass his father, Zeus swallowed his latest progeny. He then developed a headache that was only relieved when Hephaestus split his forehead, and Pallas Athene emerged fully grown and armed to the teeth (256). The epithet "Pallas" signifies "competent," "courageous," and "virginal." In the same way, Charlie fights for her father and herself. Since she is also related to Nike, the goddess of victory, this modern Pallas Athene clears the obstacles in her way and attains the decisive victory. Stronger than her father, Charlie can release her powers only after Andy has recognized and faced evil in himself.

The triangle of Charlie McGee, her father, and Rainbird is suggested most effectively through dream sequences and evokes "Beauty and the Beast." As Winter points out, Beauty's father is menaced by the Beast in his design to capture Beauty and obtain her love so as to release himself from his hideous appearance. However, instead of the elegantly resolved conflict between Beauty's love for her father and the Beast, Charlie realizes that she has been deceived by Rainbird—what he seeks is her to join

him in death (*Art,* 91). As in "Beauty and the Beast," *Firestarter*
focuses on the relationship of the heroine and the beast and is
viewed from two angles. King makes the juxtaposition of the
beautiful blonde and the half Cherokee Vietnam veteran clear
enough. "[A]s big as life and twice as ugly" (*FS,* 82), Rainbird is
depicted as "a troll, an orc, a balrog of a man" (83). Despite his
homicidal tendencies and his total amorality, he, like the original
Beast, seems almost likeable, because the reader is given some
insight into the forces that have shaped him and some sympathy
for his intentions (Notkin, 160–61). Determined to have the girl
who can light fires, Rainbird develops tender and protective feelings toward Charlie (*FS,* 135). Apart from his professional interest in Charlie, he wishes to follow her into death and decides to
look carefully into her eyes while killing her: "And then, if her
eyes gave him the signal he had looked for so long, perhaps he
would follow her" (240). Like a lover he dreams of a future together: they would step into the flames together, but "it would be
an act of love, not of destruction" (340).

Charlie's viewpoint emphasizes humanity and compassion.
The Beast's feelings do not go completely unanswered, and even
in captivity Beauty retains her ability to feel sorry for her fellow
human beings. She approaches Rainbird with a child's direct-
ness, understanding that a person cannot be judged merely by
his looks (231–32). When Rainbird finally wins her trust, Charlie
agrees to cooperate with the Shop "for John" (257). Regarding
herself as a freak, she accepts Rainbird's kindness with simple
gratitude. She likes him because of his kindness to her, sympa-
thizing and identifying with him on account of his disfigured
face (287). In her highly sexual dreams, Charlie rides a horse with
a fitting name, Necromancer, and encounters a threatening male
figure that her subconscious is able to recognize. At first she
thinks it is her father, but her joy transforms into terror when she
registers the fact that the man is "too big, too tall—and yet somehow familiar, dreadfully familiar, even in silhouette" (302).

In King the good are also subjected to suffering and pain for
the simple reason that they are human. Charlie remains loyal to
Rainbird, unlike the fairy-tale heroine who forgets her bride-
groom for a while when visiting her father. However, she is
forced to face Rainbird's betrayal and the cruel choice between
him and her father: "John or Daddy? Daddy or John?" (325).

King compares her pain to growing up: if it was about dealing with this hurt, Charlie would like to die young (325). Her essential strength, however, shows in her ability to recover. Musing on her final confrontation with the Shop agents, she grimly hopes that Rainbird will not come near either her or Andy. Finally, then, despite a strong temptation to follow Rainbird in death, she takes responsibility for her father and herself, realizing that "whatever John Rainbird might mean to her, he meant only death for her father" (360). In conclusion, in the tradition of heroic fairy tales, *Firestarter* begins with an ordeal and a persecution and ends with revenge—justice will triumph at any cost (Yarbro 69).

In *Firestarter* King treats the relationship between individual and society by means of the fantastic and in fact summarizes the function of myths and fairy tales in the novel in the afterword. Although the novel is fiction, most of its components are based on unpleasant, inexplicable, or simply fascinating real-life happenings. As King writes at the end of *Firestarter*, "[T]he world, although well-lighted with fluorescents and incandescent bulbs and neon, is still full of odd dark corners and unsettling nooks and crannies" (402–3). Progenitors of most literature, myths and fairy tales depict the most violent and treacherous behavior, and they require heroic though often harsh remedies (Yarbro, 61). Although his use of myths and fairy tales follows a long-standing literary tradition, King combines the Gothic heritage, myths, and fairy tales with realism, the very blend of which contributes to his large readership.

I T

In *It* children are depicted as the keepers and the guarantors of humanity's reputation (Warner, *Six Myths of Our Time*, 35). They have the quickest understanding of the source of danger that has come to Derry, and they should, too, because the monster preys primarily on them and is "especially hungry for boymeat" (*IT*, 19). The genesis of *It* was King's crossing a wooden bridge, listening to the hollow thump of his boot heels, and thinking of "The Three Billy Goats Gruff" (*SC*, vii). Although this fairy tale resonates throughout the novel, the troll under the bridge is depicted as "the apotheosis of all monsters" (*IT*, 18), and, instead of three goats, the bridge is crossed by Snow White and her six dwarves, that is, Beverly Marsh and the male members of the

Losers' Club. King regards *It* as his final exam in writing on child-hood (Magistrale, *Voyages*, 5). Moreover, for King, Beverly Marsh as Snow White represents the advent of manhood through the act of sex (6). Significantly, too, Bruno Bettelheim relates dwarves to prepubescent existence, "a period during which all forms of sexuality are relatively dormant" (210). Like Snow White, Beverly (Bev) escapes a parental threat, spending much of her preadoles-cent period with the dwarves/the Losers' Club before the evil queen/It disturbs her life again. Moving into adolescence, she faces a time of troubles again—however, now she is no longer a child who must passively suffer what her father inflicts on her, but a person who must take responsibility for her own life.

Although Bettelheim views the relation of Snow White and the queen as a mother-daughter conflict (210), Bev and It rep-resent good and evil in King (Magistrale, *Voyages*, 6). In Linda Anderson's view, *It* attempts to resolve the pre-Oedipal conflict through male language (112), whereas Karen Thoens regards it as "the pursuit of male mastery over a menacing female sexual-ity" (127). In contrast, King views Bev's role as that of the earth mother who brings forth adults (Magistrale, *Voyages*, 7). These different views do not necessarily exclude each other in King, whose monstrous mothers have been frequently and thoroughly documented. Just as in Bettelheim, however, King's modern Snow White remains the child in her own abusive marriage until she finally kills the queen/It (Bettelheim, 211–14; *IT*, 117). Bev's early encounters with the monster can be viewed as equivalents of the witch's stay laces, poisoned comb, and poisoned apple. In fact, one of these encounters presents the monster as the witch (*IT*, 560–68). Also, her amnesia concerning the incidents in Derry can be seen as corresponding to Snow White's deathlike sleep. Finally, the prince's kiss is later rendered as a sexual encounter between Bev and Bill Denbrough. Along the same lines as this analogy of the kiss with sex, the dwarves are also able to revive Snow White after the first two trials, but the sex-related apple re-quires a mature man to bring her to life (Bettelheim, 212–13). In the final analysis, King's treatment of Snow White as the initiator in the dwarves' rite of passage has to be regarded as a deliberate deviation from the traditional roles of these fairy-tale characters.

"Hansel and Gretel," another fairy tale to which *It* alludes (*IT*, 560–68, 1031), also discusses abandonment and child abuse, thus

reinforcing and echoing the prevalent theme of the novel. As
Yarbro points out, myths and fairy tales abound with cautionary
tales of the people who learn their lesson too late and pay for
their ignorance and obstinacy with their lives, souls, and/or fortunes (64). Like the residents of 'Salem's Lot, the townspeople of
Derry refuse to note that they might be dealing with a great danger. What is more, the manipulative, oppressive, distant, or ignorant parents contribute to their children's misery and expose
them to the monster. Both Anderson and Thoens emphasize the
maternal failure in *It* (Anderson, 111–25; Thoens, 127–40), but the
paternal failure is also evident: only Mike Hanlon has a warm relationship with his father. In addition to the incestuous Al Marsh,
Richard Macklin breaks the bones of his four-year-old stepson
with a hammer (*IT,* 255). Without disparaging the mothers' responsibility, I find it rather odd that Anderson takes the domestic violence of the fathers for granted and accuses the mothers
of their inability to protect their children (115). Although I in
part agree with Gail E. Burns and Melinda Kanner's claim that
"[f]emale reproductive potential, sexuality, and death are forged
by King in a manner that invariably locks his female characters
into particular sexually defined roles" (160), I believe that Anderson's point reinforces stereotypes. At any rate, it remains a fact
that King comments on domestic violence and both male- and
female-generated child abuse and negligence in *It.*

In the dedication of *It,* King emphasizes the function of myths
and fairy tales in his fiction: "Kids, fiction is the truth inside the
lie, and the truth of this fiction is simple enough: *the magic exists*"
(italics in original). In other words, these stories that we frequently refer to as mere fiction tell us the truth about ourselves.
"The Three Billy Goats Gruff" tells us the truth about parents who
treat their children worse than any fictional monsters ever can.
While crossing the bridge from childhood to maturity, the de-
fenseless and dependent children have to rely on the assumption
that the troll does not take the face of their own parents, as it does
in *It* (778, 891–94). "The Three Billy Goats Gruff" is introduced explicitly in the novel, since it is read aloud in the children's library.
Although some of the children giggle at Miss Davies's growling
tones of the troll, most accept "the voice of the troll as they accepted the voices of their dreams" (186). The innocent listeners

are completely unaware of the real troll whose victims King lists on the next page.

Although the monster attacks its victims in secluded places, it typically hides in sewers and under bridges. Feeding on the deepest fears of children, the beast embodies terror itself. During the reunion of the Losers' Club, Mike Hanlon remarks that the troll has returned under the bridge again (497) and, even worse, has called them back by killing nine children (506-7). In the tradition of heroic fairy tales, the club members accept the challenge without the assurance of survival or victory (519-21). And, indeed, the battle has begun: when Ben Hanscom enters the children's library, the same fairy tale is being read aloud again (535-36). The seemingly innocent children's tale changes into a tale of horror when the monster threatens the Losers' Club in words reminiscent of the Gingerbread Man from the fairy tale by the same name: *"Try to stop me and I'll kill you all!"* (718, italics in original). Like the giant from "Jack and the Beanstalk," the statue of Paul Bunyan, patron saint of fictional Derry and real-life Bangor, attacks Richie Tozier with his axe: "Unless you give me back my hen and my harp and my bags of gold, I'm going to eat you right the fuck *up!*" (578, italics in original). Undoubtedly, King plays with the contradiction between the seemingly innocent and simple children's tales and the more frightening tensions implicit in them (and in the vulgar language) in order to touch both our cultural and personal "phobic pressure points," to use King's own phrase.

Since the parents refuse to take responsibility for their children, the children must do so themselves. King alludes to *The Lord of the Rings* to emphasize the magnitude and the desperate nature of the quest. References to the fantasy classic also imply the predestination of the events and the fact that the individual club members are willing to shoulder responsibility at the risk of their lives. Mike Hanlon, the black librarian of Derry, refers to the novel's famous idea that "way leads on to way," indicating that adventures may begin on one's doorstep (*IT*, 452; Tolkien, *Rings*, 86-87). Bill Denbrough repeats the age-old question voiced by Frodo: "*Why me?*" (*IT*, 651; Tolkien, *Rings*, 74-75, italics in original) when his friends need him to tell them what to do. More than any single reference to this novel, the monster itself bears obvious resemblance to Shelob the Great, "an evil thing in spider-form" (Tolkien, *Rings*, 750). Like King's spider-monster, who has resided in Derry from the beginning of time, Tolkien's female monster entered her lair before Sauron's arrival and serves merely her own interests: "death for all others, mind and body, and for herself a glut of life, alone, swollen till the mountains could no longer hold her up and the darkness could not contain her" (751; for King's spider-monster, see "Cosmological Determinism and Fate" in chapter 3).

In addition to individual fairy tales or novels, King alludes to the Bible throughout his fiction, and *It* is no exception. In the tradition of myths and the oral tradition of Christianity, the members of the Losers' Club hold hands in a circle, and identical stigmata appear on their palms before the confrontation with the monster (*IT*, 143–44, 885–86). In contrast to the adults ironic view of God as a deity who "jerks the rug under their feet" (39), the childlike minds of their offspring approach God in concrete terms. Richie, for instance, knows that "the Bible believed in all sorts of weird stuff": ghosts, demons, and witches, and "every word of it was true—so said Reverend Craig and so said Richie's folks and so said Richie" (333). Against this background it becomes obvious that the children understand that the monster really exists, constitutes a major threat, and has to be fought against.

In King's work the symbiotic connection between myths, fairy tales, the horror genre, and realist fiction is evident. Since these genres share most functions, it comes as no surprise that they share most of their themes too. Thus, it appears only natural that King as a blender and shifter of genres would make use of these functionally and thematically interrelated genres.

3

Literary Naturalism in King's Works

In his fiction King reverts again and again to the duality between good and evil and the fact that human beings personify both. The very exercise of free will poses the major problems for the protagonists in most of his stories, and therefore it is the basis of my analysis of naturalistic traits in his fiction. The discussion of King's various types of determinism takes the individual character as the starting point and proceeds through genetic determinism and sociological determinism to cosmological determinism and, finally, to metafictional determinism, the means by which the author controls the forces controlling his fictional multiverse. In brief, the main issues analyzed in some detail are the question of whether human will is free or constrained (the section "Free Will and Responsibility") and the four types of determinism in King, including fate with its various synonyms ("Genetic and Sociological Determinism," "Cosmological Determinism and Fate," and "Metafictional Determinism").

Martin Gray defines *naturalism* as "[a] more particularised branch of *realism*" (135). Therefore, before I discuss the naturalistic traits in King, it is worthwhile to consider whether he can also be regarded as a realist. Peter Lamarque and Stein Haugom Olsen in *Truth, Fiction, and Literature* view *realism* as having three prominent features: "a certain kind of *aim*, namely, truth-telling or 'faithfulness' to the facts; a certain kind of *content*, the representation of social reality in particulars; and a certain kind of *form*, involving simplicity rather than ornateness, mirroring that

of documentary history" (311–12, italics in original). While Lamarque and Olsen define the aim of realism as a documentation
of real facts, King deals with real-life fears through allegory. He
argues that "the horror genre has been able to find national phobic
pressure points, and those books and films which have been the
most successful almost always seem to play upon and express
fears which exist across a wide spectrum of people" (*DM*, 5). Allegory is needed, because "if the shit starts getting too thick, [au-
thors and filmmakers] can always bring the monster shambling
out of the darkness again" (5). Although he explores the difficult
questions of real life and, in a sense, documents American life,
King takes liberties to advance his ideas. On a number of occasions, he has also expressed the paradox implicit in the horror
genre: "Reality *is* an unnatural order" (Winter, *Art*, 114, italics in
original) and "Fiction is the truth inside the lie" (*DM*, 403). During
his search for moral truth, King frequently surpasses the boundaries of realism and cannot thus be regarded as a realist in the
strict sense of the term.

In other words, only a few of his stories could actually take
place in real life, and even the vast majority of these stories are
borderline cases. Of all his writing, "The Body," a thinly veiled
autobiographical, coming-of-age story, presents King at his most
realistic. It relates the story of four friends who undertake a rite
of passage to find the corpse of a boy who has disappeared, but
who, in fact, has been hit by a train. When dealing with issues of
mortality, King discusses them in terms of fate. As Leonard G.
Heldreth notes, even the surname of the protagonist and King's
alter ego, Gordon Lachance, can be regarded as a pun on both
King's unexpected success as a writer and the twists of fate in
general ("Viewing 'The Body,'" 73). Also, any one of the novella's
boys could have been hit by the train in place of Ray Browner.
Similarly, it is a mere twist of fate that Lachance was the only one
to survive into manhood. Although "The Body," like a number of
other King stories, lacks the supernatural element, King admits
that "[e]lements of horror can be found in all of the tales . . .—that
business with the slugs in *The Body* is pretty gruesome" (*DS*, 502,
italics in original). In other words, King labels his most realistic
story horror.

From documented shooting incidents at schools, we know
that—unlike in *Rage*—pupils do not stay in classrooms to discuss

their personal problems with a killer when their school is surrounded by the police and their mathematics teacher lies dead on the floor. The collection *Night Shift* includes merely two stories that can in any way be regarded as documents of real life. "The Last Rung on the Ladder" relates the sad story of brother and sister drifting apart, which indirectly results in the sister's suicide, and "The Woman in the Room" depicts a man who helps his dying mother commit suicide. Although serial killers occasionally stalk among us, a man in a bloody suit looking for Norma would soon be arrested by the police ("The Man Who Loved Flowers" in *Night Shift*). Even though the resistance Bart Dawes offers to defy the circumstances he lives in might be within the limits of credence, the events of *Roadwork* appear to be too extreme. The same goes for *Cujo*. The borderline cases include such works as "Rita Hayworth and Shawshank Redemption" *(Different Seasons)*, "Apt Pupil" *(Different Seasons)*, *Misery*, *Gerald's Game*, *Dolores Claiborne*, and "My Pretty Pony" *(Nightmares and Dreamscapes)*.

As regards content and form in Lamarque and Olsen's definition of realism, that is, faithfulness to the facts, King's fiction seems equally contradictory. Although sociological concerns run through virtually all his novels, they coexist with supernatural phenomena. Furthermore, although a simple style and vernacular have become the hallmark of his fiction, King's style can seldom be regarded as purely documentary. As a blender of genres, King cannot simply be placed in a single category. What makes King's realism so effective is in part due to the contrast of realism and fantasy in his works. Also, his stories consist of blends of his own fears and experiences, which undoubtedly make them honest and real to the reader. When King is able to express these fears and experiences in a popular manner as well as couple them with wider thematic concerns, honest characters, and an intriguing narrative form, he is at his best.

Literary naturalism has to be distinguished from *realism*. If Donald Pizer is right when he states that "the form of the naturalistic novel begins to create an effect of uncertainty, of doubt and perplexity, about whether anything can be gained or learned from experience" (37), a number of distinctly naturalistic works can be distinguished in King's oeuvre, such as the early Bachman books: *Rage* (1977), *The Long Walk* (1979), *Roadwork* (1981), and

The Running Man (1982). However, confining the analysis concerning literary naturalism to these works would be to miss the point of this study. It is my task to demonstrate how Stephen King blends genres; thus, I attempt to show how the idiosyncratic balance of free will versus determinism, the four types of determinism, and fate can be detected throughout King's oeuvre. I focus on these particular aspects, because they represent the most naturalistic traits in King's fiction.

On a number of occasions, Stephen King has stated that he wrote his first novel not as a horror writer but as a literary naturalist ("Brand Name," 20). As regards naturalistic traits in his fiction, two features are especially significant: the balance between the supernatural and the rational (which is termed *magical realism* by Tony Magistrale [*Voyages*, 69], *supernational naturalism* by Jeanne Campbell Reesman [112], and *rational supernaturalism* by Douglas E. Winter [*Art*, 9]), and the various types of determinism. Winter maintains that in seeking to escape into the irrationality of horror fiction, we realize our need for reality and vice versa. King's fiction recognizes this paradox. He argues that horror is not merely an escape outward, into a kind of never-never land; it is also an escape inward, into our own selves. Hence, King's fiction is marked by the merging of the natural or the rational into the supernatural, and the reader is forced to decide whether there is some kind of order (Winter, *Art*, 112–13). Reesman provides a paraphrase of Winter's claim by arguing that "King is pursuing the American tradition of hermeneutics of doubt" (107). Since at best horror fiction is a dark analogy of reality, King's horror cannot be separated from his deterministic worldview and literary naturalism. Let me in brief illustrate my point by considering the interplay between horror and literary naturalism in *Cujo*.

The horror in *Cujo* is both predestined and real. Vic and Donna Trenton are struggling to save their marriage; little Tad Trenton fears for the monster in his closet; the stubborn car mechanic, Joe Camber, abuses his wife and raises his son to act accordingly. Despite the horror of their everyday lives, King suggests that the Castle Rock residents might in fact be confronting a supernatural threat in the form of the dead rapist-killer, Frank Dodd. The anxieties of reality are thus projected as supernatural insinuations. According to Winter, the implications of adding a supernatural factor are twofold: to efface the impression of the novel's unforgiving realism and to confirm that the evil of *Cujo* emanates from an outside source, not from the act of any character (*Art,* 109). King notes that the dog that terrorizes the town is Frank Dodd "only in the sense that there's something evil happening here, and it's outside evil; it's a visitation" (109). The writer emphasizes his naturalistic stance in the closing pages of the novel: Cujo "had never wanted to kill anybody. He had been struck by something, possibly destiny, or fate, or only a degenerative nerve disease called rabies. Free will was never a factor" (*CU,* 318).

While Winter views literary naturalism in King as *rational supernaturalism,* Reesman refers to it as *supernatural naturalism,* that is, the "tendency to join the everyday to the cosmic, conscious to unconscious, light to dark" (105). She widens Winter's definition, for instance, by taking universal fairy-tale features into consideration and by not confining the definition merely to the interplay between horror and literary naturalism. By combining archetypes and our modern reality, King's supernatural naturalism simultaneously juxtaposes and fuses the supernatural and the realistic. By modernizing and Americanizing the horror genre, he has been able to create a present-day naturalism. In King readers are able to confront their everyday anxieties in a traditional disguise, that is, in the form of a vampire tale or a ghost story. Thus, the durability of King's popularity is to some extent based on the contemporary focus of his writing (105–6). As Reesman puts it, King's characters must first realize that they exist in a naturalistic universe and then give up the realization in favor of a more expanded sense of reality that also includes the supernatural. In other words, the supernatural intrudes on our everyday awareness of contemporary culture and morals in order to shock us into an awareness of a moral reality deeper than that to which we are accustomed (109). If we widen the notion of the supernatural to encompass the Gothic and myths and fairy tales as well, Reesman's argument pinpoints an essential feature of King's oeuvre. She claims that in King's work we find "an ironic set of oppositions: supernaturalism (horror) vs. naturalism (reality), and good (unconscious knowledge) vs. evil (conscious knowledge). The first opposition causes the second to occur as a moral choice for a character, and only very morally astute characters can perceive the truth phrased as a reversal of everyday suppositions about the primacy of consciousness and rationality" (109–10). These characters are typically represented by brave children and adults who have access to their childhood memories.

In addition to the balance between the supernatural and the rational, various types of determinism shape the lives of King's characters. Most scholars seem to recognize genetic and sociological determinism as naturalistic traits in literature. Edwin J. Barton and Glenda A. Hudson point out that the premise of literary naturalism is that human beings are determined by forces beyond their control: nature, heredity, and social forces (117). M. H. Abrams also refers to authors such as Thomas Hardy who substituted a cosmic determinism for biological and environmental determinism (154). Referring to the Salem witch hunt, Hugh Trevor-Roper in *The European Witch-Craze of the Sixteenth and Seventeenth Centuries and Other Essays* argues that a Thomistic mapping of heaven and its powers prompted an extensive map of an inverted, although parallel, region below, complete with its attendant minions. He charts a peculiar internal logic by which what had been originally a matter of arcane metaphysics— witch-hunting—became at first a socially necessary effect of bully politics and then a spectacular civic rite (see also Ingebretsen, 11–30). Echoes of the Puritan cosmology, combined with sociological determinism, can be heard throughout King's fiction. I would go as far as to claim that King's brand of horror directly draws on the Puritan theological metaphysics turned into social control—and punishment. Edward J. Ingebretsen points out that in *Carrie* King adapts formulas of the captivity narrative and the spiritual autobiography to the ends of horror. Both captivity and possession have been metaphors with deep cultural resonance since Winthrop and the Great Migration (19). Throughout King's fiction, socially aberrant behavior is severely punished. In *'Salem's Lot*, for example, unrestrained sexuality turns the townspeople into vampires, whereas the reluctance to shoulder responsibility transforms the residents of Haven into outer-space aliens in *The Tommyknockers*. As regards determinism, Barton and Hudson distinguish between *hard determinism*, which views the thoughts, emotions, and activities of human beings as almost completely determined by external forces and circumstances, and *soft determinism*, which concedes that humans can exercise free will (117–18). Since King's characters have a choice

between good and evil, his various types of determinism conform to the latter.

In King humans are determined genetically (by inheritance),
sociologically (by human social relations and conditions), cosmologically (by cosmological forces), and—to use Bo Pettersson's notion and definition—metafictionally, as when his novels
begin with a plot outline (*Vonnegut*, 34). Genetic and sociological
determinism are apparently inherited from literary naturalism
and personal experience during the formative years. Although
recent research emphasizes the cooperative action of genetic and
sociological determinism and views human beings as the result
of both, the two types of determinism will be discussed in the
same section. A number of King's characters are born with a
variety of supernatural abilities that isolate them socially. In
contrast, the main cause of insanity appears to be either a character's own volition (for instance, Randall Flagg in *The Stand, The
Eyes of the Dragon,* and *The Dark Tower* series and Abe Kurtz in
Dreamcatcher) or a breakdown (for instance, Louis Creed in *Pet
Sematary* and Tansy Freneau in *Black House*). Somewhat disturb-
ingly, virtually all of King's evil characters turn out to be insane
and seemingly at the same time enjoy their mental state, unless
they are reminded of it. Breakdowns, in turn, are frequently related to unbearable mental stress (see, for instance, "Hubris and
Death [Frankenstein's Monster]" in chapter 1). However, King
distinguishes insanity from retardation, and the latter is depicted
in a positive fashion (Tom Cullen in *The Stand* and Duddits in
Dreamcatcher). Furthermore, when King explores drugs and alcohol addiction (for instance, through characters such as Father
Callahan in *'Salem's Lot,* Jack Torrance in *The Shining,* and Eddie
Dean in *The Dark Tower* series), he views various types of addiction as a social problem.

In King cosmological determinism shapes the lives of humans through three agents: (1) the mythical forces related to *The
Dark Tower* series (2) God, and (3) other extraterrestrials, such as
science-fiction aliens. One aspect of his cosmological determinism is a secularized version of the Calvinistic creed of predestination. Hence King's affinity with the origins of American literary thought, Puritanism, which in a number of ways underlies
naturalism in American literature. To a lesser extent, it is also inherited from universal myths in the form of Joseph Campbell's

ideas (Magistrale, *Decade,* 3). A third aspect of cosmological determinism in King is the extraterrestrial control of life on earth. It is, however, undercut by science-fiction parody in which the aliens are introduced as either losers *(The Tommyknockers)* or driven by their newly discovered human instincts *(Dreamcatcher).* Despite the parodical treatment of the motif, King seems to give it some credence—in his view, humans do not exist alone in the universe. In the final analysis the three approaches lead to a rather coherent cosmological view of humankind's existence in the universe. Based on a Thomistic mapping of heaven and its powers with their respective counterparts on earth, the Puritan order passed sentences on social deviants, such as witches, in times when the *polis* was threatened. In a similar vein horror fiction projects the threat of war and the fear of technological progress in the images of vampires, ghouls, and werewolves. As Edward J. Ingebretsen and Joseph Reino note, King's stories permit a glimpse into a moralistically Calvinist, Lovecraftian cosmology of distance and power, where the inscrutable Deity is also the inscrutable Wrath delivering justice (Ingebretsen, 19; Reino, 20). In the tradition of the Salem witch trials, cosmological determinism in King becomes a vehicle of sociological determinism; whether mythical creatures or outer-space aliens, the emissaries of wrath constitute a major threat to the communities they attack. James F. Smith maintains that this naturalistic vision is at the heart of the Bachman cosmos (100). I agree but would add that determinism does not predominate over free will and responsibility in King. In all three instances the determination of his characters to shoulder responsibility and take a moral stand can clear the seemingly impossible obstacles in their way.

Last, as Pettersson argues in his work on different types of determinism in Vonnegut's fiction, metafictional determinism is "a formal expression of the other types of determinism" (34), since the action is prefaced, and so determined, by either a short summary of the protagonist's life (as, for instance, in *Carrie*) or indirect hints at future events. This metafictional determinism in King seems to stem primarily from the horror tradition with its anticipation and prolepsis of horrific scenes (for instance, *The Shining*) and in the case of *Carrie* from an editorial request to add a few pages to the story. It would be tempting to explain metafictional determinism in King through the Gothic. Following the fourfold classificatory scheme suggested by Montague Summers in *The Gothic Quest*, we can see that it subsumes the historical Gothic, the natural or explained Gothic, the supernatural Gothic, and the equivocal Gothic. As Nöel Carroll points out, the historical Gothic represents a story set in the imagined past without the suggestion of supernatural events, while the natural Gothic introduces what appear to be supernatural phenomena only to explain them away (for example, Ann Radcliffe's *Mysteries of Udolpho*). The equivocal Gothic renders the supernatural origin of events in the text ambiguous by means of psychologically disturbed characters (for example, Charles Brockden Brown's *Edgar Huntley, or the Memoirs of a Sleepwalker* [1799]) (4). The explained Gothic and the equivocal Gothic presage what Tzvetan Todorov in *The Fantastic* calls the uncanny and the fantastic. Therefore, they would suit my purposes if I were explaining the contradiction between the fantastic and the realistic in King. However, metafictional determinism has little to do with the degrees of reality, but—as the term suggests—"as readers, we are repeatedly reminded that what we see is a world created and *determined* by," in this case, King (Pettersson, *Vonnegut*, 138, italics in original). Thus, the otherwise valid distinction between the fantastic and the realistic remains irrelevant; what we see is "the truth inside the lie" (King in the dedication of *It*). As I see it, the paradox reveals the secret of King's popularity. "[T]he truth of this fiction is simple enough," he tells us, "*the magic exists*" (dedication of *It*).

The body of King's fiction is strongly marked by the various types of determinism, and they feature in all his works, whether realistic or fantastic. Furthermore, humans are also determined by fate, a notion that is frequently intertwined with cosmological determinism. By endowing his fiction with Gothic and fantastic features, however, King transcends the limits of the hereditary and environmental forces of literary naturalism. The fantastic and the Gothic devices may function in a paradoxical, double way, either to alleviate the deterministic laws or to rigidify them even more. For instance, humor combined with imagination at times alleviates the rather rigorous determinism and in some cases predominates over its laws. Carrie White of *Carrie* appears resigned to her fate as an outsider and a scapegoat. Her telekinetic powers merely add to and complete the destruction that has been brought about in her childhood. *It*, in contrast, displays the power of laughter and companionship in defeating determinism. External evil has deliberately chosen Derry for its nesting place to feed on children in a twenty-seven-year cycle. Although the death rates of the town are exceedingly high, the adult population indifferently sacrifices some of its children by choosing not to realize what is happening. When finally a group of children, the so-called Losers' Club, takes action and confronts the monster, the predestined evil can be beaten. King thus underscores the importance of moral responsibility and provides an optimistic view of its possibilities. In *It* the children's close-knit friendship and at times desperate laughter bring security and human warmth to their hard lives. The dualism in King suggests that even though evil may prevail, good can conquer in the end. Reesman argues that many of King's characters defeat the forces of evil precisely because of their determination: "In a hermeneutic circle, so very like other major American writers, King moves from tentative statement to tentative statement, asking us to believe that evil exists, is a threat, and calls for moral action without the assurance even of survival, let alone victory" (110). Although bravery does not necessarily lead to a victory, it is humankind's only chance, because not taking responsibility for one's actions always leads to destruction.

Despite its numerous dimensions, King's multiverse seems relatively coherent as far as questions of free will, determinism, and fate are concerned. Similarly, each character is exposed to all these fundamental questions involved in his or her own existence. Although, for instance, Jack Torrance of *The Shining* seems predestined to commit crimes, he possesses free will at least to the extent that it would enable him to act morally. Like any other citizen of King's world, Jack, too, is determined by his genetic inheritance, social background, and the cosmological laws of the multiverse, and by the way the plot sometimes is predetermined early on in the story or novel. In addition to fate, acting morally and taking responsibility may reverse the process of history. For instance, I discuss *'Salem's Lot* and *The Shining* in all the chapters of this book to prove my claim that one and the same work by King can with good reason be viewed from different angles.

At this point I would like to remind the reader of the discussion in the introduction where I argued that literary naturalism by no means opposes the worldview of the Gothic or myths and fairy tales in King's fiction. On the contrary, the idiosyncratic balance of free will versus determinism, the four types of determinism, and fate fuse the genres in King's oeuvre to a relatively coherent whole. The slight differences in the various genres—such as fate rules humans, and humans are driven by their instincts (the Gothic) versus fate rules humans, but humans as rational beings have the ability to make moral choices (literary naturalism)—merely add layers to King's multilevel and multidimensional multiverse. Myths and fairy tales, in turn, largely share the worldview of the Gothic. Furthermore, King's naturalism is colored by the other genres implicit in his fiction in the sense that the supernatural elements either soften or emphasize the naturalistic tones. Reesman has argued that King through *supernatural realism* examines the attractions and failures of naturalism, to which he has a dualistic attitude (109). This dualistic attitude apparently derives from King's worldview, which combines Methodism and naturalism (Underwood and Miller, *Bones*, 86; Winter, *Art*, 17). In short, determinism and another force—usually called "fate," "fortune," "luck," "chance," or "destiny"—shape the lives of King's characters.

This chapter analyzes King's use of determinism, fate, and the forces counteracting them, that is, free will, responsibility, and faith. My aim is to relate literary naturalism in King to the other genres that have been detected in his oeuvre in the course of this study. Let me start, however, by viewing the extent to which King's characters are free to make choices and take responsibility for their actions.

Free Will and Responsibility

Free will and responsibility seem so interrelated in King's fiction that I will discuss both in one and the same section. King's characters always have a choice between good and evil. As his faith in the Old Testament suggests, they must also face the consequences of their actions and take responsibility for them. King is an heir of Puritan theology, according to which divine justice must be delivered on earth and thus becomes a vehicle for social control (Ingebretsen, 11–30). The Puritan witch-huntings can, in turn, be traced to a Thomistic mapping of heaven and its powers with their respective counterparts on earth (Trevor-Roper). Ingebretsen points out that the maps of heaven shaped those of earth, "as metaphysics and its imperatives came to ground in the cast-off bodies of those repudiated for the civic good" (14). Furthermore, Randall D. Larson states that King's use of religion in his fiction is based on the Judeo-Christian tradition, "freely adapted to his own mild skepticism yet lacking the dominant antagonism toward this tradition found in much modern literature" (107). Finally, Reino detects a Lovecraftian cosmology of fear and power in King. In King's stories, Reino tells us, the inscrutable Deity is the inscrutable Wrath delivering justice (20). A kind of synthesis of Calvinist morality and mythical, Lovecraftian cosmology can be detected in King. He has also been influenced by Campbell's presentations of universal myths.

It seems to me that King in his fiction combines both Puritan and mythical notions of religious justice and, more importantly, emphasizes the responsibility his characters must take for their choices, whether good or evil. In *The Moral Voyages of Stephen King*, Magistrale reaches the essence of King's moral message to his readers. First, he recognizes its two moral poles, thus underscoring that free will cannot be separated from responsibility (3). Second, he points out the implications of this dilemma: as "an agent of the norm" (*DM*, 58), King is a spokesman for social order and morality. Magistrale also argues convincingly that "[t]he horror story is the most appropriate genre for our time," because "[t]he world of the nightmare, of monsters and sadistic and grotesque occurrences, speaks to us directly from the pages of daily newspapers and the videocameras of television rooms" (*Voyages*, 4; see also Winter, *Art*, 4–5).

The question of whether human will is free or constrained has been answered in a number of ways. Furthermore, the degree of free will varies from absolute freedom through partial determinism to predestination. In this study I define *free will* as the doctrine that views humans as entirely unrestricted in their ability to choose between good and evil and which is opposed to *determinism*. This definition both emphasizes the choice between good and evil and views the concept as opposed to *determinism*. The scope of the latter includes cosmological forces—as in *The New Encyclopedia Britannica*'s definition: "[D]eterminism, theory that all events, including moral choices, are completely determined by previously existing causes that preclude free will and the possibility that man could have acted otherwise. It holds that the universe is utterly rational because complete knowledge of any given situation assures that unerring knowledge of the future is also possible" (494). That the scope of determinism ranges beyond the sphere of human actions becomes important when I analyze cosmological determinism and fate in the section titled "Cosmological Determinism and Fate." King draws on both non-deterministic and deterministic views. However, determinism predominates in his works, even to the extent of becoming *predestination*, which denotes the foreordination of all things by God, including the future bliss or sorrow of humans. However, free will and Calvinist predestination do not preclude each other in King. In his works King both advances a deterministic outlook on humankind and the universe and pleads for moral responsibility. The combination of his deterministic worldview and Methodist faith enables him to portray a freer fictional multiverse than do strict naturalists, because he has *mystery* at his disposal. In King the resolve of the characters to act morally sometimes clears obstacles and enables them to do good deeds despite determinism. In other words, free will can be demonstrated by taking moral responsibility for one's actions and bearing responsibility for future actions, which, in turn, may change the future.

I have noted that King draws on Puritan theology and both classical and Lovecraftian mythology, which both have their own definitions for *good* and *evil*. I have chosen a narrow focus: I define the term *evil* and regard *good* as its counterforce. King's definitions of the two terms (see "Hubris and Death [Frankenstein's Monster]" in chapter 1 and "The Antihero as a Generic Hybrid [Randall Flagg]" in chapter 2) will now be placed in their classical and/or Judeo-Christian contexts. The English word *evil* is of Teutonic origin, cognate with *übel* and Dutch *euvel*. Apparently, it derives from the word *ubiloz*, cognate with the prepositions *up* or *over*, and thus the etymology of *evil* connects it with the concepts of too much, exceeding due measure, over limits. Neil Forsyth in "The Origin of 'Evil': Classical or Judeo-Christian" notes that the idea is similar to the concept, common in older discussions of Greek tragedy, of *hubris*, signifying "overweening pride," "insolence," or—as I have noted in chapter 1 under "Hubris and Death (Frankenstein's Monster)"—"pride and defiance" (19). In

Poetics Aristotle introduces the term *hamartia*, which signifies a "tragic flaw" (*Poetics* 53a16; Heath, xxxi–xxxiii). Forsyth points out that English translations of Aristotle's *Poetics* are often influenced by the fact that *hamartia* is the ordinary New Testament word for *sin*, which is a matter of "offense in relation to God with emphasis on guilt" (24). In this sense the classical *hubris* and the Judeo-Christian *sin* seem to overlap. In King's terminology both are synonymous with *inside evil*, which results from "an act of free will and conscious evil—a conscious decision to do evil" (*DM*, 62) and which may be followed by guilt. Implicitly, *inside good* thus means a conscious decision to do good, to take a moral stand, and, significantly, to exercise self-control, because excess is considered a sin in both classical and Judeo-Christian thinking.

In accordance with the Calvinist concept of predestination and the unjust sufferings of Job (Bercovitch, 6–7), King defines *outside evil* as "predestinate" and "coming from outside like a stroke of lightning" (*DM*, 62). He even refers to Job's story as "[t]he most classic horror tale of this latter type" (62). Dictionary definitions of this kind of *evil* make the distinction between uses that are synonyms of *weakness* or *affliction* and uses that retain the much stronger sense, reserved for those who are barely considered human (Forsyth, 19; Pocock, 52). As regards *outside evil*, the latter meaning is relevant. Forsyth argues that no Greek word covers all that we mean by the concept of *evil*, and the so-called problem of evil was only anticipated by Epicurus (341–270 BC) (20). Epicurus could be referring to what in King is a seemingly indifferent God when he anticipates the idea of the devil in Jewish apocalyptic and then spectacularly in Christian contexts (for the demonic traits of Yahweh, see, for example, Jung, 256): "God either wishes to take away evils, and is unable; or He is able, and is unwilling; or He is neither willing nor able; or He is both willing and able. If He is willing and is unable, He is feeble, which is not in accordance with the character of God; if He is able and is unwilling, he is envious, which is equally at variance with God; if He is neither willing nor able, He is both envious and feeble, and therefore not God; if He is both willing and able, which alone is suitable to God, from what source then are evils? Or why does He not remove them?" (ch. 13.20–13.21; 270). In *Desperation* (1996) and *The Girl Who Loved Tom Gordon* (1999), King repeats the notion of God's cruelty and inability only to reject it at the end of the novels, thus shifting from the Old Testament to the New Testament. In this sense, then, classical mythology and Judeo-Christian notions are combined in King's notion of *outside evil* as both metaphysical and moral reality. Implicitly, *outside good* presupposes the existence of a benevolent creator. Forsyth refers to Plato's *Timaeus,* which provides an illustration of this outlook: when Timaeus introduces his depiction of creation, he begins with the firm statement that the creator "was good" (Forsyth, 23; Plato, *Timaeus,* 129e). Somewhat ironically, the benevolent aspect of God cannot be easily found in Judeo-Christian theology. In fact, Søren Kierkegaard, heir of the much more pessimistic Christian worldview, famously discusses the Socratic optimism in *Sickness unto Death* (218). In a similar vein King's characters are severely punished for their wrongdoings without hope of mercy. King in an 1983 *Playboy* interview with Eric Norden points out that "we are rewarded only moderately for being good, but our transgressions are penalized with absurd severity" (Underwood and Miller, *Bones,* 63). In sum, King's fiction combines the classical and Judeo-Christian notions of *good* and *evil* in all but *outside good,* in which he follows the Judeo-Christian tradition of sin and salvation—with an emphasis on sin.

I will now focus on the extent to which King's characters are free to make choices and take responsibility for their actions. I will also discuss whether the leeway for choice has grown either broader or narrower during King's literary career. In *Danse Macabre* King points out that "[t]he stories of horror which are psychological—those which explore the terrain of the human heart—almost always revolve around the free-will concept; 'inside evil,' if you will, the sort we have no right laying off on God the Father" (62).

RAGE

By the time *Carrie* was published in 1974, King had completed (if not published) five novels, including *Rage* (1977) and *The Long Walk* (1979). His experiences in high school are reflected in *Rage,* which was written during his senior year in high school; *The Long Walk* was authored in the fall of 1966 and the spring of 1967, when he was a freshman at college (*Bachman Books,* vii). Both were written under the pseudonym Richard Bachman, the origins of which were discussed in chapter 1 under "The Gothic

Double (the Werewolf)." Concerning literary naturalism, however, "Richard Bachman" allowed King to explore his darkest
fantasies and fears without the safeguard of supernatural plots.
With the exception of *Thinner* (1984), the Bachman novels relate
merely tangentially to supernatural horror (Collings, *Bachman*,
7). King has not separated the Bachman books from his others:
they explore many of the same themes from different angles, and
in their style, structure, and characterization, they are also iden-
tifiably King (Collings, *Bachman*, 15). However, the prevalent naturalism implicit in the novels considerably limits the characters'
free will, as I demonstrate in the following discussion.

On the opening page of *Rage*, King makes Charlie Decker con-
fess that he started to lose his mind two years ago. Insanity does
not, however, relieve the protagonist of moral responsibility for
his actions. On the contrary, the message of the novel seems to
imply that the seemingly insane Charlie Decker might turn out to
be one of the rare sane characters in the story. Before the incidents
of the fatal May morning that result in Charlie Decker killing two
of his teachers and holding his classmates hostage, the protagonist has not been allowed to demonstrate free will practically
anywhere. Ironically, his frustration has taken on such large proportions that its expression requires violent action, and his use of
free will thus leads to tragic consequences. Determined by his social environment—a father who hates Charlie, teachers who are
incapable of responding as human beings to the needs of their
students, and peer pressure—Charlie no longer settles for being a
pawn in the game of socialization or, as he puts it, "being mastur-
bated on" (*RA*, 21), but takes what seems to him a moral stand.

In King the American high school seemingly refuses to take
moral responsibility for the true education of its pupils. The refusal to shoulder this responsibility is reflected in the juxaposi-
tion of rationality and irrationality, which forms the basis for
the novel. Charlie's first victim, Mrs. Underwood, who teaches
mathematics, represents the former, and she dies with the novel's motto on her lips: "So you understand that when we *increase*
the number of variables, the axioms *themselves* never change"
(29, italics in original). In other words, Charlie's protest simply
manifests his own disappointment with adults and his profoundly pessimistic attitude toward life, but it does not manage to change the state of affairs. In contrast, Mrs. Underwood

represents rationality and self-control. Despite his claim that the principal "hadn't really expected any irrational act" when confronting him in his office (23), Charlie loses control over his actions from the beginning. He explicitly notes that instead of killing Mrs. Underwood he should have shot Ted Jones, a seemingly competent classmate who represents adult values in the classroom and whom the class drives insane during the four-hour ordeal. By silencing Ted, the class may have attempted to get rid of hypocritical social norms, but simultaneously the classmates silence the voice of rationality and the means of survival in society. Perhaps intentionally, Mr. Vance, a history teacher, becomes Decker's next prey. As Collings argues, Charlie and his peers have little understanding of either tradition or heritage. Controlled by passion, hatred, sex, and frustration, they drift through their adolescent lives unable to make justifiable decisions. Significantly, too, the educational system, "which should help them adjust and become part of the historical continuum[,] fails" (*Bachman*, 27–28).

However, the question of responsibility versus irresponsibility or even rationality versus irrationality finds its clearest expression in the character of Don Grace, a counselor who brings disgrace on his name. Distanced from the students he is expected to help, Grace is not able to shoulder his responsibility. Confronting Charlie over the intercom system, he hypocritically evades the facts, accusing Charlie of "a pretty antisocial act" (*RA*, 66). King criticizes contemporary psychology by making Charlie turn the tables on Grace. While Don Grace pleads for him to take responsibility for his actions, Charlie Decker triumphantly declares that the psychiatrist has been taking responsibility for other people ever since he graduated from college. The first time his responsibility seems personal and real, Grace wishes to evade it (69). In his inability to "respond rationally to irrationality," the psychiatrist is destroyed psychologically by the end of the discussion (Collings, *Bachman*, 29). Charlie sees Grace walk away like an old man and enjoys the sight (*RA*, 75).

Despite his defiance and seeming self-assurance, Charlie Decker apparently lost his free will at the age of four when confronted with insanity. At its simplest level, the novel, according to its name, discusses rage that results from a "generic disintegration of institutions—home, family, school, society" (Collings,

Bachman, 25). It suggests that adults cannot be trusted and that comfort and closeness can be given to, and received from, peers only. Relating his painful experiences with his father to his hostages, Charlie discloses the other narrative of the story. The roots of his alienation, anger, and defiance are in his home and, more precisely, in his father, who has always hated his son (*RA*, 53). An officer in the military by profession and a man of order, Charlie's father pays attention to facades. Instead of taking moral responsibility for his son, Charlie's father prefers false fronts: "My dad's motto: Keep It Tight and Keep It Right" (54).

Neither free will nor responsibility is a factor when the four-year-old Charlie Decker breaks the storm windows of his home and is thrown to the ground with full force by his father. The metaphor of a mask manifests both the emotion of rage and the contradiction between a calm surface and an inner reality: "It was like your mother coming to the breakfast table with a Halloween mask on" (56). In fact, when Charlie's mother arrives, the relative strength of the parties is changed. Observing "with what practiced and dreadful ease" his father is banished, Charlie begins to "dare to hate him back" (58). Thus, at the age of four Charlie hands over his free will to a stronger power, that is, rage. Undoubtedly, Charlie's young mind could still have been molded after the storm-window incident, but, instead of care, understanding, and responsibility, the father offers his son another fateful tool: violence. In an attempt to make his son a real man, the father and his friends take the nine-year-old Charlie hunting for a week in November. Outside the tent Charlie's father then boasts to his friends and threatens to slit his wife's nose if she turns out to be unfaithful. While accused of a violent act and awaiting the principal to discuss its consequences, Charlie encounters one of his father's friends and recalls the memory of the hunting trip. Furiously, he thinks that all those adult men should be taken to the reform school with him, because they are a part of his problem (13). Tragically, Charlie has learned a grim lesson: in addition to responding with violence, he takes no responsibility for his own actions but blames them on his father.

In *Rage* the question of free will is posed in regard to the thin line between sanity and insanity. In Charlie's vocabulary sanity means ignoring half of the facts, and free will can be demonstrated by transgressing the boundary of insanity. Similarly, taking responsibility for one's life seems to require a leap into madness. Finally, however, King raises the question of who, after all, can be regarded as sane and responsible. After the hostage incident Charlie considers life logical, prosaic, and sane, claiming that it all culminates in Mrs. Underwood's dying declaration. Sanity is maintained through the routines and logic of everyday life. As Charlie goes on to exemplify, sanity and logic also save us from the tragic element in life: "My wife and child have been critically injured in a car crash; therefore I pray" (30). Unfortunately, however, it may prevent us from thinking as well (30). The end of the novel promises little hope for the future. In correspondence with a friend called Joe Kennedy, Charlie discovers that his school friends have become exactly what was expected of them: they are duplicates of the former generation.

Charlie Decker fails miserably to demonstrate free will or to take a moral stand. By acting irrationally, he merely causes the deaths of two persons, and even his own life is saved by fate in the form of chance or dumb luck. A bullet, fired by a marksman outside the school, strikes a padlock in Charlie's pocket but does not injure him. In this early novel King seems to limit the protagonist's free will to the utmost and pose the question whether Charlie ever had an opportunity to make choices. Undoubtedly, Charlie speaks from experience when maintaining that "there's a Mr. Hyde for every happy Jekyll face, a dark face on the other side of the mirror" (30). As so often in King, the mirror reflects our own flawed humanity. Despite the seeming logic of the universe, the balance between rationality and irrationality appears so fragile that it keeps most people on the lookout for the irrational. Also, the recurring metaphor of the wheel of fortune underscores the role of fate: "It's a roulette wheel, but anybody who says the game is rigged is whining. No matter how many numbers there are, the principle of that little white jittering ball never changes. Don't say it's crazy. It's all so cool and sane" (31). In short, humans are at the mercy of chance, and rebelling against it leads either to insanity or to death.

Whereas *Rage* can be labeled a naturalistic novel, *Carrie* represents supernatural horror because of the protagonist's telekinetic ability. The two teenagers possess free will merely to the extent that they defy the sordid circumstances under which they live. Both begin in oppression and violence, and both culminate in either psychological destruction, as in *Rage,* or in physical destruction, as in *Carrie.* Demonstrating free will leads to severe punishment, and pushed too far, Carrie—like the protagonists in *Rage, The Long Walk, Roadwork,* and *The Running Man*—overreacts when taking a moral stand. In *Carrie* and *The Long Walk,* taking a stand seems more haphazard than in the other three novels, since Carrie unleashes her power without premeditation, and Raymond Garrety initially views the long walk as a game or a way to earn money to support his mother.

THE LONG WALK

The Long Walk introduces Raymond Davis Garrety, a sixteen-year-old who from a vast number of candidates has been selected to participate in a walking competition. Fully aware of the grim rules, ninety-nine athletic adolescent males enter the competition in which only the best walker survives and wins a large sum of money. No clear reason for Garrety's participation in the competition is given, but the opening pages of the novel hint at his poverty. Garrety convinces his mother that he takes the step of his own free will, because "this way is best, one way or the other" (*LW,* 181). However, it becomes obvious that the state has taken control over its citizens to the extent that parents are no longer able to bear responsibility for their children or themselves. Pushed too far, individuals seem ready to take any measures to guarantee their families a decent living.

Instead of taking responsibility for its citizens, the state deliberately entices its best young men into a deadly game. A Darwinian novel, *The Long Walk* suggests another reason for the boys' participation in the walk. Misled by the state, most of the adolescents feel both sure they will survive and honored to represent their federal states. Ironically, the survival competition has become a national sport: television broadcasts it as a commonplace program; movie theaters salute the passing competitors; and crowds follow the thinning ranks. Clearly, the crowd becomes a metaphor of the all-devouring greed of the state, which takes no moral responsibility for human lives but, on the contrary, seeks to exploit them for the purposes of entertainment. By fair means or foul, the state dulls the minds of the citizens in order to rule them more effectively and, more importantly, deprive them of their free will.

People demonstrate free will, however, by forming groups in defiance of the laws of the jungle. King's trust in close-knit communities is preserved in one of his most pessimistic novels, even if in a miniature format. King seems to suggest that human decency can survive to some degree even in the midst of the harshest Darwinian struggle. A variety of characters peoples *The Long Walk*, some of whom represent less refined and sophisticated characteristics of human nature, while others exemplify their humanity by saving lives at the risk of losing their own. One of these heroic characters, McVries, saves Garrety's life twice. In the course of the walk, McVries suggests to his companions that they support one another, all for one and one for all. And, indeed, the Three Musketeers keep company until the call for survival requires natural selection, and another competitor suggests the opposite motto "No help for anybody" (408). Aware of his debt to McVries and regarding himself an animal, Garrety stifles the voice of conscience and answers the call for survival. Of his own free will Garrety rejects humanity in order to survive: "Nothing personal. Just back to the jungle" (409). However, while succumbing to evil, Garrety subscribes to his own destruction. As King suggests, cooperation, resistance, and rebellion might have resulted in a more fortunate outcome. Unlike Garrety, Parker takes a stand, wrenching a rifle out of a soldier's hand. With a little help from McVries and Garrety, Parker might have stood a chance, but he is shot shortly after the attempt.

Having handed over his free will to the state and discovered the moral of the walk, that is, "Walk or die" (250), Garrety is likely to win the competition. While discussing it with Garrety, McVries crystallizes the lesson of the novel. Although he has known the odds, he has not "figure[d] on *people*" (250, italics in original). In other words, the drive to win and the instinct to survive rise from within. Garrety now realizes that he, unlike McVries, has known all along the true nature of the competition. However, his victory proves hollow, because he is now completely absorbed by the machinery of the state and lacks a will of his own. Thus, the user becomes the used when the greedy audience has feasted on its prey. In the Bachman books there are no winners.

Rage and *The Long Walk* can be considered naturalistic novels. However, the same worldview also prevails in King's works of other genres, such as *'Salem's Lot* and *The Stand*.

Magistrale argues that in another novel set in Maine, *Pet Sema-tary*, "the land itself stands in opposition to the mortal will" (*Voyages*, 11). In addition King's characters contribute to their own hardships by acting immorally and by not taking responsibility for their actions. The hostile and savage atmosphere of Maine reflects both malevolent supernatural energies and human nature. Although supernatural creatures threaten the lives of King's characters, it is succumbing to evil that ultimately results in their destruction. Burton Hatlen notes that, as a regionalist, King views Maine as a locale of various vices and virtues represented by distinct human personalities (49). Furthermore, Magistrale points out that most of King's Maine natives demonstrate human decency and treat others with respect. King frequently takes a critical view of small-town communities and places his individual characters in difficult situations in which the question of free will becomes of essence (*Voyages*, 1–12). The remaining section deals with these characters in his fiction.

Both free will and moral strength are required to triumph over evil in King's world. Ben Mears of *'Salem's Lot* has lost his wife, Miranda, in a motorcycle accident, in addition to which his girlfriend, Susan Norton, falls prey to the vampire Kurt Barlow. Despite his strong feelings of guilt, Ben is able to take responsibility for another human being, Mark Petrie, and for the town of Jerusalem's Lot. Unlike his peers, Mark Petrie resists the vampires by taking necessary precautions against them. Some of the characters, like Father Callahan, perish because of their naivety about evil. Callahan, an alcoholic, complains about the dilapidated state of the church, completely forgetting that the church consists of its members—including himself. While boasting of his willingness to confront evil "like Muhammed Ali against Joe Frazier" (*SL*, 150), Father Callahan does not realize that by neglecting his minor duties he has discarded the humility of being God's worthy servant and consequently his faith. Given an opportunity for heroic deeds in the field of religion, Callahan readily takes the challenge, although he no longer possesses weapons against evil.

Callahan's confrontation with Barlow turns out to be a cruel parody of Mina Harker's blood-drinking episode in *Dracula*. First, the original:

With that he pulled open his shirt, and with his long sharp nails opened a vein in his breast. When the blood began to spurt out, he took my hands in one of his, holding them tight, and with the other seized my neck and pressed my mouth to the wound, so that I must either suffocate or swallow some of the—. (Stoker, 343)

Then King's version:

And Callahan's mouth was pressed against the reeking flesh of the vampire's cold throat, where an open vein pulsed. He held his breath for what seemed like aeons, twisting his head wildly and to no avail, smearing the blood across the cheeks and forehead and chin like war paint.
Yet at last, he drank. (*SL,* 355)

Although almost identical in depiction, the passages introduce two quite different characters as regards moral strength and free will. As a virtuous Gothic heroine, Mina Harker has done nothing to deserve her evil destiny: she is struck by fate (Stoker, 343). The innocent victim is redeemed from her curse, whereas the morally weak Father Callahan finds no redemption. Praying for a second chance, he directs his steps toward Saint Andrew's to pray to the God of the Old Testament (*SL,* 360–61). Apparently, however, Father Callahan has subscribed to his own doom, for as he touches the handle of the church door, there is a blue flash of light, and he is thrown backward (361). Undoubtedly, King's God of the Old Testament delivers justice instead of "free lunches" (360), and Father Callahan is last seen entering a Greyhound and leaving the cursed town in search of some rest.

The same laws of free will and responsibility apply to King's characters both in Maine and throughout his fiction.

THE STAND

The often-repeated King maxim "evil places draw evil men" also holds true with regard to good (*SL,* 113): in *The Stand* "good places draw good men." In this "novel of journey" (Winter, *Art,* 60), the question of free will merges with the notion of predestination in a most intriguing way. To be more precise, it manifests the Calvinist idea of predestination in its purest form. Transcending the boundaries of traditional horror fiction, *The Stand* presents the post-apocalyptic United States after a worldwide catastrophe resulting from a government experiment. In addition to science fiction, the novel has been labeled "an epic story of good and evil" (Wiater, Golden, and Wagner, 81) and "epic fantasy" (Winter, *Art*, 61), to which I would add the genre horror fiction. Stanley Wiater, Christopher Golden, and Hank Wagner agree, referring both to horror and the question of free will: "[The novel's] strength also lies in the horror, the fear, the hope, and the terrifying knowledge that, ultimately, we have a choice whether to help or to hurt" (82).

The lines of demarcation between good and evil are drawn from the start in *The Stand*. Six-tenths of a percent of the world's population turns out to be inexplicably immune to Captain Trips, and shortly after the catastrophe the survivors are visited by personalized dreams involving two recurring images: a threatening dark man and an ancient black woman offering rest and peace. As Winter points out, these visions create the parameters of a choice between good and evil in which each character's intrinsic predisposition seems decisive. Implicit in the predisposition is the belief that what causes a person to choose either good or evil is at least partially predestined. The survivors seek their way either to the embodiment of the good, Mother Abagail, who aims at establishing a democratic order, or to the embodiment of evil, Randall Flagg, who attempts to decimate the world that survived the onslaught of the fatal influenza (*Art*, 65). Around Mother Abagail gathers an assortment of rather stereotypical characters, consciously paralleling the band of adventurers of J. R. R. Tolkien's *Lord of the Rings:* the self-educated mute Nick Andros, the New Hampshire sociology professor Glen Bateman, the retarded Tom Cullen from Oklahoma, the pregnant college student Fran Goldsmith, the blue-collar worker Stu Redman from Texas, and the overnight rock-and-roll sensation Larry Underwood from New York. On the opposing side around Randall Flagg are gathered Lloyd Henreid, a petty criminal who becomes one of Flagg's closest disciplines; Donald Merwin Elbert, a.k.a. the Trashcan Man, an abused child and twisted adult whose developing insanity leads to the destruction of Las Vegas; and Ace High, one of Flagg's most trusted men. The characters of Larry Underwood and Lloyd Henreid will illustrate the issue of predestination in connection with free will.

Despite his efforts to destroy his life by living in the fast lane, Larry Underwood remains good as if he were predestined to die a martyr. Like his literary predecessor, Frodo Baggins (alias

Underhill) of Tolkien's *Lord of the Rings*, Larry journeys a long way to fulfill his destiny. Despite his seeming inability to make decisions and besides his entourage of caring acquaintances, Larry is also surrounded by an aura of success. While the novel depicts the development of Larry from a drug addict to a martyr who accepts his destiny, the relationship of Larry and his mother provides an intriguing view of Larry as a person before both his drug addiction and his inner growth. From the mother's brief remarks and Larry's prejudiced and defensive interpretation of her supposed thoughts, the reader recognizes a superficial, indifferent, egoistic, and irresponsible personality who acts on the spur of the moment. Prophetically Alice observes also the good in her son. However, "this late on it would take nothing short of a catastrophe to bring it out" (*ST*, 69).

In King a minor catastrophe seldom makes a difference, and an apocalypse is required to turn Larry Underwood into a saint. His "change of soul" occurs gradually (69), and when Captain Trips hits New York, resulting in the sudden illness and death of his mother, Larry, apart from being terrified for her, feels irritated with the change of his own plans (295). When he encounters Rita Blakemoor, a middle-aged woman who becomes dependent on her new lover, Larry appears reluctant to bear responsibility for another human being. In escaping the corpse-filled city, however, he learns his lesson, and the fearful journey through an unlighted Lincoln Tunnel symbolizes a rite of passage into responsibility (387). Larry's gradual maturing is not, however, brought about without setbacks. Finding Rita dead in her sleeping bag, Larry remarkably resembles his earlier self. He feels both disgust and relief (472). Obviously this deep-seated uncertainty, the wish to prove his mother's criticism wrong combined with loneliness on the way to Nebraska, and his desperate and seemingly unanswered love for Nadine Cross, whom he encounters midway, result in Larry's "change of soul" (69).

The love he feels for Nadine Cross makes Larry voluntarily take responsibility for other human beings and realize: "*I think I've changed. Somehow. I don't know how much*" (554, italics in original). Despite his low opinion of himself, Larry becomes a prominent citizen of the Free Zone, Mother Abagail's base. Again predestination plays a decisive role in the lives of the characters when Larry passes his crucial test and proves worthy of the others' trust by rejecting Nadine in favor of Lucy (a woman for whom he develops feelings since they are not reciprocated by Nadine), that is, by rejecting passion in favor of lasting love and fidelity. To free herself from the Dark Man's spell, Nadine thrusts herself on Larry, and when her feelings are not reciprocated, she heads into the desert to become Randall Flagg's bride. Thus, Larry's moral stand results in Nadine's destruction. Having originally chosen evil, her "change of soul" occurs too late (69), unlike the spiritual transformation of Larry, who perhaps receives more than he deserves. In the end Nadine demonstrates free will by sacrificing her life and the life of her unborn baby, who would have become Flagg's heir, whereas Larry and three other men are sent to Las Vegas to confront Flagg. Having fulfilled his destiny, Larry dies in a nuclear explosion.

As regards the question of free will merged in predestination, both Harold Lauder and Lloyd Henreid present an effective counterpoint to Larry Underwood. Winter points out that Harold, too, struggles with impossible self-demands but deliberately rejects good in favor of evil. Never a truly sympathetic character, the initially obese, neurotic, and self-pitying Harold seemingly matures but in fact represses his lack of understanding when he is used and eventually cast aside by the Dark Man (*Art*, 66). At any rate, the question remains: In what respect would Larry Underwood initially be worth more than Harold Lauder or Lloyd Henreid? His visible sins, such as drug-addiction and obsession with sex, seem more than comparable with Harold's occasional voyeurism and Lloyd's petty offences, and even his decision making appears to be more than haphazard at the beginning of the novel. Therefore, the answer must be found either in the essence of the characters' being or in predestination. Despite the apparent flaws in his character, Larry is allowed moral slips that lead to major catastrophes for the other two. Nor is he the only one entitled to inner growth—both Harold and Lloyd take a moral stand before the end. Presumably, King's point is that conscious choices together with predestined inner quality determine a character's destiny.

Lloyd Henreid makes a conscious decision in favor of Randall Flagg. Beginning his career as a petty criminal, Lloyd gets involved with the insane Poke Freeman, with whom he holds up a grocery store before Captain Trips hits. Poke is shot by the store owner, whereas Lloyd ends up in prison. Randall Flagg, who comes to his rescue, demands loyalty. Making Lloyd his right-hand man, Flagg puts him "right up there with Saint Peter" (*ST*, 456). Unlike Saint Peter, Lloyd Henreid neither denies his master nor falters. He demonstrates free will and proves responsible by not leaving the Dark Man when he begins to lose the battle. Given a chance to escape, he refuses, and when forced to shoot Glen Bateman at Flagg's request, he still defends Flagg: "He told me more truth than anyone else bothered to in my whole lousy life" (1319). Like Larry Underwood, Lloyd Henreid learns to take responsibility for his actions and make a conscious stand. Since both men die in the same nuclear explosion, the biblical parable of the holy and the unholy perishing in the same fire fittingly displays their destiny.

Free will and responsibility cannot be separated from the concepts of good and evil. Placed in a difficult situation, King's characters have to take a moral stand: either to fight evil simply because it exists as a threatening force or to succumb to it. Despite the workings of fate and the four types of determinism (genetic, sociological, cosmological, and metafictional), they ultimately possess free will to choose between good and evil. The difficulties King's characters confront may seem overpowering and their alternatives severely limited, but the core of all questions revolves around good and evil. Magistrale notes that although the shape evil takes in King seems as varied as the creatures populating his fiction, it requires a human agent to manifest its authority. Evil both gains strength from earlier sins and presupposes a deliberate choice in the rejection of good. Although it constitutes an omnipresent and recurring force in King, thus resembling the concept of original sin, free will can dictate its degree of influence and even change the future. Furthermore, virtually all of King's major works include characters who embody good and evil, as the propensities for both are present in all of us (*Voyages*, 25).

Clearly recognizing the two forces, King comments on faith in *Danse Macabre:* "We fall from womb to tomb, from one blackness toward another, remembering little of the one and knowing nothing of the other . . . except through faith" (409, ellipsis in

original). His faith is that of the Old Testament, which means that
sins and wrongdoings are severely punished without any hope
of mercy. As with Job, righteous and innocent people also suffer, and the only way to be rid of this suffering is to fight the evil
forces. King is a moralist who asks both his characters and his
readers to realize that the existence of evil calls for moral action
without the assurance even of survival, let alone victory. Magistrale notes that "King's faith in the endurance of a traditional morality, based on the values of love and the resiliency of the human
spirit, power whatever light remains in a world actively pursuing
the destruction of itself and everything within it" (*Voyages*, 26).
Acting morally, taking responsibility for one's fellow human beings, and taking a moral stand remain humankind's only chance.
Evil, argues King, grows in isolation from other human beings,
whereas good and love connects people. In fact, King's evil characters appear to be either loners from the beginning or characters
who become estranged from life and human contacts after succumbing to evil. Although the members of the Losers' Club might
alone fall easy prey to the monster, together they constitute a serious threat to it by completing their circle of love and friendship.

As King has repeatedly emphasized, much of the fiction in the
horror genre reestablishes traditional values. He distinguishes
two categories of horror stories: "those in which the horror results
from an act of free will and conscious will—a conscious decision
to do evil—and those in which the horror is predestinate, coming
from outside like a stroke of lightning" (*DM*, 62; for a fuller quotation, see "Hubris and Death [Frankenstein's Monster]" in chapter 1). In representing psychological horror, the former category
seems the most significant contribution of the Gothic mode, and
in chapter 1 a number of characters were confronted with the
question of free will. Whereas the vampire Kurt Barlow appears
to be predestined to his doom, the Reverend Lester Lowe is also
struck by fate in the form of an evil destiny, but he possesses
enough free will to take a moral stand. Similarly, the werewolf
Wolf, the modern variant of Dr. Jekyll/Mr. Hyde, Thad Beaumont, and the serial killers Frank Dodd and Charles Burnside
have the freedom choose between good and evil. Note also that
my discussions in chapter 1 of the character of Louis Creed as a
late Dr. Frankenstein and of Jack Torrance to some extent also
discuss the very question of free will.

Furthermore, throughout his literary career King has explored the dilemma of choice or the forces that deprive humans of their free will. During the course of his literary career, the leeway for choice has largely remained the same, with the notable exception of the early Bachman books, where it seems rather limited. Nearly every character in King's work possesses free will to the extent of being able to take a moral standing and shoulder responsibility. Indeed, while humans are determined by forces beyond their control, free will guarantees that they can largely be held responsible for their actions.

Genetic and sociological determinism at best or worst affects an individual character before birth, during the formative years, and throughout his or her life.

Genetic and Sociological Determinism

All of Stephen King's characters are determined by genetic and / or sociological determinism in one way or another. Similarly, on both personal and social levels horror fiction feeds on our uncertainties. King puts it in visceral terms: "The thing under my bed waiting to grab my ankle isn't real. I know that, and I also know that if I'm careful to keep my foot under the covers, it will never be able to grab my ankle" (*NS*, xii). However, what we all fear are not vampires or werewolves but alienation, hate, and loneliness. By bringing up real issues (drug abuse, familial discord, the fear of technological advances beyond human means of comprehension, the xenophobia of small-town America, religious zealotry and its link to both societal and personal oppression, and the inability of social institutions to maintain their viability in the face of changing values [Magistrale, "Defining Stephen King's Horroscape," 3]), literary naturalism in general and the various types of determinism in particular create the counterbalance to the fantastic genres in King.

A number of characters are simultaneously determined by both genetic and sociological determinism. Although no clear shift from genetic to sociological determinism can be detected in the course of the analysis, I take the former as a starting point, presenting first characters born with supernatural abilities and then discussing King's mentally retarded characters. Sociological determinism will be discussed at the end of section according to the institution exerting power—the community, the government, and the church.

OVERVIEW AND DEFINITIONS

Genetic determinism views humans as determined by genetic inheritance. It affects every individual regardless of possible supernatural abilities or defects. However, since I focus on the supernatural, some further explanation is required. First, the inheritance of supernatural abilities is related to King's social criticism and illustrates determinism in his literary naturalism as a whole. Second, as this section emphasizes determinism, inherited supernatural abilities and defects determine an individual character's life to a considerably greater degree than normal genes and normal childhood. In King genetic determinism generally results in sociological determinism. In *Carrie* he presents a typical theme of a social outcast with paranormal powers. In *The Shining* Danny's precognitive talent illustrates the emotional tensions within the Torrance family. *The Stand* includes a character called Tom Cullen, whose retardedness leaves him naive and intellectually a child forever. Since Tom's goodness both represents hope for humanity and stands in defiance of the social inequality of the old order, the character of Tom will be analyzed in greater detail. *Firestarter* features Charlie McGee, who has inherited her paranormal powers from her parents, who were exposed to a parascientific experiment. Again genetic determinism is accompanied by social isolation, because Charlie is forced to flee with her father after her mother has been murdered by the government. With the notable exception of John Coffey of *The Green Mile* (1996), virtually all of King's characters with inherited supernatural powers turn out to be children. Coffey is born with the ability to heal others by inhaling their pain and then releasing it into the ether. Since *Carrie*, *The Shining*, and *Firestarter* are discussed elsewhere in this study, I confine my analysis of genetic determinism to the characters of Tom Cullen (*The Stand*) and John Coffey (*The Green Mile*).

The second kind of determinism I will deal with is *sociological determinism*. My definition of the term emphasizes both human social relations and human social conditions. King displays sociological determinism in virtually all his works, and it affects both the formative years of his characters' lives and their adolescence, adulthood as well as old age. For this reason I discuss sociological determinism according to the institutions exerting pressure on the individual: home, school, the church, the community, and the government. What led King to consider the human being's personality and actions necessarily molded by socialization, family relations, and high school in particular was most likely his family circumstances during childhood and adolescence as well as his experiences as a high school English instructor. As regards socialization King subscribes to Wordsworth's notion of the child as father to the man. Frequently, however, when the child matures into adulthood, a loss of innocence blurs his or her perception. The inevitable fall from innocence can be detected throughout King. Furthermore, King's children are depicted as perfect victims: fighting against seemingly overwhelming odds, they evoke sympathetic responses from the reader. Among the victimized children and adolescents in King's work are Carrie White *(Carrie)*, Danny Torrance *(The Shining)*, Charlie Decker *(Rage)*, Charlie McGee *(Firestarter)*, Jake Chambers (*The Dark Tower* series), Chris Chambers ("The Body"), Arnie Cunningham *(Christine)*, Bev Marsh *(It)*, and Trisha McFarland *(The Girl Who Loved Tom Gordon)*.

Most of King's fictional children and adolescents are forced to cope with the dark complexities of an adult world for which they are not responsible, either in the form of familial discord or governmental misconduct. Failure of love leads to disasters that reveal the worst of humans and fall on innocent victims, usually children. As Magistrale notes, despite their innocence or good will, King's children are both shaped and influenced by adults who are deeply involved in personal struggles with evil *(Landscape,* 78). This naturalistic theme corresponds to the Gothic theme, derived, of course, from the Old Testament, of the sins of the fathers revisited upon their children. Although King's children and adolescents personify the extremes of good and evil, the former predominate in his fiction. At the other moral pole, however, Magistrale lists "the adolescent hunters" and "the denim fascists" in *Carrie,* "Sometimes They Come Back" *(Night Shift),* and *Christine,* whose sole purpose seems to be the destruction anyone different from themselves (75). The dualism implicit in his children and adolescents also characterizes King's adult characters. Some turn out to be monsters beneath their human exterior: immature, selfish, irresponsible, and without conscience (for instance, Margaret White of *Carrie,* Greg Stillson of *The Dead Zone,* and Norman Daniels of *Rose Madder*). Magistrale notes that their systems of control (such as the church, the state, even the family itself) scarcely inhibit an undercurrent of violence that threatens to manifest itself at any moment (77). Others have been victimized during childhood or adolescence, and as a result of their victorious struggles, these characters embody maturity, altruism, and, responsibility (for instance, Ben Mears of *'Salem's Lot,* Bill Denbrough of *It,* and Mike Noonan of *Bag of Bones*).

Sociological determinism relates to human social relations, such as love. The moral survivors of King's fiction adhere to the tenet that "there is such a thing as love" (91). As a horror writer, he regards himself as "another passenger in the boat, another pilgrim on the way to whatever there is" (*DM,* 403). In other words, naturalism in King, as in the work of London, is a vehicle for humanism (Reesman, 108), and his plea for moral behavior and responsibility is rarely overridden by determinism. Although he seldom literally declares a moral stance in his fiction, he does make his position clear through his characters. Conscious of the agony in decision making, of possible escapes from responsibility, and of determinism, King first introduces several choices and then makes his point. In *Insomnia* (1994), for instance, he does not take a stand for or against abortion but emphasizes a humane view. In this and in his empathy with his characters, King seems to be retelling Twain's *Huckleberry Finn.* Magistrale points out that "in order to endure morally, the individual must balance a love for his fellow man and resolve to avoid his decadent societal institutions" (*Landscape,* 92).

To conclude, besides graphic illustrations of supernatural horror, King comments on his readers' ultimate fears, enlarging the scope beyond the personal to include a larger, cultural context. Therefore, his stories are not only excursions into a "world that never was, never could be" (*NS,* xx), but at best a "serious social fiction" (Magistrale, *Landscape,* 25). Besides the themes listed in the preceding discussion, King explores sociological determinism at work in the high school or college environment in *Carrie, Rage,* "Sometimes They Come Back" (*Night Shift*), "Apt Pupil" (*Different Seasons*), *Christine,* "Here There Be Tygers" (*Skeleton Crew*),

"Cain Rose Up" *(Skeleton Crew)*, "Suffer the Little Children" *(Nightmares and Dreamscapes)*, and *Hearts in Atlantis*, to merely mention some works in which the location plays a central role. Religious pressure is exerted in *Carrie*, "Children of the Corn" *(Night Shift)*, *The Dead Zone*, *The Gunslinger*, "The Mist" *(Skeleton Crew)*, and *Insomnia*. The social environment exerts power over its residents in *'Salem's Lot*, *It*, *Needful Things*, *Bag of Bones*, and *Storm of the Century*. The government pursues the destruction of its citizens in *The Stand*, *Firestarter*, *The Running Man*, "The Mist" *(Skeleton Crew)*, *Stephen King's Golden Years*, and *Dreamcatcher*. Far from being exhaustive, these lists indicate the width and breath of King's treatment of sociological determinism.

Two characters will be used to illustrate genetic determinism in King: John Coffey, with his inborn supernatural abilities, in *The Green Mile* (1996) and Tom Cullen, by his retardation and childlike innocence, in *The Stand* (1978).

THE GREEN MILE

Published originally in six monthly installments, *The Green Mile* follows the serial-novel form that Charles Dickens employed a century and a half ago (*GM*, vii). The deceptively simple story of John Coffey is narrated by Paul Edgecombe, a 104-year-old, retired block superintendent whose "essentially decent voice; low-key, honest, perhaps a little wide-eyed . . . is a Stephen King voice if ever there was one" (xiii). Set in prison like the novella "Rita Hayworth and the Shawshank Redemption" *(Different Seasons)*, *The Green Mile* relates the story of a black simpleton who is brought to E Block at Cold Mountain Penitentiary in the southern United States in 1932 to be executed for a crime he did not commit. Born with a supernatural healing gift, John Coffey, wrongfully convicted of having raped and murdered nine-year-old twin girls, faces with benevolence the wrongs he has suffered. In doing so he brings about transcendence to those on the Mile, that is, a row of cells that houses criminals destined for the electric chair. Apart from horror, *The Green Mile* can be labeled both a tragedy and a morality play. It discusses the existence of God, and, as Stephen J. Spignesi notes, examines the possibility that Jesus Christ has returned repeatedly to our world over the centuries only to be crucified again and again (*Essential*, 29). Indeed, John Coffey shares his initial letters with Jesus Christ, and the novel focuses on both emotional and physical mortality. Wiater, Golden, and Wagner point out that, besides prison, the system also comprises society as a whole, since racism is one of the key reasons for Coffey's wrongful imprisonment (364). To emphasize the racial aspect, King has set the novel in the southern United States.

Genetic determinism is displayed by both supernatural and realistic means in the novel: Coffey's supernatural healing ability and his race. Both isolate him from society and turn him into a freak in the eyes of his fellow human beings. Thus, by merging, genetic determinism and sociological determinism result in the destruction of John Coffey. Though subtle in presentation, the supernatural element emphasizes both the deterministic and the haphazard character of Coffey's ability. Although the gift/curse molds his entire life, Coffey did nothing to deserve it. Just as he could not choose his race, he could hardly refuse to receive his supernatural gift. The presence of the supernatural, or even the divine, becomes obvious when Coffey heals Paul Edgecombe's urinary infection, and the force of his touch lengthens Paul's life beyond his allotted lifespan—as it does in the case of the prison mouse, Mr. Jingles. As Wiater, Golden, and Wagner aptly note, despite Paul's hopes no deus ex machina appears to prevent the execution (365). Indeed, a similar regret was uttered in connection with the crucifixion of Jesus Christ. What is more, if John Coffey had been saved, King could not have made his point. Hence, the reader, too, is forced to face his own prejudices.

A strong but naive African American, John Coffey does not stand a chance against the governmental machinery. While wandering through the woods, he discovers the bodies of two white girls who have just been raped and murdered. In an attempt to revive the victims, he gets blood on his hands and is found crying over the bodies. Lacking both the wit and the will to defend himself, the simple-minded Coffey is sentenced to death for the rape and murder of the Detterick twins. Undoubtedly, his destiny is sealed the moment he comes upon the girls, because "John Coffey is a Negro, and in Trapingus County we're awful particular about giving new trials for Negroes" (*GM*, 404). King observes Coffey's race, strength, and naivety, which as genetic— and, to some extent, sociological—determinants contribute to his death sentence, convincing the white jury of his guilt: "My first thought was that he looked like a black Samson . . . only after Delilah had shaved him smooth as her faithless little hand and taken all the fun out of him" (10, ellipsis in original). Unlike most of King's characters, John Coffey remains a mystery: he is neither provided with a background, nor does the reader learn about his whereabouts during his adult life. Indeed, marked by the absence of features (14), Coffey appears to be both the personification of fate and a character struck by it.

Apart from determinism fate plays a decisive role in the novel. King suggests the existence of external evil when discussing the case of the mild-mannered Eduard Delacroix, who in an attempt to dispose of the evidence of his crime, the rape-murder of a young girl, has killed six more people. Although Delacroix is shortly to be electrocuted, neither an electric chair nor an injection can ever kill the evil as it has already found a new host: "It vacates, jumps to someone else, and leaves us to kill husks that aren't really alive anyway" (14). As noted, despite a few exceptions in his fiction, King views humans as innately good. Evil, in turn, derives from two sources, namely, external evil and socialization. The former draws on King's view of the existence of personal good/personal evil, that is, the White force/the Black force or God/the Devil. The latter has its origins in King's Wordsworthian view of children. According to this tabula rasa view of humanity, children learn anything—either good or evil—grown-ups teach them. Evil can thus be learned during the process of socialization. It can be handed down from one generation to the next, and it spreads like a contagious disease. However, King's concept of evil embraces a feeling of empathy even for his worst criminals, because in most cases he regards them as victims of unfortunate circumstances. As King emphasizes, "even the bad guy deserves to tell his side of his story" (Underwood and Miller, *Bones*, 80). Both determinism and fate in the form of evil destiny constitute strong forces in bringing about the destruction of even the best of his characters. However, despite these strong forces, by maintaining his essential humanity and moral backbone, the character deserves both King's and the reader's sympathy and respect.

As a sympathetic character, the simple and pure-hearted John Coffey succeeds in both. His lawyer cannot even find his way to the prison, as King somewhat ironically notes. The reader feels an urge to defend John Coffey, who is only capable of repeating:

"I tried to take it back, but it was too late" (*GM*, 37). Because of the hatred and prejudices of his fellow human beings, Coffey's regret is certain to be interpreted in the wrong way, and only Paul Edgecombe and his closest colleagues seem to be interested in the truth. Although rare in number, these characters making a stand bear witness to King's basic trust in human decency. By including good and courageous characters in all his novels, King seems to call both his characters and readers to take a moral stand. Despite Paul Edgecombe's efforts and to his dismay, John Coffey appears to be relieved to be executed. Because he feels "sorrow for the whole world," "something too big ever to be completely eased" (103), his life has become an unbearable burden. Certainly, in John Coffey King introduces one of his most deterministic characters. Coffey is determined genetically, sociologically, cosmologically, metafictionally, and by fate. Cosmological determinism affects him in much the same way as the other residents of King's multiverse. Metafictionally, Coffey's destiny is sealed fairly early on when Paul Edgecombe recalls the memory of Coffey's execution (66). *The Green Mile* focuses on John Coffey, the first prisoner Paul Edgecombe offers his hand to (17). In King humanity and common decency can at least offer some hope against racial and social intolerance.

THE STAND

By means of gentleness, innocence, and love typical of children, the retarded Tom Cullen of *The Stand* participates in the conflict between good and evil, an issue at the core of all of King's major stories. The handicap that has alienated Tom from others no longer seems important. His disability becomes a blessing, since innocence and naivety allow him to rise above his miserable circumstances. Furthermore, he possesses the qualities of unselfish love, loyalty, and courage essential for survival in a world where, as Magistrale notes, former values can no longer be taken for granted (*Voyages*, 70). Tom Cullen's life appears to be as determined as that of John Coffey, with the exception that Cullen is white. An outsider and victim of society's cruelty, Tom leads a life that has also been molded by fate. The crucial difference between the values of the old world and the new is manifested in the destinies of these two men with similar status and inner qualities. The world John Coffey lives in has no use for his goodness and sentences him to death, whereas Tom Cullen's special abilities contribute to the final victory of the Free Zone, Mother Abagail's base.

Tom's purity of soul seems so complete that Randall Flagg's extrasensory perception fails to detect him. Magistrale refers to Tom as the sainted idiot, whose goodness enables him to establish direct contact with God (*Voyages*, 70). Placed under hypnosis in preparation for his assignment to spy on Flagg, he is able to see the Dark Man's face, which has always been hidden from the others. Sharon A. Russell rightly notes that in King's fiction it is the ability to retain a sense of wonder that usually saves a child from destruction (120), and Tom, to be sure, has not lost his connection with childhood. He eludes Randall Flagg's searching Eye, which, as we have seen, clearly imitates that of Sauron in Tolkien's *Lord of the Rings*. Invisible to the Eye, Tom resembles Frodo Baggins and Sam Gamgee when they manage to evade Sauron's Eye in their invisible cloaks. Despite his fear Tom Cullen agrees on a westward journey or rather a crusade against Randall Flagg. By doing so he grows in stature: "I am God's Tom" (*ST* 1009). As God's good servant, he leaves the Free Zone, following the simple instructions to kill if one person sees him and to run away if more than one person sees him.

Whereas fate strikes John Coffey in the form of evil destiny, it borders on the notion of God as regards Tom. Not only does he remain immune to the Dark Man's powers of omniscience, but the previously feeble Tom turns out to be the first person to evoke fear in Flagg. Like Sauron in *The Lord of the Rings*, Flagg sends forth his searching Eye several times, but it affords him nothing (1205). Despite his disability Tom has a strong love for the people in the Free Zone. This love gives him the courage to clear the obstacles in his way. As Magistrale points out, by means of his extrasensory perception, advising him in the desert through the voice of Nick Andros, Tom rescues Stu Redman from certain death (*Voyages*, 71). Indeed, love or the lack of it also makes the difference between the communities of Las Vegas and the Free Zone. What was missing in Las Vegas, King has Tom decide, was simply love: "Love didn't grow very well in a place where there was only fear, just as plants didn't grow very well in a place where it was always dark" (*ST*, 1249–50). In King selfish urges alienate individuals from love, which presupposes sacrifices and a sense of community. According to Jonathan P. Davies, King's works "serve to argue that society needs a collective good will" (85). The sacrifices of Glen Bateman, Tom Cullen, Dayna Jurgens, Stu Redman, and Larry Underwood are made of their own free will, and it is precisely this unselfish love that King regards as the hope for humanity's future.

ROADWORK

Sociological determinism is strongly marked in both *Roadwork* and *Needful Things*. In the former the institutions exerting pressure on humans are society and the government, whereas the latter focuses on the close-knit community and the church. *Roadwork* is an example of King's naturalistic work, whereas *Needful Things* exemplifies traditional horror or even the Gothic. King argues that *Roadwork* is an effort to make sense of his mother's painful death from cancer (Winter, *Art*, 202–3). Indeed, Barton George Dawes's secure life changes tragically when his son Charlie dies from an inoperable brain tumor. Subtitled *A Novel of the First Energy Crisis*, the majority of the story occurs between November 20, 1973, and January 20, 1974. Wiater, Golden, and Wagner note that in that brief timespan of the United States' nationwide energy shortage brought on by the Middle East Oil crisis, we witness the protagonist's disintegration as he is deprived of his livelihood, his marriage, and his cherished home (400).

In *Roadwork* genetic and sociological determinism together result in the destruction of the protagonist. The former presents itself in the form of the incurable tumor; the latter as a breakdown in human communication between the couple and as governmental indifference to the citizens' needs and wishes. An executive at the Blue Ribbon Laundry, Barton George Dawes is on the verge of a breakdown when the state government decides to build a freeway extension that will pass through both his laundry and his neighborhood. Having lost his son and about to lose his wife, Dawes maintains his routines without letting himself think about them. However, he is deeply shaken by the meaninglessness of life. Comparing the freeway extension with Charlie's tumor, Dawes considers God responsible for doing "a little roadwork on their son Charlie's brain" (*RW*, 620). He then draws the conclusion that "if a collection of bad cells no bigger than a walnut" could actually destroy all valuable things in life, life couldn't be trusted, and he would be "justified in stepping out of his car" (624–25). But even death is a cold comfort to Dawes, because life seems "a preparation for hell" (625). Indeed, it is the death of his son that alienates Dawes from both his colleagues and his wife. Dawes cannot cry over Charlie, whereas Mary is healed by doing so. Despite the couple's shared experiences, Mary leaves her husband, because he appears to be too unstable. Again a breakdown in human communication dissolves a marriage, since, unable to find consolation in each other, Mary and Bart drift into a crisis.

Dawes defies the deterministic forces in his life by taking action or, as he sees it, by shouldering the responsibility for his own life and for his close-knit community. Regarding his fellow human beings as cowards, he decides to take a stand and purchases a 460 Weatherby gun for his cousin Nick Adams, a passionate hunter from Michigan. To prevent the freeway extension from being constructed, Dawes takes direct measures in the manner of Nick Adams in Hemingway. Firebombing the construction site only to discover that the project is only going to be delayed, Dawes finally admits having suffered defeat after defeat. As Winter maintains, Dawes's life seems "nothing but a memorial to mindlessness" (*Art*, 203). Before his final act of violence, Dawes gives in to temptation and makes love to an attractive hitchhiker with whom he discusses the roadwork:

> "What do you think of it?" he asked her.
> "Am I supposed to think something?" She was fencing, trying to figure this out.
> "You must think of something," he said.
> She shrugged. "It's a roadwork, so what? They are building a road in a city I'll probably never be in again. What am I supposed to think? It's ugly." (*RW*, 552)

In short, what outlines the framework and content of life to one person means nothing to another. Also, if viewed from another angle, the state government has little empathy for an individual character's suffering and pain. Ironically, the seemingly insane Bart turns out to be the one character acting morally. He sets up a trust fund for the hitchhiker, Olivia Brenner, using the money from the sale of his home. While she, in turn, uses the money to get her life together and enrolls in business school, Dawes's unselfish act appears to be the only positive achievement in the novel. Again King seems to underscore that love, which is so sadly lacking, should come from within—it cannot be taken for granted as coming from the government or from any other authorities, for that matter. As Winter notes, in desperation Bart Dawes finally wires his home with explosives and waits for the authorities and the news cameras, "with the hope that once, just once, people will think" (*Art*, 204).

In *Roadwork* no one will—even though, of course, its readers might. By not revealing the name of Dawes's small city or that of the state, King makes the point that Dawes's fate could become anybody's fate. Wiater, Golden, and Wagner argue that despite the lack of the supernatural to soften the blows of harsh reality, the novel quickly becomes surreal in the sense that "everything that befalls Dawes is like a personal solar eclipse" (401). Experiencing no joyful sequences to balance the unremitting series of small catastrophes, Dawes is consumed by the darkness around him. Obsessive and violent, he can only receive the reader's pity. In King life is unjust, and the attempts of Charlie Decker, Ray Garrety, Bart Dawes, and Ben Richards to take a moral stand prove effortless and lead to destruction. Whether other options exist goes unanswered in the Bachman books.

In the four Bachman books, sociological determinism shapes the lives of King's characters through home (*Rage* and to some extent *The Long Walk*), school (*Rage*), the community, and the government (all the works). The novels have protagonists who are sociologically so tightly determined and whose free will is so limited that they find violence and self-destruction as their only means to take a stand and defy the prevailing circumstances. While realizing their defeat, Charlie Decker (*Rage*) and Bart Dawes (*Roadwork*) take violent measures in order to take a stand; while realizing their victory, Ray Garrety (*The Long Walk*) and Ben Richards (*The Running Man*) no longer give it any credit. Despite the victory their lives remain unfair and their fate remains meaningless. However, the battle is worth fighting, because in the Stephen King multiverse the moral message is that dedication, determination, and will power may sometimes overcome seemingly impossible odds.

NEEDFUL THINGS

In *Needful Things* cosmological determinism in the form of religious zealotry becomes a vehicle for societal and personal oppression. The novel focuses on sociological determinism through the fictional microcosm of Castle Rock and its religious segregation. Having examined small-town pathology with its calm surface and rotten heart in Derry and Jerusalem's Lot, King demonstrates that small-town America exerts pressure on its citizens in various ways. In Castle Rock the rules of social behavior and etiquette are applied to the smallest detail, from addressing a tourist to paying a visit to a new shop for the first time. Hypocrisy and moral corruption characterize this American pastoral, which condemns anybody who is different. Religious double standards thrive, even to the extent of the two congregation leaders of Castle Rock embroiling themselves in a vendetta. Deriving its name from a Frank Sinatra song, Castle Rock also figures in the Castle Rock trilogy (*The Dark Half* [1989], "The Sun Dog" [1990], and *Needful Things* [1991]), *The Dead Zone* (1979), *Cujo* (1981), and "The Body" (1982). Located near Durham, Maine, where King moved at the age of eleven, and modeled after the Durham of his youth, Castle Rock in *Needful Things* brings back not only the familiar setting but also important characters (Beahm, *Story*, 19, 27). The action covers eight days, from October 8 to October 15, during which the town of Castle Rock is totally destroyed.

The gossipy information of the introduction sets up the meshes of personal conflicts that both shape the lives of the Castle Rock residents and eventually result in the destruction of the town. The folksy narrator begins by welcoming the reader to participate in the action of this traditional horror novel in which characters, despite their apparently social actions, are motivated by evil. Having led the reader to the steps of the bandstand where Alma Frechette was raped and murdered by Frank Dodd in *The Dead Zone*, the narrator introduces the passersby and gossips about their relationships, concentrating on the tensions between various characters. By drawing parallels to readers' experiences, on the one hand, and by bringing them up to date on some of the past history of Castle Rock, on the other hand, the narrator clearly indicates that catastrophic future events might happen in any town (*NT*, 8). Inviting the reader to witness the future events, the narrator now reveals that real trouble is on its way. "The bad feeling seems to come" from Needful Things, a new store that is about to welcome its first customer (9).

In a small town like Castle Rock, havoc can be wreaked by the sudden appearance of a malevolent stranger who brings the web of social conflicts and sociological determinism to the surface. "Things just feel *wrong*" (10, italics in original) when the shop owner, Leland Gaunt, welcomes his first customer, the eleven-year-old Brian Rusk, with the words echoing Count Dracula's salute to Jonathan Harker in *Dracula:* "Come in, my friend. Enter freely, and leave some of the happiness you bring!" (23). Despite his momentary fear, Brian develops an instant liking for the tall, kind Leland Gaunt, who claims to be from Akron, Ohio. Like Kurt Barlow (*'Salem's Lot*), Randall Flagg (*The Stand, The Eyes of the Dragon, The Dark Tower* series), and Andre Linoge (*Storm of the Century*), Gaunt embodies supernatural evil. He regards himself as "an electrician of the human soul" and delights in "cross-wiring" his victims to achieve chaos (339). Comparing the towns-people to fuse boxes lined up neatly side by side, he considers his work quickly accomplished: "All it took was an understanding of human nature" (339). More importantly, he collects souls like trophies by getting people to tell him what they want most in the world. In the tradition of the humorously anarchic Trickster, however, "it was mostly amusement, not souls, that kept him going" (340). In exchange for his bargain, Brian engages himself with something that involves his neighbor. Similarly, Gaunt will involve the whole town in a network of "deeds" (37).

The social structure and the unwritten rules of the town are broken by Polly Chalmers, who ironically brings Leland Gaunt a devil's-food cake, ignoring the fact that "Certain things are simply Not Done" (39). Ordinary behavior is not even expected of Polly, who does not play by the rules and who is therefore considered "Eccentric" (41). Despite her suspicions, Polly, too, purchases a locket called an Azka to relieve her arthritis. As payment she plays a trick on Ace Merrill, an ex-convict and character who appears in "The Body" and "The Sun Dog." By the end of the first section, Leland Gaunt has most of the townspeople in his power. Only the protagonist, Sheriff Alan Pangborn, has the will power to stop Gaunt. There is further destruction when, in the first section, Nettie Cobb and Wilma Jerzyck fight to the death. As is common in King, the introductory section covers the longest period of time, from Tuesday through Sunday, and it puts into motion the accelerating action of the second section.

Because society fails to provide its citizens with security, Gaunt is able to exploit their human defects and loneliness. In King, as Russell points out, civilization seems a thin coating over our violent impulses, and he gives little credit to our abilities to live together in harmony. As the social structures of Castle Rock begin to fall apart, King proves how weak the traditional supports of a community are (122). Teaming up with the petty criminals Ace Merrill and Buster Keeton, Gaunt reaps the fruits of his labor in the course of the second section. Having finally left the burning town, Polly answers the question, "What happened?" with the words, "There was a sale. The biggest going-out-of-business sale you ever saw . . . but in the end, some of us decided not to buy" (*NT*, 730, ellipsis in original). Not all of us, says King, subscribe to evil impulses. Therefore, sociological determinism is not all-powerful. Though Gaunt himself is not a force of sociological determinism, his evil is instilled early on by social indifference.

In *Needful Things* King explores the relationship between the individual and the close-knit community and develops the theme in a new way by combining it with two other themes noted by Russell: the importance of childhood and the destructive impact of an evil presence (121). As Wiater, Golden, and Wagner state, this premise derives from a long tradition in American literature for chronicling events in small towns, from Sherwood Anderson's *Winesburg, Ohio* and Thornton Wilder's *Our Town* to Don Robertson's *Paradise Falls* (154)—not to mention classic stories by Irving, Hawthorne, and Twain. As Wiater, Golden, and Wagner go on to point out, the horror genre has similar examples where a stranger comes to town, wreaking havoc for his own purposes, most notably Ray Bradbury's *Something Wicked This Way Comes,* Charles Beaumont's *Intruder,* and Richard Matheson's short story "The Distributor" (154). Most of the characters are defined by their needful things and, more importantly, what they are willing to do in order to get them. Gaunt argues that "*everything is for sale*" (*NT*, 82, italics in original), because "it's *really* a question of supply and demand" (339, italics in original). He also refers to the people's free will and free trade (722). Tragically,

however, most of the needful things have no value in themselves, and virtually everybody falls prey to Gaunt, even the
basically decent people who simply wish to fulfill one of their
dreams. Concerned with how far people will go in their quest for
personal gratification and afraid that it can destroy society, King
explores Castle Rock and uses Leland Gaunt and his store to test
the rules of the microcosm. Russell claims that if *The Stand* views
"what happens after a civilization is destroyed," then *Needful
Things* "details the process of destruction" (122). To be more precise, Gaunt compares his victims to sheep without a shepherd
whom he deceives by selling them illusions and more dangerous
yet: "At the end, Mr. Gaunt always sold them weapons . . . and
they always bought" (*NT*, 584, ellipsis in original).

Society's failure extends to all the organizations we normally
trust: the sheriff's office, the state government, and the church. As
Russell notes, when individuals become antagonistic, no higher
organization can prevent the violence from escalating (122). Similarly, parent-child relationships also fail in *Needful Things*. Alan
Pangborn, a surrogate father to Brian Rusk, fails to reach the boy
before he commits suicide. Norris Ridgewick is drawn to Gaunt's
shop by the promise of regaining connection with his father.
Since neither Brian nor Norris can admit what they have done in
exchange for their bargains, however, the baseball card and the
fishing rod isolate them from human relations. Realizing that
material goods cannot substitute for parent-child relationships,
both get rid of their special things.

In sum, although sociological determinism plays a decisive
role both in *Needful Things* and in King in general, Leland Gaunt
represents evil that comes from outside. Again "evil places call
evil men" (*SL*, 113; Winter, *Art*, 44), and Leland Gaunt opens his
store in the same building that belonged to Pop Merrill, an evil
character in "The Sun Dog." External evil represented by Gaunt
cooperates with the horror of human evil. In essence the latter
appears to be more destructive than the former, and despite the
supernatural devices, the horror implicit in *Needful Things* remains realistic. Only a few people are able to break away from
Gaunt's control, and they will have to live with and take responsibility for the consequences of their actions. In King the supernatural manifestations of evil seem symbolic representations of a

cultural crisis. As Magistrale claims, evil fills the void created by the absence of healthy personal relationships, responsible government, and a supportive system of religious faith (*Landscape*, 40). Determinism in King focuses on this misconduct of human nature. Unlike the strictest literary naturalists such as Emile Zola, King only seldom leaves his characters completely at the mercy of indifferent forces, but allows them to discover humanity, even morality, in their fellow human beings—not to mention, through occasional interventions of cosmological forces.

Cosmological Determinism and Fate

Cosmological determinism and fate seem interrelated in King's works. King has created a relatively coherent oeuvre in which the individual works largely reflect a compatible worldview and, indeed, obey the same laws. However, King has not deliberately been building his multiverse from the beginning of his writing career, and it would be both unrealistic and implausibly teleological to assume a cosmological consistency in his works. Of course, the weighting of the various types of determinism shifts from novel to novel, but the principal determinants of human behavior remain the same. King's stories often provide a moralistically Calvinist, Lovecraftian cosmology of distance and power, where the inscrutable Deity at times is the inscrutable Wrath delivering justice. In the tradition of New England Puritanism, cosmological determinism in King becomes the vehicle of sociological determinism; the emissaries of wrath take a variety of guises, such as the mythical Beast *(The Dark Tower)*, the God of the Lost *(The Girl Who Loved Tom Gordon)*, and alien weasels *(Dreamcatcher)*, but they always constitute a major threat to the communities they attack. Reino argues that basic to the philosophy of virtually all of King's stories is Lovecraft's concept of cosmic fear (20). H. P. Lovecraft defines this kind of horror as a "certain atmosphere of breathless and unexplainable dread" that expresses "a malign and particular suspension or defeat of those fixed laws of Nature that are our only safeguard against the assaults of chaos and the daemons of unplumbed space" (*Horror*, 15). While King does not harp on universal and/or divine malevolence with Lovecraft's psychopathic insistence (Reino, 21), he at times substitutes twists of fate for Lovecraft's hostility against God. Therefore, cosmological determinism and fate are inseparable in King's fiction.

Fate constitutes a prevalent motif throughout King's works. In fact, at the heart of all his writing is the role fate plays in our lives. However, cosmological determinism appears to be even more complex, because the realistic setting of, for instance, the Bachman books finds no easy equivalent in that of, for instance, Roland the Gunslinger, whose mythical quest takes him through a number of more or less fantastic worlds in the King multiverse. King has repeatedly suggested that our universe may exist within a larger one, which, in turn, exists within an even larger universe, and that these may be interrelated (see, for instance, *GS*, 207–9). Wiater, Golden, and Wagner sum up most of the interrelations, maintaining that with the publication of the simultaneously written *Desperation* (1996, published by King) and *The Regulators* (1996, published by Bachman), King consciously incorporates the Bachman books into his multiverse. As they go on to argue, the references seem infrequent (Ellen Carver in *Desperation* is a fan of Paul Sheldon's Misery novels) and the connecting characters minor (Cynthia Smith from *Rose Madder* appears in *Desperation*), but King finally allows the world of Richard Bachman to fuse with his other parallel realities. More importantly, the characters of *Desperation* and *The Regulators* are involved in a cosmic battle of good versus evil, order versus chaos, or the Purpose versus the Random (387–88). In this section I suggest that in King's multiverse human behavior is determined by cosmological forces. Cosmological determinism appears in three forms: (1) mythical forces related to *The Dark Tower* series (2) God/the Devil, and (3) other extraterrestrials, such as science-fiction aliens. The first two suggest a cosmological principle of predestined order, whereas the third focuses on extraterrestrial control of life on earth. The three forms of cosmological determinism are interrelated and reflect a rather coherent worldview. The forces will be dealt with in this order with a focus on fate.

Virtually all of King's stories suggest human bondage to fate. When defining King as a writer, Reino refers to fate by wondering how anybody can be popular with such a grim "view of himself, his readers, his state (Maine), his nation, and the malevolent universe into which he had the misfortune to be born" (1). Later, when focusing on King's fiction, instead of his personality, he claims that "a God-hostile point of view permeates much of King's work" (20–21). Thus, he suggests that chaos, evil destiny, or inscrutable fate wait to devour his characters when the fixed laws of nature cease to protect them (20–21). In a similar vein Harold Bloom in the introduction to *Bloom's BioCritiques: Stephen King* traces King's brand of horror to the "sub-literary" prose of Poe and H. P. Lovecraft (1). Rather than being hostile to God, King seems to project some wrath of the inscrutable Puritan Deity in fate, which "kills the very good and the very gentle and the very brave impartially" (Hemingway, *Farewell to Arms*, 249). A number of critics seem to share Ben P. Indick's grim view of fate in King as he considers *Cujo* "an existentialist application of a blind, uncaring universe purposelessly destroying" whatever comes its way ("Supernatural," 12). Surely, in its destructive aspect fate is King's way of warning us to be on our guard and to prepare ourselves for the forces of reality and death.

The pessimistic aspect may seem overpowering, but it is still only one facet of King's conception of fate. In fact, he embraces three different meanings of *fate* in his fiction. First, fate borders on the notion of God. In this aspect it denotes a predetermined and inevitable necessity, that is, the power that is thought to determine one's future, success, or failure. In King fate conspires against evil forces (as in, for instance, *Insomnia*), which indicates that the notion of fate might often border on that of God, thus equaling his notions of "fate," "purpose," "necessity," and "destiny." Second, fate may resemble "chance" or "blind coincidence" (see, for instance, the Bachman books). Third, fate can indicate "evil destiny," "doom," and "destruction," even "death" (see, for instance, *The Shining* and *Storm of the Century*). Generally speaking, the first notion of fate is tantamount to God, and the third one borders on the devil, since the twists and turns in which it involves his characters seem haphazard or evil. When analyzing *Thinner* (1984), Magistrale aptly characterizes the second notion of fate by arguing that "other agents are involved when a human tragedy occurs—including the absence of dumb luck" (*Decade*, 62). This is exactly what fate denotes in *Thinner*: a lack of substance, a lack of luck.

Somewhat surprisingly, the conception of *fate* and the word *fairy* (as in *fairy tale*) derive from the same origin. Marina Warner argues that the word *fairy* in the Romance languages indicates a meaning of the fairy tale, because it goes back to a Latin word, *fata*, a rare variant of *fatum* (fate), referring to a goddess of destiny. The fairies and the goddess of destiny resemble each other, for both know the course of fate. Fate, or *fatum*, means literally "that which is spoken," and the past particle of the verb *fari*, "to speak," gives French *fée*, Italian *fata*, Spanish *hada*, all meaning "fairy" and including connotations of fate (*Beast*, 14–15; for the relation between religion and fairy stories, see Tolkien, "On Fairy-Stories"). Thus, all the genres and modes analyzed in this study regard fate as one of their key notions. Western culture seems to have adopted these notions from Greek mythology, in which Atropos, Lachesis, and Clotho were three sisters who together made up the three aspects of Fate. King is aware of the three Fates, and in *Insomnia* (1994) he has simply changed their gender but preserved the names. As the daughters of Zeus and Themis (the goddess of law), maidenly Clotho ("the spinner") spun the thread of each human's life, middle-aged Lachesis ("the apportioner") selected the length of each thread, and the hag Atropos ("the inflexible") cut through it, thus causing the end of each life (Forty, 274). In *Insomnia* these creatures are called "little bald doctors" by the protagonist (216) and "physicians of the last resort" by themselves (388). As in King the three Fates stood above the interplay between gods and humans, taking little part in earthly matters. In fact, they were nearly outside time itself (Forty, 274). In King, Clotho and Lachesis serve the Purpose, that is, meaningful death, whereas Atropos—the hag—remains an agent of the Random, that is, random death.

In King's individual works, cosmological determinism is intertwined with fate. While fate includes an aspect of predestination, even the works that do not specifically deal with cosmological determinism, may, however, be exposed to it in the form of fate. For instance, the protagonist of *Rage*, Charlie Decker, who appears to be at the mercy of irrational forces, stays alive despite a marksman's bullet, because fate interferes in the form of chance or coincidence. Also, although cosmological determinism as such is not treated in *Carrie* or *'Salem's Lot*, both Carrie and Count Barlow are struck by fate in the form of evil destiny. Thus, no clear distinctions can be made as regards cosmological determinism, and it is constantly blended with fate. My objective here is to explore the implications of what cosmological determinism and fate can mean in King's fiction. Ultimately, both reflect his personal worldview, which presupposes the existence of these forces. In King humans are not the masters of their fate but are shaped by various forces. However, this strict determinism is alleviated by free will, responsibility, and at times religious faith.

King was raised in an atmosphere of a secularized version of the Calvinistic creed of predestination. In the mid-eighties he then became acquainted with Joseph Campbell's works on universal myths and was influenced by them. Although some of King's characters have been molded after mythical models, not all of them can be traced to Campbell for the obvious reason that some of the books in which such characters figure, for instance, *The Stand* (1978) (Randall Flagg) and *The Gunslinger* (1982) (Roland the Gunslinger), were published before King had even read Campbell's study. Hence, as difficult as it appears to locate a precise influence, we should also keep in mind that mythical influences are derived from various sources. We absorb them from childhood on through comics, books, and films. Significantly, King acknowledges his debt to the works he read during his formative years: the Bible and *King Arthur's Tales* (Magistrale, *Decade*, 3). Although the journey motif, for instance, is found in all literature—Northrop Frye explored the idea with his class of 1932 and has expressed it in *Anatomy of Criticism* in 1957—King has applied Campbell's representation of cosmology to his fiction, and it will therefore be emphasized in this section. The first form of cosmological determinism in King deals with fate and the mythical good and evil.

FATE AND THE MYTHICAL GOOD AND EVIL

The mythical representatives of good and evil can be detected in *The Dark Tower* series and the works related to it. The mysterious Crimson King (*Insomnia, Hearts of Atlantis*, and *The Dark Tower*) inhabiting the Dark Tower is either equated with or at least of the same species as the title character of *It*. Indeed, the Crimson King's cursed son, Mordred, can take spider form. Therefore, let me begin my discussion with *It*. "It" is a spider monster that can take human form and that symbolizes all of King's mythical representatives of evil, while the counterforce of It is the Turtle, and the creator of them both is the Final Other, an equivalent to

Aristotle's unmoved mover (that is, the Creator who creates without moving).

It brings the reader back to Derry, a fictional town in New England, where the members of the Losers' Club return to confront the supernatural creature that terrorized their youth. The title character, an amorphous being from outer space that is shaped by people's imaginations and fears, changed their lives in 1958, when, masquerading as a clown trapped in the sewer, it killed the six-year-old George Denbrough. Discovering that the monster surfaces from a sewer every twenty-seven years to feed on the primal fear of children, Richie Tozier, Bill Denbrough, Beverly Marsh, Ben Hanscom, Mike Hanlon, and Eddie Kaspbrak return to kill it. Both predestination and fate (tantamount to God) play a decisive role in *It*. When the Losers' Club welcomes its seventh member, Mike Hanlon, Bill and Richie realize that they are all together now (*IT*, 689). Again, when the childhood friends return to Derry in 1985, Ben Hanscom notes that in a much-quoted line in King's fiction free will had never been a factor (536).

The Final Other seems to be the power behind the formation of the Losers' Club. Although he only seldom intervenes in human events, he attempts to restore the balance of the multiverse, which is threatened by It. The Losers' Club is aware of the good force, maintaining that the Final Other wanted them "to stay alive and do the job" (884). To strengthen the unity of the club and perhaps even to address the Final Other, the members close their mythical circle. Reminiscent of biblical stigmata, their hands begin to bleed. Symbolizing the universal round, that is, the cosmogonic circle (Campbell, *Hero*, 261), the club members feel the power of the completed circle (*IT*, 886). In King the completed circle also epitomizes love and friendship as the only lasting defense against evil: *"The love is what matters, the caring . . . it's always the desire, never the time. Maybe that's all we get to take with us when we go out of the blue and into the black"* (887–88, italics and ellipsis in original). Indeed, the monster attempts to attack the members of the Losers' Club individually, because it realizes that the strength of the club lies in its unity.

Having long indulged itself with feelings of omnipotence, It senses a new kind of threat in the Losers' Club. Before confronting the children in the summer of 1958, It assumes that before the universe there had been only itself and the Turtle, whom It considers stupid or even dead by now (989). King explains that the character of the Turtle derives in part from a Native American story about a turtle holding up a man who holds up the world and in part from the myth of Atlas holding the world on his shoulder. In his view the Turtle symbolizes everything that is stable and solid in the universe. Embodying sanity in an unstable world, the slow and strong Turtle constitutes a durable force. With him a strong force for good dies (Magistrale, *Decade*, 12-13). When thrown into the void of eternity, Bill encounters the Turtle, who, indeed, can be considered passive: *"I'm the Turtle, son. I made the universe, but please don't blame me for it; I had a bellyache"* (*IT*, 1034, italics in original). When Bill pleads with the Turtle to help him, he refers to It as his brother, maintaining: *"I take no stand in these matters. My brother—has his own place in the macroverse; energy is eternal"* (1034, italics in original). Since in the cosmogonic cycle good and evil take their ordained course, myths seldom make moral judgments. Campbell maintains that it seems universal to cast the antagonist in the role of the clown—and so does King with Pennywise the Clown. These devils may triumph in our world, but they suffer a defeat when the perspective shifts to the transcendental (*Hero*, 294).

The major force of King's mythical multiverse belongs to the Final Other, who, despite his seeming passivity, plays an active role as a cosmological force. Exploring the indifference of God in mythical terms in *It* (just as he explores God in religious terms in *The Stand, Desperation*, and *The Girl Who Loved Tom Gordon*), King draws the conclusion that despite the seeming indifference of God, he is ultimately an active agent. The Turtle reveals that this Final Other dwells in a void beyond this one and has created both the Turtle, who only watches, and It, who only eats. He considers this Final Other "a force beyond the universe, a power beyond all other power, the author of all there is" (*IT*, 1035). Like Aristotle's unmoved mover (primarily a principle), to which the Olympian gods and the three Fates were subjected (Reino, 99), King's Final Other makes things happen of their own accord. The unmoved mover figures in a number of mythologies and, as Campbell states, shapes the universe with a miraculous spontaneity (*Hero*, 281). In King God requires humans to help themselves and their fellow human beings and may therefore seem indifferent. Although the Turtle sounds harsh when he tells Bill to fend for himself, the Final Other has provided the Losers' Club with strength and courage to triumph over evil and to fulfill its destiny.

In its focus on human fate and destiny, *Insomnia* can be considered one of King's distinctly cosmological novels. Centering on the lives of two senior citizens, it has explicit ties to Roland the Gunslinger's world, referring to both Roland and the Crimson King. *Insomnia* also includes the three Fates. Mike Noonan in *Bag of Bones* comments on the death of the protagonist of *Insomnia*, Ralph Roberts, who has made a pact with the Purpose in order to save the life of Natalie Deepneau. Her destiny would have been to die in a car accident, but having fulfilled his own purpose, Ralph sacrifices himself to save her life. The Crimson King, a powerful figure of evil, recurs on a larger scale in *Black House* and serves the Beast of the Tower. Ed Deepneau, a research scientist at Hawking Labs who is driven insane by Atropos, likens him to King Herod, regarding Herod as one of the Crimson King's incarnations. Like the evil in *The Green Mile*, the Crimson King leaps from body to body and generation to generation in search of the Messiah (*IS*, 81–82). While escaping the court of the Crimson King, Ralph Roberts thinks of "deadlights," the deadly gaze of the spider monster of *It*, as though the evil of the Crimson King had leapt into the spider's body.

In *Insomnia* King suggests a strict cosmological determinism. If the Wheel of the Universe is in balance, good triumphs over evil, which indicates that the Wheel represents necessity or the Purpose in *Insomnia*. Both poles have their preordained destinies to fulfill, but at times the Random attempts to interfere in human events and earthly matters. In *Insomnia* Atropos uses Ed Deepneau as his pawn in order to kill Patrick Danville, a young boy who is predestined to save Roland the Gunslinger's life later in *The Dark Tower* series. Patrick, too, dreams about Roland and refers to him as a king. He also draws a picture featuring Roland squaring off against the Red King, that is, the Crimson King, against the backdrop of the Tower. Patrick has a decisive role in the final battle, and after he has been saved, "upon all the levels of the universe, matters both Random and Purposeful resumed their ordained courses. Worlds which had trembled for a moment in their orbits now steadied, and in one of those worlds, in a desert that was the apotheosis of all deserts, a man named Roland turned over in his bedroll and slept easily once again beneath the alien constellations" (617). King suggests that both his characters and the reader have roles to play by participating in the realization of some cosmic plan. King has Ralph realize that "[*l*]*ife is a wheel*" and that "[*s*]*ooner or later everything you thought you'd left behind comes around again*" (656, italics in original).

In *Insomnia* King focuses on the role of fate and portrays it in mythical terms. Ralph Roberts and Lois Chasse form a *ka-tet* and Clotho and Lachesis another *ka-tet* in order to save Patrick Danville. In mapping out the forces at work in the universe, Clotho and Lachesis explain the four constants of existence (life, death, the Random, and the Purpose) and the hierarchy of short timers (normal mortals), long timers (enchanted mortals, such as Dorrance Marstellar, a peculiar guardian angel, and the three Fates), and all timers (immortals, such as the Final Other) (393, 405). When explaining King's cosmological determinism, Clotho and Lachesis claim that all universes exist in "the same tower of existence" (405). Wiater, Golden, and Wagner draw parallels between these cosmological forces: "Between the Random and the Purpose—or, to use terms from other King works, the Beast and the Other—a kind of chess game is being played, but still there is mystery aplenty in life" (112–13). In brief, despite predestination, the cosmic plan can be altered by acting morally and bearing responsibility for one's fellow human beings. As if to underscore this stance, King has added a number of literary references to Greek mythology, the Bible, *Morte D'Arthur,* and *The Lord of the Rings.*

In *Hearts in Atlantis* King suggests more firmly than ever that one should act morally, play one's role in life and the cosmic plan, and take responsibility when required. Shunning moral responsibility, the protagonist loses his direction in life for many years. The novel portrays both the Vietnam War era and the world of *The Dark Tower* series. The first of the five loosely interconnected stories, "Low Men in Yellow Coats," focuses on Bobby Garfield, whose path is tracked throughout the tales and whose wheel of existence is touched by "other worlds than these" (*GS,* 191). The eleven-year-old Bobby is living with his widowed mother in a boardinghouse in Connecticut when Ted Brautigan, a mysterious middle-aged man, moves into the house in 1960.

Bobby and Ted form a friendship, and eventually Bobby learns Ted's secret: he is evading the low men in yellow coats, the supernatural trackers of the Crimson King. Ted is tracked down, because he is regarded as a skillful breaker, that is, a being who can break the beams leading to the Dark Tower. Tragically, Ted is practically handed over to the low men by Bobby's mother, who discloses his hiding place. When given the choice of trying to help Ted or leaving him, Bobby chooses not to fight (*HA*, 287). Again predestination appears in the form of *ka-tet*, and Bobby's crime takes on vast dimensions, because Ted turns out to be his karmic soul brother, *te-ka*, for whose well-being he is responsible. Having lost his faith in himself, Bobby becomes a juvenile delinquent for many years. Only when Bobby receives a message from Ted does he change heart and rid himself of guilt. Having escaped from the Crimson King, Ted has filled the envelope with rose petals, a recognizable image of the Tower in *The Dark Tower* series. The red rose that Jake Chambers finds growing alone in the middle of a wasteland in New York (in *The Waste Lands*) contains all of King's universes much in the same way as the Tower and the title object of *The Talisman*.

By his love and responsibility, Ted saves the boy's life and allows him to redeem himself later in life. Because the multiverse is held together by beams that Ted can shatter, thus giving him a barganing chip, he can negotiate Bobby's release. Shaped in the treadmill of various types of determinism, King's characters may triumph over these forces if they remain true to themselves and do not falter when responsibility should be taken. Regardless of the terms used, good and evil obey the same laws both in King's mythical works related to *The Dark Tower* series and in his works treating these forces according to traditional notions of God and the devil. Such different works as *The Eyes of the Dragon, Rose Madder,* and "Little Sisters of Eluria" (*Everything's Eventual*) include references to the world of Roland the Gunslinger. A number of cross references make clear that King has deliberately been building his multiverse since around the time of *The Talisman*'s publication. It is likely that the collaboration with Peter Straub encouraged him to experiment with new ideas, such as multiple dimensions, which then resulted in the construction of the multiverse.

GOOD AND EVIL IN RELIGIOUS TERMS / FATE

The second form of cosmological determinism in King centers on the role of God as a cosmological determinant. Since the devil has been discussed in connection with Randall Flagg in chapter 2 under "The Antihero as a Generic Hybrid (Randall Flagg)," personified evil will only be referred to here when relevant. This is because King's view of good and evil can likewise be applied to his mythical forces by using different terms. The novels *Desperation* (1996) and *The Girl Who Loved Tom Gordon* (1999) demonstrate that, despite the range of fantastic creatures, King has created a rather coherent oeuvre in which the individual works reflect a common worldview. In addition both King's mythical works related to *The Dark Tower* series and his more realistic stories always focus on real-life issues. With the aid of supernatural creatures and events, King examines the naturalistic forces that shape human existence on earth and determines how much control humans have over their own lives.

It is of crucial importance to distinguish a writer's personal religious conviction from his writing. King comments on faith in *Danse Macabre*, in which he states that faith is all humans can lean on in their existential anguish (409). On another occasion he explains his stance in greater detail, maintaining that no one can say what God is like and that Christ's divinity has not been proven (Larson, 107). Hence, based on the Old Testament and the Judeo-Christian tradition, King's use of religion amounts to an exploration of morality and the seemingly unjust sufferings of innocent people such as Job. Larson notes that King's use of religion varies from the depiction of religious fanaticism in *Carrie* and "The Mist" *(Skeleton Crew)* to the portrayal of the power of a very real God in *The Stand* and Johnny Smith's acceptance of his fate in *The Dead Zone* (107). Winter notes that King's stories tend to "celebrate the existence of good, while graphically demonstrating its cost" (*Art*, 104–5). In an interview with Peter S. Perakos (1978), King affirms this stance, considering God an active agent and rejecting the argument that in most works of the horror genre, evil triumphs over good (Underwood and Miller, *Feast*, 65). Perhaps King's pervasive suspicions of religious organizations partly contribute to his treatment of good and evil beyond established religions. The forces of White and Black may appeal more than any church to a writer who claims that he has "never been crazy about the Catholics, where the men make the rules and the women wash the underwear" (*OW*, 61). King regards himself as "religious in terms of White," that is, elemental good. He does not go to church, because the institution focuses on making morals (Underwood and Miller, *Feast*, 65). This, incidentally, links King with Emerson, who believed in good and evil but distrusted religious institutions.

The question of good versus evil even dominates sociological determinism, another prevalent theme in King, since it epitomizes and sums up the core of all his writing. In a 1988 interview with Janet Beauliau, King argues that, above all else, he is interested in whether there are powers of good and evil outside ourselves. He places these concepts in "the human heart," but while exploring the possibility of external good and evil, he views them through God and the devil (Spignesi, *Essential*, 62). Spignesi notes the spiritual/metaphysical bent of some of King's "more thoughtful recent works" (such as *The Green Mile*, *Desperation*, and *The Girl Who Loved Tom Gordon*), underscoring, however, that religion has been central in King's works throughout his writing career (61). He also refers to King's comments on religion in his letter to reviewers that King included with the review copies of *The Girl Who Loved Tom Gordon*: "I have been writing about God—the possibility of God and the consequences for humans if God does exist—for 20 years now, ever since *The Stand*" (62).

Companion novels, such as *Desperation* and *The Regulators*, have the theme of God in common but treat it differently. *Desperation* analyzes humankind's relationship with God and his divine intervention in human events. *The Regulators* introduces the human being as God, stating that a human in the position of God only wreaks havoc. As in *'Salem's Lot* and *The Stand*, the God of *Desperation* resembles that of the Old Testament. God works through intermediaries, such as Moses, Mother Abagail *(The Stand)*, and David Carver *(Desperation)* and, as Wiater, Golden, and Wagner note, "seems content to sit on the sidelines and observe, unless forces beyond human ken come into play" (416). Although both *Desperation* and *The Girl Who Loved Tom Gordon* show God as an active agent, he remains a mystery in King. David Carver's first encounter with God recalls Moses on Mount

Horeb. While asking, *"Who are you?"* he is answered, *"Who I am"* (*DE*, 137, italics in original). In King the mythical Final Other and God resemble each other in passivity. Only when the balance of King's multiverse seems endangered do they intervene in human events.

As in virtually all of King's works, fate constitutes a cosmological force in *Desperation* and is tantamount to God. The novel relates the story of a group of people who, while traveling on Interstate 50 through the Nevada desert, are arrested by a police officer possessed by Tak, an ancient demon. The characters unanimously repeat the age-old question: "Why are some chosen, while others are killed?" The survivors soon conclude that they were chosen by Tak, who acts like "the Angel of Death in Exodus" (277). Cosmological determinism is displayed in the form of the Old Testament narratives. King frames the novel by introducing the story of Moses and the water springing from the rock (145). He begins by suggesting that the eleven-year-old David Carver might be a worthy successor of the Old Testament prophet. When the Israelites ask to whom their thanks for the water should be directed, Moses says that they can thank Moses himself. In contrast, David takes no credit for the recovery of his friend, Brian. More important seems the thematic echo the story produces: like his biblical predecessor, David will be displaced when it is time to lead the survivors to safety. King here repeats the notion of God's cruelty only to reject it at the end of the novel. The drunk Reverend Martin reveals one of our worst fears about God's nature—cruelty and indifference to human pain: "'Just one little misstep in a long, hardworking life in the service of the Lord,' Reverend Martin said cheerfully, 'but God kept him out of the Promised Land for it. Joshua led 'em across the river'" (144). Because of its seeming imbalance, the young David Carver's battle with the demonic Tak resembles the conflict between David and Goliath. David also recalls an Old Testament story of Daniel in the lion's den (192–93), whereas another character cites the phrase "And a little child shall lead them" (266). Performing miracles, the Christ figure David Carver pleads with God to lift the burden placed on his shoulders. Like Mother Abagail of *The Stand*, David underscores the importance of taking a moral stand: "[I]f we leave Desperation without doing what God sent us here to do, we'll pay the price" (415).

Despite his obvious omnipotence, King's God requires human assistance and acts through human vessels. A year before the main narrative of the novel, David Carver has faced a tragedy when his best friend, Brian, was critically injured by a drunk driver. While walking in the woods in his agony, David hears the voice of God. In exchange for God's saving his friend's life, he promises to become God's servant. Shortly thereafter Brian returns to health, whereas God instructs David to seek out the Reverend Martin, who becomes the boy's spiritual guide. Chosen by God, David is prepared for his mission in Desperation. Only when Tak captures his family does he realize that the events are predestined and that he has to fulfill his own destiny. Under the impression that God has chosen him to battle Tak, David escapes from his prison cell and releases his fellow inmates. Like Moses of the Old Testament, he discovers that somebody else has been chosen to finish the mission. Humbling his heart before God, David leaves Desperation with the conviction that God is a loving deity: "First John, chapter four, verse eight. 'God is love'" (546).

"The world had teeth and it could bite you with them anytime it wanted" reads the opening line of *The Girl Who Loved Tom Gordon,* which goes on to discuss the nature of God. A purely situational novel, it introduces Trisha McFarland, a nine-year-old schoolgirl, who gets lost in the woods. In an effort to combat her mounting fear, she imagines that Tom Gordon, the Boston Red Sox relief pitcher, is there with her. King's God seems a creator-preserver-destroyer, which reflects one of the numerous conceptions of myth. In this respect Campbell refers to the paradox of the dual focus: "Just as at the opening of the cosmogonic cycle it was possible to say 'God is not involved,' but at the same time 'God is creator-preserver-destroyer,' so now at this critical juncture, where the One breaks into many, destiny 'happens,' but at the same time 'is brought about'" (*Hero,* 288). Similarly, King has divided his creator-preserver-destroyer God in *The Girl Who Loved Tom Gordon* into three different god figures: Mr. Bork, the Subaudible, and the God of the Lost, respectively. Mr. Bork, who resembles Trisha's science teacher at Sanford Elementary School, represents the God of Tom Gordon, the "one he points up to when he gets the save" (*GWLTG,* 168). Although Tom's God in principle can be reached, he does not generally intervene in earthly matters. The Subaudible is Larry McFarland's name for a protective but weak God (72). The third figure is referred to as the God of the Woods or the God of the Lost, and, according to his destroyer nature, he is merely waiting for Trisha McFarland to mature.

The question of the nature of God is intertwined with fate in *The Girl Who Loved Tom Gordon.* While musing on her parents' divorce and her brother's recurring question why the children have to pay for what their parents do wrong, Trisha draws the same conclusion as a number of other King characters: "just because" (166). She survives because she accepts the facts of life and even the role of fate in it (166). In the woods Trisha also encounters the three gods: two in white robes, one in a black robe. The second white-robed god, the Subaudible, looks like her father. As Trisha has suspected all along, this god turns out to be so weak that he has to take the shape of someone she knows in order to appear. The figure in the black robe has no face, only a deformed head made of wasps. The black-robed figure affirms Trisha's worst fears concerning the world: "The skin of the world is woven of stingers, a fact you have now learned for yourself. Beneath there is nothing but bone and the God we share" (171).

In his fiction King rather seldom uses characters as mouthpieces for his moral views. In *The Girl Who Loved Tom Gordon,* however, he forcefully points out who the real God is. When the God on the left steps forward, Trisha recognizes Tom Gordon's God, Mr. Bork from Sanford Elementary School. Mr. Bork can be seen to epitomize King's ambiguous relationship to God: in principle he should be imminent, but the person in need can never *truly* count on him. When Trisha asks Tom Gordon about "that pointin thing," he explains: "I point because it's God's nature to come on in the bottom of the ninth. . . . Especially when the bases are loaded and there's only one out" (185). Tom's God is desperately needed, and Trisha begins to develop a direct link to him, while the God of the Lost keeps her company on her journey. Having found the road, she knows where to point. While awaiting the inevitable confrontation with the God of the Lost, Trisha negotiates with the God of Tom Gordon, attempting to establish trust in him. Afraid that he might be occupied with something more important, however, she decides to make a leap of faith. In Trisha's prayer King crystallizes humankind's agony before the invisible God: "'God, if You can't be a Red Sox fan, be a Tom Gordon fan,' she said. 'Can you do that much, at least? Can you *be* that much?'" (235, italics in original). In *The Girl Who Loved Tom Gordon,* he can.

Throughout King, God requires human assistance. While the God of the Lost announces his terms, commanding her to worship him, Trisha realizes that she must "close" (246), that is, end the game. Later in the hospital Trisha has a message for her father. Pointing to Tom Gordon's and, more importantly, to her own God, she never takes her eyes from her father. King underscores the importance of love: "The smile which lit his face from the eyes down was the sweetest, truest thing she had ever seen. If there was a path, it was there" (262). Good often triumphs over evil both in King's mythical works related to *The Dark Tower* series and in the works that explore the existence of good and evil in traditional terms. In both, responsibility and compassion for one's fellow human beings can overcome seemingly overwhelming obstacles. Also, despite God's seeming passivity, he comes to the aid of those who help themselves.

EXTRATERRESTRIAL CONTROL AND FATE

The third form of cosmological determinism comprises extraterrestrial control of life on earth. King depicts evil through aliens. However, the aliens are not allowed to reign free, but rather good forces challenge them in the form of courageous and independent individuals. In its science-fiction form King has dealt with this force in the novels *The Tommyknockers* and *Dreamcatcher.* Aliens also exert influence on humans in such stories as "I Am the Doorway" *(Night Shift),* "The Lonesome Death of Jordy Verrill" *(Creepshow),* "Beachworld" *(Skeleton Crew),* "Home Delivery" *(Nightmares and Dreamscapes),* and "The Ten O' Clock People" *(Nightmares and Dreamscapes).* In both *The Tommyknockers* and *Dreamcatcher,* King mocks scientific pretensions. Again he deftly uses science-fiction conventions when writing horror stories (for science-fiction conventions, see Aldiss, 350–52; Knight, 63; Parrinder, 17; Scholes and Rabkin, 89; Sutherland "American Science Fiction since 1960," 162). In doing so, he shows how technology for its own sake may not be progress at all *(The Tommyknockers)* and how little the government takes responsibility for its citizens *(Dreamcatcher).* By acknowledging that scientific progress has done little for humans as moral beings, King pleads for the restoration of the dignity of the human being. Furthermore, cosmological determinism is undercut in both novels by means of humor and imagination. Both also underscore the importance of moral action and responsibility.

Reminiscent of H. P. Lovecraft's classic 1927 tale "The Colour Out of Space," *The Tommyknockers* conveys the fears King felt as a child growing up during the Cold War. Having had his formative years during the 1950s, King evinces a fear of both radiation from the atomic bomb and the threat of Communism. While noting that the effects of the uncovered Tommyknocker ship mimic radiation poisoning, Wiater, Golden, and Wagner observe the novel's similarities with classic cinematic parables of paranoia, such as *Invaders from Mars* (1953) and *Invasion of the Body Snatchers* (1956) (258). *The Tommyknockers* was written in the spring and summer of 1986, when King was in the throes of cocaine addiction, and his own version of the novel reads as follows: A forties-style science-fiction tale, *Tommyknockers* introduces a writer-heroine who discovers a spaceship buried in the ground. The crew is still on board, alive but hibernating. These aliens enter one's head and start tommyknocking, that is, haunting there. Drawing parallels with his cocaine addiction, King then adds: "What you got was energy and a kind of superficial intelligence. . . . What you gave up in exchange was your soul. It was the best metaphor for drugs and alcohol my tired, overstressed mind could come up with" (*OW*, 97).

As in virtually all of King's major works, humans are determined by fate in *The Tommyknockers*. In the form of evil destiny, fate strikes the unsuspecting residents of Haven (note the ironic name), as it strikes the residents of Castle Rock, Derry, and 'Salem's Lot—in all of which the question, Why us? goes unanswered. Indeed, the first section is concerned with the question of fate: "For want of a nail the kingdom was lost—that's how the catechism goes when you boil it down. In the end, you can boil *everything* down to something similar—or so Roberta Anderson thought much later on. It's either all an accident . . . or all fate. Anderson literally stumbled over her destiny in the small town of Haven, Maine, on June 21, 1988. The stumble was the root of the matter; all the rest was nothing but history" (*TK*, 13, italics and ellipsis in original). Contrary to her inner warnings, Bobbi is drawn to the spaceship, and she seems unable to resist the temptation.

As if to underscore the predestined nature of the event, King maintains: "Not even discovering some part of her had known she would end up here in spite of whatever foolish conceptions of free will the rest of her mind might possess disturbed her" (67).

Free will, however, remains a factor, both in King's personal life while writing *The Tommyknockers* and in the novel. Drinking and using drugs, he was given the choice between his family and the addiction. King recalls the memory in *On Writing:* "I was afraid that I wouldn't be able to work anymore if I quit drinking and drugging, but I decided . . . that I would trade writing for staying married and watching the kids grow up" (98). King's conception of free will, fate, and determinism has been molded by both his Methodist upbringing and personal experience. It is strongly reflected in *The Tommyknockers,* where Bobbi succumbs to the temptation, but Ruth McCausland, Haven's police chief and its "heart and conscience" (379), resists becoming mentally enslaved. Unable to resist the Tommyknockers, Ruth sacrifices herself by blowing up the clock tower in order to warn the neighboring towns.

In the prefatory note to *The Tommyknockers,* King explains the origins of the title, referring to *The Oxford Unabridged Dictionary.* According to this dictionary, "Tommyknockers are the ghosts of miners who died of starvation, but still go knocking for food and rescue" (7). Instead of ghosts, Bobbi Anderson has fallen under the influence of "a race of highly advanced intergalactic gypsies" (Wiater, Golden, and Wagner, 259). Despite their seemingly high technology, the Tommyknockers have not been able to create anything truly innovative, and even their mediocre inventions appear to be useless when they end up fighting a mortal combat in the spaceship. By means of science-fiction parody King makes the point that technological progress cannot be equated with intelligence. Furthermore, he distrusts technology and frequently equates it with evil. Most of the Havenites voluntarily hand over their free will to the Tommyknockers or rather—as King's subtext reads—to technology. When steering the spaceship into outer space, Jim Gardener both pleads with God and expresses an often-repeated King maxim: "*I met the Tommyknockers, and they were us.* [—] Please help me, God, just a little help, okay?" (*TK,* 730, italics in original). King emphasizes that the face of the Tommyknocker is the one we encounter in the bathroom mirror every morning. What is more, God remains a prevalent force in *The Tommyknockers* and *Dreamcatcher* despite the aliens. Since both novels also view humans as their own worst enemy—indeed, worse than any imaginable alien—I will discuss *Dreamcatcher* mainly as a science-fiction parody.

Both *The Tommyknockers* and *Dreamcatcher* have the same moral: uncontrolled scientific progress leads to destruction. The aliens taking over earth prove no better than the human race. Despite their seemingly more developed technology or rather because of it, the extraterrestrials have been forced to leave their own polluted and destroyed planets. Having landed on earth, they attempt to exert pressure on humans, who in their eternal quest for progress sell their souls for mediocre inventions. King emphasizes humanistic values when he points out that the survivors of these alien attacks realize the importance of love and moral responsibility and act accordingly. As the first novel-length work King wrote after having been hit by a van in 1999, *Dreamcatcher* depicts a similar accident. It also criticizes both the government's lack of responsibility for its citizens and the citizens' lack of responsibility for their fellow human beings and ultimately pleads for human dignity. Including both dream sequences and numerous shifts in time, the complex novel has three levels. It can be viewed as a science-fiction parody, as a tale of horror, and as a comment on the absence of responsibility.

Dreamcatcher thematizes extraterrestrial control of life on earth, fate, and responsibility. In November 2001 four childhood friends have gathered for their annual reunion in a hunting cabin where the dreamcatcher, an old Indian charm, dangles from the ceiling. Going through difficult times, Beaver, Pete, Henry, and Jonesy recall happy memories of the year 1978, when they met Douglas Cavell, nicknamed Duddits, a boy with Down's syndrome and extrasensory abilities. Duddits had taught them to "see the line" (*DCA*, 154), an ability that makes Jonesy resistant to Mr. Gray, or rather an outer space alien inhabiting Jonesy's mind after an alien spaceship crashes in the woods near the cabin. Jonesy also encounters in the woods a confused and lost hunter, Richard McCarthy, who gives birth to an alien parasite (note the possible allusion to the communist-hating senator). Promising to solve the situation in twenty-four to forty-eight hours, the government aims at killing the people in the area and sets up a covert camp for that purpose. Reminiscent of an action movie, the third part of the novel consists of an all-out chase through a wintry landscape as Jonesy attempts to reach Duddits in order to gain powers from the past.

In *Dreamcatcher* the aliens are not only hostile but also fertile, and they can spread terrible diseases. Unable to adapt to the cold climate of Maine, the dying aliens spread an infection that affects people in one of two ways. When the aliens decay, the infection spreads to human hosts: the lucky ones come down with a case of red fungus and telepathic powers; the unlucky ones become host to a parasite that is referred to as a cancer. Although the novel opens with an assorted collection of news clippings deal-ing with unexplained sightings in the sky, the reader may not be prepared for King's version of an alien. Attacked by the creature to which McCarthy gave birth, Beaver is unable to offer enough resistance: "It looked like some kind of freak weasel—no legs but with a thick reddish-gold tail" (164). Having returned to the cabin after the accident, Henry discovers an alien who has recently given birth to a hundred new earth invaders (233). Bev Vincent points out the novel's similarities with *Invasion of the Body Snatchers* and *Aliens* (Spignesi, *Essential,* 104), in the latter of which a monstrous mother both lays eggs in her slimy nest and produces progeny to occupy human bodies.

The visceral and violent scenes in *Dreamcatcher* are undercut by science-fiction parody and humor. Seizing the "gross-out" level, which, in his view, "can be done with varying degrees of artistic finesse, but [which is] always there" in horror fiction (*DM*, 4), King depicts McCarthy's four missing teeth, his "meth-ane swamp-gas farts" (*DCA*, 59), his "mighty belches" (60), and his unlucky visit "to the john" (92). In a similar vein, while turn-ing to escape, Jonesy encounters Mr. Gray, who may be con-nected with the title character of *It*. When Mr. Gray's head ex-plodes and releases a cloud of ether-smelling particles, Jonesy breathes the creature in (170). Although toward the end of the novel he refers to himself as "the only man on earth who truly understood what it was to be raped" (596), Jonesy shares some hilarious moments with Mr. Gray as he shares bodies with him. Unable to feel anything, Mr. Gray gets inside Jonesy's head, stealing his emotions, memories, and even the taste for bacon— in brief, Jonesy's basic personality. Fighting for control over his own mind, Jonesy is forced to lead Mr. Gray to the Quabbin Reservoir, where the alien attempts to spread the infection by water. Finding Jonesy's emotions very disturbing at first, Mr. Gray begins to enjoy his life as a human being. As King seems to suggest, in light of human cruelty, Mr. Gray turns out to be a decent human being (326). The newly adopted human nature does not, however, stop Mr. Gray from attempting to finish his mission.

In *Dreamcatcher* King does what in *Danse Macabre* he calls one of the basic functions of horror fiction: "express[es] fears which exist across a wide spectrum of people" (5). These "phobic pressure points" (5) of *Dreamcatcher* are summed up in the closing paragraphs of the novel. The two survivors, Henry and Jonesy, finally recall their memories of the events while drinking beer on the porch of Jonesy's cottage in Ware, Maine. Both men have undergone a treatment with Terry Gerritsen, a navy psychologist, who assumes that an important question has now been answered: we are not the only intelligent beings in the universe. As in *The Tommyknockers*, however, the protagonists do not regard the creatures as truly intelligent (*DCA*, 593). Despite the amoral aliens and their equally immoral human counterparts, God remains a major force in *Dreamcatcher*. As a possible reflection of King's near-fatal accident, Henry refers to "God, who had crept back into his life over these last few months" (595). In Henry's view it is God "[w]ho sings the lullaby, helps us to go to sleep when we're sad and scared" (595). The title object becomes the symbol of fate bordering on the notion of God in the novel. In our eternal attempt to outrun him, we may run as fast and as far as we can, but we can "never run off the dreamcatcher" (592). Moreover, neither Jonesy nor Henry believes in coincidence. Therefore, King has Henry add, "we are a *species* living in the dreamcatcher" (596, italics in original). Sooner or later these or other aliens will return, and then humanity will once again need the dreamcatcher.

King's stories typically provide a moralistically Calvinist cosmology of order, which is repeatedly attacked by Lovecraftian chaos and where the inscrutable Deity at times becomes the inscrutable Wrath delivering justice. In the tradition of New England Puritanism, cosmological determinism in King becomes the vehicle of sociological determinism; the emissaries of wrath take a variety of guises, such as the mythical Beast *(The Dark Tower)*, the God of the Lost *(The Girl Who Loved Tom Gordon)*, and alien weasels *(Dreamcatcher)*, but they always constitute a major threat to the communities they attack. Similarly, the good forces fighting the evil ones are represented by such different beings as the mythical Final Other *(It)*, God of the New Testament *(The Girl Who Loved Tom Gordon)*, and the writer Jim Gardener *(The Tommyknockers)*. Significantly, all of King's science-fiction aliens are evil. Thus, despite his three different approaches to cosmology, King focuses on the struggle between good and evil, placing his characters in the middle. They, too, must take a moral stand, because cosmological forces typically require human agents to manifest their authority.

In a similar vein fate is manifested in three forms in King's fiction. In *It* and *Insomnia*, as we have noted, it borders on the notion of God, who restores the balance of the multiverse. On the other hand, in the distinctly naturalistic Bachman books, in which the protagonists appear to be at the mercy of indifferent and overpowering forces, fate resembles chance or coincidence. In *Thinner* a strawberry pie becomes the metaphor for the absence of luck, the second form of fate. Bill Halleck, an overweight lawyer with wife and daughter, is cursed by a gypsy man for accidentally hitting and killing his daughter. Losing two pounds every day and gradually turning into a skeleton, the well-off Halleck becomes an outcast of society—in a word: a gypsy. In an attempt to remove the curse, Halleck has a gangster trace the gypsy who placed the curse on him. The old man insists that the curse cannot be completely lifted, merely transferred to someone else. The curse is temporarily transferred to a strawberry pie, which Halleck offers to his wife but which is accidentally shared by his beloved daughter. Resignedly, Billy cuts himself a piece of the cursed pie, thus completing the circle of vengeance. Although Halleck finally accepts his own "piece of the pie," he argues that other agents are also involved when a human tragedy occurs—including the absence of luck. His acknowledged responsibility does not change the fact that, like the woman he accidentally kills, he remains a victim of fate's twists and turns. Tony Magistrale draws parallels with other Bachman protagonists and argues that Bill Halleck also "finds himself trapped in circumstances over which he is essentially powerless. Even the destruction of his daughter, the only person in Halleck's life to whom he remains devoted, is the result of yet another accident" (*Decade*, 62).

In *The Shining* and *Storm of the Century*, the protagonists are struck by fate in the form of evil destiny. The recurring motif of wasps becomes the symbol of Jack Torrance's troubled life in the former. When a big, lazy-moving wasp stings him on the roof of the Overlook Hotel, Jack finds its nest between himself and the ladder, both literally and metaphorically. Recalling his failures and experiences in life, Jack feels that he has "unwittingly stuck his hand into The Great Wasps' Nest of Life" (*SH*, 122). He reasons that in such pain one can neither act morally nor love anybody, not to mention be held responsible for one's actions. Finding common decency impossible, Jack defends himself by stating that he has by no means made a pact with the devil; rather, "it just happened to you. Passively, with no say, you ceased to be a creature of the mind and became a creature of the nerve endings" (123). To prove Jack wrong and unreliable, King has him finish: "They would pay for stinging him" (129). Tragically, however, Jack makes his son pay by giving him the large wasps' nest he assumes to be empty. Again the sins of the fathers are visited on their sons as Jack contently states: "I had one in my room when I was a kid. My dad gave it to me" (133). Of course, the intoxicated and angry wasps attack the innocent Danny at night with near-fatal consequences.

In a similar vein *Storm of the Century* continues King's analysis of the dilemma of free will, responsibility, and fate, but takes it a step further by enlarging the scope of responsibility. The isolated residents of Little Tall Island are visited by a demon who threatens to destroy the community unless he is handed a child to be raised as his protégé. Mike Anderson, the constable of the island, remains the only parent to offer resistance and refuse the ultimatum. In *Storm of the Century*, King draws the conclusion that pulling together is not always for the common good (*SC*, ix). Reminiscent of Shirley Jackson's "Lottery," the residents select the child by drawing lots. Of course, the lot falls on Ralph Anderson, whose father has been the only one to take a moral stand. In fact, the evil destiny of the novel seems tantamount to the devil as the demon has obviously chosen his protégé before the lottery. Although innocent himself, Mike is thus forced to bear responsibility even for the evil actions of his community, that is, not merely "pay as you go" (1) but "pay as your community goes."

In King's fiction cosmological determinism merges with fate and its numerous synonyms in a kind of synthesis. A prevalent theme, fate has been discussed in connection with '*Salem's Lot* ("Abnormal and Repressed Sexuality [the Vampire]" in chapter 1), *Pet Sematary* ("Hubris and Death [Frankenstein's Monster]" in chapter 1), *Cycle of the Werewolf* ("The Gothic Double [the Werewolf]" in chapter 1), *The Shining* ("The Gothic Melodrama [the Ghost]" in chapter 1), and throughout this section. From Carrie White of *Carrie* (1974) to Ned Wilcox of *From a Buick 8* (2002), King's characters are exposed to these influences. Although fate is manifested in three forms in King, in most of his fiction he tends to view fate as the ultimate deterministic force along the same lines as the ancient Greeks *(moira)* rather than as the naturalistic, haphazard nature of the course of events. Some of King's works, however, seem to treat fate according to Anna Wierzbicka's view: "*Fate,* as it is used in modern English, doesn't suggest any impenetrable mystery behind the events. . . . It breathes the atmosphere of English empiricism, and scepticism" (92–93). At any rate, the fact that fate is "a deterministic concept" (Pettersson, *Vonnegut,* 124) may explain King's rather frictionless synthesis of determinism and fate.

Shaped by the treadmill of determinism and fate, King's characters are also subject to a fourth kind of determinism, metafictional determinism, which is the ultimate force determining their world.

Metafictional Determinism

Metafictional determinism denotes the way in which "the course of action is established by an outline early on" in a work of art (Pettersson, *Vonnegut,* 138). One of its devices denotes the way in which the author "makes his own presence known in his fiction" (138), either by framing his novels by rough plot outlines or by hinting at future events. In the last volumes of *The Dark Tower* series he also intrudes in the novels as a more or less autobiographical persona. In a personal letter to the author of this monograph, King has commented on aspects of metafictional determinism.

When writing the last three volumes of *The Dark Tower* series, he has rediscovered a little of that urgency of his early works—the feeling that the story is writing *him* instead of the other way around. That sense, he states, is stronger in these books, where he finds himself an actual character—neither quite fact nor fiction, but a mingling of the two. In a similar vein, King appears in virtually all the films made of his stories, in minor roles ranging from a priest to a news reporter.

Shlomith Rimmon-Kenan cites the opening of Nabokov's *Laughter in the Dark* as an example of "summary" in fiction (53–54), but, as Pettersson states, "the passage is also a supreme instance of metafictional determinism because of its initial position and the limits it sets to the story" (*Vonnegut,* 138). After the three-line summary of the protagonist's life, Nabokov comments on the tragedy as follows: "This is the whole story and we might have left it at that had there not been profit and pleasure in the telling; and although there is plenty of space on a gravestone to contain, bound in moss, the abridged version of a man's life, detail is always welcome" (5). Similarly, in King the reader is at times reminded that what he experiences is a multiverse created and *determined* by the author Stephen King.

Since he is also aware that his fiction is not read for plot alone, King provides a rough plot outline of the future tragedy in *Carrie:* "We have only skimpy hearsay evidence upon which to lay our foundation in this case, but even this is enough to indicate that a 'TK' potential of immense magnitude existed within Carrie White. The great tragedy is that we are now all Monday-morning quarterbacks" (6). Far from providing an exhaustive plot summary, King settles for hinting at the consequences of Carrie's quirky ability. Unlike the natural or explained Gothic presented by Montague Summers in *The Gothic Quest,* King does not wait until the closing pages but explains the seemingly supernatural events at the outset of the novel. By deploying quasi-scientific explanations and by means of gradual exposition, he heightens the reader's curiosity as to *how* and *why* the action took place. This becomes even more obvious in *Christine,* in which the plot summary is rendered in a paragraph, separated from the beginning of the story with an empty line: "This is the story of a lover's triangle, I suppose you'd say—Arnie Cunningham, Leigh Cabot, and, of course, Christine. But I want you to understand that Christine was there first. She was Arnie's first love, and while I wouldn't presume to say for sure (not from whatever heights of wisdom I've attained in my twenty-two years, anyway), I think she was his only true love. So I call what happened a tragedy" (1). Narrating the book partially in the first person, King uses Dennis Guilder as his mouthpiece to indicate the premise of the story. Although the reader is not expecting a happy outcome after this introduction, his interest is directed to character psychology and narrative form.

In the same way, in the form of a newspaper clipping *'Salem's Lot* offers detailed information on individual characters at the beginning of the novel. The editor, John Lewis, begins by setting place and time: 'Salem's Lot, a little over a year ago. He then indicates the situation: people begin to disappear. Next, he lists several survivors of the vampire plague: Parkins Gillespie, Charles James, Pauline Dickens, and Rhoda Curless. Finally, Lewis enumerates some of the missing persons, hinting at natural reasons for their disappearance: "Lawrence Crockett, a local real estate agent who has disappeared with his wife and daughter, has left a number of questionable business ventures and land deals behind him. . . . The Royce McDougalls, also among the missing, had lost their infant son earlier in the year and there was little to hold them in town" (xvi). By revealing some of the survivors and some of the victims of the vampire town, King both directs the reader's interest to the motives underlying their actions and heightens the degree of suspense. Remarkably, however, the whereabouts of such central characters as Susan Norton, Matt Burke, and Jimmy Cody are not even hinted at, which undoubtedly leaves a number of roads to be taken. Presumably, too, King's lengthy novels become more digestible in this way.

Such summaries are only seldom included in King's novels, however. In *The Shining* the future tragedy is uncovered both by anticipative or proleptic dreams in which Tony either warns Danny or shows future events and by creating a threatening atmosphere that anticipates a disaster. The latter includes, for instance, characterization (Jack Torrance appears to be doomed from the beginning), comparison of past events with the present (Delbert Grady versus Jack Torrance), metaphors (the wasps' nest), and reference to the reader's common knowledge about relations between cause and effect (Jack's violent behavior under pressure). In the same way, in *The Dead Zone* Johnny Smith's skating accident at the age of six anticipates his tragic destiny. Johnny recovers, but shortly thereafter Chuck Spier loses an eye in an accident. Johnny's religious mother, Vera, who later turns into a fanatic, declares that it is owing to God's mercy that Chuck has not lost both eyes. Johnny goes with his father to visit him in the hospital a week after the accident: "The sight of Big Chuck lying in that hospital bed, looking oddly wasted and small, had shaken Johnny badly—and that night he dreamed it was *him* lying there" (*DZ*, 4, italics in original). However, he never connects his occasional hunches with the accident on the ice:

It was not until the night of the country fair and the mask that anything very startling happened. Before the second accident.
Later, he thought of that often.
The thing with the Wheel of Fortune had happened *before* the second accident.
Like a warning from his own childhood. (4, italics in original)

Johnny, too, will be lying on a hospital bed similar to Big Chuck's, and his mother will regard it as a blessing that he is at least alive. The omniscient narrator reveals to the reader more than the protagonist knows about his own condition, thus hinting at the future relevance of both the hunches and the Wheel of Fortune.

Most of King's novels rely on the same devices. Even the thriller *Firestarter* and the naturalistic *Cujo* deploy anticipation and prolepses to heighten tension. In *Firestarter* Andy McGee tells Charlie that "[e]verything's fine," but the narrator adds: "But as it turned out, nothing was fine. Nothing" (15). Before the disaster in *Cujo*, the narrator matter-of-factly states that Cujo "was a Saint Bernard in his prime, five years old, nearly two hundred pounds in weight, and now, on the morning of June 16, 1980, he was pre-rabid" (21) and so anticipates the future with the rabid Cujo. In *The Talisman* the narrator shares the bad news with the reader before the protagonist hears it: "But Uncle Tommy was already dead; it was just that the news was still on the other end of a lot of telephone wires" (4). In *The Gunslinger* (1982) King's narrator remains in the background, distributing information by other means and using characters as his mouthpieces. For instance, Walter reveals sequences of Roland the Gunslinger's future by looking at tarot cards: "[A] mixture of the standard deck and a selection of my own development. Watch closely gunslinger. [—] I'm going to tell your future, Roland" (*GS*, 200).

Instead of interrupting the third-person narration, King discreetly adds to suspense by distributing information within it. This device seems typical of King throughout his fiction, and the following example illustrates its effectiveness with regard to the quick spread of the lethal virus in *The Stand:*

Joe Bob felt fine; dying was the last thing on his mind. Nevertheless, he was already a sick man. He had gotten more than gas at Bill Hapscomb's Texaco. And he gave Harry Trent more than a speeding summons.

Harry, a gregarious man who liked his job, passed the sickness to more than forty people during that day and the next. How many those forty passed it to is impossible to say—you might as well ask how many angels can dance on the head of a pin. If you were to make a conservative estimate of five apiece, you'd have two hundred. Using the same conservative formula, one could say those two hundred went on to infect a thousand, the thousand five thousand, the five thousand *twenty*-five thousand. (93, italics in original)

Instead of detailed plot summaries, King prefers to use gradual exposition. In the quoted passage, the narrator delights in flaunting that he possesses more information than the reader: he knows that the seemingly healthy Joe Bob will soon die, and he is aware that the population of earth will be virtually extinguished within less than three weeks. Most of King's novels rely on this technique, and it is at its most effective in King's short, laconic remarks after a lengthy depiction. Heading for Las Vegas with Glen Bateman, Ralph Brentner, and Larry Underwood, Stu Redman hurts his leg and is unable to continue the mission: "Larry went up the bank quickly and joined the other two. They stood and waved down. Stu raised his hand in return. They left. And they never saw Stu Redman again" (*ST*, 1300). Without stating it, King leads the reader to believe that the wounded Stu Redman will not survive. The short sentences both add to the atmosphere of destiny and heighten the suspense, which later culminates in the reader's realization that he has drawn wrong conclusions all along: it is the expedition that will not survive, whereas Stu Redman will.

Analyzing Vonnegut's fiction, Pettersson maintains that plot summaries seem redundant in novels with straightforward narrators, and that "metafictional determinism by plot outline demands some anachrony" (*Vonnegut*, 139–40). Despite their undeniable logic, the two statements only partially hold true in relation to King. Although the early Bachman books include neither plot outlines nor hints at future events, the protagonist of the deceptively simple *Dolores Claiborne* declares in the opening pages of the novel that she pleads not guilty of the crime of which she is accused but guilty of another: "I didn't kill that bitch Vera Donovan, and no matter what you think now, I intend to make you believe that. I didn't push her down that frigging staircase. It's fine if you want to lock me up for the other, but I don't have none of that bitch's blood on my hands. [—] I want you to get every goddam word, startin with this: twenty-nine years ago, when Police Chief Bissette here was in the first grade and still eatin the paste off the back of his pitchers, I killed my husband, Joe St. George" (20–22). However, there are some anachronic features in *Dolores Claiborne*, which she admits herself: "Instead of telling her front to back or back to front, I'm gonna start in the middle and just kinda work both ways" (24). Of course, it remains the writer's decision to deploy whatever devices he chooses to advance the story, but by revealing the secret of a suspense story on the opening page the narrator takes a conscious risk, and he must have a solid trust in his own ability to *retell* the story in a fresh manner. In *Dolores Claiborne*, for instance, King comments on familial discord, violence, and child abuse, to mention the most prevalent themes inherent in the novel. Centering on a plain and poor widow with three children, King captures the reader's interest by his thematic concerns and the novel's intriguing narrative form.

Perhaps due to his personal preferences and the Gothic tradition of narrative techniques, King relies on anticipatory hints and prolepses rather than plot outlines in his fiction. (As I noted earlier in this chapter, some of his stories fall into the natural or explained Gothic [for example, *Gerald's Game*], others into the supernatural Gothic ['*Salem's Lot*], and yet others into the equivocal Gothic ["The Boogeyman"] in Montague Summers's classificatory scheme.) A plot summary and repeated prolepses seem mutually exclusive, because, as Pettersson notes, the former would only take the sting out of the latter (*Vonnegut*, 140). In the anachronic *It*, King sets the limits to the story by metafictional determinism; however, he does so without revealing future events, but by indicating the duration of the tragedy: "The terror, which would not end for another twenty-eight years—if it ever did end—began, so far as I know or can tell, with a boat made from a sheet of newspaper floating down a gutter swollen with rain" (15). By setting the timespan, the first-person narrator makes the repeated shifts in time more digestible. Vaguely he also hints at the fortunate outcome of the series of events, leaving, however, all questions concerning how and why unanswered (for different types of narrating, see Genette, 217).

Despite this fairly discreet way to conduct his fictional orchestra, King remains an omnipotent force in his multiverse. However, despite the omnipotence within his own creation, the writer, too, is shaped by the various types of determinism, including fate in our world. At times even the writer appears to be at the mercy of metafictional determinism when some stories make up their own mind. In *The Dark Tower* series Roland's *ka-tet* must save King's life in the real world so that he can finish the final volumes and save the multiverse. Similarily, King's attitude toward the unexpected death of the child protagonist, Tad Trenton, summarizes his views on the interdeterminism of author and character. King has never been comfortable with the child's death in the closing pages of *Cujo*, but "the pessimistic stance of the novel was, in King's words, 'almost demanded'" (Winter, *Art*, 115). In regard to author, character, and reader, the degrees of free will and determinism vary considerably. If the character is determined by King's imagination, both King and the reader in turn are shaped by various types of determinism and fate. To be more precise, if Wiater, Golden, and Wagner are right in their claim that the reader is a character of King's imagination and, although not created by King, certainly coopted by him (xvii), both the author and the reader seem to have a dual citizenship in both King's multiverse and the real world.

King distrusts conscious plotting, because our lives are largely plotless, and because plotting and the spontaneity of real creation are not compatible (*OW*, 163). He prefers to place his characters in a difficult situation and see whether they can handle it.

Since they sometimes can and sometimes cannot, "the twists of fate are already apparent in the event of writing" (Renman, 25). In other words, while writing King seldom knows how the novel will develop and is therefore able to enjoy the process of writing as much as the reader enjoys the process of reading (Underwood and Miller, *Bones*, 81–82). Knowing something about how King writes his stories, I would presume that his rough plot outlines, anticipations, prolepses, and authorial interventions have been added to the text after the first draft.

In sum, the weighting of genetic, sociological, cosmological, and metafictional determinism as well as fate may shift from novel to novel, but the principal determinants of human behavior remain the same. Furthermore, although King's characters are subject to forces beyond their control, they always possess enough free will to take a moral stand and shoulder responsibility. This seems merely logical, because what purpose would morals serve, if humans were completely determined by the four types of determinism and fate.

Conclusion

We have now wandered through King's fictional chamber of horrors, from the basement to the attic. It has become obvious that his fictional art consists of generic hybrids. In combining elements of the Gothic tale with other genres (such as myths, fairy tales, and literary naturalism), King enriches his fiction at the same time as he challenges the traditional limits associated with these genres and modes. I have emphasized the fact that King has been simultaneously influenced by the contradictory impulses of free will and determinism in order to highlight a core tension in his oeuvre, and I have supported this contention through the analysis of the gothic, myths, and fairy tales. The end product of King's genre blending can be called horror fiction, but in its diversity and versatility his brand of horror fiction is unique by virtue of the many genres merged. If the Gothic basement of King's fictional chamber of horrors provides his stories with a historical perspective, then myths and fairy tales reside in its lodgings in an airy atmosphere of timelessness. King's reliance on mythical paradigms and fairy tales throughout his writing career creates a balance between the Gothic and literary naturalism and unifies his fiction by linking the events within his stories with larger patterns of human behavior. Finally, in the attic we have literary naturalism, which features in all of King's fiction regardless of its degree of realism. It is the idiosyncratic blend of free will and determinism that combines the different aspects of the fantastic and realistic in King and makes his horror fiction so unique.

I have focused on the functions of the genres King employs to demonstrate that the genres are interrelated largely by their common functions. Presumably, King takes his thematic concerns as a starting point in his fiction, and these concerns may in part determine his choice of the genre. Most of King's novels and stories are generic hybrids. By using genres that reinforce each other thematically, he often expands their limits and redefines them. Thus, *The Shining*, for example, can be labeled both a Gothic novel with fairy-tale influences and a tale of horror with naturalistic traits. Partially overlapping, the functions of the genres King uses may explain the formula and the characteristics of his works. King's works have a structure similar to that of myths and fairy tales, and they also draw on literary naturalism, focusing on human beings' struggle against seemingly overpowering forces, viewing humans as determined by forces beyond their control and returning to the past to explain the present.

Determinism connects the fantastic and the realistic genres and modes in King. The leitmotif of determinism in King combines the ultimately realistic basis of two of its types (genetic and sociological) with the partly fictional origins of the other two (cosmological and metafictional). Through his dualistic view of determinism, King merges fact with fiction and comments on common social taboos and fears. Hence, literary naturalism forms a realistic counterforce to the fantastic Gothic, myths, and fairy tales, and this adds depth to his fiction. By using various types of determinism, King is able to blend the realistic and the fantastic in ways that heighten the credibility and suspense of his works. In King's world the realism in the Bachman books coexists with the fantastic dimensions of Wolf (*The Talisman*) and Roland the Gunslinger (*The Dark Tower* series), since they largely obey the same deterministic laws. In short, three factors affect the balance of the supernatural and the realistic in King: (1) literary naturalism as a realistic genre versus the fantastic genres of the Gothic, myths, and fairy tales (2) the tension between the four types of determinism (genetic, sociological, cosmological, and metafictional) and fate in his works, and (3) his dualistic worldview, which paradoxically blends faith and naturalism. In this system religious faith is often combined with literary naturalism and its rather grim view of reality. However, the four types of determinism in King fuse these viewpoints into a surprisingly coherent whole. In fact, determinism features in all of King's fiction regardless of the degree of realism.

Although according to Alastair Fowler genres lack stability and although every literary work changes the genre it employs (11, 23), what King has done to the horror genre since the publication of *Carrie* clearly entails more than a matter of minute or indirect modulations. These changes involve major modulations and departures from generic codes, on the one hand, and blends of genres, on the other. By means of the former, King departs from the conventions of the horror genre by emphasizing contemporary social and political anxieties and by focusing on individual characters. By means of the latter, he reinforces the same effect: literary naturalism confronts these social and personal "phobic pressure points" head on, whereas the Gothic, myths, and fairy tales approach them indirectly. At the beginning of our literary journey, I presented the hypothesis that King's characters, his Constant Reader, and his effective genre blending or genre shifting contribute to his large readership. Obviously, all these factors are both interrelated and genre generated. For instance, when he departs from the horror formula and focuses on the ordinary life of his ordinary protagonist, King simultaneously enriches the horror genre with developed, realistic characters, who seldom people traditional horror fiction, and deviates from the formula by devoting at best the first half of a novel to character development. By enriching his horror with, for instance, literary naturalism, he also adds realistic traits and depth to his characters.

The Gothic basement of King's fictional chamber of horrors provides his stories with literary roots. In a sense King writes like the original Gothic writers in the eighteenth and nineteenth centuries. Concerned with death, decay, disorder, and ruin, the Gothic novel was born as a reaction against the Enlightenment in the late eighteenth century. Drawing from the past, it gave way to the realist novel at the beginning of the nineteenth century but did not become completely extinct: Jane Austen parodied the Gothic novel in *Northanger Abbey* (1818), and Charles Dickens created generic hybrids in his broodingly Gothic but fairly realistic characters, such as Oliver Twist and Miss Havisham. As a whole, however, the Gothic mode descended to the level of cheap entertainment and survived primarily in the short story format to the twentieth century. What King did in the 1970s was what Dickens did well over a century earlier: he merged the Gothic with literary realism and the recognizable archetypes of myths and fairy tales. With his long novels King has simply reestablished the primacy of the novel in comparison to the short story within the genre. What is more, by being able to communicate to those readers who would not normally choose a Gothic or a horror novel, he has restored the genre to its original use: to comment on contemporary phobias. In our rational and scientific era, King has voiced criticism of uncontrolled scientific progress and of the omnipotence and omnipresence of rationalism, just as Horace Walpole, Matthew Lewis, and Ann Radcliffe, in their own way, spoke for the romantic rebellion against the Age of Enlightenment. King's fiction often underscores that we live in the center of mystery, that humans can neither comprehend nor dominate the universe.

Myths and fairy tales reside in the lodgings of King's chamber of horrors, thus bridging the seeming gap between the Gothic and literary naturalism. Furthermore, the Gothic atmosphere permeates King's myths and fairy tales, which share several traits with the Gothic mode and the horror genre. When the function of the horror story is compared to Bruno Bettelheim's paradigm, we find that both horror and myths/fairy tales take us back to childhood anxieties by erasing the distinction between child and adult. While fairy tales conform to the way children experience their environment (45), horror fiction subverts the manner adults perceive their environment by challenging their faith in the secure foundations of modern society (Magistrale, *Voyages,* 5). Both, however, focus on the dark side of the human psyche. Bettelheim claims that a child, not having his id under conscious control, needs tales that permit fantasy satisfaction of these negative tendencies (52), whereas horror fiction allows us to transcend the world of darkness. King's use of such characters as Roland the Gunslinger and Randall Flagg, the recurring hero and antihero, respectively, is another aspect that unifies his work. As Sharon A. Russell notes, King "explores related genres with characters who share many traits" (25). Therefore, I call them generic hybrids. Myths, for instance, are seen through the eyes of Roland the Gunslinger, who goes on a classic hero's journey, and his antagonist Randall Flagg, who as a composite of many traits and genres brings about destruction wherever he wanders. On the floors of his fictional chamber of horrors, King also has rooms for other genres, subgenres, and modes, such as science fiction, suspense, and fantasy. As Michael R. Collings maintains, science-fiction

stories, for instance, show signs of the same "generic indecisive-
ness" that characterizes all of King's work: they begin with a
science-fiction framework but edge into horror (*Facets*, 15). In
this way different genres add their special seasonings to King's
blend of horror.

Finally, in the attic we have literary naturalism, because it features in all of King's fiction regardless of the degree of realism. To
be sure, the Gothic mode and the horror genre share a number of
traits with literary naturalism, of which the grim view of reality
constitutes the most significant. Perhaps the dramatic rise in horror fiction in the 1970s is grounded in the baby-boomers' Gothic-
naturalistic realization that the American dream often turns out
to be the American nightmare. Under the pressure of the Emersonian drive, horror fiction provides a channel to express the dark
side of the dream—as the Gothic did in the eighteenth and nineteenth centuries. Literary naturalism also ties the fantastic to
everyday life in King. In all his stories, reality shifts. As Alan Ryan
points out, King repeatedly pulls the rug from under the feet of
his ordinary characters living in their ordinary world (193–94).
The safe world dissolves, giving way to horrors beyond human
control. Focusing on the struggle, King places his decent and
basically good characters at the mercy of indifferent forces, with
survival depending on their moral strength and the responsibility they may take for their fellow human beings. In most of
his novels, King underscores a humane stance and love as humankind's only weapon against dehumanization and evil.

Apart from genres King's popularity is based on his simultaneously stereotypical and well-developed characters; his deep-
seated respect for his Constant Reader, whom he genuinely
cherishes and to whom he offers prefaces and afterwords to explain the backgrounds of his stories; and his visual and visceral
imagination derived in part from his dedication to horror films
(see, for instance, Warren, 125; LaBrie, 52–53). King's characters
are frequently placed in situations where they must rise above
their capacities and often difficult backgrounds in order to
reach a heroic stance. In the multiverse King has created, characters, events, and settings are interrelated. This multiverse has
been constructed to provide the settings for Gothic, mythical,
fairy-tale, and naturalistic narratives. More importantly, the
characters of the multiverse are involved in a cosmic battle of

good versus evil, order versus chaos, or the Purpose versus the Random. This seems in accordance with King's moral message to his readers, who are encouraged to take a moral stand and participate in the development of his stories. Since King practices what he teaches, namely, that "imagery does not occur on the writer's page; it occurs in the reader's mind" (Magistrale, *Voyages*, 6), the Constant Reader also plays an important role in explaining his popularity.

Since King lays such strong emphasis on characters, I discussed the characteristics of the genres implicit in his works through them. For instance, the contradiction between King's everyday characters and monsters displays another common feature in his fiction, that is, realism versus the supernatural. By juxtaposing the two worlds, he explores issues arising from the subtext. King's ordinary characters are accessible, people with whom most readers can identify. King argues that his readers feel comfortable in "the Steve King hammock," because they know the characters and respond to them: "You don't have unease about who they are," King tells us, "you have unease about the circumstances that they find themselves in. And that's where the suspense comes from" (Winter, *Faces*, 251). Hence, these decent characters become the victims of monsters like Kurt Barlow, Randall Flagg, and Leland Gaunt. On a more general level, this brings us to Hans Robert Jauss's reader-response theory and his notion of *sympathetic identification*, by which he means "the aesthetic affect of projecting oneself into the alien self, a process which eliminates the admiring distance and can inspire feelings in the spectator or reader that will lead him to a solidarization with the suffering hero" (172). In his definition Jauss, by identifying the reader's feelings of "solidarization with the suffering hero," suggests the seeds of a moral attitude, based on sympathy, on the part of the reader. King could not agree more, since it is by inviting such sympathy that he pleads for humanity and responsibility in his works.

King's consideration of his Constant Reader borders on both Stanley Fish's notion of interpretative communities (483) and Bo Pettersson's notion of popular imagination as a "shared frame of mind" ("Imagination," 23–34). Pettersson traces popular imagination to the oral tradition of myths (12), and King also stresses the oral tradition and the fact that his family often read

Dickens's stories and others aloud in his childhood home: "It was a rare chance to enjoy a written work as we enjoyed the movies we went to and the TV programmes *(Rawhide, Bonanza, Route 66)* that we watched together; they were a family event" *(GM,* xi). The points I wish to make here are, first, that King's both visual (seeing stories as images before writing them) and oral (vernacular) style of writing—or, as Michael J. Collins terms it, "the vivid prose of Stephen King" (110)—relates him to the oral tradition of storytelling and, second, that this contributes to the special qualities of his fiction. Furthermore, while *"folk,* later *popular,* today largely *mass* culture" (Pettersson, "Imagination," 26, italics in original) and popular imagination in particular consist of "a host of individual interpretations" (34), King views his role as a medium in this process. Like John Coffey he inhales the pain and suffering of his fellow human beings and "expels it in a horrid, visible form, not unlike the demon rising from the ruins of the Overlook Hotel in *The Shining,*" that is, in the form of his fiction (Wiater, Golden, and Wagner, 365). King considers horror stories "a basket loosely packed with phobias; when the writer passes by, you take one of his imaginary horrors out of the basket and put one of your real ones in—at least for a time" *(NS,* xviii). King does not confine popular imagination with its shared frame of mind to the present but enlarges the scope to the past. For example, he notes that only after many years did he discover that Dickens's stories had been consumed by families in nineteenth-century Britain and America in the same fashion as his own family did *(GM,* xi). In short, King continues this tradition of mythmaking by means of visual images, vernacular, and—most importantly— fascinating stories. He maintains that "the story value holds dominance over every other facet of the writer's craft; characterization, theme, mood, none of those things is anything if the story is dull. And if the story does hold you, all else can be forgiven" *(NS,* xx; see also Terrell, 16).

King's popularity has been broader than that of a genre writer. As a matter of fact, John Sutherland in *Fiction and Fiction Industry* regards bestsellers as generic categories in themselves (12), which, somewhat ironically, makes *bestsellerdom* another genre in King's brand of horror. In his later study *Bestsellers: Popular Fiction in the 1970s,* Sutherland defines the term *bestseller* as follows: "The bestseller expresses and fills certain needs in the reading public. It consolidates prejudice, provides comfort, is therapy, offers vicarious reward or stimulus. In some socially controlled circumstances it may indoctrinate or control a population's ideas on politically sensitive subjects. In other circumstances, especially where sexual mores are concerned, it may also play a subversive social role, introducing new codes and licence" (34, see also Escarpit, 84; C. Bloom, 6). This understanding of a change in publishing that occurred during the 1970s is related to Sutherland's second main observation of the period in which genre fiction grew. In brief, the day and age of technological revolutions and social changes was ready for King's brand of horror. In *Bloom's BioCritiques: Stephen King*, Harold Bloom points out that King—like such mainstream bestsellerists as Tom Clancy, John Grisham, and Danielle Steele—does not seem "a borderline literary phenomenon, whose works will have the status of period pieces" (1). In *Modern Critical Views: Stephen King*, Bloom goes as far as to claim that hundreds of thousands of American schoolchildren turn to King in the same way that their parents resort to Danielle Steel and Tom Clancy (2). With the possible exceptions of Clive Barker and Anne Rice, few other genre writers have been able to attract even nearly as many readers outside their respective genres as has King. As a fundamentalist in questions of morality (Underwood and Miller, *Bones*, 193), King may have lost some readers to Barker and Rice, who seem to employ a playful attitude toward good and evil in their fiction. Tellingly, Bloom considers King "preferable to the sadistic Anne Rice, whose fictions are profoundly unhealthy, and whose style is even more tedious than King's" (*Views*, 2).

King's popularity as a horror writer is clear, but what is it about his brand of horror that appeals to readers who are not usually interested in the genre? Clive Bloom in *Bestsellers: Popular Fiction since 1900* argues that King not only "reinvented the horror genre," but he is also the best-selling American writer of all time (215). When *Carrie* was published in 1974, it turned out to be a moderate hardcover success. Its success as a paperback, however, was phenomenal. Although Ira Levin's *Rosemary's Baby* (1967) and William Peter Blatty's *Exorcist* (1971) had paved the way for King's fiction, their success cannot explain King's durability. One of the reasons, according to Gary Hoppenstand and Ray B. Browne, might be termed King's storytelling ability, which they admiringly call the "dazzle effect." In their view by his fiction King is able to take readers out of themselves so that they become oblivious to style or even the written word in their desire to be swept away by the author's vision (2).

This argument certainly holds some truth. Even though King offers only quasi-scientific explanations of various phenomena and gory details, readers ignore these obvious defects in both fact and style and go on reading his stories. Obviously, King possesses an intimate understanding of what his audience expects from his work. Without changing the fundamental motifs of the horror story (the haunted house or the vampire), he is able to adapt them to the emotional needs of the audience. And undoubtedly the emotional needs of male readers may not always be compatible with those of teenage and female readers. Hoppenstand and Brown point out that, unlike Robert Bloch and Richard Matheson, King is able to communicate to those people who otherwise would never choose a horror novel (5). In his fiction King seems to deal with what Victor Turner calls "social dramas" and Hoppenstand and Browne call "social melodramas, that is, stories that are based on cultural paradigms, such as the nuclear family (Turner, 141–68; Hoppenstand and Browne, 6–9). While female readers discover in King's stories social melodrama as the crucial angle of his fiction, adolescents recognize in his works young protagonists who face life's difficult choices in much the same way as they do. For example, in *Pet Sematary* the supernatural motif of the novel is the evil spirit, but the actual horror elements of the story center on the disintegration of the Creed family.

In *Faces of Fear* Douglas E. Winter interviews seventeen horror writers from Britain and the United States: V. C. Andrews, Clive Barker (Br.), William Peter Blatty, Robert Bloch, Ramsay Campbell (Br.), John Coyne, Dennis Etchison, Charles L. Grant, James Herbert (Br.), Stephen King, T. E. D. Klein, Richard Matheson, Michael McDowell, David Morrell, Alan Ryan, Peter Straub, and Whitley Strieber. Not surprisingly, these writers share many traits, and at least three seem to be best-selling ones, Stephen King in particular. As Winter points out, ten of the writers were born between 1943 and 1947 (*Faces of Fear*, 7). Furthermore, the writers admire and are primarily influenced by one another's fiction and the classics of the genre. Finally, many of the interviewees have deeply held religious beliefs (*Fear*, 8).

Despite the homogeneity of the group, Stephen King sells considerably better than any of them. James Herbert, the best-selling horror writer in Britain in 1985, points out some reasons for his own success and that of King. Herbert argues that he writes for pleasure, and the public "tunes into him," just as they did into Stephen King, the Beatles, and the Rolling Stones (Herbert in Winter, *Fear*, 107). Significantly, the three constituents of his popularity seem identical to those of King's: "the humanity of his characters" (104), the "strong moral tone" of his books (104), and faith: "I *am* a Catholic. . . . And I am—in a funny way—very, very religious" (105, italics in original). Several peers seem to recognize this combination as the bedrock of King's large readership. What is more, David Morrell and Peter Straub refer to King's compulsion to write on a regular basis and his sheer hard work (Morrell in Winter, *Fear*, 91–92; Straub in Winter, *Fear*, 228). Also, both Charles L. Grant and John Coyne also consider colloquial language and style one of King's hallmarks (Grant in Winter, *Fear*, 119; Coyne in Winter, *Fear*, 156). According to Coyne, all horror writers try to "carry whatever is real one step further." The reason that the Gothic returned as a popular genre, he tells us, is that writers such as Blatty and King "moved it into the colloquial and made it commonplace, so that [they're] not talking about vampires and Dracula, [they] are talking about the girl next door or the girl in the next seat" (Coyne in Winter, *Fear*, 156). Grant concludes by arguing that nobody has been able to reveal the final secret of King's popularity: publishers are "really confused as to why Peter Straub sells a lot of books but still isn't as big as Stephen King" (Grant in Winter, *Fear*, 120–21). I claim that one final truth about King's great success can be found in the dedication of *It*: "Kids, fiction is the truth inside the lie, and the truth of this fiction is simple enough: *the magic exists*" (italics in original). King's readers "tune into" the truths of his magical fiction and find them true and valid in their own lives.

Tony Magistrale points out that King has long ago reached the point in his writing career where more is required to satisfy his ambition than the sale of books (*Voyages*, i). Although his latest work, regardless of its critical reception or topic and by virtue of the author's name alone, instantaneously reaches the top of the bestseller lists, King expresses his need of recognition by using the writer-protagonist of *Misery*, Paul Sheldon, as his mouthpiece:

"So what was the truth? The *truth*, should you insist, was that the increasing dismissal of his work in the critical press as that of a 'popular writer' (which was, as he understood it, one step—a small one—above that of a 'hack') had hurt him badly" (286, italics in original). In addition to recognition, King hopes that his fiction will prove durable, so that after his death some little boy will find one of his dusty novels on a library shelf (King in Collings, "King and the Critics," 65). Tim Underwood, however, would not allow King's fiction that honor but maintains that his "work probably won't last . . . , stories like 'The Raft' or *The Mist* may have the power to disturb, but their effects are ephemeral" (Underwood and Miller, *Kingdom*, 255). Shortly thereafter Underwood goes on to claim that King's fiction is "not primarily concerned with the higher centers of the brain; his aim is visceral" (257). Magistrale counters, stating that visceral elements are central in Shakespeare (*Voyages*, iii). Indeed, the horror genre has always been plagued by its fascination with the grotesque. In this study, however, I have attempted to show more reasons for King's popularity than the visceral.

In the introduction of his latest short-story collection, *Everything's Eventual* (2002), King acknowledges that he expects the collection to "end up on the best-seller lists for awhile." He also takes delight in the fact that he has succeeded in keeping his craft new. He writes "[n]ot for money, not even precisely for love, but as a kind of dues-paying" (xv). For these reasons—and those mentioned earlier in this discussion—I believe that King's fiction will last. It has already received critical recognition. For instance, "The Man in the Black Suit" *(Everything's Eventual)* won both the 1994 World Fantasy Award for best short fiction and the 1996 O. Henry Award for best American short story. Most recently, in 2003, the National Book Foundation gave its annual medal for distinguished contribution to American letters to Stephen King. In fact, King's selection is the first time that the somewhat conservative organization has awarded its medal to an author best known for popular genres, such as tales of horror, science fiction, and thrillers. According to the *New York Times* (September 15, 2003), the board members chose to honor Mr. King for several reasons: his promotion of less-established authors, his donations to libraries and schools, his storytelling skill, and the sheer volume of his work, which has attracted a multitude of readers. Several board members said that they also considered the cultural influence of King's many works adapted for film and television. Furthermore, the durability of King's work is based on his abiding exploration of human nature, moral responsibility, and literary genres, on his respect for the craft, and, quite simply, on his love of writing.

Appendix: A Note on
Previous Criticism

Bibliography

Index

Appendix
A Note on Previous Criticism

So much writing and research about Stephen King has been published since the 1980s that it is difficult to avoid turning a brief exposition into a bibliography. I will therefore confine myself to a few remarks on the references that have particular relevance to this work. Given the extent of King criticism—about forty books have been published about King and/or his work in the United States alone (Wiater, Golden, and Wagner, 460)—its quality varies considerably. Since popular criticism and academic criticism are not necessarily mutually exclusive, I prefer to comment on these works in the rough order of their original publication, discussing, however, the works by one and the same critic together.

Tim Underwood and Chuck Miller have published three collections of essays on King's work (*Reign of Fear: The Fiction and Films of Stephen King*, however, is edited by Don Herron, although published by Underwood and Miller [1988]) and two collections of interviews with him. *Fear Itself: the Horror Fiction of Stephen King* (1982) contains the first collection of essays on King, with a foreword by King, an introduction by Peter Straub, and an afterword by George Romero. The essays vary from Alan Ryan's unsuccessful attempt to view *'Salem's Lot* (1975) as a fairy tale for grownups, to Chelsea Quinn Yarbro's thorough analysis of mythical and fairy-tale themes in King's work and Don Herron's insightful comparison of King's fiction with earlier works in the genre. Although most of the critics in *Kingdom of Fear: The World of Stephen King* (1986) have a positive view of King's work, both Tony Magistrale and Stanley Wiater, Christopher Golden, and Hank Wagner note that the editor Tim Underwood's essay "The Skull beneath the Skin" looks on it most unfavorably (Magistrale, *Voyages*, ii–iv; Wiater, Golden, and Wagner, 461), in claiming that King's "work probably won't last" (255).

Both interview collections, *Bare Bones: Conversations on Terror with Stephen King* (1988) and *Feast of Fear: Conversations with Stephen King* (1989), are compiled from various sources and are organized by theme.

A friend of King's, Douglas E. Winter, provides what he calls "a critical appreciation": an intermingling of biography, literary analysis, and interviews (xiii). *Stephen King: The Art of Darkness* (1984), an updated and expanded version of *The Reader's Guide to Stephen King* (1982), is the first and only authorized study of King. The third edition in 1986 also reveals the details of how King has employed the Richard Bachman pseudonym. Winter's enthusiastic effort serves as a useful reader's guide to King, but, as Magistrale notes, he must sometimes sacrifice analytical depth "in favor of tracing the broad sweep of King's prolific canon" (*Landscape*, 1). Winter takes Stella Flanders's journey in "The Reach" (1981) as a starting point in viewing King's fiction. Winter claims: "To ask why we read horror fiction is to ask why Stella Flanders took that walk [to the unknown] on that cold winter's day of the storyteller's imagination" (*Art*, 1). Winter has also edited *Faces of Fear: Encounters with the Masters of Modern Horror,* which includes an interview with King.

In *Discovering Stephen King* (1985), one of the first collections of critical essays on King's early writings, the editor, Darrell Schweitzer, analyzes the state of King criticism and includes a brief King biography as well as synopses of his early fiction. Such contemporaries as Randall D. Larson, Debra Stump, and Leonard G. Heldreth focus on the discovery of sin and its moral consequences, free will and responsibility, and mortality versus immortality in the horror genre, respectively, whereas Michael R. Collings discusses the various genres in *The Stand* (1978), and Robert M. Price examines how King reflects H. P. Lovecraft's visions of horror. In addition to the wide range of topics, the quality of the essays is uneven.

Michael R. Collings provides both quality and quantity. In 1985 Collings authored three monographs and coauthored a fourth with his student David A. Engebretson. The cooperation brought about *The Shorter Works of Stephen King,* which analyzes King's short stories and the four novellas in *Different Seasons* (1982). Collings maintains that while "King is known primarily for his novels, he has also produced a substantial body of short stories, including some of the finest examples of supernatural horror" (*The Shorter Works of Stephen King,* 1). With this view he joins the long line of literary critics, starting with Poe, who consider the concise short-story form the most suitable to produce the effect of horror. Collings's other contributions in 1985 include *The Many Facets of Stephen King,* which views King as a pop-culture phenomenon; *The Stephen King Concordance;* and, for my purposes particularly interesting,

Stephen King as Richard Bachman. In addition to giving reasons for the pseudonym, the latter work also examines the naturalistic worldview of the Bachman books. Collings has also assessed film adaptations of King's novels in *The Films of Stephen King* (1986), as well as compiled a primary and secondary bibliography on King's works, *The Annotated Guide to Stephen King: A Primary and Secondary Bibliography of the Works of America's Premier Horror Writer* (1986). The bibliography was later expanded and updated, and both editions were "designed as a research tool for the increasing number of scholars and critics responding to King's work and to criticism of King" (*Guide*, 1-2).

Two book-length analyses link King directly to the Gothic tradition, namely, *The Gothic World of Stephen King: Landscape of Nightmares* (ed. Ray Browne and Gary Hoppenstand, 1987) and Tony Magistrale's *Landscape of Fear: Stephen King's American Gothic* (1988). The former is particularly concerned with *Pet Sematary* (1983), a latter-day version of Mary Shelley's *Frankenstein,* but it also deals with King's other major work. Among others it includes James Egan's intriguing essay "*The Dark Tower:* Stephen King's Gothic Western." However, Egan emphasizes the Gothic atmosphere of the series, while I view it primarily as a hero's journey and thus have discussed it primarily in chapter 2. Undoubtedly, both approaches can be justified, and they only prove the versatility of King's fiction; in my detailed analysis of *The Dark Tower,* the Gothic characteristics were foregrounded. Similarly, Magistrale's *Landscape of Fear* views King as an heir to the American Gothic tradition and refers to him as a critic of American values and institutions.

King's seminal and recurring themes are sensitively dealt with in Tony Magistrale's *Moral Voyages of Stephen King* (1989). Like Carroll F. Terrell in *Stephen King: Man and Artist* (1990), Magistrale is also concerned with religious questions and the moral polarities of good and evil in King's fiction. Moreover, Magistrale's book-length analysis— *The Second Decade,* Danse Macabre *to* The Dark Half (1992)—covers the second decade of King's career and thus constitutes an independent sequel to Joseph Reino's *First Decade: From* Carrie *to* Pet Sematary (1988). Although Magistrale regards King as one of the best writers in America today, he notes King's tendency to overwrite his texts. In Magistrale's view more important than the number of books King has published is the range of literary genres and traditions he has incorporated into his art, which "belies the easy reductive characteristics condescending academics often ascribe to horror and popular fiction" (*Decade*, ix). Besides these monographs, Magistrale has edited the two readers, *Discovering Stephen King's* The Shining (1991) and *A Casebook on* The Stand (1992), both of which consist of critical essays and focus on a single novel. He has also edited *The Dark Descent: Essays Defining Stephen*

King's Horrorscape (1992) and (with Michael A. Morrison) *A Dark Night's Dreaming: Contemporary American Horror Fiction* (1996), which compares King to his contemporary American peers. What is more, Magistrale has recently completed a new book on King's film adaptations. It is titled *Hollywood's Stephen King* and was published in November 2003.

In a number of works the popular culture authority George Beahm covers King's biography and fiction, which he finds flawless. *The Stephen King Companion* (1989, revised 1995) includes essays, anecdotes, and interviews and covers different aspects of King's writing, critical reception, and personal life. *The Stephen King Story* (1991, revised and updated 1993) provides a literary profile of the author, emphasizing King's early years as an author. *Stephen King: America's Best-Loved Boogeyman* (1998) continues along the same lines, but considers the influences that shaped both King's oeuvre and his personal life in somewhat greater depth. *Stephen King from A to Z: An Encyclopedia of His Life and Work* (1998) provides a handy reference in an easy-to-read format but no real insights for serious literary scholars. Finally, *The Stephen King Country* (1999) presents pictures of the locations of King's real Maine as well as of the inspirations for some of his horror scenes.

In *Stephen King and Clive Barker* (1990), James Van Hise interviews the two writers and regards the latter as King's heir to the throne. Van Hise himself does not draw further conclusions, but an observant reader cannot help comparing King's moralistic stance to Barker's playful attitude toward good and evil. In King's presence the Constant Reader feels safe enough to touch "the shape under the sheet" (*NS*, xx). After all, despite the twists of fate, King subscribes to good, whereas Barker is devoted to the postmodern principle of refusing to allow either pole in a system—good or evil—to "become the centre and guarantor of presence" (Selden, Widdowson, and Brooker, 170–71). In an essay on Stephen King's fiction Barker states: "Darkness has a place in all of us; a substantial place that must, for our health's sake, be respected and investigated" (33). If it holds true that we feel safe within the framework of such dichotomies as evil/good, beautiful/ugly, and God/devil, then this may add another factor to King's large readership.

However odd in its ranking system, Stephen J. Spignesi's *Shape under the Sheet: The Complete Stephen King Encyclopedia* (1991), which was expanded and updated as *The Essential Stephen King: A Ranking of the Greatest Novels, Short Stories, Movies, and Other Creations of the World's Most Popular Writer* (2001), is worth mentioning in this connection, because the latter, in particular, provides useful character listings of the ranked stories. In *The Unseen King* (1989), Tyson Blue, in contrast, emphasizes texts that are often overlooked by King critics: poetry, screenplays, and King's early writing as a columnist for the University of

Maine, Orono, student newspaper. Focusing on King's unpublished short stories, Blue takes this early writing as a starting point for King's later fiction. Apart from his two aforementioned works and two quiz books on King, Spignesi has authored *The Lost Work of Stephen King* (1998), which in fact is—as the title page announces—an invaluable "guide to the unpublished manuscripts, story fragments, alternative versions, and oddities."

Five more critical volumes are worth mentioning. Sharon A. Russell's selective monograph, *Stephen King: A Critical Companion* (1996), is structured on a chronological principle and discusses every novel separately. In contrast to many other analyses, Russell provides alternative readings of individual novels and comments on both the specific genre of each novel and generic conventions in general. The most critical assessment of King's fiction is presented by Harold Bloom, who in the introduction of *Modern Critical Views: Stephen King* (1998) claims that "King has replaced reading" and that "the triumph of the genial King is a large emblem of the failures of American education" (2). In an introduction to *Bloom's BioCritiques: Stephen King* (2002), he lists King's "obvious inadequacies: cliché-writing, flat characters who are names upon the page [!], and in general a remarkable absence of invention for someone edging over into the occult, the preternatural, the imaginary" (1–2). In addition to these pointedly provocative arguments, the collections include insightful essays by serious scholars.

King would have lost many Constant Readers if they had been introduced to his fiction by Kathleen Margaret Lant and Theresa Thompson's (eds.) *Imagining the Worst: Stephen King and the Representation of Women* (1998), which is an interesting analysis of the female monsters in King's oeuvre. Although the study is partially marred by far-fetched psychoanalytic theorizing, it provides both traditional scholarship and unexplored territory. The editors start by musing on the reasons for King's strong appeal to female readers. From there they go on to eroticize the relationship between writer and reader by referring to King's preface in *Night Shift* (1978), in which the writer guides his reader to the fountainheads of horror. According to Lant and Thompson, King's "depiction of the horror writer as a man who 'enfolds' your hand in his own and 'puts your hands on the shape under the sheet,' asserts an intimacy that, as he directs us to feel 'here . . . here . . . and *here*,' becomes increasingly erotic and provocative" (Lant and Thompson, 5, quoting *NS*, xx, italics and ellipses in original). The editors evidently have a point, because horror and sex are often blended in horror fiction. However, when in another paper we are reminded of King's worst sexual nightmares—"the *vagina dentata*" (the vagina with teeth) (Cassuto, 62; Underwood and Miller, *Bones*, 195) and the pregnancy in "The Breathing

Method" (*DS* [1982]; Underwood and Miller, *Bones,* 195)—the sexism implicit in the book becomes pointedly Freudian and unintentionally comic as such. As noted, Stanley Wiater, Christopher Golden, and Hank Wagner's *Stephen King Universe: A Guide to the Worlds of the King of Horror* (2001) takes as a starting point the view that all of King's individual works are intertwined through overlapping narrative threads, with the world of the Dark Tower as their nexus. Covering all of King's fiction, this reference book may not provide literary-critical insights but offers a central research tool for scholars and critics.

Bibliography

Works by Stephen King

Bag of Bones. 1998. New York: Pocket Books, 1999.
Black House. London: HarperCollins, 2001.
Carrie. 1974. New York: Pocket Books, 1999.
Cat's Eye. Original screenplay, 1985. (Directed by Lewis Teague).
Christine. London: Hodder & Stoughton, 1983.
Creepshow. 1982. Turnhout, Belgium: Proost International Book Production, 1992.
Cujo. 1981. New York: Signet, 1982.
Cycle of the Werewolf. 1983. New York: Signet, 1985.
Danse Macabre. 1981. New York: Berkley Books, 1983.
The Dark Half. 1989. New York: Signet, 1990.
The Dark Tower: Dark Tower VIII. London: Hodder & Stoughton, 2004.
The Dead Zone. 1979. New York: Signet, 1980.
Desperation. 1996. New York: Signet, 1997.
Different Seasons. 1982. New York: Signet, 1983.
Dolores Claiborne. New York: Signet, 1993.
The Drawing of the Three: Dark Tower II. 1987. New York: Plume, 1989.
Dreamcatcher. London: Hodder & Stoughton, 2001.
The Eyes of the Dragon. 1987. New York: Signet, 1988.
Everything's Eventual. London: Hodder & Stoughton, 2002.
Firestarter. 1980. New York: Signet, 1981.
Four Past Midnight. 1990. New York: Signet, 1991.
From a Buick 8. London: Hodder & Stoughton, 2002.
Gerald's Game. 1992. New York: Signet, 1993.
The Girl Who Loved Tom Gordon. 1999. New York: Pocket Books, 2000.
The Green Mile. 1996. New York: Plume, 1997.
The Gunslinger: The Dark Tower I. 1982. New York: Plume, 1988.

Hearts in Atlantis. 1999. New York: Pocket Books, 2000.

"The Horror Writer and the Ten Bears." In *Kingdom of Fear: The World of Stephen King*, ed. Tim Underwood and Chuck Miller. New York: New American Library, 1986.

"Imagery and the Third Eye." *The Writer*, October 1980, 11–14.

Insomnia. 1994. New York: Signet, 1995.

It. 1986. London: Hodder & Stoughton, 1987.

The Long Walk. In *The Bachman Books: Four Early Novels by Stephen King: Rage, The Long Walk, Roadwork, The Running Man*, 171–433. 1979. New York: Signet, 1986.

Misery. 1987. New York: Signet, 1988.

Needful Things. 1991. New York: Signet, 1992.

Nightmares and Dreamscapes. 1993. New York: Signet, 1994.

Night Shift. 1978. New York: Signet, 1979.

"The Novelist Sounds Off." *Time*, Oct. 6, 1986, 80.

"On Becoming a Brand Name." In *Fear Itself: The Horror Fiction of Stephen King*, ed. Tim Underwood and Chuck Miller, 15–42. New York: New American Library, 1985.

On Writing. New York: Scribner, 2000.

Pet Sematary. 1983. New York: Signet, 1984.

Rage. In *The Bachman Books: Four Early Novels by Stephen King: Rage, The Long Walk, Roadwork, The Running Man*, 3–170. 1977. New York: Signet, 1986.

The Regulators. 1996. New York: Signet, 1997.

Roadwork. In *The Bachman Books: Four Early Novels by Stephen King: Rage, The Long Walk, Roadwork, The Running Man*, 435–708. New York: Signet, 1986.

Rose Madder. 1995. New York: Signet, 1996.

The Running Man. In *The Bachman Books: Four Early Novels by Stephen King: Rage, The Long Walk, Roadwork, The Running Man*, 709–923. New York: Signet, 1986.

'Salem's Lot. 1975. New York: Signet, 1976.

The Shining. 1977. New York: Signet, 1978.

Skeleton Crew. 1985. New York: Signet, 1986.

Sleepwalkers. Original screenplay, 1992. (Directed by Mick Garris).

Song of Susannah: The Dark Tower VI. London: Hodder & Stoughton, 2004.

The Stand. 1978. Complete and uncut edition. New York: New English Library, 1990.

Stephen King's Golden Years. Original television series, 1991.

Storm of the Century. New York: Pocket Books, 1999.

The Talisman (with Peter Straub). 1984. New York: Berkley, 1985.

Thinner. 1984. New York: Signet, 1985.

The Tommyknockers. 1987. New York: Signet, 1988.
The Waste Lands: The Dark Tower III. 1991. New York: Plume, 1992.
Wizard and Glass: The Dark Tower IV. 1997. New York: Signet, 1998.

Secondary Sources

Abrams, M. H. *A Glossary of Literary Terms.* 1957. New York: Holt, Rine-
hart & Winston, 1984.
Aldiss, Brian W. *Billion Year Spree: The History of Science Fiction.* 1973.
London: Corgi, 1975.
Anderson, Linda. *"'OH DEAR JESUS IT IS FEMALE':* Monster as
Mother/Mother as Monster in Stephen King's *It."* In *Imagining
the Worst: Stephen King and the Representation of Women,* edited by
Kathleen Margaret Lant and Theresa Thompson, 111–25. Westport,
Conn.: Greenwood Press, 1998.
Aristotle. *Poetics.* Translated and with an introduction by Malcolm
Heath. London: Penguin, 1996.
Babcock, Barbara. *"'A Tolerated Margin of Mess': The Trickster and His
Tales Reconsidered."* In *Critical Essays on Native American Literature,*
edited by Andrew Wiget, 153–85. Boston: G. K. Hall & Co., 1985.
Badley, Linda. "Love and Death in the American Car: Stephen King's
Auto-Erotic Horror." In *The Gothic World of Stephen King: Landscape of
Nightmares,* edited by Gary Hoppenstand and Ray B. Browne, 84–
94. Bowling Green, Ohio: Bowling Green State University Popular
Press, 1987.
———. "Stephen King: Viewing the Body." In *Modern Critical Views: Ste-
phen King,* edited by Harold Bloom, 163–90. Philadelphia: Chelsea
House, 1998.
———. *Writing Horror and the Body: The Fiction of Stephen King, Clive
Barker, and Ann Rice.* Westport, Conn., and London: Greenwood
Press, 1996.
Barker, Clive. "Surviving the Ride." In *Modern Critical Views: Stephen
King,* edited by Harold Bloom, 27–33. Philadelphia: Chelsea House,
1998.
Barthes, Roland. *Mythologies.* 1957. Selected and translated from the
French by Annette Lavers. London: Vintage, 2000.
Barton, Edwin J., and Glenda A. Hudson. *A Contemporary Guide to Liter-
ary Terms with Strategies for Writing Essays about Literature.* Boston:
Houghton Mifflin Company, 1997.
Baudrillard, Jean. *The Transparency of Evil: Essays on Extreme Phenomena.*
Translated by James Herbert. London: Verso, 1999. Originally pub-
lished as *La transparency du mal: Essai sur les phénomenes extremes*
(1990).

Baym, Nina, et al. "Native American Trickster Tales." In *The Norton Anthology of American Literature*, 55–56. 1979. New York: W. W. Norton & Company, 1999.

Beahm, George. *Stephen King: America's Best-Loved Boogeyman*. Kansas City, Mo.: Andrews & McMeel, 1998.

———, ed. *The Stephen King Companion*. 1989. Kansas City, Mo.: Andrews & McMeel, 1995.

———. *The Stephen King Country*. Philadelphia: Running Press, 1999.

———. *Stephen King from A to Z: An Encyclopedia of His Life and Work*. Kansas City, Mo.: Andrews & McMeel, 1998.

———. *The Stephen King Story: A Literary Profile*. 1991. London: Little, Brown & Company, 1993.

Benton, Richard B. "The Problems of Literary Gothicism." *Emerson Society Quarterly* 18 (1972): 7–8.

Bercovitch, Sacvan. *The Puritan Origins of the American Self*. New Haven, Conn.: Yale University Press, 1975.

Bettelheim, Bruno. *The Uses of Enchantment: The Meaning and Importance of Fairy Tales*. 1975. London: Penguin, 1991.

Birkhead, Edith. *The Tale of Terror: A Study of the Gothic Romance*. London: Constable & Company, 1921.

Bloom, Clive. *Bestsellers: Popular Fiction since 1900*. New York: Palgrave, 2002.

Bloom, Harold. Introduction to *Bloom's BioCritiques: Stephen King*, edited by Harold Bloom, 1–2. Philadelphia: Chelsea House, 2002.

———. Introduction to *Modern Critical Views: Stephen King*, edited by Harold Bloom, 1–3. Philadelphia: Chelsea House, 1998.

———. *Poetics of Influence*. New Haven, Conn.: Schwab, 1988.

Blue, Tyson. *The Unseen King*. Mercer Island, Wash.: Starmont House, 1989.

Bosky, Bernadette Lynn. "The Mind's a Monkey: Character and Psychology in Stephen King's Recent Fiction." In *Kingdom of Fear: The World of Stephen King*, edited by Tim Underwood and Chuck Miller, 241–76. 1986. New York: Signet, 1987.

———. "Stephen King and Peter Straub: Fear and Friendship." In *Discovering Stephen King*, edited by Darrell Schweitzer, 55–82. Mercer Island, Wash.: Starmont House, 1985.

Briggs, Julia. *Night Visitors: The Rise and Fall of the English Ghost Story*. London: Faber & Faber, 1977.

Browning, Robert. *The Works of Robert Browning*. 1833–89. Ware, Hertfordshire: Wordsworth Editions, 1994.

Bullough, Edward, "'Psychical Distance' as a Factor in Art and an Aesthetic Principle." In *Critical Theory since Plato*, edited by Hazard Adams, 758. New York: Harcourt Brace Jovanovich, 1971.

Burke, Edmund. *A Philosophical Enquiry into the Origin of Our Ideas of the Sublime and the Beautiful.* 1757. Edited by Adam Phillips. Oxford: Oxford University Press, 1990.

Burns, Gail E., and Melinda Kanner. "Women, Danger and Death: The Perversion of the Female Principle in Stephen King's Fiction." In *Sexual Politics and Popular Culture,* edited by Diane Raymond, 158–71. Bowling Green, Ohio: Bowling Green State University Popular Press, 1990.

Calder, Jenni. *There Must Be a Lone Ranger.* London: Hamish Hamilton, 1974.

Campbell, Joseph. *The Hero with a Thousand Faces.* 1949. London: Fontana Press, 1993.

———. *Transformations of Myth through Time.* 1990. New York: Harper-Perennial, 1999.

Carroll, Noël. *The Philosophy of Horror, or, Paradoxes of the Heart.* New York: Routledge, 1990.

Carter, Margaret L. *Shadow of a Shade: A Survey of Vampirism in Literature.* New York: Gordon Press, 1975.

Casebeer, Edwin F. "The Art of Balance: Stephen King's Canon." In *A Dark Night's Dreaming: Contemporary American Horror Fiction,* edited by Tony Magistrale and Michael A. Morrison, 42–54. Columbia: University of South Carolina Press, 1996.

———. "The Ecological System of Stephen King's 'The Dark Half,'" in *The Doppelganger in Contemporary Literature, Film, and Art.* Special issue, *Journal of the Fantastic in the Arts* 6, nos. 2–3 (1994): 126–42.

Cassuto, Leonard. "Repulsive Attractions: 'The Raft,' the *Vagina Dentata,* and the Slasher Formula." In *Imagining the Worst: Stephen King and the Representation of Women,* edited by Kathleen Margaret Lant and Theresa Thompson, 61–78. Westport, Conn.: Greenwood Press, 1998.

Cawelti, John G. *Adventure, Mystery, and Romance: Formula Stories as Art and Popular Culture.* Chicago: University of Chicago Press, 1976.

———. *The Six-Gun Mystique.* Bowling Green, Ohio: Bowling Green State University Popular Press, 1984.

Chase, Richard. *The American Novel and Its Tradition.* New York: Doubleday Anchor, 1957.

Clemens, Valdine. *The Return of the Repressed: Gothic Horror from* The Castle of Otranto *to* Alien. Albany, N.Y.: State University of New York, 1999.

Clery, E. J. Introduction to *The Castle of Otranto,* by Horace Walpole. 1764. Oxford: Oxford University Press, 1996.

Collings, Michael R. *The Annotated Guide to Stephen King: A Primary and Secondary Bibliography of the Works of America's Premier Horror Writer.* Mercer Island, Wash.: Starmont House, 1986.

————. *The Films of Stephen King*. Mercer Island, Wash.: Starmont House, 1986.

————. "King and the Critics." In *Bloom's BioCritiques: Stephen King*, edited by Harold Bloom, 63–79. Philadelphia: Chelsea House, 2002.

————. *The Many Facets of Stephen King*. Mercer Island, Wash.: Starmont House, 1985.

————. "*The Stand:* Science Fiction and Fantasy." In *Discovering Stephen King*, edited by Darrell Schweitzer, 83–90, Mercer Island, Wash.: Starmont House, 1985.

————. *Stephen King as Richard Bachman*. Mercer Island, Wash.: Starmont House, 1985.

————. *The Stephen King Concordance*. Mercer Island, Wash.: Starmont House, 1985.

————. *The Stephen King Phenomenon*. Mercer Island, Wash.: Starmont House, 1987.

Collings, Michael R., and David Engebretson. *The Shorter Works of Stephen King*. Mercer Island, Wash.: Starmont House, 1985.

Collins, Michael J. "Culture in the Hall of Mirrors: Film and Fiction and Fiction and Film." In *A Dark Night's Dreaming: Contemporary American Horror Fiction*, edited by Tony Magistrale and Michael A. Morrison, 110–22. Columbia: University of South Carolina Press, 1996.

Cotterell, Arthur. *A Dictionary of World Mythology*. 1979. Oxford: Oxford University Press, 1986.

Curran, Donald T. "Complex, Archetype, and Primal Fear: King's Use of Fairy Tales in *The Shining*." In *The Dark Descent: Essays in Defining Stephen King's Horrorscape*, edited by Tony Magistrale, 33–46. Westport, Conn.: Greenwood Press, 1992.

Davis, Jonathan P. "The Struggle for Personal Morality in America." In *Bloom's BioCritiques: Stephen King*, edited by Harold Bloom, 81–93. Philadelphia: Chelsea House, 2002.

Day, William Patrick. *In the Circles of Fear and Desire: A Study of Gothic Fantasy*. Chicago: University of Chicago Press, 1985.

Deleuze, Gilles. *Masochism:* Coldness and Cruelty *by Gilles Deleuze and* Venus in Furs *by Leopold von Sacher-Masoch*. New York: Zone Books, 1991.

Deleuze, Gilles, and Felix Guattari. *A Thousand Plateaus: Capitalism and Schizophrenia*. 1987. London: Athlone Press, 1999.

Deloria, Vine Jr. *Spirit and Reason: The Vine Deloria Jr. Reader*. Golden, Colo.: Fulcrum, 1999.

Demos, John. *Entertaining Satan: Witchcraft and the Culture of Early New England*. Oxford: Oxford University Press, 1982.

Derrida, Jacques. "'Eating Well,' or the Calculation of the Subject: An Interview with Jacques Derrida." In *Who Comes after the Subject?*

edited by Eduardo Cadava, Peter Connor, and Jean-Luc Nancy. London: Routledge, 1991.

Douglas, Susan. *Where the Girls Are: Growing Up Female with the Mass Media*. New York: Times Books, 1994.

Dyson, Cindy. "Biography of Stephen King." In *Bloom's BioCritiques: Stephen King*, edited by Harold Bloom, 3–47. Philadelphia: Chelsea House, 2002.

Eberhart, John Mark. "As Final Installments Loom, Stephen King Shores Up First Book in Dark Tower Series." *Kansas City Star*, June 29, 2003.

Edmundson, Mark. *Nightmare on Main Street: Angels, Sadomasochism, and the Culture of Gothic*. 1997. Cambridge, Mass.: Harvard University Press, 1999.

Egan, James. "Stephen King's Gothic Western." In *The Gothic World of Stephen King: Landscape of Nightmare*, edited by Gary Hoppenstand and Ray B. Browne, 95–106. Bowling Green, Ohio: Bowling Green State University Popular Press, 1987.

———. "Technohorror: The Dystopian Vision of Stephen King." In *Modern Critical Views: Stephen King*, edited by Harold Bloom, 47–58. Philadelphia: Chelsea House, 1998.

Eliade, Mircea. *Myth and Reality*. 1963. Translated from the French by Willard R. Trask. Prospect Heights, Ill.: Waveland Press, 1998.

Emerson, Ralph Waldo. *Nature*. 1836. In *The Essential Writings of Ralph Waldo Emerson*, edited by Brooks Atkinson and with an introduction by Mary Oliver. New York: Random House, 2000.

Epicurus. *On the Anger of God*. In *Ante-Nicene Fathers*, 7:270. Grand Rapids, Mich.: Eerdmans, 1985.

Escarpit, Robert. *Sociology of Literature*. 1958. Translated from the French by Ernest Pick. London: F. Cass, 1971.

Fiedler, Leslie A. *Freaks: Myths and Images of the Secret Self*. New York: Simon & Schuster, 1978.

———. *Love and Death in the American Novel*. 1960. New York: Dell, 1969.

Fish, Stanley. "Interpreting the *Variorum*." *Critical Inquiry* 2, no. 3 (1976): 465–85.

Fokkema, Douwe. "Concluding Observations: Is There a Future for Research on Postmodernism?" In *Exploring Postmodernism*, edited by Matei Calinescu and Douwe Fokkema, 233–41. Amsterdam: John Benjamins, 1987.

Forsyth, Neil. "The Origin of 'Evil': Classical or Judeo-Christian?" *Perspectives on Evil and Human Wickedness* 1, no. 1 (Jan. 2002): 17–52.

Forty, Jo. *Mythology: A Visual Encyclopedia*. London: PRC, 1999.

Foucault, Michel. *The History of Sexuality*. Volume 1, *An Introduction*. 1976. Translated from the French by Robert Hurley. New York: Vintage Books, 1990.

Fowler, Alastair. *Kinds of Literature: An Introduction to the Theory of Genres and Modes.* 1982. Oxford: Clarendon Press, 2000.

Frank, Frederick S. *The First Gothics: A Critical Guide to the English Gothic Novel.* London: Garland, 1987.

———. "The Gothic Romance." In *Horror Literature: A Historical Survey and Critical Guide to the Best of Horror Literature,* edited by Marshall A. Tymn. New York: Bowker, 1981.

———. *Guide to the Gothic: An Annotated Bibliography of Criticism.* Metuchen, N.J.: Scarecrow Press, 1984.

Franz, Marie-Louise von. *The Interpretation of Fairy Tales.* 1970. Boston: Shambala, 1996.

Frye, Northrop. *Anatomy of Criticism: Four Essays.* 1957. London: Penguin, 1990.

———. *Myth and Metaphor: Selected Essays, 1974-1988.* 1990. Charlottesville: University Press of Virginia, 2000.

Gafford, Sam. "Lovecraft's Influence on Stephen King." *Crypt of Cthulhu* 3, no. 2 (1983).

Gallagher, Bernard J. "Reading Between the Lines: Stephen King and Allegory." In *The Gothic World of Stephen King: Landscape of Nightmares,* edited by Gary Hoppenstand and Ray B. Browne, 37-48. Bowling Green, Ohio: Bowling Green State University Popular Press, 1987.

Genette, Gérard. *Narrative Discourse: An Essay in Method.* Translated by Jane E. Lewin. Ithaca, N.Y.: Cornell University Press, 1983. Originally published as "Discours du récit," a portion of *Figures III* (1972).

Gennep, Arnold Van. *The Rites of Passage.* 1960. Chicago: University of Chicago Press, 1984.

Goldstein, Bill. "King of Horror." *Publishers Weekly,* Jan. 24, 1991.

Gottschalk, Katherine K. "Stephen King's Dark and Terrible Mother, Annie Wilkes." In *Modern Critical Views: Stephen King,* edited by Harold Bloom, 121-30. Philadelphia: Chelsea House, 1998.

Grant, Charles L. "Grey Arena." In *Fear Itself: The Horror Fiction of Stephen King,* edited by Tim Underwood and Chuck Miller, 165-71. 1982. New York: New American Library, 1985.

Gray, Martin. *A Dictionary of Literary Terms.* Harlow, Essex: Longman, York Press, 1984.

Gray, Paul. "Stephen King: Master of Postliterate Prose." *Time,* Aug. 30, 1982, 87.

Halberstam, Judith. *Skin Shows: Gothic Horror and the Technology of Monsters.* 1995. Durham, N.C.: Duke University Press, 2000.

Hall, David. *Worlds of Wonder, Days of Judgment: Popular Religious Belief in Early New England.* New York: Knopf, 1989.

Hanson, Clare. "Stephen King: Powers of Horror." In *American Horror*

Fiction: From Brockden Brown to Stephen King, edited by Brian Docherty, 135–54. New York: St. Martin's Press, 1990.

Hatlen, Burton. "Beyond the Kittery Bridge." In *Fear Itself: The Horror Fiction of Stephen King,* edited by Tim Underwood and Chuck Miller, 45–60. 1982. New York: New American Library, 1985.

Hawthorn, Jeremy. *A Glossary of Contemporary Literary Theory.* London: Arnold, 1998.

Heath, Malcolm. Introduction to *Poetics,* by Aristotle. London: Penguin, 1996.

Heldreth, Leonard G. "The Ultimate Horror: The Dead Child in Stephen King's Stories and Novels." In *Discovering Stephen King,* edited by Darrell Schweitzer, 141–52. Mercer Island, Wash.: Starmont House, 1985.

———. "Viewing 'The Body': King's Portrait of the Artist as Survivor." In *The Gothic World of Stephen King: Landscape of Nightmares,* ed. Gary Hoppenstand and Ray B. Browne, 64–74. Bowling Green, Ohio: Bowling Green State University Popular Press, 1987.

Hemingway, Ernest. *A Farewell to Arms.* New York: Scribner's, 1929.

———. *The Nick Adams Stories.* 1972. New York: Scribner's, 1999.

Hennessy, Brendan. "The Gothic Novel." In *British Writers,* vol. 3. New York: Charles Scribner's Sons, 1980.

Herron, Don. "Horror Springs in the Fiction of Stephen King." In *Fear Itself: The Horror Fiction of Stephen King,* edited by Tim Underwood and Chuck Miller, 75–99. 1982. New York: New American Library, 1985.

———, ed. *Reign of Fear: The Fiction and Films of Stephen King.* Columbia, Pa: Underwood & Miller, 1988.

Hicks, James E. "Stephen King's Creation of Horror in 'Salem's Lot: A Prolegomenon towards a New Hermeneutic of the Gothic Novel." In *The Gothic World of Stephen King: Landscape of Nightmares,* edited by Gary Hoppenstand and Ray B. Browne, 75–83. Bowling Green, Ohio: Bowling Green State University Popular Press, 1987.

Hirsch, E. D., Jr. "In Defense of the Author." In *Intention and Interpretation,* edited by Gary Iseminger, 11–23. Philadelphia: Temple University Press, 1992.

Hochman, Baruch. *Character in Literature.* Ithaca, N.Y.: Cornell University Press, 1985.

The Holy Bible. New International Version. 1980. London: Hodder & Stoughton, 1987.

Hoppenstand, Gary, and Ray B. Browne. "The Horror of It All: Stephen King and the Landscape of the American Nightmare." In *The Gothic World of Stephen King: Landscape of Nightmares,* edited by Gary Hoppenstand and Ray B. Browne, 1–19. Bowling Green, Ohio: Bowling Green State University Press, 1987.

Horton, Rod W., and Herbert W. Edwards. *Backgrounds of American Literary Thought.* 1952. Englewood Cliffs, N.J.: Prentice-Hall, 1974.

Hyles, Vernon. "Freaks: The Grotesque as Metaphor in the Works of Stephen King." In *The Gothic World of Stephen King: Landscape of Nightmares,* edited by Gary Hoppenstand and Ray B. Browne, 56–63. Bowling Green, Ohio: Bowling Green State University Press, 1987.

Indick, Ben P. "King and the Literary Tradition of Horror and the Supernatural." In *Fear Itself: The Horror Fiction of Stephen King,* edited by Tim Underwood and Chuck Miller, 175–88. 1982. New York: New American Library, 1985.

———. "What Makes Him So Scary?" In *Discovering Stephen King,* edited by Darrell Schweitzer, 9–14. Mercer Island, Wash.: Starmont House, 1985.

Ingebretsen, Edward J. "Cotton Mather and Stephen King: Writing/ Righting the Body Politic." In *Imagining the Worst: Stephen King and the Representation of Women,* edited by Kathleen Margaret Lant and Theresa Thomson, 11–30. Westport, Conn.: Greenwood Press, 1998.

Jameson, Fredric. *Postmodernism, or, The Cultural Logic of Late Capitalism.* 1991. London: Verso, 1999.

Jancovich, Mark. *Horror.* London: Batsford, 1992.

Jauss, Hans Robert. "Levels of Identification of Hero and Audience." *New Literary History* 5, no. 2 (Winter 1974).

Johansson, Annika. *Världar av ljus, världar av mörker.* Lund: Bibliotekstjänst, 1996.

Joyce, James. *Finnegans Wake.* 1939. London: Penguin, 1999.

Jung, Carl. G. *The Archetypes and the Collective Unconscious.* 1959. London: Routledge, 1991.

Kaplan, Harold I., Benjamin J. Sadock, and Jack A. Grebb. *Kaplan and Sadock's Synopsis of Psychiatry: Behavioral Sciences, Clinical Psychiatry.* 1972. Baltimore: Williams & Wilkins, 1994.

Kayser, Wolfgang. *The Grotesque in Art and Literature.* Translated by Ulrich Weisstein. New York: McGraw-Hill, 1966. Originally published as *Das Groteske: Seine Gestaltung in Malerei und Dichtung* (1957).

Keesey, Douglas. "Patriarchal Mediations of *Carrie*: The Book, the Movie, and the Musical." In *Imagining the Worst: Stephen King and the Representation of Women,* edited by Kathleen Margaret Lant and Theresa Thomson, 31–45. Westport, Conn.: Greenwood Press, 1998.

Kierkegaard, Søren. *The Sickness unto Death: A Christian Psychological Exposition of Edification and Awakening by Anti-Climacus.* Translated by Alastair Hannay. Princeton, N.J.: Princeton University Press, 1954.

Kinnunen, Hannele. "Gothic Features in *Misery* and *The Shining* by Stephen King, or, The Legacy of *The Castle of Otranto.*" Master's thesis, University of Turku, 1995.

Knight, Damon. "What Is Science Fiction?" In *Turning Points,* edited by Damon Knight, 62–69. New York: Harper & Row, 1977.

Kristeva, Julia. *Powers of Horror: An Essay on Abjection.* Translated by Leon S. Roudiez. New York: Columbia University Press, 1982. Originally published as *Pouvoirs de l'horreur* (1980).

LaBrie, Aimee. "Stephen King: Exorcising the Demons." In *Bloom's Bio-Critiques: Stephen King,* edited by Harold Bloom, 49–61. Philadelphia: Chelsea House, 2002.

Lamarque, Peter, and Stein Haugom Olsen. *Truth, Fiction, and Literature: A Philosophical Perspective.* Oxford: Oxford University Press, 1994.

Lant, Kathleen Margaret. "The Rape of Constant Reader: Stephen King's Construction of the Female Reader and Violation of the Female Body in *Misery.*" In *Imagining the Worst: Stephen King and the Representation of Women,* edited by Kathleen Margaret Lant and Theresa Thomson, 159–81. Westport, Conn.: Greenwood Press, 1998.

Lant, Kathleen Margaret, and Theresa Thompson. "Imagining the Worst: Stephen King and the Representation of Women." In *Imagining the Worst: Stephen King and the Representation of Women,* edited by Kathleen Margaret Lant and Theresa Thomson, 3–8. Westport, Conn.: Greenwood Press, 1998.

Larson, Randall D. "*Cycle of the Werewolf* and the Moral Tradition of Horror." In *Discovering Stephen King,* edited by Darrell Schweitzer, 102–8. Mercer Island, Wash.: Starmont House, 1985.

Leiber, Fritz. "Horror Hits a High." In *Fear Itself: The Horror Fiction of Stephen King,* edited by Tim Underwood and Chuck Miller, 103–21. 1982. New York: New American Library, 1985.

———. "A Literary Copernicus." In *H. P. Lovecraft: Four Decades of Criticism,* edited by S. T. Joshi. Athens: Ohio University Press, 1980.

Lewis, Matthew. *The Monk: A Romance.* 1796. London: Penguin, 1998.

Lovecraft, H. P. "The Dunwich Horror" (1929). In *The Dunwich Horror and Others.* New York: Jove, 1978.

———. "Nyarlathotep." In *The Doom That Came to Sarnath and Other Stories,* edited by Carter Lin. New York: Ballantine Books, 1982.

———. *Supernatural Horror.* 1945. New York: Dover Publications, 1973.

Madden, Edward. "Cars Are Girls: Sexual Power and Sexual Panic in Stephen King's *Christine.*" In *Imagining the Worst: Stephen King and the Representation of Women,* edited by Kathleen Margaret Lant and Theresa Thomson, 143–58. Westport, Conn.: Greenwood Press, 1998.

Magistrale, Tony, ed. *A Casebook on* The Stand. Mercer Island, Wash.: Starmont House, 1992.

———. "Defining Stephen King's Horroscape: An Introduction." In *The Dark Descent: Essays Defining Stephen King's Horroscape,* edited by Tony Magistrale, 1–4. Westport, Conn.: Greenwood Press, 1992.

———, ed. *Discovering Stephen King's* The Shining. San Bernardino, Calif.: Borgo Press, 1998. Originally published as *The Shining Reader* (Mercer Island, Wash.: Starmont House: 1991).

———. *Hollywood's Stephen King.* New York: Palgrave Macmillan, 2003.

———. *Landscape of Fear: Stephen King's American Gothic.* Bowling Green, Ohio: Bowling Green State University, Popular Press, 1988.

———. *The Moral Voyages of Stephen King.* Mercer Island, Wash.: Starmont Studies, 1989.

———. *Stephen King: The Second Decade,* Danse Macabre *to* The Dark Half. New York: Twayne, 1992.

Magistrale, Tony, and Michael A. Morrison, eds. *A Dark Night's Dreaming: Contemporary American Horror Fiction.* Columbia: University of South Carolina Press, 1996.

Malakoff and Co. "Stephen King." http://www.malakoff.com/sking.htm.

Manchel, Frank. "What about Jack? Another Perspective on Family Relationships in Stanley Kubrick's *The Shining.*" In *Discovering Stephen King's* The Shining, edited by Tony Magistrale, 82–94. San Bernardino, Calif.: Borgo Press, 1998.

Maturin, C. *Melmoth the Wanderer.* 1820. Oxford: Oxford University Press, 1998.

McHale, Brian. "Writing about Postmodernist Writing." *Poetics Today* 3, no. 3 (Summer 1982): 211–27.

Moore, R. I. *The Formation of a Persecuting Society: Power and Deviance in Western Europe, 950–1250.* New York: Basil Blackwell, 1987.

Mustazza, Leonard. "Fear and Pity: Tragic Horror in King's *Pet Sematary.*" In *The Dark Descent: Essays Defining Stephen King's Horroscape,* edited by Tony Magistrale, 73–82. Westport, Conn.: Greenwood Press, 1992.

Nabokov, Vladimir. *Laughter in the Dark.* London: Penguin, 2001. Originally published in Russian in 1933.

New Encyclopaedia Britannica, Micropaedia, vol. 3. Chicago: Encyclopaedia Britannica, 1983.

Newhouse, Tom. "A Blind Date with Disaster: Adolescent Revolt in the Fiction of Stephen King." In *The Gothic World of Stephen King: Landscape of Nightmares,* edited by Gary Hoppenstand and Ray B. Browne, 49–55. Bowling Green, Ohio: Bowling Green State University Popular Press, 1987.

Newton, K. M., ed. *Twentieth-Century Literary Theory: A Reader.* 1988. New York: St. Martin's Press, 1997.

Notkin, Deborah L. "Stephen King: Horror and Humanity for Our Time." In *Fear Itself: The Horror Fiction of Stephen King,* edited by Tim Underwood and Chuck Miller, 151–62. 1982. New York: New American Library, 1985.

O'Hehir, Andrew. "The Salon Interview: Stephen King." http://archive
.salon.com/books/int/1998/09/cov_si_24int.html.

Ong, Walter J. *Orality and Literacy: The Technologizing of the Word*. New
Accents. London: Methuen, 1982.

Opie, Iona, and Peter Opie. *The Classic Fairy Tales*. 1974. London: Gra-
nada, 1980.

Overlook Connection Press. "Horror Plum'd: An International Stephen
King Bibliography and Guide—1960–2000." http://www.overlook
connection.com/kingbib.htm.

Parrinder, Patrick. *Science Fiction: Its Criticism and Teaching*. London:
Methuen, 1980.

Pettersson, Bo. "On the Study of Imagination and Popular Imagination:
A Historical Survey and a Look Ahead." In *Popular Imagination*, ed-
ited by S.-K. Klinkman, 11–50. Åbo, Finland: Nordic Network for
Folklore, 2002.

———. *The World According to Kurt Vonnegut: Moral Paradox and Narrative Form*. Åbo, Finland: Åbo Akademi University Press, 1994.

Pharr, Mary. "A Dream of New Life: Stephen King's *Pet Sematary* as a
Variant of Frankenstein." In *The Gothic World of Stephen King: Landscape of Nightmares*, edited by Gary Hoppenstand and Ray B. Browne,
115–25. Bowling Green, Ohio: Bowling Green State University Popular Press, 1987.

———. "Publisher's Review of Heidi Strengell's *Stephen King's Chamber
of Horrors*. Unpublished letter to the publisher. October 2003.

———. "Partners in the *Danse:* Women in Stephen King's Fiction." In
The Dark Descent: Essays Defining Stephen King's Horroscape, edited by
Tony Magistrale, 19–32. Westport, Conn.: Greenwood Press, 1992.

Pizer, Donald. *Realism and Naturalism in Nineteenth-Century American Literature*. Rev. ed. Carbondale: Southern Illinois University Press, 1984.

Plato. *The Republic*. Mineola, N.Y.: Dover, 2000.

———. *Timaeus*. With an introduction by Donald J. Zeyl. London: Hack-
ett, 2000.

Pocock, David. "Unruly Evil." In *The Anthropology of Evil*, edited by
David Parkin. Oxford: Blackwell, 1985.

Poe, Edgar Allan. "The Fall of the House of Usher." In *The Fall of the
House of Usher and Other Writings: Poems, Tales, Essays and Reviews*.
London: Penguin, 1967.

———. "Lionizing." An E-Book Reader. Amazon.com, 2003.

Price, Robert M. "Stephen King and the Lovecraft Mythos." In *Discovering Stephen King*, edited by Darrell Schweitzer, 106–22. Mercer Island, Wash.: Starmont House, 1985.

Propp, Vladimir. *Morphology of the Folktale*. Translated by Laurence
Scott. 1968. Austin: University of Texas Press, 2000. Originally published in Russian in 1928.

Punter, David. *The Literature of Terror: A History of Gothic Fictions from 1765 to the Present Day.* Vol. 1, *The Gothic Tradition.* Harlow, Essex: Pearson Education, 1996.

———. *The Literature of Terror: A History of Gothic Fictions from 1765 to the Present Day.* Vol. 2, *The Modern Gothic.* Harlow, Essex: Pearson Education, 1996.

Radcliffe, Ann. *The Mysteries of Udolpho.* 1794. Oxford: Oxford University Press, 1998.

Rafferty, Terrence. "Bad Blood." Review of *The Dark Half,* directed by George Romero. *New Yorker,* May 3, 1993, 105–6, 107.

Railo, Eino. *The Haunted Castle: A Study of the Elements of English Romanticism.* New York: Humanities Press, 1964.

Reese, Ben. "A King and His Tower: An Interview with Stephen King." www.amazon.com/exec/obidos/tg/feature/-/455676/104-96637 09-8831121.

Reesman, Jeanne Campbell. "Stephen King and the Tradition of American Naturalism in *The Shining.*" In *Modern Critical Views: Stephen King,* edited by Harold Bloom, 105–19. Philadelphia: Chelsea House, 1998.

Reino, Joseph. *Stephen King: The First Decade,* Carrie *to* Pet Sematary. Boston: Twayne, 1988.

Renman, Roger. "Realism and Fate in Stephen King's Early Fiction." Master's thesis, University of Helsinki, 2001.

Rickels, Laurence A. *The Vampire Lectures.* Minneapolis: University of Minnesota Press, 1999.

Ricoeur, Paul. *Oneself as Another.* Translated by Kathleen Blamey. Chicago: University of Chicago Press, 1992. Originally published as *Soi-même comme un autre* (1990).

Rimmon-Kenan, Shlomith. *Narrative Fiction: Contemporary Poetics.* London: Methuen, 1983.

Roberts, Garyn G. "Of Mad Dogs and Firestarters: The Incomparable Stephen King." In *The Gothic World of Stephen King: Landscape of Nightmares,* edited by Gary Hoppenstand and Ray B. Browne, 31–36. Bowling Green, Ohio: Bowling Green State University Popular Press, 1987.

Romero, George A. Afterword to *Fear Itself: The Horror Fiction of Stephen King,* edited by Tim Underwood and Chuck Miller, 253–57. 1982. New York: New American Library, 1985.

Russell, Sharon A. *Stephen King: A Critical Companion.* Westport, Conn.: Greenwood Press, 1996.

Ryan, Alan. "The Marsten House in '*Salem's Lot.*" In *Fear Itself: The Horror Fiction of Stephen King,* edited by Tim Underwood and Chuck Miller, 191–202. 1982. New York: New American Library, 1985.

Sage, Victor. *Horror Fiction in the Protestant Tradition.* 1988. London: Palgrave Macmillan, 1999.

Scholes, Robert, and Eric S. Rabkin. *Science Fiction: History — Science — Vision.* London: Oxford University Press, 1977.

Schroeder, Natalie. "'Oz the Gweat and Tewwible' and 'The Other Side': The Theme of Death in *Pet Sematary* and *Jitterburg Perfume.*" In *The Gothic World of Stephen King: Landscape of Nightmares,* edited by Gary Hoppenstand and Ray B. Browne, 135-41. Bowling Green, Ohio: Bowling Green State University, Popular Press, 1987.

Schuman, Samuel. "Taking Stephen King Seriously: Reflections on a Decade of Best-Sellers." In *The Gothic World of Stephen King: Landscape of Nightmares,* edited by Gary Hoppenstand and Ray B. Browne, 107-14. Bowling Green, Ohio: Bowling Green State University Popular Press, 1987.

Schweitzer, Darrell, ed. *Discovering Stephen King.* Mercer Island, Wash.: Starmont House, 1985.

Sedgwick, Eve Kosofsky. *Between Men: English Literature and Male Homosocial Desire.* New York: Columbia University Press, 1985.

———. *The Coherence of Gothic Conventions.* New York: Methuen, 1986.

———. *Epistemology of the Closet.* Berkeley: University of California Press, 1990.

Selden, Raman, Peter Widdowson, and Peter Brooker. *A Reader's Guide to Contemporary Literary Theory.* 1985. Harlow, Essex: Prentice Hall, 1997.

Senf, Carol A. "Blood, Eroticism, and the Vampire in Twentieth-Century Popular Literature." In *The Gothic World of Stephen King: Landscape of Nightmares,* edited by Gary Hoppenstand and Ray B. Browne, 20-30. Bowling Green, Ohio: Bowling Green State University Press, 1987.

———. "*Gerald's Game* and *Dolores Claiborne:* Stephen King and the Evolution of an Authentic Female Narrative Voice." In *Imagining the Worst: Stephen King and the Representation of Women,* edited by Kathleen Margaret Lant and Theresa Thomson, 91-107. Westport, Conn.: Greenwood Press, 1998.

Shackleton, Mark. "Native Myth Meets Western Culture: The Plays of Tomson Highway." In *Migration, Preservation, and Change,* edited by Jeffrey Kaplan, Mark Shackleton, and Maarika Toivonen, 47-58. Renvall Institutes Publications 10. Helsinki: Renvall Institute, 1999.

Shelley, Mary. *Frankenstein.* 1818. London: Penguin Books, 1994.

———. *Frankenstein.* In *Frankenstein/Dracula/Dr. Jekyll and Mr. Hyde.* With an introduction by Stephen King. New York: Signet, 1978.

———. *Frankenstein, or the Modern Prometheus.* With an introduction by Stephen King. New York: Dodd, Mead, 1983.

Sjögren, Olle. "Kirottu kynnys: Kauhuelokuva modernina siirty-märiittinä." In *Uhka silmälle*, edited by Tilda-Maria Forselius and Seppo Luoma-Keturi, 13–51. Helsinki: Like, 1989.

Smith, James F. "'Everybody Pays . . . Even for Things They Didn't Do': Stephen King's Pay-out in the Bachman Novels." In *The Dark Descent: Essays Defining Stephen King's Horroscape*, edited by Tony Magistrale, 99–112. Westport, Conn.: Greenwood Press, 1992.

Snyder, Gary. "The Incredible Survival of Coyote." In *The Old Ways: Six Essays*. San Francisco: City Lights, 1975.

Spignesi, Stephen J. *The Essential Stephen King: A Ranking of the Greatest Novels, Short Stories, Movies, and Other Creations of the World's Most Popular Writer*. Franklin Lakes, N.J.: New Page, 2001.

——. *The Lost Work of Stephen King: A Guide to Unpublished Manuscripts, Story Fragments, Alternative Versions, and Oddities*. Secaucus, N.J.: Birch Lane Press, 1998.

Stanton, Michael N. "Once Out of Nature: The Topiary." In *Discovering Stephen King's* The Shining, edited by Tony Magistrale, 11–18. San Bernardino, Calif.: Borgo Press, 1998.

Starkey, Marion. *The Devil in Massachusetts: A Modern Enquiry into the Salem Witch Trials*. New York: Knopf, 1949.

Stephens, John. "Myth/Mythology and Fairy Tales." In *The Oxford Companion to Fairy Tales: The Western Fairy Tale Tradition from Medieval to Modern*, edited by Jack Zipes. Oxford: Oxford University Press, 2000.

Stevenson, Robert Louis. *The Strange Case of Dr Jekyll and Mr Hyde*. 1886. London: Penguin, 1994.

Stoker, Bram. *Dracula*. 1897. London: Penguin, 1994.

Straub, Peter. "Meeting Stevie." In *Fear Itself: The Horror Fiction of Stephen King*, edited by Tim Underwood and Chuck Miller, 7–13. 1982. New York: New American Library, 1985.

Strengell, Heidi. "Women Characters in Stephen King's Novels." Long essay, University of Helsinki, 2001.

Stump, Debra. "A Matter of Choice: King's *Cujo* and Malamud's *The Natural*." In *Discovering Stephen King*, edited by Darrell Schweitzer, 131–52. Mercer Island, Wash.: Starmont House, 1985.

Summers, Montague. *The Gothic Quest: A History of the Gothic Novel*. London: Fortune, 1938.

Sutherland, John. "American Science Fiction since 1960." In *Science Fiction: A Critical Guide*, edited by Patrick Parrinder, 62–86. London: Longman, 1979.

——. *Bestsellers: Popular Fiction in the 1970s*. London: Routledge, 1981.

——. *Fiction and the Fiction Industry*. London: Athlone Press, 1978.

Tatar, Maria. *The Hard Facts of the Grimm's Fairy Tales*. Princeton, N.J.: Princeton University Press, 1987.

———. *Off with Their Heads! Fairy Tales and the Culture of Childhood.* Princeton, N.J.: Princeton University Press, 1992.

Terrell, Carroll F. *Stephen King: Man and Artist.* Orono, Me.: Northern Lights, 1990.

Thoens, Karen. "*It:* A Sexual Fantasy." In *Imagining the Worst: Stephen King and the Representation of Women,* edited by Kathleen Margaret Lant and Theresa Thomson, 127–40. Westport, Conn.: Greenwood Press, 1998.

Thomas, Keith. *Religion and the Decline of Magic.* New York: Scribner's, 1976.

Thompson, C. J. S. *The Mystery and Lore of Monsters.* London: Williams & Norgate, 1930.

Thompson, Theresa. "Rituals of Male Violence: Unlocking the (Fe)Male Self in *Gerald's Game* and *Dolores Claiborne.*" In *Imagining the Worst: Stephen King and the Representation of Women,* edited by Kathleen Margaret Lant and Theresa Thomson, 47–58. Westport, Conn.: Greenwood Press, 1998.

Todorov, Tzvetan. *The Fantastic: A Structural Approach to a Literary Genre.* Translated by Richard Howard. Ithaca, N.Y.: Cornell University Press, 1975. Originally published as *Introduction á la littérature fantastique* (1970).

Tolkien, J. R. R. "On Fairy-Stories." In *The Monsters and the Critics,* edited by Christopher Tolkien. London: HarperCollins, 1983.

———. *The Lord of the Rings.* 1954–55. London: Unwin, 1989.

Trevor-Roper, Hugh. *The European Witch-Craze of the Sixteenth and Seventeenth Centuries and Other Essays.* New York: Harper, 1969.

Tropp, Michael. *Images of Fear: How Horror Stories Helped Shape Modern Culture (1818–1918).* Jefferson, N.C.: McFarland, 1990.

Turner, Victor. "Social Dramas and Stories about Them." *Critical Inquiry* 7 (Autumn 1980): 141–68.

Underwood, Tim. "The Skull beneath the Skin." In *Kingdom of Fear: The World of Stephen King,* edited by Tim Underwood and Chuck Miller, 255–56. New York: New American Library, 1986.

Underwood, Tim, and Chuck Miller, eds. *Bare Bones: Conversations on Terror with Stephen King.* 1988. Sevenoaks, Kent: New English Library, 1989.

———, eds. *Fear Itself: The Horror Fiction of Stephen King.* 1982. New York: New American Library, 1985.

———, eds. *Feast of Fear: Conversations with Stephen King.* 1989. New York: Carroll & Graf, 1992.

———, eds. *Kingdom of Fear: The World of Stephen King.* New York: New American Library, 1986.

Van Hise, James. *Stephen King and Clive Barker: The Illustrated Masters of the Macabre.* Las Vegas: Pioneer Books, 1990.

Walpole, Horace. *The Castle of Otranto*. 1764. Oxford: Oxford University Press, 1996.

Warner, Marina. *From the Beast to the Blonde: On Fairy Tales and Their Tellers*. 1994. London: Vintage, 1995.

——. *No Go the Bogeyman: Scaring, Lulling, and Making Mock*. 1998. London: Vintage, 2000.

——. *Six Myths of Our Time: The Reith Lectures 1994*. London: Vintage, 1994.

Warren, Bill. "The Movies and Mr. King." In *Fear Itself: The Horror Fiction of Stephen King*, edited by Tim Underwood and Chuck Miller, 125–48. 1982. New York: New American Library, 1985.

Waugh, Patrick. *Metafiction: The Theory and Practice of Self-Conscious Fiction*. London: Methuen, 1984.

Weller, Greg. "The Masks of the Goddess: The Unfolding of the Female Archetype in Stephen King's *Carrie*." In *The Dark Descent: Essays Defining Stephen King's Horroscape*, edited by Tony Magistrale, 5–17. Westport, Conn.: Greenwood Press, 1992.

Wiater, Stanley, Christopher Golden, and Hank Wagner. *The Stephen King Universe: A Guide to the Worlds of the King of Horror*. Los Angeles: Renaissance, 2001.

Wierzbicka, Anna. *Semantics, Culture, and Cognition: Universal Human Concepts in Culture- Specific Configurations*. New York: Oxford University Press, 1992.

Wilde, Alan. *Horizons of Assent: Modernism, Postmodernism, and the Ironic Imagination*. Baltimore: Johns Hopkins University Press, 1981.

Wilson, Colin. *The Outsider*. London: Victor Gollanz, 1956.

Winter, Douglas E. *Faces of Fear: Encounters with the Creators of Modern Horror*. New York: Berkley Books, 1985.

——. "The Night Journeys of Stephen King." In *Fear Itself: The Horror Fiction of Stephen King*, edited by Tim Underwood and Chuck Miller, 205–51. 1982. New York: New American Library, 1985.

——. *Stephen King: The Art of Darkness*. 1984. New York: Signet, 1986.

Yarbro, Chelsea Quinn. "Cinderella's Revenge: Twists on Fairy Tale and Mythic Themes in the Work of Stephen King." In *Fear Itself: The Horror Fiction of Stephen King*, edited by Tim Underwood and Chuck Miller, 61–71. 1982. New York: New American Library, 1985.

Ziolkowski, Theodore. *Disenchanted Images: A Literary Iconology*. Princeton, N.J.: Princeton University Press, 1977.

Zipes, Jack. *Fairy Tale as Myth/Myth as Fairy Tale*. Lexington: University Press of Kentucky, 1994.

——. "Introduction to *Spells of Enchantment: The Wondrous Fairy Tales of Western Culture*, edited by Jack Zipes, xi–xxxii. London: Penguin, 1991.

Index

This list includes the names of persons and fictional characters, the titles of King's works and other reference books mentioned in the text, from the introduction to the opening note in the bibliography. Mythical and Old Testament names are included when they have relevance to King's work. The names, titles, and references in parentheses are excluded.

A RAY AND PAT BROWNE BOOK

Murder on the Reservation: American Indian Crime Fiction
Ray B. Browne

Profiles of Popular Culture: A Reader
Edited by Ray B. Browne

Goddesses and Monsters: Women, Myth, Power, and Popular Culture
Jane Caputi

Mystery, Violence, and Popular Culture
John G. Cawelti

Baseball and Country Music
Don Cusic

Popular Witchcraft: Straight from the Witch's Mouth, 2nd edition
Jack Fritscher

The Essential Guide to Werewolf Literature
Brian J. Frost

Popular Culture Theory and Methodology: A Basic Introduction
Edited by Harold E. Hinds Jr., Marilyn F. Motz, and Angela M. S. Nelson

Rituals and Patterns in Children's Lives
Edited by Kathy Merlock Jackson

Images of the Corpse: From the Renaissance to Cyberspace
Edited by Elizabeth Klaver

Dissecting Stephen King: From the Gothic to Literary Naturalism
Heidi Strengell

Walking Shadows: Orson Welles, William Randolph Hearst, and Citizen Kane
John Evangelist Walsh

Spectral America: Phantoms and the National Imagination
Edited by Jeffrey Andrew Weinstock

King of the Cowboys, Queen of the West: Roy Rogers and Dale Evans
Raymond E. White